PRECEDENTS AND CASE-BASED REASONING IN THE EUROPEAN COURT OF JUSTICE

Past cases are the European Court of Justice's most prominent tool in making and justifying the rulings and decisions which affect the everyday lives of more than half a billion people. Marc Jacob's detailed analysis of the use of precedents and case-based reasoning in the Court uses methods such as doctrinal scholarship, empirical research, institutional analysis, comparative law and legal theory in order to unravel and critique the how and why of the Court's precedent technique. In doing so, he moves the wider debate beyond received 'common law' versus 'civil law' figments and 'Eurosceptic' versus 'Euromantic' battlelines, and also provides a useful blueprint for assessing and comparing the case law practices of other dispute resolution bodies.

MARC JACOB is a member of the international arbitration group of a leading international law firm, where he advises and represents sovereign and corporate entities in cross-border commercial disputes, investment treaty arbitrations and public international law matters. He is also a lecturer at the University of Tübingen, Germany.

PRECEDENTS AND CASE-BASED REASONING IN THE EUROPEAN COURT OF JUSTICE

Unfinished Business

MARC JACOB

CAMBRIDGE UNIVERSITY PRESS

CAMBRIDGE
UNIVERSITY PRESS

University Printing House, Cambridge CB2 8BS, United Kingdom

Published in the United States of America by Cambridge University Press, New York

Cambridge University Press is part of the University of Cambridge.

It furthers the University's mission by disseminating knowledge in the pursuit of
education, learning, and research at the highest international levels of excellence.

www.cambridge.org
Information on this title: www.cambridge.org/9781107045491

© Marc Jacob 2014

First published 2014

Printed in the United Kingdom by Clays, St Ives plc

A catalogue record for this publication is available from the British Library

Library of Congress Cataloguing in Publication data
Jacob, Marc A., 1979– author.
Precedents and case-based reasoning in the European Court of Justice : unfinished business /
Marc A. Jacob.
p.   cm.
Includes bibliographical references and index.
ISBN 978-1-107-04549-1 (hardback)
1. Court of Justice of the European Communities   2. Stare decisis – European Union
countries.   3. Case-based reasoning – European Union countries.   4. Judgments – European
Union countries.   I. Title.
KJE5461.J32   2014
341.242'2284 – dc23   2013030433

ISBN 978-1-107-04549-1 Hardback

Meiner Familie

CONTENTS

LIST OF FIGURES

ACKNOWLEDGEMENTS

This book aims to provide a fresh eye on a topic that is both abiding and acute, and to deliberately do so by an amalgam of various juxtapositions: European law and international law, common law and civil law, doctrine and theory, legal academe and practice. Whether or not it succeeds, this work could not have been written without the contributions of many.

Over the years, I have benefitted greatly from the insights of talented individuals too numerous to mention. My three intellectual homes – University College London, Harvard Law School and the Max Planck Institute for Comparative Public Law and International Law – have all deeply influenced this work in their own unique way. Many of the people I met there have become good friends, and I would like to thank them individually and collectively for their inspiration, collegiality and sense of humour. In many respects, they are the forgotten sources of this book.

I am deeply indebted to Professor Armin von Bogdandy, Director at the Max Planck Institute, who first suggested this project to me in the context of a doctoral thesis at the University of Frankfurt. Like many others, I owe much to the intensity of his love for law as a science, and for his provision of a wonderfully vital environment in Heidelberg that allowed me to work in confidence and under the best conditions possible. His constructive criticism has profoundly shaped this book. Special thanks also to the members of the *Dienstagsrunde*, past and present, whose ideas have greatly enriched my thinking. I miss the banter.

At the University of Frankfurt, Professor Rainer Hofmann provided extremely helpful comments on my original thesis. Professor Stefan Kadelbach kindly agreed to chair my PhD committee in October 2012 and kept me on my toes.

I owe a special gratitude to the many members of the Court of Justice of the European Union, and in particular to Judge Allan Rosas, who very generously allowed me to put my ideas to them during my stay in Luxembourg and who graciously shared candid insights into their everyday work.

At Cambridge University Press, Elizabeth Spicer and Richard Woodham deserve thanks for what has been a quality publishing process.

Most importantly, I wish to thank my family, big and small, for their unfailing support, encouragement and patience. This book is dedicated to them.

LIST OF ABBREVIATIONS

AG	Advocate General
BIT	bilateral investment treaty
CFI	Court of First Instance
CFREU	Charter of Fundamental Rights of the European Union
CJEU	Court of Justice of the European Union
DSU	Final Act Embodying the Results of the Uruguay Round of Multilateral Trade Negotiations, Annex 2, Understanding on Rules and Procedures Governing the Settlement of Disputes
ECJ	European Court of Justice
ECHR	European Convention on Human Rights
ECtHR	European Court of Human Rights
EEC	European Economic Community
EU	European Union
FCC	(German) Federal Constitutional Court
GATT	General Agreement on Tariffs and Trade
GC	General Court
ICJ	International Court of Justice
ICSID	International Centre for Settlement of Investment Disputes
ICSID Convention	Convention on the Settlement of Investment Disputes between States and Nationals of Other States
NAFTA	North American Free Trade Agreement
NBSM	not binding, but subsidiary means
PCIJ	Permanent Court of International Justice
TEU	Treaty on European Union
TFEU	Treaty on the Functioning of the European Union
VCLT	Vienna Convention on the Law of Treaties
WHO	World Health Organization
WTO	World Trade Organisation

1

Introduction

A Mapping the prolific juggernaut

This is a study of precedents in the European Court of Justice ('ECJ', 'the Court'). In a legal context, the term 'precedent' is normally associated with an earlier decision of a court and tribunal that is later referred to by adjudicatory bodies, involved parties or commentators, usually, but not exclusively, in the context of dispute resolution. Precedents are a fundamentally important tool of the ECJ in making and justifying its decisions. They inform influential rulings and profoundly shape legal landscapes, sometimes at break-neck speed, at other times over the undulating course of time.

That matter is unfinished business in more than one sense. First, the content and structure of precedents is dynamic. Secondly, the Court has struggled to come up with a consistent and satisfactory practice that is independent from the supposed cunning of history and not afraid of discourse, dissent and political re-imagination. Thirdly, existing scholarly approaches, even progressive ones, often have a difficult time fitting this practice into adequate conceptual arrangements. The underlying premise of this work is that legal scholarship can make a relevant contribution that nudges the larger debate beyond seductive yet unrealistic images that tend to cast the ECJ either in the role of the Machiavellian manipulator or the Solomonic saviour. Taking a cue from doctrinal, theoretical and interdisciplinary approaches, the present work is prompted by two observations and a curiosity.

An initial observation is that the ECJ's output matters immensely. The general rise to prominence of courts and tribunals, in particular those that do not operate in a purely domestic setting, is well-documented.[1] At

---

[1] See e.g. H. Lauterpacht, *The Function of Law in the International Community* (Clarendon Press, Oxford, 1933), pp. 26–42 (surveying various arbitration conventions); P. Sands, 'Turtles and Torturers: The Transformation of International Law', *New York University Journal of International Law & Politics*, 33 (2001), 527, 553 ('powerful new international

least since the second half of the twentieth century, judges and litigants in many parts of the world slowly but surely rival legislators, reformers and professors as pivotal agencies in law.[2] Granted, not all spheres of law have experienced judicialisation to the same extent. Some remain decidedly more transactional and less pervaded by dispute settlement. But it holds true for the supranational European sphere, where the idea of a transformation not only of law but also of entire polities through adjudication is a household theme.[3] The ECJ is a prolific juggernaut. It rules without possibility of appeal on a plethora of matters ranging from the institutional architecture of the European Union ('EU') via basic principles of market freedoms to sundry matters such as consumer protection concerning package tours. Its pronouncements are watched keenly, not least by national (constitutional) courts. With this ascendance of the judiciary, authoritative impromptu pronouncements on legal norms and nimble case-by-case balancing profoundly set the tone for discourse about law a decade into the twenty-first century. Simultaneously, comprehensive codification attempts and claims about absolute legal 'truths' are widely discredited as fanciful and rule scepticism is nurtured. Even neo-formalist responses to post-modern legal thought, let alone interdisciplinary approaches, stress the *who* and *why* over the *what*; in other words, actors and processes rather than the abstract divination of meaning are the central battlegrounds.[4] While this has seriously dented dubious textualism, it has also stifled re-imagination.

The second observation ties in with this. Precedents matter. In the process of justifying decisions, adjudicators, including those at the ECJ,

judiciary'); Y. Shany, 'No Longer a Weak Department of Power? Reflections on the Emergence of a New International Judiciary', *European Journal of International Law*, 20 (2009), 73, 75–6, 90 (highlighting remaining deficits and limitations); A. von Bogdandy and I. Venzke, 'Beyond Dispute: International Judicial Institutions as Lawmakers', *German Law Journal*, 12 (2011), 979 (noting a quantitative and qualitative shift).

[2] See D. Kennedy, 'Two Globalizations of Law & Legal Thought: 1850–1968', *Suffolk University Law Review*, 36 (2003), 631, 632–3; R. Hirschl, 'The New Constitutionalism and the Judicialization of Pure Politics Worldwide', *Fordham Law Review*, 75 (2006–2007), 721, 722 (observing an expansion in terms of geography and scope). Cf. J. Waldron, *Law and Disagreement* (Clarendon Press, Oxford, 1999), pp. 9, 213 (sensing democratic participation on the decline).

[3] See e.g. J. H. H. Weiler, 'The Transformation of Europe', *Yale Law Journal*, 100 (1990–1991), 2403; A. Arnull, 'Me and My Shadow: The European Court of Justice and the Disintegration of European Union Law', *Fordham International Law Journal*, 31 (2008), 1174, 1175–7.

[4] On the recent mainstream fixation with conditionalities rather than 'abstract theory' see G. Shaffer and T. Ginsburg, 'The Empirical Turn in International Legal Scholarship', *American Journal of International Law*, 106 (2012), 1.

often draw heavily on prior cases. The practice gives courts and tribunals a degree of self-sufficiency, and hence power. This triggers a host of big questions, many of them ageless classics of law, poltics and philosophy, and it is here that the question of judicial precedent becomes acutely important beyond individual legal situations.

The curiosity is that the use of precedents by the ECJ is far-reaching but rarely, if ever, explicated in detail as an intricate legal technique in its own right.[5] At a time when EU law regularly and deeply affects hundreds of millions of people, a comforting yet numbing consensus coagulates, according to which 'there is no binding doctrine of precedent akin to the Anglo-American *stare decisis* doctrine' (or similar). But that can only be the beginning of a thorough inquiry. The present work addresses that gap.

This book is not just about adjudicators and their attitudes, behaviour and strategies. Political scientists have done important work on the broader topic, not least by introducing and applying concepts such as precedent density, network centrality, inward or outward citations and authority and hub scores. Still, legal scholarship adds a significant dimension. For all the advances in measuring and empirically quantifying precedent usage or placing it in broader political contexts, any statistical framework has to be vested with meaning, and legal discourse remains a distinct field of inquiry. To truly understand precedent, one also needs to dig into the legal method of the Court. The present work examines different concepts and archetypes on offer to get a theoretical and methodological grip on precedent from a lawyer's perspective and supplements this with an analysis of the ECJ's technique. At the same time, an important approach incorporated here is that adjudicatory bodies like the ECJ should indeed be seen and researched as complex institutions affected by a diverse range of contextual incentives and constraints.[6]

The Court is a prime candidate for a study of precedent. A necessary but not sufficient consideration is that this dispute resolution body

---

[5] Cf. Y. Lupu and E. Voeten, 'Precedent in International Courts: A Network Analysis of Case Citations by the European Court of Human Rights', *British Journal of Political Science*, 42 (2012), 413, 414 (on the dearth of research on the use of precedents by international judges).

[6] The work hence combines the study of autonomous legal ideas with their transformation and management in practice. Cf. D. Kennedy, 'The Move to Institutions', *Cardozo Law Review*, 8 (1987), 841, 843; B. Kingsbury, 'International Courts: Uneven Judicialisation in Global Order' in J. Crawford and M. Koskenniemi (eds.), *The Cambridge Companion to International Law* (Cambridge University Press, 2012).

has produced ample legal material to work with.[7] Moreover, the stakes are high. The EU represents the most successful innovation in political and legal authority of the last century.[8] It has now emerged as a full-blown global actor, for instance as a part of the so called Quartet on the Middle East. Its legal system has challenged the predominant paradigm of world order that emerged sixty years ago.[9] At home, there can be no doubt that its institutions profoundly shape the everyday lives of the inhabitants of its Member States. But this is not a book about European integration in general. Rows of library shelves have been filled with that topic.[10] Instead, this book takes a closer look at a crucial part of the inner workings of one of its central actors, the ECJ, which sits at the helm of the triadic Court of Justice of the European Union ('CJEU').[11] The European project may have begun as a treaty-based project of legislation, but it is famously considered to have unfolded as a half-century of bold judicial innovation and constitutionalisation. Even a cursory treatment of the EU would seem incomplete without mentioning how the ECJ spearheaded the development of many of the central features of this unique hybrid intergovernmental and supranational organisation and legal order, promoting integration while simultaneously often

[7]   By contrast, as of April 2013, the International Tribunal for the Law of the Sea in Hamburg has had twenty-one cases since its inauguration in 1996.
[8]   See K. R. McNamara, 'Constructing Authority in the European Union' in D. D. Avant, M. Finnemore and S. K. Sell (eds.), *Who Governs the Globe?* (Cambridge University Press, 2010), p. 153.
[9]   Cf. D. Halberstam and E. Stein, 'The United Nations, the European Union, and the King of Sweden: Economic Sanctions and Individual Rights in a Plural World Order', *Common Market Law Review*, 46 (2009), 13.
[10] See e.g. A. Grimmel and C. Jakobeit (eds.), *Politische Theorien der Europäischen Integration* (VS Verlag, Wiesbaden, 2009). Perspicacious portrayals avoid the simple and tautological *sui generis* label. See e.g. J. Neyer and D. Wolf, 'The Analysis of Compliance with International Rules: Definitions, Variables, and Methodology' in M. Zürn and C. Joerges (eds.), *Law and Governance in Postnational Europe: Compliance Beyond the Nation-State* (Cambridge University Press, 2005); R. Schütze, *From Dual to Cooperative Federalism: The Changing Structure of European Law* (Oxford University Press, 2009), pp. 59–60, 71.
[11] This new title was introduced by the Treaty of Lisbon. See Consolidated Version of the Treaty on European Union ('TEU') [2012] OJ C326/13 Art. 19(1); Consolidated Version of the Treaty on the Function of the European Union ('TFEU') [2012] OJ C326/47 Arts. 251–81; Consolidated Version of Protocol (No. 3) on the Statute of the Court of Justice of the European Union ('CJEU Statute'), annexed to the Treaties, as amended by Regulation (EU, Euratom) No. 741/2012 of the European Parliament and of the Council of 11.8.2012 [2012] OJ L228/1. This work focuses on the ECJ's use of precedent. The General Court ('GC') and Civil Service Tribunal are largely outside its scope.

enhancing its own position.[12] Consistent enlargement of the Union has further enhanced the position of the Court vis-à-vis the Member States, given that an increased likelihood of political differences generally tends to favour adjudicatory solutions. Nor is this slipping of (often very sensitive) issues to Luxembourg always unwelcome.[13] Over time, the ECJ has risen like Cinderella from the soot and obscurity of its working-class background in the former European Coal and Steel Community to slide on the glittering slipper of human rights and citizenship.[14] The whole episode has rightly been called Europe's 'most powerful and diffused' meta-narrative.[15] Not infrequently, this attracts outspoken disapproval.[16]

[12] See e.g. the classic expositions by P. Pescatore, *The Law of Integration* (Sijthoff, Leiden, 1974), pp. 89–90; R. Lecourt, *L' Europe des juges* (reprint edn, Bruylant, Brussels, 2008 (1976)), pp. 216–19, 236–42; E. Stein, 'Lawyers, Judges, and the Making of a Transnational Constitution', *American Journal of International Law*, 75 (1981), 1, 24–7; Weiler (n. 3 above), pp. 2413, 2426. More recent contributions include D. Edward, 'Richterrecht in Community Law' in R. Schulze and U. Seif (eds.), *Richterrecht und Rechtsfortbildung in der Europäischen Rechtsgemeinschaft* (Mohr Siebeck, Tübingen, 2003), pp. 75–80; A. Stone Sweet, 'Conclusion' in A. Stone Sweet (ed.), *The Judicial Construction of Europe* (Oxford University Press, 2004), pp. 235–41; U. Haltern, *Europarecht und das Politische* (Mohr Siebeck, Tübingen 2005), pp. 280–93; J. Schwarze, 'Grenzen des Richterrechts in der Europäischen Rechtsordnung' in G. Müller, E. Osterloh and T. Stein (eds.), *Festschrift für Günter Hirsch zum 65. Geburtstag* (C. H. Beck, Munich, 2008), pp. 169–70; J. Komarek, 'Precedent and Judicial Lawmaking in Supreme Courts: The Court of Justice Compared to the US Supreme Court and the French Cour de Cassation', *The Cambridge Yearbook of European Legal Studies*, 11 (2009), 399, 400.

[13] See K. J. Alter, 'Agents or Trustees? International Courts in their Political Context', *European Journal of International Relations*, 14 (2008), 33, 53–4.

[14] See e.g. Joined Cases C-402/05 P and C-415/05 P *Yassin Abdullah Kadi and Al Barakaat International Foundation* v. *Council and Commission* (Grand Chamber) [2008] ECR I-6351; Case C-34/09 *Gerardo Ruiz Zambrano* v. *Office national de l'emploi (ONEm) (Grand Chamber)* [2011] ECR I-1177.

[15] A. Vauchez, 'The Transnational Politics of Judicialization: Van Gend en Loos and the Making of EU Polity', *European Law Journal*, 16 (2010), 1, 2.

[16] See e.g. H. Rasmussen, *On Law and Policy in the European Court of Justice* (Nijhoff, Dordrecht, 1986), pp. 12–14, 31–3, 61–5; H. Rasmussen, 'Between Self-Restraint and Activism: A Judicial Policy for the European Court', *European Law Review*, 13 (1988), 28, 37 ('teleological, pro-Community crusade', 'few cancer-cells . . . able to ruin completely the healthiest body'); P. Neill, 'The European Court of Justice: A Case Study in Judicial Activism' (European Policy Forum, 1995); J. Coppel and A. O'Neill, 'The European Court of Justice: Taking Rights Seriously?', *Legal Studies*, 12 (2006), 227, 237, 244–5; R. Herzog and L. Gerken, 'Stoppt den Europäischen Gerichtshof', *Frankfurter Allgemeine Zeitung* (Frankfurt, 8 September 2008) (castigating the ECJ for 'interfering massively' with Member States' legal orders and its 'arrogant' reasoning in Case C-144/04 *Werner Mangold* v. *Rüdiger Helm* (Grand Chamber) [2005] ECR I-9981); P. Hilpold, 'Unionsbürgerschaft und Bildungsrechte oder: Der EuGH-Richter als "Künstler"' in G. H. Roth and P. Hilpold (eds.), *Der EuGH und die Souveränität der Mitgliedstaaten* (Stämpfli, Bern, 2008),

Tensions flare at different levels of abstraction, ranging from broad questions on the proper allocation of powers amongst the Union's institutions or the reach of EU directives to concrete issues of social policy and labour law. Throughout all of this, the question of the Union's democratic accountability and finality looms large.[17]

Faced with these antagonistic assertions of authority – pluralistic *forces* – it might seem quaint to care about what could be considered *legal method*. But there is little that is fusty about looking over the shoulder of the European judicial elite as it shapes social reality by deciding cases with the help of its routine toolkit.[18] Problems of legal theory are real legal problems.[19] At the very least, this helps to develop a vocabulary for a critique of what has become a semi-autonomous process. The alternative, pragmatism with a sprinkling of psychology or sociology, is hardly satisfying. Even if it were possible to discover 'law-like regularities in judicial decision-making', thinking about law and its practice should not be reduced to theory-starved recounting of social phenomena. The abrogation of critical thinking in favour of practical compatibility, a charge not only levelled against common lawyers,[20] and a legal scholarship that is simply the handmaiden of a particular project, are of little use.[21]

B Four theses

This book sets out to map the ECJ's case law technique in detail. This is done with a view to contributing to a deeper understanding of

---

pp. 12, 52–3; Q. L. Hong, 'Constitutional Review in the Mega-Leviathan: A Democratic Foundation for the European Court of Justice', *European Law Journal*, 16 (2010), 695, 708 ('blatantly political decisions').

[17] Cf. U. Haltern, 'On Finality' in A. von Bogdandy and J. Bast (eds.), *Principles of European Constitutional Law* (2nd edn, Hart and C. H. Beck, Oxford and Munich, 2010), p. 234 (on constitutional dialogue with the Court).

[18] It is possible to distinguish between (re)solving cases and legal method, but the position taken here is that the latter is in any event essential to the former. Cf. F. Müller and R. Christensen, *Juristische Methodik: Grundlagen* (9th edn, Duncker & Humblot, Berlin, 2004), p. 29.

[19] See A. Somek, *Rechtliches Wissen* (Suhrkamp, Frankfurt am Main, 2006), pp. 14, 108. The obvious caveat of course being that these are real rather than imagined problems.

[20] For a German perspective see B. Schlink, 'Die Entthronung der Staatsrechtswissenschaft durch die Verfassungsgerichtsbarkeit', *Der Staat*, 28 (1989), 161.

[21] Cf. R. A. Posner, 'The Deprofessionalization of Legal Teaching and Scholarship', *Michigan Law Review*, 91 (1993), 1921, 1928: 'But where is it written that all legal scholarship shall be in the service of the legal profession? Perhaps the ultimate criterion of scholarship is utility, but it need not be utility to a particular audience.'

case-based reasoning and jurisprudence, both at the Court and elsewhere. Four specific theses are pursued.

First, the incessant and often acrimonious debate over whether the ECJ 'makes law' by way of usurping other institutions or the Member States is too crude to be useful. Conceptually, the situation is far messier than this particular variant of the 'epic rivalry' can convey, with a myriad of points made in a multitude of form-independent instances read in a certain way making law. In order to get past this intellectual stagnation it is necessary to go back to epistemological basics and rethink adjudication in terms of contestable claims based on the available legal information. Normatively, the underlying concerns can nonetheless be taken seriously, since this realisation enhances, rather than diminishes, critical potential. Law and legal practice also remain viable.

Secondly, the ECJ primarily uses precedents to bolster its legitimacy and acceptance and to fend off outside challenges. While there are also other potential reasons for case citations, including envisaged efficiency gains, the Court above all refers to past decisions to resolve cases, demonstrate the coherence of EU law and thus enhance its credibility vis-à-vis other actors in the European legal space, notably the Member States (and in particular their courts) and other EU institutions. This explains the Court's precedent practice better than traditional approaches that focus on bindingness or the absence thereof. It is also preferable to an overly schematic juxtaposition between arguments from authority and arguments from reason. Finally, it gets past one-dimensional arguments that the judges either care solely about practical compliance or solely about legal doctrine.

Thirdly and closely connected, the ECJ's precedent technique is complex and situational. It is not hostage to abstract (and, to boot, often imprecise) legal traditions or families that continue to float around through legal textbooks, law school classrooms and even the odd judicial opinion, but instead owed to the real-world circumstances the Court is faced with and its very own operational modalities. Comparisons with other forms of non-national dispute settlement, in particular investor–state arbitration under international law, further bring this out. This reinforces the view that neat categorical separations – an 'age of innocence', as one observer called it – are rapidly coming to an end.[22] The broader insight is that precedent usage is receptive and contextual.

---

[22] G. A. Bermann, 'Reconciling European Union Law Demands with the Demands of International Arbitration', *Fordham International Law Journal*, 34 (2011), 1193, 1194.

Fourthly, the ECJ has not yet fully developed the techniques and features that one would expect from a mature and satisfactory system of adjudication that takes case law seriously. Even when viewed as a semi-autonomous system that should by all means bolster its own legitimacy and acceptance, it falls short in important respects and endangers legitimacy rather than fostering it. The main problem is a lack of contestability. The Court's precedent practice is prone to offload responsibility, stifle heterogeneity of solutions and promote a self-satisfied institutional platform. More concretely, the ECJ relies too heavily on repetition for legitimacy, which gives rise to the familiar 'authority not reason' accusations. But the argument developed here is not driven by tired nationalistic Euroscepticism. There is in fact little reason to assume that the ECJ is not sincere, pragmatic or technically competent. On the contrary, the problem is that it is at times too well-intended and pragmatic and overly afraid of fragmenting the European legal order, thus obstructing progressive re-imagination. It fails to realise the true promise of a post-nationalistic Europe. Nor is this critique speculative or mired in despair: it has practical implications and leads to concrete recommendations and alternatives.

C The course of the book

The dual dimension of precedent informs the structure of this study. Precedent can both licence and require coercion.[23] On one hand, it plays a vital role in forming EU law. The decisions resulting from ECJ adjudication are important building blocks of the European legal order. On the other hand and at the same time, precedents can impact and channel subsequent reasoning.

Hence the book proceeds as follows. After this initial sketch of the study's ambit and theses (Chapter 1), the next chapter deals with setting precedents (Chapter 2). It tackles the notion of judge-made law, which may be termed *positive precedent*, and develops a conceptual approach. The argument is that the ECJ makes law, and that it is important to appreciate this. In considering the creative or generative side of adjudication, the chapter unfolds and assesses different models on offer that deal with the phenomenon.

---

[23] Cf. B. A. Garner (ed.), *Black's Law Dictionary* (8th edn, Thomson West, St Paul, MN, 2004), p. 1214 (reflecting the dual sense of precedents making law and furnishing a basis for decisions).

The largest part of this work is dedicated to the ECJ's use of precedents outside the same set of proceedings. It deals with the channelling or constraining facet of prior decisions that may be termed *negative precedent*. Following an examination of what is relevant in a prior case (Chapter 3), the book unfolds the general citation practice or precedent-application by the Court (Chapter 4). Subsequently, an account of the Court's avoidance techniques, including distinguishing prior cases (Chapter 5) and departing from precedents (Chapter 6), is presented. Contextual explanations for this practice are later synthesised (Chapter 7). The book then addresses the debate on the binding force and normativity of ECJ precedents (Chapter 8). The final chapter summarises the various findings and offers suggestions for the ECJ's practice to evolve (Chapter 9).

2

Setting precedents

Law made in Luxembourg

A The different meanings of precedent

'Precedent' is a complex concept.[1] Used as a noun and stripped down to its basics, three points can be discerned. First, something happened before. In that respect, it looks to the past. Secondly, it can provide a reason for doing something. In this respect, precedent looks to the future. Its heart is an appeal to or against repetition. Past events should or should not happen again. Hence it is not only a thing, but also an argument. Thirdly, the bond between the past and present decision is that they are in some respect similar. This is often implicit.

In its raw form precedent is not exclusive to law, let alone legal dispute settlement in the EU. Examples can be homely or grand, such as children demanding treatment akin to elder siblings[2] or the Allied powers deciding not to treat the question of German reparations after World War II as they had previously done in the Treaty of Versailles following World War I. In a legal context, precedent often acquires certain peculiarities. For example, the past events tend to be decided cases.[3] They might be afforded special normative quality, in which case the existence of a precedent can provide a reason for deciding in a particular way, regardless of individual beliefs or contrary reasons. This can serve to differentiate precedent from experience, namely observational knowledge about the world,[4] which is instead revised when it turns out to be wrong.

---

[1] Little however turns on the difference between 'precedent' and 'precedents'.

[2] An illustration used by F. Schauer, 'Precedent', *Stanford Law Review*, 39 (1986–1987), 571, 572.

[3] This emerges very clearly from the term common in German legal scholarship: *Präjudiz*. Indeed, a precedent might be considered to *prejudge* a matter.

[4] See N. Duxbury, *The Nature and Authority of Precedent* (Cambridge University Press, 2008), pp. 2–3.

Collectively, precedents on a particular subject form something commonly called 'case law' or a functional equivalent.[5] Such case law is rarely 'pure', but often an interpretive gloss on or an elaboration of treaty standards or legislation.[6] Fitting this case law into received categories of jurisprudential thought often causes considerable head-scratching. As will be elaborated in due course, reasoning by precedent usually involves bouncing between a general idea and its particular application. This allows for various extensions of reasoning, be it to different times or situations. Besides their common use as a synonym for earlier decisions,[7] precedents are typically approached in roughly three ascending degrees of abstraction.

First and at a concrete level, precedents are used to make claims about *norms*. Examples abound. For instance, one might say that according to precedent the principle of fiscal neutrality in EU law does not preclude a taxable person advancing VAT and temporarily bearing a cash-flow burden.[8] In this conception, precedent is a vehicle or shell for a normative proposition. The present work is not a study of the substantive norms found in ECJ precedents; those are discussed amply in the respective literature.

Secondly and more abstractly, *doctrines or rules of precedent* seek to assert control over the use of prior decisions. They are guidelines stipulating how precedents operate in practice in a given legal system. This can be done either through methodological instruction, explicit regulation or through 'inherent' substantive principles such as legal certainty or the protection of legitimate expectations. Sometimes this might involve constitutional considerations.[9] Where doctrines of precedent are methodological in nature, their misapplication does not necessarily result in an

---

[5] See e.g. Case C-406/09 *Realchemie Nederland BV* v. *Bayer CropScience AG* (Grand Chamber) [2011] ECR I-9773 (paras. 38–9).

[6] Cf. N. MacCormick, 'Why Cases Have Rationes and What These Are' in L. Goldstein (ed.), *Precedent in Law* (Clarendon Press, Oxford, 1987), p. 155; A. Burrows, 'The Relationship between Common Law and Statute Law in the Law of Obligations', *Law Quarterly Review*, 128 (2012), 232, 234, 258.

[7] See e.g. Case C-51/10 P *Agencja Wydawnicza Technopol sp. z o.o.* v. *OHIM* (First Chamber) [2011] ECR I-1541(para. 72).

[8] See Case C-274/10 *Commission* v. *Republic of Hungary* [2011] ECR I-7289, Opinion of AG Bot (para. 59).

[9] See e.g. the German Basic Law Art. 20(3), according to which the judiciary is bound 'by law and justice'. This is the official (and slightly curious) translation of 'die Rechtsprechung [ist] an Gesetz und Recht gebunden'.

incorrect judgment. It is however conceivable that underlying rules or principles could indirectly be violated, thereby triggering some form of legal consequence.

Doctrines of precedent can be fairly detailed, in particular in legal systems in which case law is openly acknowledged to play a crucial role.[10] But they can also be implicit, terse or prohibitive. As will be unfolded over the course of this study, this tends to be the case regarding the ECJ. Nevertheless, care should be taken not to confuse such doctrines or rules with their contents. Negative stipulations are perfectly possible, for example 'in European Union law, the Court's judgments do not constitute binding precedents'.[11] That does not mean that there is no doctrine of precedent at all. Quite the contrary, assuming that this statement is correct, it demonstrably rules out binding authority of past cases.

Thirdly, *theories of precedent* take a step back and examine the essence and potential of judicial pronouncements.[12] They often make no claim to proscribe or even represent the precise workings of precedents in the everyday legal practice of a specific legal system or adjudicatory body. Rather, they provide an analytical or normative framework for understanding precedent in a more general jurisprudential sense. They will likely inquire into whether and how precedents work, how they relate to analogy, the concept of legal norms, different ideologies regarding precedent, the proper role of the judge (usually folded into a discussion of the separation of powers), the various advantages and disadvantages of assorted precedent models and possible approaches and limits to the extrapolation, interpretation and application of precedents. A particular classic is the question whether precedents are law properly so called.

B The attraction of precedent

Why might the ECJ refer to past decisions? Assuming it is not otherwise compelled, adducing an older case might at first blush resemble taking

---

[10] Cf. R. Cross and J. W. Harris, *Precedent in English Law* (4th edn, Clarendon Press, Oxford, 1991), pp. 3–38.

[11] Case C-163/09 *Repertoire Culinaire Ltd* v. *The Commissioners of Her Majesty's Revenue & Customs* [2010] ECR I-12717, Opinion of AG Kokott (para. 61).

[12] See e.g. R. Siltala, *A Theory of Precedent: From Analytical Positivism to a Post-Analytical Philosophy of Law* (Hart, Oxford, 2000); P. Chiassoni, 'The Philosophy of Precedent: Conceptual Analysis and Rational Reconstruction' in T. Bustamente and C. Bernal Pulido (eds.), *On the Philosophy of Precedent* (Franz Steiner, Stuttgart, 2012).

computer advice given in the 1990s or even before. Not only that, it can likely be assumed that adequate case-based reasoning is in principle costly in terms of being an effort the Court has to exert.[13] Nonetheless, it remains very popular in many different fora. Various *raisons d'être* are commonly mentioned in connection with national settings and will be sketched briefly.[14] Roughly speaking, they can be divided into two categories.

i Substantive

First, there are substantive concerns with an individual dimension. Precedent is said to be a function of equality by treating like cases alike. Equality and non-discrimination are fundamental principles of EU law.[15] The Union considers itself a project of exporting the rule of law beyond the nation state, famously taking pride in being a supranational 'community of law'.[16] Amongst other things, this involves affording individuals a predictable legal environment in which they can reasonably ascertain their rights and obligations. Legal certainty, predictability and previsibility are considered cardinal principles.[17] Whether or not this takes an unduly optimistic view as to people's appetite for case reports and the lucidity of the latter, it seems fair to assume that decision-making in accordance with established pronouncements will afford proper respect to people's reliance interests and reasonable expectations.

---

[13] Cf. J. R. Lax and C. M. Cameron, 'Bargaining and Opinion Assignment on the US Supreme Court', *Journal of Law, Economics & Organization*, 23 (2007), 276, 277.

[14] For general discussion see e.g. M. Kriele, *Theorie der Rechtsgewinnung* (2nd edn, Duncker & Humblot, Berlin, 1976), pp. 259–68; Z. Bankowski *et al.*, 'Rationales for Precedent' in N. MacCormick and R. Summers (eds.), *Interpreting Precedents: A Comparative Study* (Ashgate, Aldershot, 1997), pp. 481–500; Duxbury (n. 4 above), pp. 150–82.

[15] See e.g. TEU Preamble, Arts. 2, 3(3), 4(2), 9, 21; TFEU Arts. 8, 18, 153(1), 157, 199; Charter of Fundamental Rights of the European Union ('CFREU') [2000] OJ C364/1 Preamble, Arts. 20–23. Moreover, the core fundamental freedoms logic is to a large extent premised on preventing nationality-based discrimination. Cf. M. Poiares Maduro, *We the Court: The European Court of Justice and the European Economic Constitution* (Hart, Oxford, 1998), pp. 36–42 (while drawing attention to necessary refinements).

[16] The German term *Rechtsgemeinschaft* is usually attributed to Walter Hallstein, the first President of the Commission of the European Economic Community. See W. Hallstein, *Die Europäische Gemeinschaft* (5th edn, Econ, Düsseldorf and Vienna, 1979), p. 53.

[17] See e.g. Joined Cases C-189/02 P, C-202/02 P, C-205/02 P to C-208/02 P and C-213/02 P *Dansk Rørindustri and ors v. Commission* (Grand Chamber) [2005] ECR I-5425; Joined Cases C-201/09 P and C-216/09 P *ArcelorMittal Luxembourg SA v. Commission* (Grand Chamber) [2011] ECR I-2239 (para. 68).

ii Systemic

Other perceived benefits of arguing by precedent revolve around system maintenance. For one, precedents can increase efficiency and save time when used as convenient shorthand, polished phrases or ready-made building blocks in later reasoning processes. They bring an element of industrialisation to dispute settlement through standardised argumentation patterns. This practicality of precedents, which includes facilitating internal communication within the Court, has been suggested to play an important role in EU litigation.[18]

Besides efficiency, precedents can be a tool to boost the external persuasiveness of an argument even in systems that do not pretend to abide by any bindingness doctrine. Precedents immediately add their influence to what is being said. At the very least, this has *ceteris paribus* logic on its side: assuming everything else is the same, why change anything?[19] Unsettling things without argument to the contrary seems arbitary, and doing something for the first time can exert a psychological inhibition. Looking at the broader picture, a good argument is often one that fits smoothly within a larger systemic whole. As will be addressed later, precedents are an excellent way to demonstrate coherence with the broader legal framework and to showcase internal consistency. The unity of the EU legal order has always been a cardinal theme, not least as a corollary of its self-ascribed autonomous nature.[20] Used judiciously, case citations suggest a continued trajectory rather than novel alarm and surprises. Adjudication then acquires the tranquil air of organic fit or growth. Its perceived effects are de-personalisation and neutrality. This implies constraint and direction, to the point that judges cannot be faulted for a decision. More sulkily, blame can be laid at a different door.[21] Precedent is outsourcing in more than just one sense.

It is already here that the strategic dimension of embedding decisions starts to shine through. Precedent can acquire a (faux) populist tilt. To take a historical example, before the existence of the modern state, precedent

---

[18] See e.g. K. Schiemann, *Vom Richter des Common Law zum Richter des Europäischen Rechts* (Vorträge und Berichte Nr 145, Zentrum für Europäisches Wirtschaftsrecht, Rheinische Friedrich-Wilhelms-Universität, Bonn, 2005), pp. 8–9.

[19] Cf. J. Bengoetxea, N. MacCormick and L. Moral Soriano, 'Integration and Integrity in the Legal Reasoning of the European Court of Justice' in G. de Búrca and J. Weiler (eds.), *The European Court of Justice* (Oxford University Press, 2001), p. 46.

[20] See D. Chalmers, G. Davies and G. Monti, *European Union Law: Text and Materials* (2nd edn, Cambridge University Press, 2010), p. 160.

[21] This tactic is particularly viable in hierarchical settings. Cf. Case T-85/09 *Yassin Abdullah Kadi* v. *Commission* (Seventh Chamber) [2010] ECR II-5177 (para. 123).

served a very direct unificatory purpose in medieval England. Long before there was a parliament, the king's judges travelled the shires from the second half to the twelfth century on to set up court and pacify the realm, all of this of course without a statute book in hand.[22] Their activities had a strong executive flavour, but this has traditionally been depicted as an orderly act of fusing diverse local customs into a more-or-less unitary body of law, called the 'common law', which in its original meaning was said to be the 'universal custom of the realm' or *lex et consuetudo Angliae*.[23] Of course, communal systems of justice were already in place at the time. The common law was hardly entirely native, with the Norman conquest, Roman law, canon law, the law merchant and the peculiar system of equity all leaving their mark over time. The native origin narrative, however, remained a linchpin of its legitimacy even when the separation of powers was no longer anachronistic. The rules enunciated by the judges were supposed to be known through the experience of everyday life, since they allegedly sprang from English soil.[24] As this declaratory account became increasingly hard to maintain, the binding character of judicial decisions stepped in to fulfil this function.[25] Yet it cannot be assumed that this common law was particularly coherent, not least since law reporting only began at the end of the thirteenth century and was for a long time a rather slapdash affair. But the purpose of prior judicial decisions lay not only – or even primarily – in establishing hard-and-fast rules, but also in furnishing a looser network of principles for what seemed analogous situations, as emerges from the work attributed to Bracton.[26] In other words, the king's law may not have been universal or consistent, but its unifying and legitimising force prevailed over time, albeit more as a matter of expedience and ritualised symbiosis with practice than anything else.

Contemporary lawyers similarly often draw on connections to existing structures for legitimacy, since it shrinks the distance between ('permissible since real') *lex lata* and ('impermissible since wishful') *lex ferenda*, thus fitting with ingrained expectations concerning legal discourse. Consider only the references of the ECJ to the legal traditions of

---

[22] See J. H. Baker, *An Introduction to English Legal History* (4th edn, Butterworths, London, 2002), pp. 12–29.

[23] G. Simonds, 'Law' in E. Barker (ed.), *The Character of England* (Clarendon Press, Oxford, 1947), pp. 115–16.

[24] Cf. D. J. Davies, *The Book of English Law* (John Murray, London, 1953), p. 24.

[25] See e.g. Simonds (n. 23 above), p. 116.

[26] See T. Twiss (ed.), *Henrici de Bracton: De Legibus et Consuetudinibus Angliae*, 6 vols. (William S. Hein, Buffalo, 1990 (1878)), I, p. xxxvii.

the Member States, for instance in establishing Member State liability, in assessing no-fault Union liability or in entrenching fundamental rights. It is an accustomed element in opinions of Advocates General, pleadings of the Commission and judicial deliberations.[27] Even if the judgments themselves often eschew the term 'comparative law', the method remains an important legitimatory source for the ECJ's pronouncements and is a means of diplomacy with domestic legal orders and other addressees.[28] Indeed, at the Court, that particular technique is institutionalised in two respects. First, the judges roughly match the individual Member State legal traditions in equal proportion. Secondly, the Research and Documentation department of the CJEU is staffed by a few dozen lawyers drawn from the various jurisdictions and produces comparative law studies at the behest of one of the three courts. This is done not to arithmetically divine a solution common to the largest number of Member States, but rather to support normative choices and to ensure that the Court does not flatly cut across domestic legal orders without knowing this. In other words, this shows a semblance of coherence and bolsters acceptance. As will be developed over the course of this monograph, the ECJ's case citation practice seeks to meld conceptions of law and reality and gel external communication; this is vital to ensure the legitimacy of the Court, which in turn is crucial to its long-term survival.[29]

C Factors conducive to positive precedent

i Brevity and fecundity of (treaty) language

Several factors encourage the use of precedents in the ECJ. First, the substratum of the supranational European legal system is rather thin.

---

[27] See P. Pescatore, 'Le Recours, dans la jurisprudence de la Cour de justice des Communautés européennes, à des normes déduites de la comparaison des droits des états membres', *Revue Internationale de Droit Comparé*, 32 (1980), 337, 338.

[28] See K. Lenaerts, 'Interlocking Legal Orders in the European Union and Comparative Law', *International and Comparative Law Quarterly*, 52 (2003), 873, 874, 906.

[29] Cf. R. A. Cichowski, *The European Court and Civil Society: Litigation, Mobilization and Governance* (Cambridge University Press, New York 2007), pp. 41–4; Y. Lupu and E. Voeten, 'Precedent in International Courts: A Network Analysis of Case Citations by the European Court of Human Rights', *British Journal of Political Science*, 42 (2012), 413, 413–4 ('uncertain compliance environment'). That is of course not to deny that other factors also affect legitimacy, e.g. political independence. See E. Benvenisti and G. W. Downs, 'Prospects for the Increased Independence of International Tribunals', *German Law Journal*, 12 (2011), 1057, 1058 (calling political independence a 'necessary, if not sufficient, condition for the perceived legitimacy' of judicial activity).

The TEU numbers 55 Articles, the TFEU 358. Unsurprisingly, like many foundational instruments, these treaties consist of clauses of a general nature requiring elaboration to be operable in practice. At least in the eyes of certain users, they are 'incomplete'. And almost to add insult to injury, many basic points that might be considered essential for a project as ambitious as the EU are not found directly in the treaties, including legal sources and the relationship between the supranational and national levels, perhaps precisely because of the staggering ambition of the endeavour.[30] Moreover, only fairly recently have ideas such as civil liberties and fundamental rights found their way into the treaties.

Coupled with a vast array of highly receptive concepts, this *traité-cadre* provides ample opportunity for actors to put forward their designs based on this slender framework, often through the use of amorphous general principles.[31] In-built multilingualism adds another dimension of complexity. It has always been a powerful reason for not adopting a narrow literal approach to the understanding of supranational legal provisions.[32] Hence AG Jacobs noted in *HAG II*: 'In keeping with its nature as a *traité-cadre*, the EEC Treaty does not purport to lay down an exhaustive code of rules . . . in Community law. It merely provides a skeleton. The task of putting flesh on the bones falls to the Community legislature and to the Court of Justice.'[33] The ECJ agrees. As the Court famously noted in *Les Verts*, the treaties are but 'the basic constitutional charter'.[34]

ii Absence of widespread codification

Closely related to the previous point, the EU legal order has never experienced extensive codification in its secondary law. Compared to

---

[30] On this 'strange [linguistic] economy' see T. Koopmans, 'The Birth of European Law at the Crossroads of Legal Traditions', *American Journal of Comparative Law*, 39 (1991), 493, 495.

[31] See T. Tridimas, *The General Principles of EU Law* (2nd edn, Oxford University Press, 2006), p. 18; K. Lenaerts and K. Gutman, '"Federal Common Law" in the European Union: A Comparative Perspective from the United States', *American Journal of Comparative Law*, 54 (2006), 1, 7–16; M. K. Moser, 'Allgemeine Rechtsgrundsätze in der Rechtsprechung des EuGH als Katalysatoren einer europäischen Wertegemeinschaft', *Zeitschrift für Europarecht, Internationales Privatrecht & Rechtsvergleichung*, 53 (2012), 4, 17.

[32] See Case C-461/03 *Gaston Schul Douane-expediteur BV* v. *Minister van Landbouw, Natuur en Voedselkwaliteit* [2005] ECR I-10513, Opinion of AG Ruiz-Jarabo Colomer (para. 56).

[33] Case C-10/89 *SA CNL-SUCAL NV* v. *HAG GF AG ('HAG II')* [1990] ECR I-3711, Opinion of AG Jacobs (para. 10).

[34] Case 294/83 *Parti écologiste "Les Verts"* v. *Parliament* [1986] ECR 1339 (para. 23).

many domestic legal orders, it is relatively novel, almost experimental. Codification typically has three features:[35] (i) it aims to be comprehensive concerning a particular subject matter, (ii) it is systematic in presenting its *sujet* as a closed, rational entity and (iii) it is made by a centralised legislature. It cannot and does not attempt to shut out adjudicatory creativity, but it focuses the actors' minds differently by providing a specific matrix of legal information and at least nominally instils an order of precedence. While some areas of EU law have seen tenacious attempts to put the sprawling case law of the Court on a more organised footing,[36] vastly important swathes, including the free movement of goods, have never received such methodical attention.

iii Finality, recognition and effective enforcement

Besides this considerable latitude, the ECJ enjoys independence in a very practical sense. There is no appeal from its judgments. They are binding from the date of delivery.[37] The Court may decide thoroughly unconvincingly, but it does so with the force of law. Enforcement is rarely problematic, perhaps because it is careful not to overplay its hand in this respect.[38] This contrasts noticeably with general international law and the ICJ, where Security Council action under UN Charter Art. 94(2) remains a rather speculative possibility.[39]

iv Multiplicity of influences and polycentricity of actors

Whenever there is a confluence of multiple legal and political influences and a convergence of different actors it becomes all the more important who has the last say. To be sure, even a confident adjudicatory body cannot in the end thrive when contravening a uniform position of influential political stakeholders. But it can certainly benefit from the absence of

---

[35] See R. Zimmermann, 'Codification: History and Present Significance of an Idea', *European Review of Private Law*, 3 (1995), 95, 95–7.

[36] See e.g. Directive 2006/123/EC of the European Parliament and of the Council of 12 Dec. 2006 on services in the internal market [2006] OJ L376/36.

[37] See ECJ Rules of Procedure Art. 91(1); C. F. Germelmann, *Die Rechtskraft von Gerichtsentscheidungen in der Europäischen Union* (Mohr Siebeck, Tübingen, 2009), p. 333.

[38] Cf. TFEU Arts. 260, 280, 299; H. G. Schermers and D. F. Waelbroeck, *Judicial Protection in the European Union* (6th edn, Kluwer Law International, The Hague, 2001), pp. 745–6.

[39] Charter of the United Nations of 24 Oct. 1945, 1 UNTS XVI.

the latter by drawing on a wide range of different ideas and concepts, depending on the situation. That need not be an invariably cynical exercise, as this allows adjudication to give effect to views other than blunt majoritarianism. Resolving such differences is an important facet of ECJ law-making.

The EU is undoubtedly diverse. The ever-closer union programmatically referred to in the Preamble and Art. 1 of the TEU does not aspire to singularity. Rather, the EU is a context for interaction, a 'plurality of collective wills'.[40] While the supranational element is one of its commonly touted hallmarks, the EU plays host to a wide range of competing models of organisation, governance and democracy that have spawned many political and philosophical classifications and an unmanageable literature.[41] This diversity of influences has often led to a flight into the widely used albeit unsatisfactory 'sui generis' label. Yet it is neither high-faluting theorising nor simply a description of the diverse aims contained in the foundational instruments. Not only are there more than two dozen individual legal orders and traditions, the EU's diversity can be broken down into a myriad of very live issues, ranging from the multiple actors involved in law-making to the decentralised effectuation of EU law.

The ECJ constantly plays upon this. It utilises evaluative comparative methodology and frequently sets important baseline standards that are then left to the Member State legal orders to flesh out, as in the interplay between EU remedies and national procedural autonomy. Writers assert that this is apposite since it shows deference and limits excesses.[42] Private individuals have been particularly welcome catalysts for judicial creativity, with most landmark cases springing from preliminary reference proceedings according to what is now TFEU Art. 267.[43] These requests make up

---

[40] D. Halberstam, 'Constitutional Heterarchy: The Centrality of Conflict in the European Union and the United States' in J. L. Dunoff and J. P. Trachtman (eds.), *Ruling the World? Constitutionalism, International Law, and Global Governance* (Cambridge University Press, 2009), p. 340.

[41] See J. H. H. Weiler, 'European Models: Polity, People and System' in P. Craig and C. Harlow (eds.), *Lawmaking in the European Union* (Kluwer Law International, London, The Hague & Boston, 1998), pp. 9–32.

[42] See G. Conway, 'Levels of Generality in the Legal Reasoning of the European Court of Justice', *European Law Journal*, 14 (2008), 787, 805.

[43] Out of a dozen 'classics' of EU law contained in a recent collection, eleven involved preliminary references: M. Poiares Maduro and L. Azoulai (eds.), *The Past and Future*

the largest part of the Court's workload,[44] a practice that is reflected in the addition of a separate title to the ECJ Rules of Procedure in 2012 (Arts. 93–118).[45] Over time, this perspective has shifted notably from a functional understanding of individuals as facilitators of market integration to citizenry as an end in itself. It is hard to deny that all of this enhances the Court's position.

More pragmatically, the Court is evidently not a lone wolf. First, the Member States of course craft the treaties and allocate competences. This was not just a once and forever decision long ago; primary law can be revised, as the Lisbon Treaty shows and the single currency crisis portended. Secondly, other EU organs are vital. Secondary law decisively shapes the face of the Union. The Commission or Council also seek to steer the boat, at times leaping to the Court's aid. Thirdly, national courts and governments fire warning shots or acquiesce, thus influencing the course of the ECJ. In short, the view that the Court simply does one entity's bidding as a conscious agent or unconscious automaton is not plausible.[46]

D Models denying ECJ law-making

Examples of the importance of ECJ precedents – many of them abundantly familiar classics – could be taken from almost every sphere of social interaction, including the constitutional buildings blocks of the EU,[47]

---

of EU Law: The Classics of EU Law Revisited on the 50th Anniversary of the Rome Treaty (Hart, Oxford, 2010). See also T. Koopmans, 'La Procédure préjudicielle – victime de son succès?' in F. Capotorti et al. (eds.), Du droit international au droit de l'intégration: Liber amicorum Pierre Pescatore (Nomos, Baden-Baden, 1987), pp. 347–57; U. Haltern, Europarecht: Dogmatik im Kontext (2nd edn, Mohr Siebeck, Tübingen, 2007), p. 187; K. Lenaerts and J. A. Gutiérrez-Fons, 'The Constitutional Allocation of Powers and General Principles of EU Law', Common Market Law Review, 47 (2010), 1629, 1635.

[44] See R. Mackenzie, C. Romano and Y. Shany, Manual on International Courts and Tribunals (2nd edn, Oxford University Press, 2010), p. 263.

[45] Rules of Procedure of the Court of Justice (September 2012) [2012] OJ L265/1 ('ECJ Rules of Procedure').

[46] See A. Stone Sweet, 'Conclusion' in A. Stone Sweet (ed.), The Judicial Construction of Europe (Oxford University Press, 2004), p. 235; P. P. Craig, 'The ECJ and Ultra Vires Action: A Conceptual Analysis', Common Market Law Review, 48 (2011), 395, 396.

[47] See e.g. Case 26/62 NV Algemene Transport- en Expeditie Onderneming van Gend & Loos v. Netherlands Inland Revenue Administration [1963] ECR 1; F. Mancini, 'The Making of a Constitution for Europe', Common Market Law Review, 26 (1989), 595, 600.

fundamental freedoms,[48] fundamental rights,[49] citizenship,[50] social and labour law,[51] private international law[52] and state liability.[53] But whether or not adjudicators actually 'make law' remains a topic for the ages. The following sections analyse two models frequently employed in order to put the lie to statements to the effect that judges, irrespective of whether they operate in a national, international or supranational setting, are law-makers. What the models have in common is that they separate the application and the creation of law. They differ with regard to the scope they allow for legal development in the course of adjudication.

i The binary model: static sources or the tyranny of the letter

The binary model employs the most austere and straightforward conceptual apparatus (see Figure 2.D.i.). It is twofold in the sense that there are mutually exclusive possibilities according to which actors either make law or not, in which case they will be interpreting, clarifying or applying it. The actors are typecast: state parties and legislators create law, adjudicators do not. Only the former craft sources, which are the sole font of normativity. There is an important corollary to this bifurcation. The law does not change through adjudication. The ideal is that it remains static,

---

[48] See e.g. Case 8–74 *Procureur du Roi* v. *Benoît and Gustave Dassonville* [1974] ECR 837; A. Rosas, 'Life after *Dassonville* and *Cassis*: Evolution but No Revolution' in M. Poiares Maduro and L. Azoulai (eds.), *The Past and Future of EU Law* (Hart, Oxford and Portland, 2010), p. 436 ('cited *ad nauseam* in subsequent case law').

[49] See e.g. Case 29/69 *Erich Stauder* v. *City of Ulm – Sozialamt* [1969] ECR 419; P. Pescatore, 'Les Droits de l'homme et l'intégration européenne', *Cahiers de Droit Européen*, 4 (1968), 629, 635–6.

[50] See e.g. Case C-184/99 *Rudy Grzelczyk* v. *Centre public d'aide sociale d'Ottignies-Louvain-la-Neuve* [2001] ECR I-6193; S. Kadelbach, 'Union Citizenship' in A. von Bogdandy and J. Bast (eds.), *Principles of European Constitutional Law* (2nd edn, Hart and C. H. Beck, Oxford and Munich, 2010), p. 464.

[51] See e.g. Case 43–75 *Gabrielle Defrenne* v. *Société anonyme belge de navigation aérienne Sabena* [1976] ECR 455; A. Rosas, 'Finis Europae Socialis?' in J.-C. Piris *et al.* (eds.), *Chemins d'Europe: mélanges en l'honneur de Jean-Paul Jacqué* (Dalloz, Paris, 2010), p. 592.

[52] Note this telling title: A. Borrás, 'Legislation through Individual Case Law: The ECJ's Handwriting in the Brussels I Regulation', *The European Legal Forum*, 5(6) (2010), 241. Cf. European Parliament Resolution of 7 Sep. 2010 (INI/2009/2140) Implementation and review of Council Regulation (EC) No. 44/2001 on jurisdiction and the recognition and enforcement of judgments in civil and commercial matters (Brussels I) (mentioning ten particularly important ECJ precedents in a recital).

[53] See e.g. Joined Cases C-6/90 and C-9/90 *Andrea Francovich and Danila Bonifaci and ors* v. *Italian Republic* [1991] ECR I-5357.

BINARY MODEL

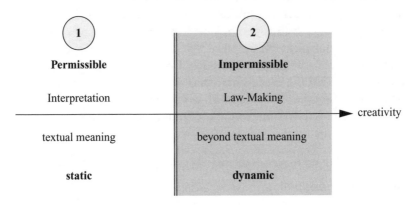

Figure 2.D.i Binary model

like a prehistoric fly encased in amber. Three types of considerations prop up this model: doctrinal, epistemological and substantive.

The ECJ does not display an overwhelming affinity for this model. Beyond national legal orders, the binary model remains particularly prevalent in public international law.[54] This is largely explicable due to the historically rather fragile position of international courts and tribunals, as evidenced by the widespread importance attached to consent and voluntary submission to adjudication. States do not like their own judiciaries telling them what to do, let alone distant ones. As is familiar, Art. 38(1)(d) of the Statute of the International Court of Justice ('ICJ') considers judicial decisions to be 'subsidiary means for the

---

[54] On the traditional consent-based and state-centric underpinnings see W. Grewe, *Epochen der Völkerrechtsgeschichte* (Nomos, Baden-Baden, 1984), pp. 591–601. But see V. Lowe, 'The Function of Litigation in International Society', *International and Comparative Law Quarterly*, 61 (2012), 209, 214 ('Cases make law. However one might finesse the technically nonbinding, non-precedential force of judgments and awards in international law, the principles that are laid down, refined and applied in particular cases are a part of the architecture of the legal system.'); ITLOS, Case No. 16, *Dispute Concerning Delimitation of the Maritime Boundary Between Bangladesh and Myanmar in the Bay of Bengal (Bangladesh/Myanmar)*, Declaration of Judge Wolfrum of 14 Mar. 2012 (pp. 2–3) (expressing doubts that the role of 'case law' is adequately described as a 'means for identifying the applicable sources', speaking of a 'law-making function' of international courts and stating that their 'case law constitutes an *acquis judiciare*, a source of international law', while couching this in 'progressive development' terms with an apparent appreciation for Holmesian delegated law-making).

determination of rules of law'.[55] Sources are properly treaties, custom and general principles. Sometimes, a guarded position regarding precedent-following is taken to obviate the possibility of judicial law-making, thereby eliding positive and negative precedent.[56] Equally famous is the age-old disbelief and scorn that this professed – and often professional – jurisprudential asceticism attracts.[57] The modern mainstream acknowledges the criticism *in abstracto*, but considers it misplaced rather than unfounded.[58] In its view, for all the protestation, Art. 38 has not caused any particularly worrisome problems.[59] Indeed, the mainstream would not be the mainstream if it did not pay heed to practical reality, which demands paying close attention to international adjudication.[60] Decisions are thus often presented as records of how abstract rules have fared in practice. Accordingly, many acts of judicial creativity are reformulated as the discovery or declaration of (customary international) law.[61] Overall, 'difficult theories of judicial legislation' are avoided.[62] Adopting this view also

---

[55] Statute of the International Court of Justice ('ICJ Statute') of 26 Jun. 1945, 33 UNTS 993. Cf. R. Y. Jennings and A. Watts, *Oppenheim's International Law*, I: *Peace* (9th edn, Longman, Harlow, 1992), para. 13 ('subsidiary and indirect'); W. Graf Vitzthum, 'Begriff, Geschichte und Rechtsquellen des Völkerrechts' in W. Graf Vitzthum (ed.), *Völkerrecht* (5th edn, De Gruyter, Berlin, 2010), p. 66.

[56] See Jennings and Watts (n. 55 above), para. 13; *Burlington Resources Inc.* v. *Republic of Ecuador*, ICSID Case No. ARB/08/05, Decision on Jurisdiction of 2 Jun. 2010 (Kaufmann-Kohler, Orrego Vicuña, Stern) (para. 100) (Arbitrator Stern considered it her role 'to decide each case on its own merits, independently of any apparent jurisprudential trend').

[57] See e.g. H. Kelsen, *Reine Rechtslehre* (Franz Deuticke, Leipzig and Vienna, 1934), p. 78; G. G. Fitzmaurice, 'Some Problems Regarding the Formal Sources of Law' in F. M. van Asbeck (ed.), *Symbolae Verzijl: présentées au Prof. J. H. W. Verzijl, á l'occasion de son LXX-ième anniversaire* (Nijhoff, La Haye, 1958), pp. 153–76.

[58] See e.g. A. Pellet, 'Article 38' in A. Zimmermann, K. Oellers-Frahm and C. Tomuschat (eds.), *The Statute of the International Court of Justice: A Commentary* (Oxford University Press, 2006), m.n. 79 (with further references to critiques and responses). For a nuanced understanding of sources see A. Verdross and B. Simma, *Universelles Völkerrecht: Theorie und Praxis* (3rd edn, Duncker & Humblot, Berlin, 1984), para. 619.

[59] See S. Besson, 'Theorizing the Sources of International Law' in S. Besson and J. Tasioulas (eds.), *The Philosophy of International Law* (Oxford University Press, 2010), p. 164 ('placative confidence').

[60] See e.g. S. M. Schwebel, 'The Contribution of the International Court of Justice to the Development of International Law' in W. P. Heere (ed.), *International Law and The Hague's 750th Anniversary* (TMC Asser Press, The Hague, 1999), p. 407.

[61] See H. Lauterpacht, *The Development of International Law by the International Court* (Stevens, London, 1958), p. 368.

[62] S. Rosenne, *The Law and Practice of the International Court 1920–2005*, 4 vols. (4th edn, Martinus Nijhoff, Leiden, 2006), III, p. 1553.

nurtures tendencies not to believe strongly in the restrictive force of precedents.

That the binary model has had much less purchase concerning the ECJ can to an extent be traced to the far more assured and integrated position the supranational Court enjoys in comparison to international courts and tribunals. Vis-à-vis domestic courts, it never had a strong unitary legislator to rival it. Doctrinally, unlike international law and its ICJ Statute Art. 38, the ECJ does not have a single provision that is understood to comprehensively and compulsorily set out what it can work with. This is both a cause and a consequence of the EU's maturity; the true quantum leap that launched the EU legal order beyond conventional regional international organisations is its effective auto-generative capacity.[63]

This lack of a single provision instructing the ECJ does not of course prevent a more orthodox enumeration of what the sources of EU law might be.[64] But judgments of the ECJ are not included in traditional enumerations of primary law, secondary law or international treaties with 'third countries', namely non-Member States, or international organisations. This is perhaps understandable from the perspective of not wanting to offend democratic sensitivities, but a powerful case has been made that the EU has come a long way from a rudimentary and functional separation of powers and a rigidly orthodox conception of legal sources.[65] TEU Art. 19(1), which purports to define the role of the ECJ, nebulously speaks of the Court ensuring that 'the law is observed' in the interpretation and application of the treaties. Even a cursory glance at the Court's case reports will yield an abundance of references to its 'case law'. Such references are also very common in secondary legislation.[66]

This flies in the face of the static binary model. Instead of 'case law', 'jurisprudence' would seem a more felicitous expression, as used in

---

[63] See C. W. A. Timmermans, 'General Aspects of the European Union and the European Communities' in P. J. G. Kapteyn and P. VerLoren van Themaat (eds.), *The Law of the European Union and the European Communities* (4th edn, Kluwer Law International, Alphen aan den Rijn 2008), p. 73.

[64] See e.g. T. C. Hartley, *The Foundations of European Union Law* (7th edn, Oxford University Press, 2010), p. 84; K.-D. Borchardt, *Die rechtlichen Grundlagen der Europäischen Union* (4th edn, Facultas, Vienna, 2010), pp. 69–78.

[65] Cf. F. C. Mayer, 'Art. 19 EUV' in E. Grabitz, M. Hilf and M. Nettesheim (eds.), *Das Recht der Europäischen Union* (C. H. Beck, Munich, 2010), m.nn. 23–33.

[66] See e.g. Directive 2006/123/EC of the European Parliament and of the Council of 12 Dec. 2006 on services in the internal market [2006] OJ L376/36; Council Implementing Regulation (EU) No. 282/2011 of 15 Mar. 2011 laying down implementing measures for Directive 2006/112/EC on the common system of value added tax [2011] OJ L77/1.

the Romance languages (French: *jurisprudence*, Italian: *giurisprudenza*, Spanish: *jurisprudencia*, Portuguese: *jurisprudência*). According to those expressions, judgments display perception of the law, namely the courts' cognisance of legal reality. What they do not do is alter it. In other words, they merely talk about the legal situation, as arguably borne out by the German *Rechtsprechung* or the Dutch *rechtspraak*.[67] Judgments can be either right or wrong, depending on whether they are within the realm of legal reality or not. But they cannot move the borderline. They might help us understand the law, but they are not the stuff of law itself.[68] They are exemplary at best.

From time to time the ECJ itself entertains the idea of merely clarifying or interpreting what is statically contained in 'official' sources of law.[69] In particular its earlier and more impersonal judgments that appear to echo the *Conseil d'État* (the French Council of State) can read like a denial of law-making.[70] This supposed passivity also comes to the fore explicitly in statements to the effect that the ECJ simply 'confirms' certain propositions of law in its case law.[71]

Yet the paint is peeling noticeably, even if one leaves aside the issue of stretching the ordinary meaning of norms almost infinitely via *effet utile* logic. The Advocates General in particular are noticeably more intrepid and often appear quite happy to state how the ECJ has developed 'its case

[67] Cf. P. Kirchhof, 'Recht Sprechen ist Sprechen über das Gesetz' in G. Müller, E. Osterloh and T. Stein (eds.), *Festschrift für Günter Hirsch zum 65. Geburtstag* (C. H. Beck, Munich, 2008), pp. 584–8.

[68] This distinction is brought out by the rival German concepts *Rechtsquelle* and *Rechtserkenntnisquelle*, which differentiate between sources of law and sources of legal cognition.

[69] See e.g. Case 61/79 *Amministrazione delle finanze dello Stato* v. *Denkavit italiana Srl* [1980] ECR 1205 (para. 16) (interpreting a rule 'as it must be or ought to have been understood and applied from the time of its coming into force'); *ibid.* Opinion of AG Reischl (p. 1232); Case C-209/03 *The Queen, on the application of Dany Bidar* v. *London Borough of Ealing and Secretary of State for Education and Skills* (Grand Chamber) [2005] ECR I-2119 (para. 66).

[70] Cf. J. J. Barceló, 'Precedent in European Community Law' in N. MacCormick and R. Summers (eds.), *Interpreting Precedents: A Comparative Study* (Ashgate, Aldershot, 1997), p. 411 (calling its style of reasoning 'deductive, legalistic and magisterial').

[71] See e.g. Joined Cases 16 to 20/79 *Criminal proceedings against Joseph Danis and ors* [1979] ECR 3327 (para. 8); Case 176/82 *Théo Nebe* v. *Commission* (Second Chamber) [1983] ECR 2475 (para. 21); Case C-138/02 *Brian Francis Collins* v. *Secretary of State for Work and Pensions* [2004] ECR I-2703 Opinion of AG Ruiz-Jarabo Colomer (para. 70); Case C-546/07 *Commission* v. *Federal Republic of Germany* [2010] ECR I-439, Opinion of AG Mazák (para. 38); Case C-389/08 *Base NV and ors* v. *Ministerraad* [2010] ECR I-9073 Opinion of AG Cruz Villalón (para. 38).

law' rather than just interpreted provisions.[72] The possessive pronoun clearly suggests the Court is the font of law, not the Member States or the Union. Perhaps surprisingly, Member States and the Council chime in similarly in the course of making submissions.[73] Indeed, judgments of the ECJ itself are gradually willing to let their guard down in this respect.[74] Increasingly liberal translations also contribute to this.[75] Candid commentary has long since played its part.[76]

To a large degree, the particular usage is a function of the respective legitimacy demands. State liability is an example. *Francovich* defensively probed its point by stating the remedy to be 'inherent' in the treaties.[77] In 2012, the Grand Chamber in *Dominguez* had no qualms about presenting the ECJ's precedents as the foundation of state liability.[78] After all, the

---

[72] See e.g. Case C-44/93 *Namur-Les Assurances du Crédit SA* v. *Office National du Ducroire and the Belgian State* [1994] ECR I-3829, Opinion of AG Lenz (para. 70); Case C-9/93 *IHT Internationale Heiztechnik GmbH and Uwe Danzinger* v. *Ideal-Standard GmbH and Wabco Standard GmbH* [1994] ECR I-2789, Opinion of AG Gulman (para. 56); Case C-302/00 *Commission* v. *French Republic* [2002] ECR I-2055, Opinion of AG Alber (para. 53); Case C-72/03 *Carbonati Apuani Srl* v. *Comune di Carrara* [2004] ECR I-8027, Opinion of AG Poiares Maduro (fn. 61); Case C-131/03 P *R.J. Reynolds Tobacco Holdings, Inc. and ors* v. *Commission* [2006] ECR I-7795, Opinion of AG Sharpston (para. 101).

[73] See e.g. Case C-482/08 *United Kingdom of Great Britain and Northern Ireland* v. *Council* (Grand Chamber) [2010] ECR I-10413 (paras. 33, 40); Case C-409/06 *Winner Wetten GmbH* v. *Bürgermeisterin der Stadt Bergheim* (Grand Chamber) [2010] ECR I-8015 (para. 63).

[74] See e.g. Case C-232/99 *Commission* v. *Kingdom of Spain* (Fifth Chamber) [2002] ECR I-4235 (paras. 20–1); Case C-193/01 P *Athanasios Pitsiorlas* v. *Council and Banque centrale européenne* (Fifth Chamber) [2003] ECR I-4837 (para. 24); Case C-337/06 *Bayerischer Rundfunk and ors* v. *GEWA – Gesellschaft für Gebäudereinigung und Wartung mbH* (Fourth Chamber) [2007] ECR I-11173 (para. 53); Case C-265/09 P *OHIM* v. *BORCO-Marken-Import Matthiesen GmbH & Co. KG* (First Chamber) [2010] ECR I-8265 (para. 25).

[75] Sometimes the French version on which the judges agreed upon is still a little more guarded than the official English translation. See e.g. Case C-243/01 *Criminal proceedings against Piergiorgio Gambelli and ors* [2003] ECR I-13031 (para. 64), where the English version reads 'conditions laid down by the case-law of the Court' while the French original speaks of 'conditions qui ressortent de la jurisprudence de la Cour'.

[76] See e.g. U. Everling, 'On the Judge-Made Law of the European Community's Courts' in D. O'Keeffe and A. Bavasso (eds.), *Judicial Review in European Union Law: Liber Amicorum in Honour of Lord Slynn of Hadley*, 2 vols. (Kluwer Law International, The Hague, London and Boston, 2000), I, pp. 30, 35. Indeed, leading academic journals such as the Common Market Law Review plainly place 'case law' alongside other items such as 'articles', 'book reviews' and 'survey of literature' in their table of contents.

[77] Joined Cases C-6/90 and C-9/90 *Andrea Francovich and Danila Bonifaci and ors* v. *Italian Republic* [1991] ECR I-5357 (para. 35).

[78] Case C-282/10 *Maribel Dominguez* v. *Centre informatique du Centre Ouest Atlantique and Préfet de la région Centre* (Grand Chamber) [2012] ECR I-0000 (para. 43).

previous two decades had gone by relatively smoothly, largely because the floodgates did not open. Hence there is support not only for the view that the judges themselves, despite occasional statements to the contrary, hardly buy into the binary model, but also that they are increasingly prepared to dispense with it publicly as the Court becomes an ever more robust and accepted part of everyday life in the EU. This is significant, since even if one is prepared to pardon 'case law' as an otiose slip of the tongue or imprecise shorthand, 'development' thereof clearly crosses the bright dividing line assumed to exist by the binary model and unsettles its stillness.[79] At the same time, 'activism' remains a dirty word even in the most optimistic and frank circles.

What is perhaps less conspicuous about the binary model is the underlying epistemic premise that is required to make it operable: the law exists as an objectively ascertainable totality of relevant rules. In other words, if there is meaning to text, it cannot be what it is simply taken to mean by somebody at a specific time. Otherwise it would have no real meaning at all, the argument goes. In this conception, there is no triangle between text, author and interpreter that creates meaning.[80] Meaning is buried in things, waiting to be excavated. Refuge can be sought in lexical definitions contained in a dictionary, 'that haven against the harshness of reality' as one Advocate General of the ECJ once called it.[81]

For this model, what is claimed to be the law, no matter by whom, does not affect the law itself. The latter exists as a self-sufficient 'thing in itself'. A proposition of law either reflects legal reality or it is off the mark and hence mistaken, perhaps wishfully or wilfully so. In this dichotomy, you are either within the law or outside of it. What counts as valid law is defined by specific mechanisms or rules, which stake out the scope of legal reality.[82] Sources are the most obvious proxies, but not the only ones. Seen through this prism, adjudication becomes the sweaty but plain labour of separating the wheat from the chaff. But the wheat and chaff are already there. Law only changes when the relevant rules are amended, for which

[79] The concept of legal 'development' plays a central role in the ternary model, to be discussed next.

[80] Cf. R. Christensen, 'Postmoderne Methodik oder: Überlebt der König seine Enthauptung in der Regel?', *Kritische Justiz*, 43 (2010), 223, 225.

[81] Case C-506/06 *Sabine Mayr* v. *Bäckerei und Konditorei Gerhard Flöckner OHG* [2008] ECR I-1017, Opinion of AG Ruiz-Jarabo Colomer (para. 38) (tasked with determining the meaning of 'pregnancy').

[82] The paragon remains H. L. A. Hart, *The Concept of Law* (2nd edn, Oxford University Press, 1997), pp. 94–5, 105.

there are prescribed techniques, such as TEU Art. 48 (for EU primary law) and TFEU Art. 294 (i.e. the EU's ordinary legislative procedure) or Arts. 39–41 of the Vienna Convention on the Law of Treaties of 1969[83] (for international law). True, in order to remain workable and avoid a recurrent *non liquet*, the binary model frequently has to work out the trajectory of a source. The free movement of goods provisions say nothing about jet skis, but they, too, can of course in principle benefit from basic market access guarantees.[84] The binary model also does not presuppose complete agreement on what sources imply, nor does it pretend perfection. But at the end of the day, it eschews an evolutionary or fragmentary conception of meaning and law-making by adjudication.

This view that judges like those at the ECJ are solely in the business of authoritatively rendering legal reality intelligible is as old as it is famous. Its patron saint – or, depending on one's perspective, whipping boy – is Charles-Louis de Secondat, Baron de La Brède et de Montesquieu, a colourful character and one of the great minds of the Enlightenment. His celebrated metaphor regarding inanimate judicial articulation of the law refuses to go away.[85] Yet it has long since been debunked as a myth in many national legal systems,[86] where it is widely recognised that any court faced with at least moderately complex disputes does a lot more than just decide them. Judges ask hypothetical questions for that very reason, namely to test wider ramifications. If all that was required was a decision on ultimately conflict-free legal material appellate courts would hardly exist. Courts and tribunals at the apex of their respective systems do not primarily decide for one or two parties, but in the interest of the legal

---

[83] Vienna Convention on the Law of Treaties ('VCLT') of 23 Jun. 1969, 1155 UNTS 331, Part IV.

[84] See Case C-142/05 *Åklagaren* v. *Percy Mickelsson and Joakim Roos* (Second Chamber) [2009] ECR I-4273.

[85] See Montesquieu, *De l'ésprit des lois*, 31 vols. (Éditions Gallimard, Paris 1995 (1758)), XI, ch. VI. Cf. V. Constantinesco, 'The ECJ as a Law-Maker: Praeter aut Contra Legem?' in D. O'Keeffe and A. Bavasso (eds.), *Judicial Review in European Union Law: Liber Amicorum in Honour of Lord Slynn of Hadley*, 2 vols. (Kluwer Law International, The Hague, London and Boston, 2000), I, pp. 73–4. For the view that the hallowed mouthful was in fact intended as a smokescreen to enable quite the opposite, namely the capacity to review legislative acts, see K. M. Schönfeld, 'Rex, Lex et Judex: Montesquieu and *la bouche de la loi* Revisited', *European Constitutional Law Review*, 4 (2008), 274.

[86] See e.g. C. Möllers, *Die drei Gewalten: Legitimation der Gewaltengliederung in Verfassungsstaat, europäischer Integration und Internationalisierung* (Velbrück, Weilerswist, 2008), p. 94; M. Eckertz-Höfer, '"Vom guten Richter" – Ethos, Unabhängigkeit, Professionalität', *Die Öffentliche Verwaltung*, 62 (2009), 729, 733; G. Hager, *Rechtsmethoden in Europa* (Mohr Siebeck, Tübingen, 2009), pp. 210–2.

system over the long haul. Even if the *Conseil d'État* adamantly sticks to its guns, most French lawyers have long discarded the supposedly wholesome parable that *jurisprudence* is 'revealed' rather than made.[87] With respect to the ECJ, it is a claim so steep it topples over backwards.[88]

It is not that the binary model is unworkable in practice, given enough lip service and chutzpah. But it is somewhere between redundant and misleading. It is redundant because it cannot satisfactorily tackle the weighty significance of adjudication in modern legal practice and the precarious power of the ultimate interpreter.[89] Ironically, this supposedly matter-of-fact model fails to account for everyday lawyering in Luxembourg and elsewhere. Legal practice is intellectually marginalised. Endless efforts are devoted to 'law-identification' (i.e. separating 'law' from 'non-law'), when the real battleground is the meaning itself rather than its supposed divination.

It is misleading because the model struggles to achieve what it set out to do even when examined on its own terms. Its Achilles' heel is that it replaces one circularity with another. There is no way for the human mind to know the law without knowing it. In other words: the meaning of a legal source begs the very question. That is the first circularity that has forever bedevilled any form of understanding, including legal interpretation.[90] Rules famously do not explain their application. That understanding *is* interpretation has long become the 'interpretive orthodoxy'.[91] The binary model however seeks to resolve this problem and quell any creativity through a self-defeating doctrine of legal method of legal doctrine:[92] legal method, logically prior to doctrinal arguments, is made dependent on doctrine. 'Look at the materials we're supposed

---

[87] See e.g. M. Troper and C. Grzegorczyk, 'Precedent in France' in N. MacCormick and R. Summers (eds.), *Interpreting Precedents: A Comparative Study* (Ashgate, Aldershot, 1997), p. 114.

[88] See C. Tomuschat, 'Das Europa der Richter' in J. Bröhmer *et al.* (eds.), *Internationale Gemeinschaft und Menschenrechte: Festschrift für Georg Ress zum 70. Geburtstag* (Carl Heymanns, Cologne, 2005), pp. 857, 869; Lenaerts and Gutiérrez-Fons (see n. 43 above), p. 1668.

[89] On the latter see F. Müller and R. Christensen, *Juristische Methodik: Grundlagen* (9th edn, Duncker & Humblot, Berlin, 2004), p. 290.

[90] Kant famously drew attention to this in his *Critique of Pure Reason*. See W. Weischedel, *Die philosophische Hintertreppe* (38th edn, DTV, Munich, 2009), p. 184. The idea has been recycled and forgotten in roughly equal measure ever since.

[91] D. Patterson, 'The Poverty of Interpretive Universalism: Towards the Reconstruction of Legal Theory', *Texas Law Review*, 72 (1993), 1.

[92] See A. Somek, *Rechtliches Wissen* (Suhrkamp, Frankfurt am Main, 2006), p. 80 (in German: 'eine wunderbar zirkuläre Dogmatik der Methode der Dogmatik'; original emphasis).

to render intelligible,' the model exclaims, 'they will tell us how to make use of them.' It is deliberately relegated to its closed set of limited tools and patterns for legal work, such as Arts. 38 and 59 of the ICJ Statute. It mistrusts cases and non-canonical devices – many of which are popular in a supranational context[93] – such as harmonious interpretation, sincere co-operation, comparative law and general principles, which are either made to fit the canon or disavowed altogether. The flaw is that the binary model pegs its hopes on a rigid scheme that is dependant on understanding itself. The upshot is a superfluous ontology of legal method, starved of ambition and innovation, forever and endlessly confined to repeat, like a broken record, the '*de facto*' or 'practical' significance of precedent.[94] The artificiality of such terminology is demonstrated by the fact that the common law could also be said to be a '*de facto*' system of precedent, not only if one adopts an originalist understanding of, for instance, the US Constitution, but also when one considers how rarely a common law court faced with at least a modicum of complexity genuinely considers its answer irredeemably set out by a precedent.

One commentator chides, 'Legal Positivism is dead, isn't it? We are all legal realists now.'[95] So why is the dichotomous approach not abandoned? There are two key reasons besides simplicity sustaining it and the declaratory view of adjudication.

First, it protects the respective normative enterprise. This appeals especially to public international law dispute settlement bodies and tribunals, given that they do not enjoy the same level of institutional reassurance that the ECJ does. Adjudicators and those seeking to persuade them know that the legitimatory pressures weighing on their shoulders ease off immensely if what they are engaged in is portrayed as a simple matter of saying out loud what is part of a fixed and predetermined state of affairs. This is more likely to coax acceptance and to allow for bolder decisions. The decisions and long-term results are then up to 'the law'. Arbitrators and judges can at most be blamed for getting it wrong this time, but not for a general state of dissatisfaction. Adjudicators are postmen – they simply deliver the bad news. The binary model is then not a deeply reflected or elaborated

---

[93] Cf. M. W. Hesselink, 'A Toolbox for European Judges', *European Law Journal*, 17 (2011), 441, 446–51.

[94] See e.g. Jennings and Watts (n. 55 above), para. 13 ('judges do not *in principle* make law'; emphasis added); *International Thunderbird Gaming Corporation* v. *United Mexican States*, *Ad Hoc* NAFTA Arbitration under UNCITRAL Rules, Separate Opinion of Arbitrator Wälde of 26 Jan. 2006 (para. 129).

[95] A. Somek, 'The Spirit of Legal Positivism', *German Law Journal*, 12 (2011), 729.

theoretical position, but an instinct regarding practical compatibility, namely the capacity to connect to and submerge within majority expectations.[96] It is the name of the game in many legal contexts, and where an actor transcends these rules he or she is quickly in trouble.

This allure of the 'automaton' theory of adjudication is universal. All kinds of legal systems and traditions flirt with the binary model, including common lawyers.[97] The common law has long entertained its own version of the declaratory theory, according to which a judicial decision (i.e. the common law) is merely evidence of long-established customs or general principles. Contrary to what is often believed and taught, understanding precedents as sources was often controversial in England.[98] The influential writings of Blackstone and Hale supported variants of the binary model.[99] Traces remain omnipresent. The current Chief Justice of the US Supreme Court, for example, drew on this during his confirmation hearings before the Senate Judiciary Committee, couched in folksy baseball terms:

> Judges and Justices are servants of the law, not the other way around. Judges are like umpires. Umpires don't make the rules, they apply them. The role of an umpire and a judge is critical. They make sure everybody plays by the rules, but it is a limited role. Nobody ever went to a ball game to see the umpire . . . I will remember that it's my job to call balls and strikes, and not to pitch or bat.[100]

---

[96] Cf. N. Luhmann, *Soziale Systeme: Grundriß einer allgemeinen Theorie* (Suhrkamp, Frankfurt am Main, 1984), p. 159.

[97] In the common law world, this eternal debate is often conducted under the headings of formalism and realism, with supporters of the binary model rallying under the banner of the former, and those opposing the declaratory theory often subscribing to the latter. See B. Tamanaha, *Beyond the Formalist-Realist Divide: The Role of Politics in Judging* (Princeton University Press, 2010).

[98] In *R* v. *Bembridge* (1783) 3 Doug 327, 332, Lord Mansfield, a famously bold judge, opined that 'the law does not consist of particular cases but of general principles, which are illustrated and explained by these cases'.

[99] See J. H. Langbein, 'Blackstone on Judging' in W. Prest (ed.), *Blackstone and his Commentaries: Biography, Law, History* (Hart, Oxford, 2009), pp. 65–78; M. Hale, *The History of the Common Law of England* (reprint edn, Rothman, Littleton, 1987 (1713)), p. 68 ('[T]he Decisions of Courts of Justice . . . do not make a Law properly so called, (for that only the King and Parliament can do); yet they have a great Weight and Authority in Expounding, Declaring, and Publishing what the Law of this Kingdom is, especially when such Decisions hold a Consonancy and Congruity with Resolutions and Decisions of former Times').

[100] Statement of the Nominee, Confirmation Hearing on the Nomination of John G. Roberts, Jr. to be Chief Justice of the United States, Senate Committee on the Judiciary, S. Hrg. 109–58, 12–15 Sep. 2005 (pp. 55–6).

The legitimacy demands in that particular scenario should be obvious. As homely as this picture might be to politicians and the public, its professed tameness has triggered fits of despair and mockery from others, for the reasons touted above and because it insulates adjudication from critique.[101]

But this caginess need not be purely cynical. A second motivation is more enlightened and goes back to the basic idea of ensuring accountability and democratic participation. Even the dyed-in-the-wool positivists of the nineteenth century were likely unpersuaded by an elementary black-and-white model of legal decision-making.[102] Instead, the fixation with strict typologies of sources and methods stems from a fundamental desire to rationalise and systematise the law – a closed and coherent legal *order* – and move from organic and fickle dominion to artificial and acquiescent authority. It is in many respects the story of the rise of modern political organisation. The root of the project is emancipation. It strives for autonomy and universalisation; ultimately, it is about freedom, collective self-government, pluralism and dissent. The fanciful positivism espoused by the binary model has become a target that is easy to ridicule, but one should bear in mind that it is the reduction of more complex themes into a simplistic 'apply-don't-make-law' pastiche of adjudication and crude methodological prescription that primarily deserves derision. At the very least, the model provides a vocabulary to utter concerns, rudimentary as it may be.[103] The matter remains particularly acute in non-domestic legal settings, such as the EU, where institutional back-ups and democratic counterweights to effective adjudication are often few and far between.

All the same, care needs to be taken not to elide the general concern that adjudicators should not exert a stranglehold over law-making, and hence a wide range of social life, with a blunt observational claim that they do not make law. Quite the contrary, only a forthright acknowledgement of

---

[101]   See e.g. B. N. Cardozo, *The Nature of the Judicial Process* (Yale University Press, New Haven 1925), p. 166 ('not discovery, but creation'); G. Williams, *Salmond on Jurisprudence* (11th edn, Sweet & Maxwell, London, 1957), p. 164 ('the declaratory theory must be totally rejected if we are to attain to any sound analysis and explanation of the true operation of judicial decisions'); M. Shapiro, 'Judges as Liars', *Harvard Journal of Law & Public Policy*, 17 (1994), 155, 165 (claiming that 'judges must always deny that they make law' and that 'judges necessarily lie because that is the nature of the activity they engage in'); E. W. Thomas, *The Judicial Process* (Cambridge University Press, 2005), p. 3 (decrying that 'the belief that judges do not make law is hopelessly out of date' and insisting that they do so even when not extending an existing doctrine or principle).

[102]   See T. Vesting, *Rechtstheorie* (C. H. Beck, Munich, 2007), pp. 50–1.

[103]   See Eckertz-Höfer (n. 86 above), p. 734.

the positive power of precedents can really further the broader concerns regarding accountability and legitimacy. The blinkered approach does more harm than good.

In conclusion, EU law is far less partial to the binary model than public international law, altogether a more fragile and contractarian enterprise. The ECJ does draw on it when legitimacy concerns appear particularly urgent. But doctrinal and epistemic support for this model is weak. The underlying substantive idea fares better and triggers continued attempts to come up with a more accurate conceptualisation of adjudication and law-making that is nevertheless respectful of the basic concerns. One such effort will be considered next.

ii The ternary model: dynamic development or having one's cake and eating it

A term often encountered in decisions of the ECJ to describe an important aspect of precedents is *development* of the law.[104] Whereas the binary model sees adjudication in stark contrasts of black and white or 'making' and 'applying' law, the ternary model adds a shade of grey in between those polar extremes: 'developing' the law (see Figure 2.D.ii.). On paper, the activity of adjudicators can thus neatly be divided into three categories as concerns their creativity. In ascending order of initiative these are: (i) interpretation, (ii) legal development and (iii) law-making.[105]

TERNARY MODEL

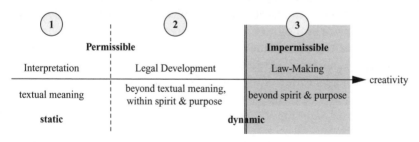

Figure 2.D.ii Ternary model

---

[104] For examples see n. 74 above.
[105] Cf. K.-D. Borchardt, 'Auslegung, Rechtsfortbildung und Rechtsschöpfung' in R. Schulze, M. Zuleeg and S. Kadelbach (eds.), *Europarecht: Handbuch für die deutsche Rechtspraxis* (2nd edn, Nomos, Baden-Baden, 2010), p. 568.

This is relevant because the former two are considered legitimate, while the third category is branded as impermissible and off limits. In order to differentiate between the three types of activity, the model posits that interpretation sticks to the possible meaning of the wording of a legal provision, legal development takes place outside of this but within the spirit and purpose of a provision and law-making in turn goes beyond the spirit and purpose of a provision.[106]

The draw of this model is that it appreciates the creativity of the ECJ yet nevertheless tries to not let it run rampant; there remains a categorical distinction between legal development and law-making. Development suggests hybridity and fluidity. Pronouncements are both old and new at the same time. The law changes through adjudication while remaining the same. That is the essence of *Rechtsfortbildung*.

It is particularly well suited to codification projects, which explains its popularity in Continental European legal systems. The underlying message is that, for all their ostensible stringency and formality, codes are not prison cells.[107] After all, it almost goes without saying that scepticism regarding any *ratio scripta* is an abiding theme.[108] Codes accommodate this. In particular broadly drafted general clauses sought to improve on hopelessly detailed former legislation projects that got lost in a thicket of particularistic instructions. Indeed, the instinctive fix to judicial law-making might be to try to map out every possible application of law in advance in minute detail. Such was the aim of the *Allgemeines Landrecht für die Preußischen Staaten* (General Law of the Prussian States) of 1794, which, as is well known, unsuccessfully sought to comprehensively codify not only civil law but also constitutional, administrative and criminal law in thousands upon thousands of paragraphs. This ultimately futile enterprise was driven by the idea that exhaustive codification would obviate the need for creative adjudication. Savigny's doubts regarding naïve beliefs that written sources would automatically ensure wholly equal, foreseeable and prompt application of the law and his insistence on a multiplicity of relevant actors would appear vindicated in that respect.[109]

---

[106] See e.g. M. Klatt, *Making the Law Explicit: The Normativity of Legal Argumentation* (Hart, Oxford, 2008), pp. 5–18; K. F. Walter, *Rechtsfortbildung durch den EuGH* (Duncker & Humblot, Berlin, 2009), pp. 41–3.

[107] See Zimmermann (see n. 35 above).

[108] Cf. H. Coing, 'Philologie und Jurisprudenz: Eine Analyse der "Dialogi" des Gentilis' in D. Simon (ed.), *Gesammelte Aufsätze zu Rechtsgeschichte, Rechtsphilosophie und Zivilrecht: 1947–1975*, 2 vols., (Klostermann, Frankfurt 1982), II, p. 223.

[109] Cf. F. C. von Savigny, *Vom Beruf unsrer Zeit für Gesetzgebung und Rechtswissenschaft* (2nd edn, J. C. B. Mohr, Heidelberg, 1828), p. 11.

Hence a different technique was pursued by those codes exemplified by the French *Code civil* of 1804 or the Austrian *Allgemeines Bürgerliches Gesetzbuch* (General Civil Code) of 1811. Besides a narrower thematic focus on private law, they proved to be more workable in that they did not set out to regulate every conceivable eventuality in explicit detail. Such codes provide general rules which can be 'developed' (rather than 'made') by adjudicators in individual cases, such as the delictual clause of Art. 1382 of the *Code civil*. This is already a lot more reminiscent of the EU treaties; consider only the clipped mention of the Union's values, fundamental freedoms or Union liability.

Yet even then the nagging question remains how effective such deliberate attempts at nipping casuistry or the universalisation of decisions in the bud really are. François Gény launched his celebrated attack on the 'fétichisme de la loi écrite et codifiée' at the end of the nineteenth century.[110] He did not contest the general allocation of legislative competence as such, but rather the idea of the law as a complete and final product that required nothing but interpretation in the sense of automatic application.[111] The corollary of this thought is the shattering of the supposed unity of law and legislation and a reinstating of judges and commentators as vital players. Indeed, Art. 4 of the French *Code civil* rules out bland refusals to rule upon complicated cases,[112] perhaps after all hinting at a more co-operative relationship between judiciary and legislature and a less hermetic separation of powers. To the present day, these borders between adjudication and legislation remain disputed. As Raymond Saleilles noted in the preface to Gény's seminal work at the turn of the century, the battle cry of the likes of Gény and later Rudolf von Jhering was 'Par le Code civil, mais au-delà du Code civil!' But in the same breath he mischievously pointed out that there were those who would rather have inverted the order of that motto to soften its bold implications and cling on to the fictional vestiges of stability.[113]

This hybrid development approach is very attractive for the ECJ. The terseness of the treaty terms is no obstacle, yet their creativity is legitimate if it remains within certain bounds. In many respects, the ternary model is a response to the binary model just examined (i.e. allegations that law-making is simply not for the Court). The main critique is taken on board,

---

[110] See F. Gény, *Méthode d'interprétation et sources en droit privé positif*, 2 vols. (Libr. Générale de Droit et de Jurisprudence, Paris 1919), I, no. 35.

[111] See Gény (n. 110 above), nos. 20–5, 57.

[112] Art. 4 reads: 'Le juge qui refusera de juger, sous prétexte du silence, de l'obscurité ou de l'insuffisance de la loi, pourra être poursuivi comme coupable de déni de justice.'

[113] See Gény (n. 110 above), p. xxv.

but ample leeway is built into the system. State liability is again a good example. Faced with the assertion that only the legislature could fashion such a remedy, the Court in *Brasserie du Pêcheur* noted that the general thrust underlying the admittedly not directly applicable treaty text was on its side.[114] At the ECJ, talk of 'development' is particularly noticeable in submissions of Advocates General and judgments of chambers of three and five judges, formations that do not have the same legitimatory heft as the Grand Chamber and hence are often more coy about the novelty of their solution.

Indeed, as to the creation of state liability by the ECJ, many (Continental) critiques did not deplore that the Court developed the law, but rather that it did so *improperly*.[115] The shift from wording to spirit and purpose brings with it a heightened sensitivity for context and substance. *Francovich* was claimed to be apodictic in the sense that it was simply not a convincing legal development.[116] The question becomes not so much whether the ECJ is creative, but rather how it goes about doing so. The limits rather than the fact of innovation become central. Indeed, even the *Bundesverfassungsgericht* (the German Federal Constitutional Court, 'FCC'), hardly the biggest cheerleader of the ECJ,[117] has explicitly and repeatedly accepted the concept of legal development through the Luxembourg court, for instance in its *Honeywell* judgment of 2010.[118] What it demanded instead of complete abstinence or unconvincing self-denial was a transparent method to differentiate legal development from free-form 'political' law-making.[119] In this it echoed the modern German

---

[114] Joined Cases C-46/93 and C-48/93 *Brasserie du Pêcheur SA* v. *Bundesrepublik Deutschland* [1996] ECR I-1029 (para. 29).

[115] See e.g. W. Dänzer-Vanotti, 'Unzulässige Rechtsforbildung des Europäischen Gerichtshofs', *Recht der Internationalen Wirtschaft*, (1992), 733, 740–2.

[116] Cf. F. Ossenbühl, 'Der gemeinschaftsrechtliche Staatshaftungsanspruch', *Deutsches Verwaltungsblatt*, 107 (1992), 993, 994; T. von Danwitz, 'Zur Entwicklung der gemeinschaftlichen Staatshaftung', *Juristenzeitung*, 49 (1994), 335, 338.

[117] Its scepticism, including highlights *Solange I* and *Maastricht* but also the more ambiguous *Lisbon* decision, is well known. The *Bundesverfassungsgericht* has to date never made a reference to the ECJ. Cf. J. A. Frowein, 'Kritische Bemerkungen zur Lage des deutschen Staatsrechts aus rechtsvergleichender Sicht', *Die Öffentliche Verwaltung*, 51 (1998), 806; J. E. K. Murkens, 'Identity Trumps Integration: The Lisbon Treaty in the German Federal Constitutional Court', *Der Staat*, 48 (2009), 517, 534.

[118] BVerfG, 2 BvR 2661/06, *Honeywell*, 2. Senate, 6 Jul. 2010 (m.n. 62) (with further references). See also U. Steiner, 'Richterliche Rechtsfortbildung und Grundgesetz' in G. Müller, E. Osterloh and T. Stein (eds.), *Festschrift für Günter Hirsch zum 65. Geburtstag* (C. H. Beck, Munich, 2008), p. 614.

[119] BVerfG, 2 BvR 2661/06, *Honeywell*, 2. Senate, 6 Jul. 2010, m.n. 64.

constitutional tradition of seeking to strictly separate law from politics, with an ever-present and thinly veiled distrust of the latter. All the same, the shift from discovery to justification was welcome. The Danish *Højesteret* (Supreme Court) has made similar indications concerning legal development by the ECJ.[120]

For this liberal, middle-of-the-road, Dworkinian position, judges are good, perhaps even heroic archetypes, but they should not be philosopher kings. The law changes, but it is still thought to remain a larger, systemic affair in the sense that judges do not impose personal preferences. *Gesetzesbindung*, the link to democratic participation, is not severed. For the EU, this means that the rule of law of TEU Art. 2 and the interpretation and application of the treaties according to TEU Art. 19(1) are observed. Indeed, even international courts like the European Court of Human Rights ('ECtHR') that plainly wear their heart on their sleeve as concerns dynamic judicial evolution take great care not to take things too far and give the impression that they are outright legislating and hence look for a societal basis or emergent consensus.[121]

But like so many solutions that look good on paper, the ternary model suffers from several difficulties. A preliminary hint perhaps lies in the fact that, outside German-speaking legal scholarship, the tripartite development *model* (as opposed to the mere *idea* of legal development) never really caught on. It is certainly not expressly in use at the ECJ. That need not of course be fatal, but it prompts further inquiry as to why that may be the case. Three points stick out regarding this schematic triad.

An initial issue is that the first partition is an academic battle line.[122] Irrespective of the feasibility of the distinction, given that both interpretation and development in accordance within the object and purpose of a norm are permissible, any differentiation would appear to serve the glory of a perfect scholarly superstructure more than anything else. The real bone of contention is the second mark between permissible and impermissible adjudicative activity, which would also explain why the ternary model is rarely explicated fully in practice and often lapses back into a variant of the binary approach.

---

[120] See R. Hofmann, 'Der Oberste Gerichtshof Dänemarks und die europäische Integration', *Europäische Grundrechte-Zeitschrift*, 26 (1999), 1, 3.

[121] See e.g. ECtHR, *Hirst* v. *United Kingdom (No. 2)*, Application No. 74025/01, Joint Dissenting Opinion of Judges Wildhaber, Costa, Lorenzen, Kovler, and Jebens of 6 Oct. 2005 (para. 6).

[122] Cf. S. Vogenauer, *Die Auslegung von Gesetzen in England und auf dem Kontinent*, 2 vols. (Mohr Siebeck, Tübingen 2001), I, pp. 141–6.

The second point relates to demarcating the boundaries. As to the first line, the difference between interpretation and development of the law again presupposes a preconceived notion as to where the ordinary meaning of a textual provision ends.[123] The 'thing in itself' is back. Yet precisely this will normally be hotly disputed or simply impossible to fathom. For instance, when is an eatery not a 'restaurant and catering service'?[124] Of course, extreme cases will be apparent enough and quickly exposed as irritating sophistry with predictable regularity, but many cases that are litigated at the ECJ will be much closer to call, not least because they will usually have seen various rounds of prior contestation. This is not the place to tackle the never-ending philosophical question of whether textual meaning is always up in air or not, but for practical purposes much in the end depends on educated reflexes.[125] At the very least, the boundary is a very fluid one, and the model does nothing to address this uncertainty.

Correspondingly, concerning the crucial second dividing line, it will in practice be fiendishly difficult to determine what is still covered by the object and purpose of a provision and what goes beyond that. As the criticism that the ECJ state liability decisions attracted indicates, even those who have no truck with legal development through adjudication as such can argue endlessly over what precisely the *telos* of a norm is.

It would be short-sighted to dismiss this as a 'purely practical' problem. The issue again goes deeper than 'merely tricky' application; the model rests on a flawed epistemic assumption. The boundary between the (permissible) second category and the (impermissible) third category does not solve the enduring circularity already encountered when examining the binary model. Distinguishing between law and non-law according to whether something is covered by the spirit and purpose of a norm rather than its ordinary textual meaning simply reformulates the intractable question. The spirit and purpose is no more intrinsic to a treaty provision than textual meaning. In fact, even the reasoning employed will be very similar with textual interpretation reinforcing purpose just as purpose can reinforce textual interpretation. Ultimately, only by knowing the law 'as it already is' can one grasp law 'as it is now being made'. One needs to know what is old to say what is new. This double standard was exposed

---

[123] See J. Esser, *Vorverständnis und Methodenwahl in der Rechtsfindung* (Athenäum, Frankfurt 1970), pp. 175–7; Kriele (n. 14 above), p. 222.

[124] Joined Cases C-497/09, C-499/09, C-501/09 and C-502/09 *Finanzamt Burgdorf v. Manfred Bog* (Third Chamber) [2011] ECR I-1457.

[125] See Hager (n. 86 above), pp. 287–91.

among others by Henry Maine: before a decision is rendered it is taken for granted that some rule covers the situation, otherwise it would not be possible to argue the point according to existing rules. Once a decision is rendered, it is admitted that a novel train of thought or modification of law has been established.[126]

Again, as with the contested ordinary meaning of sources, there are ways to deal with this in practice, chiefly by submitting rival arguments to adjudication and simply not worrying about this infinite logical regression. One common, albeit not mandatory, routine for judges to argue that development was fitting and necessary is to claim that it fills a gap or lacuna. There are provisions that encourage such reasoning. TEU Art. 19(1) could be understood in such a manner. But, for the reasons mentioned above, from a theoretical point of view the concept of gap-filling remains as unsatisfactory and inconclusive as the question whether the hole forms part of the doughnut. Essentially, the basic positions have not changed since Kelsen's notorious disdain almost eighty years ago.[127]

Thirdly, even if one can agree on precise partitions and assuming that one manages to situate an ECJ ruling in one of the categories, the question arises why proclaiming something to be in accordance with the supposed purpose or trajectory of a norm is not a creative act. Even if a development does in fact fit snugly into a larger systemic whole, the fact that it is not identical to what already exists itself suggests novelty. Undeniably, a degree of creativity is integral to the development model in order to differentiate it from static binary accounts. The thrust is that through referencing the broader aims of a norm the judge is confined in his or her leeway to shape law. The democracy and legitimacy concerns are again well taken, but it seems artificial to nevertheless doggedly deny law-making in such a situation.[128] A decision like *Francovich* may certainly be said to fit into the larger scheme of the treaties (i.e. be within the permissible second category), but looking at the issue of legal protection available to individuals in a situation where directives are not directly effective one can just as well say it made law. The same could be said about the direct effect of treaty provisions conferring rights in claims against private individuals before and after *Defrenne*.[129] The examples are endless. What is more, the

---

[126] See H. S. Maine, *Ancient Law* (Routledge, London, 1905), p. 35.

[127] See Kelsen (n. 57 above), p. 106.

[128] The alternative doctrinal objection of lacking bindingunion acness is examined in Ch. 8.

[129] Case 43–75 *Gabrielle Defrenne* v. *Société anonyme belge de navigation aérienne Sabena* [1976] ECR 455.

ternary scheme provides no further argument as to why the third category should necessarily be illegitimate.[130] In this sense it is as canonical and closed as the binary model.

To wrap up on the ternary model, it does well to appreciate the inevitability of changing context and to at least attempt to avoid falling into insignificance or intransigence, as happens to most approaches denying judicial law-making. Its main achievement lies in making demands regarding judicial creativity, rather than obsessing about its very existence. Comparable 'creative interpretation' solutions similarly hope to take judges down a notch and implicitly affirm legislative superiority.[131] But unless one is taken by the argument that legal theory conditions political reality, such an intended effect is more likely a product of *ex post* ratiocination than a real causal relationship. The one legal order clinging most obstinately to notions of parliamentary sovereignty, that of the United Kingdom,[132] also gave birth to what is widely considered to be the most unabashed common law system. The relationship between judicial and legislative power is more complicated than a seesaw in which one side invariably goes up when the other goes down. But the ternary model provides a more refined vocabulary for critique than the binary approach.

Yet, in the end, it is also embarrassed by its inability to let go of self-defeating modes of inquiry. The original problem is repackaged in 'development' terminology. Claims about the meaning of a source become claims about the purpose of a norm. The ontological baseline that all judicial law-making is by definition off limits is not explored. For all its neatness, this suggests that method can replace questions of substance and sustains a perennial predicament of changing law without making law.

E Models recognising ECJ law-making

i The pragmatic model: the tyranny of the lawyer

Pragmatic approaches acknowledge the law-making property of adjudication. They spring from *ex post* observations that, in the end, judges do much more than resolve disputes or apply law in accordance with the rules of evidence and proof. But this is easier to put in terms of political

---

[130] Cf. Borchardt (n. 105 above), pp. 570–3.
[131] See e.g. J. Komárek, 'Judicial Lawmaking and Precedent in Supreme Courts', *LSE Law, Society and Economy Working Papers 4/2011* (2011), p. 28.
[132] See e.g. the recent European Union Act 2011 (c. 12), s. 18.

science than jurisprudence. The former can point to larger corollaries of judging such as policy-making, social control, regime legitimation, norm advancement and the acceleration of a more coherent legal system.[133] This is a far cry from traditional views that mainly limit the judicial function to determining facts, interpreting law, filling in gaps and perhaps developing the law incrementally.[134] But it is more difficult to put in terms of legal theory. Pragmatic approaches ultimately rely on descriptions of what they consider to be actual legal practice or predictions of official action. Out of the models presented so far, the ECJ's own approach to judicial law-making comes closest to pragmatism, assuming that it can be anthropomorphised as a single actor in this respect. Yet there are two exceptions, one fake and one real. They will be explained shortly.

It should first, however, be noted that there is no one-and-only pragmatic model. Approaches include theories of legal decision-making that focus solely on acceptance and outright attacks on pretenses nurtured by 'deluded' judges.[135] Others more moderately claim that legal process does not care about neat textbook-like separations between different sources or assert dispassionately that law is made by decision-makers when 'authority and power coincide'.[136] Indeed, this broad variety often gives rise to misconceptions and mischaracterisations. For instance, as has been observed concerning one particular strand of domestic pragmatism, most portrayals of what became known as US legal realism are 'false or trivial or both', chiefly on account of insinuating far too much rule-scepticism.[137] Bearing this in mind, three recurring features can usually be traced in an archetypal pragmatic model.

First and foremost, the pragmatic model does not buy into any *bouche qui prononce les paroles de la loi* mysticism. A formal statement of rules

---

[133] See e.g. H. Jacob, *Courts, Law, and Politics in Comparative Perspective* (Yale University Press, New Haven, 1996), p. 3; E. Benvenisti and G. W. Downs, 'National Courts, Domestic Democracy, and the Evolution of International Law', *European Journal of International Law*, 20 (2009), 59, 61.

[134] See e.g. A. Barak, *The Judge in a Democracy* (Princeton University Press, 2006), p. 37.

[135] See C. Schmitt, *Gesetz und Urteil: Eine Untersuchung zum Problem der Rechtspraxis* (Liebmann, Berlin, 1912), pp. 111–14; J. Frank, *Law and the Modern Mind* (Brentano, New York, 1930), pp. 8–10.

[136] See W. G. Friedmann, 'General Course in Public International Law', *Recueil des Cours/ Académie de Droit International de La Haye*, 127 (1969), 41, 131–72 (stressing 'newer and more flexible sources'); R. Higgins, *Problems and Process: International Law and How We Use It* (Clarendon Press, Oxford, 1994), p. 15.

[137] W. Twining, *General Jurisprudence* (Cambridge University Press, 2009), pp. 299–300 (recalling Corbin's work on the Restatement of Contracts and Llewellyn's reporting on the Uniform Commercial Code).

demoting prior judicial decisions is insufficient to describe 'what is really going on'. Claims that doctrine or theory can fully account for and restrict what counts as law are met with incredulity. Such assertions 'ignore the reality' that judges 'play a major law-making role'.[138] Instead, dispute settlement occupies much of the limelight.

Secondly, the pervading law-making propensity of precedents is down to a blend of cause and effect, to historical, political, economic and psychological patterns and to policy-oriented social conceptions of law. Consequences reign supreme. A decision like *Defrenne* made law because it patently changed a legal state of affairs *ex nunc*.[139] Likewise, in *Test-Achats*, the ECJ made law because it profoundly upset an entire industry premised on mathematically sound actuarial calculations for a fundamental cause.[140] The Court's healthcare case law is 'real' law since it decisively impacts national systems.[141] And had *Francovich* and its progeny been ignored or rebelled against, it would likely not be possible to sensibly invoke EU law state liability.[142]

Thirdly, the operation of precedent is not impersonal. On the contrary, one has to look closely at the lawyers involved and their context, including their place and function in society. In line with this, the meaning of legal text is ultimately reduced to the last authoritative exposition thereof, thereby becoming inextricably linked to the judges. Here, too, there is no triangle of meaning. But unlike in the binary model, it is the interpreter (rather than the text or author) who is the last man standing.

Pragmatic approaches to precedent-setting come in different shades of cynicism. Caustic versions have little patience for idealism and conceptualise adjudication in terms of raw power relations, personal interest and rational choice.[143] Unsurprisingly, given their hurtful effects on perceptions of institutional legitimacy, they tend to be the preserve of scholars

---

[138] Cf. A. E. Boyle and C. M. Chinkin, *The Making of International Law* (Oxford University Press, 2007), p. 268.

[139] Case 43–75 *Gabrielle Defrenne* v. *Société anonyme belge de navigation aérienne Sabena* [1976] ECR 455.

[140] Case C-236/09 *Association Belge des Consommateurs Test-Achats and ors* v. *Conseil des ministres* (Grand Chamber) [2011] ECR I-773 (paras. 33–4).

[141] Cf. A. J. Obermaier, *The End of Territoriality? The Impact of ECJ Rulings on British, German and French Social Policy* (Ashgate, Farnham, 2009).

[142] Joined Cases C-6/90 and C-9/90 *Andrea Francovich and Danila Bonifaci and ors* v. *Italian Republic* [1991] ECR I-5357.

[143] See e.g. H. Rasmussen, *On Law and Policy in the European Court of Justice* (Nijhoff, Dordrecht, 1986), chs. 8–10; E. A. Posner and J. Yoo, 'Judicial Independence in International Tribunals', *California Law Review*, 93 (2005), 1, 72.

rather than serving judges. In more upbeat variants, which accord in particular to the romantic ideal of the common law judiciary, adjudicators have a 'legitimate law-making function' and seek to keep the law 'abreast of current social conditions and expectations'.[144] At the same time, any impersonal declaratory theory is firmly rejected for being 'at odds with reality'.[145] In order to avoid both being ruled by the proverbial dead hand from the grave and flouting the basic separation of powers, legal development can here again be an opportune way to describe the task of adjudicators to be 'limited', although this is then not based on a high-fidelity and ultimately negative theory such as the ternary model analysed above, but rather on an appeal to common sense or political merit.[146] In this optimistic version of pragmatism, the judge becomes a virtuous, level-headed and self-disciplined Solomon.[147] Somewhere in between, adjudicators are more-or-less emergency legislators that are simply trying to come up with the most reasonable outcome in a specific context.[148]

Even if it does not always mirror all of the archetypal features outlined earlier, the ECJ routinely defaults to milder variants of pragmatism. It regularly declares itself to be in the driving seat by noting that '*the Court* has previously held',[149] '*the Court* has stated several times',[150] '*the Court* has acknowledged in its decisions'[151] and so on. Even if one insists on recasting all of these expressions in declaratory or evidentiary terms to avoid the notion of pragmatic judicial law-making, the near ubiquitous mention of its own 'case law', both by itself and other institutions, cannot easily be ignored. This can be traced back to at least 1958, long before common law legal orders joined the predecessor of the EU.[152] Case law is

---

[144] See e.g. *National Westminster Bank plc* v. *Spectrum Plus Ltd and ors* [2005] 2 AC 680 (para. 32) (Lord Nicholls).

[145] *Ibid.* para. 34.   [146] *Ibid.* paras. 31–2.   [147] Cf. Cardozo (n. 101 above), p. 121.

[148] See R. A. Posner, 'Pragmatic Adjudication' in M. Dickstein (ed.), *The Revival of Pragmatism: New Essays on Social Thought, Law, and Culture* (Duke University Press, Durham 1998), p. 244; Thomas (n. 101 above), pp. 77–84, 254–65.

[149] See e.g. Case C-163/10 *Criminal proceedings against Aldo Patriciello* (Grand Chamber) [2011] ECR I-7565 (para. 18).

[150] See e.g. Case C-34/09 *Gerardo Ruiz Zambrano* v. *Office national de l'emploi (ONEm) (Grand Chamber)* [2011] ECR I-1177 (para. 41).

[151] See e.g. Case C-212/08 *Zeturf Ltd* v. *Premier ministre* (Eighth Chamber) [2011] ECR I-5633 (para. 41).

[152] See Case 2–57 *Compagnie des Hauts Fourneaux de Chasse* v. *High Authority of the European Coal and Steel Community* [1958] ECR 199, 206. On 'declaratory' adjudication see Ch. 2, D.i.

arguably an even bolder expression than positive precedent, since – at least according to certain common law theories – the latter is an encapsulation of principle rather than a source of law.[153]

Turning now to the fake exception to the ECJ's pragmatism, which reaffirms rather than denies this stance, the Court is at times pressured into defensive denial.[154] Yet as both classic cases like *Brasserie du Pêcheur* and more recent decisions like *West Tankers* show, there is little to suggest that rigid jurisprudential strictures seriously limit the Court when it comes to setting precedents.[155] Like most busy adjudicators, the ECJ does not ponder deeply the ontology of norms or the 'essence of things'. It flirts with semantic approaches like pseudo-objective gap-filling and deference to the EU legislator just as it reasons consequentially,[156] often all in the same decision and in the service of getting reasonable answers to pressing real-world problems while keeping as many players happy as possible. The ECJ takes a robust approach to law-making, sometimes pushing for more development, sometimes for less, often – but by no means inevitably – depending on the broader context.[157]

The real exceptions to pragmatism are the Court's flashes of idealism. The thrust then becomes one of particular needs and efforts transforming social reality in the European legal space. The examples above regarding its more intrepid exertions over the course of the last half-century bear ample witness to this idealistic drive.[158] A common technique in this respect are the ECJ's references to broader systemic demands.[159] Idealism nevertheless remains the exception rather than the rule, since the majority of cases decided by the Court do not engage in inspired re-imagination of life in the EU. Both its daily dispute-settlement task and its long-term viability act as dampeners. Quite when the stars align, namely when an

---

[153] See M. Zander, *The Law-Making Process* (6th edn, Cambridge University Press, 2004), pp. 298–302.

[154] On the ECJ 'merely confirming' propositions of law see Ch. 2, D.i.

[155] Joined Cases C-46/93 and C-48/93 *Brasserie du Pêcheur SA* v. *Bundesrepublik Deutschland* [1996] ECR I-1029; Case C-185/07 *Allianz SpA and Generali Assicurazioni Generali SpA* v. *West Tankers Inc.* (Grand Chamber) [2009] ECR I-663 (para. 29) (combining three possible sources when ruling that 'an anti-suit injunction . . . is contrary to the general principle which emerges from the case-law of the Court on the Brussels Convention').

[156] See Joined Cases C-46/93 and C-48/93 *Brasserie du Pêcheur SA* v. *Bundesrepublik Deutschland* [1996] ECR I-1029 (paras. 20–1, 79).

[157] Cf. K. Alter and L. R. Helfer, 'Legal Integration in the Andes: Law-Making by the Andean Tribunal of Justice', *European Law Journal*, 17 (2011), 701, 705.

[158] See Ch. 2, D.ii. But it does not follow that creativity is exceptional.

[159] Cf. Ch. 4, C.ii. below on its general precedent citations.

idealistic moment outweighs routine pragmatism, is impossible to predict with legal tools only.

A broader assessment of pragmatism is not called for in this study.[160] But three important and interrelated points concerning positive precedent should be noted. First, unflinching pragmatism hazards a degree of inconsistency. This is particularly likely where, as at the ECJ, the case-load is high and many different legal minds are involved in decision-making. Some pragmatists may embrace a chaotic state of affairs, but as long as one has to work within an enforced legal order like the EU that can hardly be the end of the matter.

Secondly, the pragmatic model breeds an ever-stronger reliance on precedent.[161] It is very much self-reinforcing, since there is little by way of an external irritant. The more cases there are, the more cross-reference takes place, since this is where 'the real law' plays out, to the point where EU law is reduced to what the Court says or is claimed to have said. Regardless of the merits of a particular aspect of judge-made law, inside and outside perceptions can, over time, fall apart more and more, until the bubble threatens to be burst from the outside. The ever-louder criticism of the ECJ bears witness to this.

Thirdly, pragmatic recognition alone adds nothing beyond the necessary – but as such insufficient – acknowledgement of judicial law-making. There is no deeper discussion of what this entails. Potential for criticism and self-transformation is sorely lacking. Normativity is marginalised and in the end replaced with sheer compatibility and interconnection.[162] Facticity is privileged. Might and right are elided when it is thought that, quasi-automatically, 'over time, the unfit [precedents] will perish'.[163] Of course there is much to be said for not being baited into believing EU law to be a perfect creation that can be traced back flawlessly to a handful of pristine axioms; but at the same time, only the subjugated, servile or superstitious endure bizarre or idiosyncratic law-making in the long run. Ironically, pragmatism itself can become highly insensitive to systemic

---

[160] For a scathing critique see M. Koskenniemi, 'Constitutionalism as Mindset: Reflections on Kantian Themes about International Law and Globalization', *Theoretical Inquiries in Law*, 8 (2007), 9, 14–17. For deeper waters see D. Parfit, *Reasons and Persons* (Clarendon Press, Oxford, 1987), ch. 3.

[161] See P. S. Atiyah, *Pragmatism and Theory in English Law* (The Hamlyn Lectures, Stevens, London, 1987), pp. 91–2, 125–9 (cautioning against rampant '*ad hockery*').

[162] Cf. Somek (n. 92 above), p. 80.

[163] C. McLachlan, L. Shore and M. Weiniger, *International Investment Arbitration: Substantive Principles* (Oxford University Press, 2007), p. 75 (intoning a 'Darwinian reality').

effects, with the judge permitted to run free as a 'wise elder' with minimal constraints.[164]

The challenge lies in taking pragmatism on board without letting it take over the rudder entirely. In other words, how can ECJ law-making be conceptualised more satisfactorily without ramming square pegs into round holes?

ii An alternative model: avoiding the tyranny of letter and lawyer

What follows is an alternative reconstruction. It argues that all courts and tribunals, including the ECJ, invariably make law and apply law at the same time. Intellectual efforts should be directed to possible responses. Two key points set this model apart from those above. First, tiresome allegations concerning the fact of law-making by the Court are neither particularly damning nor helpful. Secondly, a critical vocabulary is imperative and available. *Consensus creat ius* is not the end of the matter.

What can be salvaged from the previous observations is that law-making in the EU is not only a matter for one discrete entity endowed with a monopoly.[165] It is a collective enterprise of a plurality of law-makers in which courts (and the Court) also play an undeniably important part. A strict tripartite separation of powers was never very convincing for the EU. For instance, the Commission and Council both exert multiple functions. At the same time, any model must be judged by whether is avoids the 'dirty little secrets'[166] of (pragmatic) jurisprudence: legal and social determinism and discomfort with democracy.

Since this is a reconstruction, it needs to be able to explain current practice, although it need not condone it. First, in purely observational terms, the alternative model latches on to the rich popularity of case-based reasoning and raw creativity of ECJ adjudication explicated above. The second aspect is that it must be arguable in doctrinal terms. This is more of a problem for public international law and select national legal systems than for EU law, given the latter's moderate agnosticism

---

[164] See A. Vermeule, *Judging under Uncertainty* (Harvard University Press, Cambridge, MA, 2006), pp. 52–9.

[165] Cf. A. von Bogdandy, *Gubernative Rechtsetzung* (Mohr Siebeck, Tübingen, 2000), pp. 100–2; Besson (n. 59 above), p. 164; P. P. Craig, 'Competence and Member State Autonomy: Causality, Consequence and Legitimacy' in H. W. Micklitz and B. de Witte (eds.), *The European Court of Justice and the Autonomy of Member States* (Oxford Legal Studies Research Paper No. 57/2009, 2010).

[166] R. M. Unger, *What Should Legal Analysis Become?* (Verso, London, 1996), p. 72.

as concerns sources of law and especially in light of the absence of a black-letter obstacle such as ICJ Statute Art. 38.[167] But even that would not have to be fatal, since existing provisions cannot be immunised from renewed understanding.[168] What emerges is akin to a privity-burden rule (i.e. that it is in principle unfair to impact a party who may not have had a stake in the process) that demands treating autonomy with care, rather than a rigid doctrinal construct that dabbles in 'world creation'.[169] That is arguably the true heart of any positivist project.[170] Such re-imagination is not 'pie in the sky' stuff. If anything, the prevailing understanding is unreal.

(a) Limited cognition and legal information

Law as an outgrowth of human society and culture is saddled with the thankless task of capturing 'the infinite within the finite'.[171] As a professional discipline and method of social interaction, it is formulaic and recursive; but the human mind, an indispensable ingredient, is often neither. The latter has the eternal potential to transform received wisdom and come up with new answers to both novel and familiar situations. Views on precedent need to appreciate this.

The argument that the ECJ makes law proceeds in three steps. The starting point can be treated fairly briefly, given its prominence and maturity.[172] Our cognition of things – understood as the intellectual capacity for representational perception and inference, as opposed to

---

[167] ICJ Statute Art. 59 and *extra partes* effect are a different matter concerning negative (i.e. constraining) precedent.

[168] While this cannot be pursued here in detail, a rebuttal of the orthodox understanding would centre on the wording ('shall apply' rather than sources terminology), the ambiguity of the 'source' concept, the plurality of grounds for judgments (legal text, factual evidence, logical operations, linguistic arguments, consequentialist considerations etc.), a refutation of the 'thing in itself' view, the express possibility of other bases for judicial decision-making (such as *ex aequo et bono* rulings) and the progressive weakening of private law-esque consent fetishism in international law.

[169] Cf. Somek (n. 92 above), p. 56.

[170] See Somek (n. 95 above), p. 733 ('a sting in the flesh of complacent orthodoxy').

[171] On this theme see R. M. Unger, *The Self Awakened: Pragmatism Unbound* (Harvard University Press, Cambridge, MA, 2007), pp. 239–43.

[172] See Ch. 2, D.i. See in particular R. Langton, *Kantian Humility: Our Ignorance of Things in Themselves* (Oxford University Press, 1998), pp. 15–47. See also Kelsen (n. 57 above), pp. 96–9; Koskenniemi (n. 160 above), pp. 9–11; A. von Bogdandy and I. Venzke, 'Beyond Dispute: International Judicial Institutions as Lawmakers', *German Law Journal*, 12 (2011), 979, 984–6 (on inferential linguistic approaches).

human experience, intention or ambition – is limited.[173] This applies to language, the main working material of lawyers, as it does to everything else, including legal paraphernalia such as precedents and treaty provisions. One need not go so far as to claim that words are eternally indeterminate. It is sufficient to note that the relationship between words and the things to which they refer is something that has engaged, and will always engage, the human mind. Absolute certainty is out of reach. In that respect, lawyers have just as much or as little grasp on 'the law' as scientists have on 'reality'.[174] Attempts to 'get to the bottom of things' are doomed to infinite regression if pursued obstinately with a naturalistic essence of law in mind. What humans have is their best possible understanding of something. This is the core of a critical reconstruction.[175]

Secondly, once this epistemic humility is accepted, law as a 'thing in itself' dissolves into information about law. This is recorded and conveyed in claims about law, for which legal positivism to the present day remains an important medium of communication and which explains its enduring popularity.[176] Many of its other pretensions are however rightly and widely discredited.[177]

In many subtle ways, legal practice reflects this humility, even if actors at times profess to be doing something more. Entities insisting on a certain application of law bring 'claims'. Legal know-how comes at a premium, measurable in billable hours. Propositions are submitted. Presumptions are used. The ECJ retires to deliberate and debate matters. It decides claims on a balance of probabilities with 'sufficient' proof,[178] not by way of (pseudo-)objective verification. Advocates General routinely state that

---

[173] In Kant's famous metaphor, we are stranded on an island 'surrounded by a vast and stormy ocean, where illusion properly resides and many fog banks and much fast-melting ice feign new-found lands. This sea incessantly deludes the seafarer with empty hopes as he roves through his discoveries, and thus entangles him in adventures that he can never relinquish, nor ever bring to an end.' See I. Kant, *Critique of Pure Reason* (Hackett, Indianapolis, 1996 (1781)), p. 303.

[174] See Müller and Christensen (n. 89 above), pp. 32–8.

[175] Cf. D. Kennedy, 'A Left Phenomenological Alternative to the Hart/Kelsen Theory of Legal Interpretation' in D. Kennedy (ed.), *Legal Reasoning: Collected Essays* (Davies, Aurora, 2008), p. 170.

[176] See F. Schauer and V. J. Wise, 'Legal Positivism as Legal Information', *Cornell Law Review*, 82 (1996–1997), 1080, 1081–2, 1095; Eckertz-Höfer (n. 86 above), p. 734. Cf. G. Roellecke, 'Zur Unterscheidung von Rechtsdogmatik und Theorie', *Juristenzeitung*, 66 (2011), 645, 646, 652.

[177] See Schauer and Wise (n. 176 above), pp. 1080–1.

[178] See e.g. Case 107/82 *Allgemeine Elektrizitäts-Gesellschaft AEG-Telefunken AG v. Commission* [1983] ECR 3151 (paras. 134–6).

they are 'convinced' or 'not persuaded' by a contention.[179] All of this eschews the absolutist language of truth – that is to say, a genuine correlation of a statement with fact or reality. When the ECJ does trespass into language that suggests correspondence of its statements with actual conditions, this tends to be a reassuring convenience or a flexing of authority rather than a deep belief in a material state of affairs.[180]

Thirdly, in this world of limited cognition and contested approximations, EU law is made up of various form-independent bits and pieces of legal information. It is not solely divulged in a static or tidy fashion, but as a collection of multiple heterogeneous entry and exit points – as a rhizome rather than a root-tree order, to use a well-known botanical metaphor.[181] More modern imagery might look to internet hyperlinks or publicly visible Twitter tweets. Crucially, information about law can just as well be contained in a precedent. In this sense ECJ adjudication is a law-making process, since it generates these units of legal information.[182] The following diagram illustrates how a certain legal proposition can be transported from one case to another.

The flat hierarchy and disorderly nature of legal information are immediately apparent. The arrows indicate how the references were made by the Court at the respective time, but – absent further reasoning – there is no reason why it could not have connected cases differently or included other cases that do no appear here at all. Such isolated cases could also be on point, but they do not form part of this particular citation network.[183]

The pattern shows that, like most other adjudicatory bodies, the ECJ often cites a handful of decisions for the same legal proposition, despite

---

[179] See e.g. Case C-376/10 P *Pye Phyo Tay Za* v. *Council* [2012] ECR I-0000, Opinion of AG Mengozzi (para. 108).

[180] While the parties are usually 'not persuaded' or 'not convinced' of certain points, the Court as the decision-maker rejects arguments in more absolute terms, e.g. when it states that a suggestion or analysis 'cannot be accepted'. See e.g. Case C-442/09 *Karl Heinz Bablok and ors* v. *Freistaat Bayern* (Grand Chamber) [2011] ECR I-7419 (paras. 87, 95).

[181] Commonly attributed to G. Deleuze and F. Guattari, *A Thousand Plateaus* (reprint edn, Continuum, London, 2003 (1987)), ch. 1.

[182] Note that this differs from the familiar 'precedents as evidence' view, which is a half-way house by considering other materials to be more than just evidence of law.

[183] On citation network analysis in general see J. H. Fowler *et al.*, 'Network Analysis and the Law: Measuring the Legal Importance of Precedents at the U.S. Supreme Court', *Political Analysis*, 15 (2007), 324, 325–32 (observing that '[p]recedent plays a central role in the judiciary by providing information to judges' and that law is often thought of as an 'interconnected set of legal rules resulting from the repeated use and interpretation of those rules in different cases over time').

the fact that the cases were quite disparate. In Figure 2.E.ii, the Court in a preliminary reference on the common system of VAT reiterated that it was, pursuant to the co-operative mechanism of TFEU Art. 267 and subject to certain limited exceptions, obliged to give a ruling on questions submitted by national courts concerning the interpretation of a provision of EU law.[184] In doing so, the ECJ referred to three cases. Those are united by virtue of a common rationale on this point – one might say they convey the same legal information in this regard – but their actual decisions were poles apart.[185] They in turn refer to each other and to further cases, which again cite other previous judgments.

One can thus chart a web of over thirty cases, which ultimately trace their origins back to at least five cases which do not refer to other decisions but appear to ground their reasoning solely on the treaty text. This interlocking network, collectively referred to as the ECJ's case law or jurisprudence on this issue, was built over a period of forty years by an ever-changing Court. The individual cases dealt with very different matters. But in terms of their legal information on this discrete point, they are considered equal, namely instances of one and the same class or group. As will be elaborated upon later, the ECJ reinforces this by frequently prefacing references to prior cases with the qualifiers 'inter alia' or 'in particular', signifying that it would consider other citations similarly apposite. While most cases refer to decisions that are chronologically proximate, some are quite happy to leapfrog judgments in their selection, again underscoring the generality of the legal rationale beyond the individual case.

An entire branch of empirical legal research, network analysis, mines this very real web of case law for further insights. Extracting

---

[184] Case C-392/09 *Uszodaépítő kft* v. *APEH Központi Hivatal Hatósági Főosztály* (Third Chamber) [2010] ECR I-8791 (para. 22). It is for the national court to determine in light of the particular circumstances both the need for a preliminary ruling in order to deliver judgment and the relevance of the questions which it submits to the ECJ.

[185] The three cases cited and their decisions, briefly put, were: Case C-379/98 *PreussenElektra AG* v. *Schleswag AG* [2001] ECR I-2099 (certain provisions concerning private electricity undertakings are neither state aid nor precluded by the free movement of goods); Case C-103/08 *Arthur Gottwald* v. *Bezirkshauptmannschaft Bregenz* (First Chamber) [2009] ECR I-9117 (the primary law prohibition of discrimination allows legislation restricting the issue of a free motorway toll pass to resident or ordinarily resident disabled persons); Case C-82/09 *Dimos Agiou Nikolaou Kritis* v. *Ypourgos Agrotikis Anaptyxis kai Trofimon* (Fourth Chamber) [2010] ECR I-3649 (definitions contained in a regulation on forestry do not prevent the adoption of different definitions in situations not covered by the secondary legislation in question).

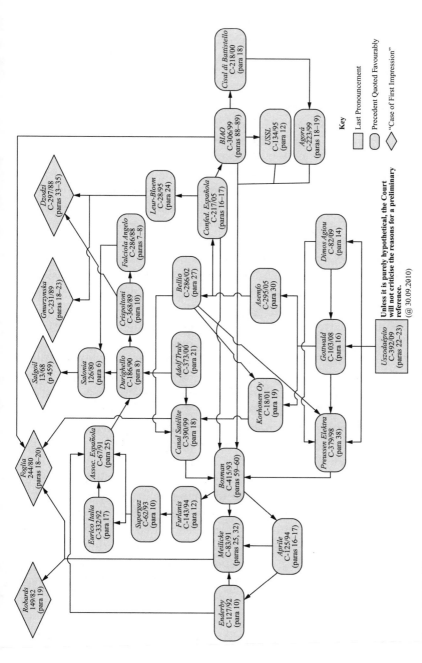

Figure 2.E.ii Heterogeneous flow of legal information from precedent to precedent

data from such a network one could quantitatively identify important 'authorities' (i.e. widely cited precedents) and 'hubs' (i.e. cases that cite a lot of other decisions). For instance, in the sample above, the *Bosman* judgment stands out.[186] The case is without doubt one of the more well-known ECJ decisions, as a quick glance at the extensive list of corresponding *notes de doctrine* corroborates. But even such figures resulting from diligently programmed algorithms need to be treated with care. An awareness of the interconnection of legal information does not dispense with the need for interpretation and context-sensitivity.

To begin with, network analysis says nothing about whether the precedent links are coherent or convincing. It also cannot, without more, explain how and why courts develop their practice of precedent.[187] One needs to be wary of the fact that cases are cited at different times for different reasons. In the present example, *Bosman* appears to be a popular precedent on the ECJ's general reluctance to criticise the terms of a preliminary reference. It is, however, much better known as an authority in the sphere of economic mobility and competition in professional sports. Aggregating citations elides such nuances; disaggregating them risks telling only part of a bigger story.

Similar caveats apply to hub scores. High hub scores can denote cases where the Court thought it particularly necessary to justify a specific decision by reference to precedents. This might indicate a particularly difficult context in which acceptance hung by a thread and the ECJ thought it especially necessary to shore up its legitimacy with ample case citations. But it could also be a rather banal matter of personal opinion, writing style or a nod to in-house citation guidelines,[188] an interpretation of a particular case law doctrine or the fortuitous absence of isolating factual specificities. At other times, it might be opportune to say less rather than more about a particularly controversial legal proposition, or there simply is no precedent upon which to rely. Indeed, the ECJ is routinely taken to task for what comes across as apodictic parsimony. The point here is that quantitative analysis can indeed be a useful tool, in particular to question received views and explore counterintuitive blind spots, but ultimately legal information and case-based reasoning retains a mercurial quality that is impossible to pin down via social mathematics alone.

---

[186] Case C-415/93 *Union royale belge des sociétés de football association ASBL* v. *Jean-Marc Bosman* [1995] ECR I-4921.
[187] Cf. Lupu and Voeten (n. 29 above), p. 439.   [188] Cf. Ch. 4, C. below.

The concept of legal information also explains why the ECJ is willing to consider the jurisprudence of other courts. This is not an act of subordination or erroneous application of 'foreign' law. Rather, such precedents, too, are potentially valuable units of legal information. For instance, the Court regularly refers to decisions of the ECtHR when concerned with fundamental rights matters.[189] It has also cited the ICJ when dealing with international law.[190] It does not however normally invoke precedents of domestic courts or the General Court ('GC', formerly the Court of First Instance ('CFI')). But the concepts of limited cognition and legal information are not antagonistic to strategic manoeuvring or causal forces. Rather, attempts to make sense of semantic content often run alongside patterns of stimulus and response. While Member State courts' decisions could of course also contain valuable nuggets of legal information – such as German jurisprudence on proportionality – the lack of such citations is once more down to considerations regarding acceptance. The ECJ does not want to privilege one national legal order over two dozen other ones. In its citation practice, the Court also does not pander to particular Member States' legal systems, such as the respondent state in infringement proceedings or the legal order of a referring court in a preliminary reference. This bolsters both its autonomy and the legitimacy of its judicial output in the long term, even if this might cause friction in individual cases where national legal orders routinely handle a particular point of law differently. Concerning the GC, the dynamics of tiered jurisdiction come into play.

This practice of cross-tribunal citation by the ECJ has, properly understood, nothing to do with non-applicable law determining a legal dispute or outsourcing decision-making to 'foreign' adjudicators. The point is far more basic. It again relates to fundamental modes of intellectual attainment. The human mind is inquisitive and discursive. Looking around is an intrinsic part of forming and testing beliefs. This does not stop at jurisdictional borders, governing law or typologies of legal sources. In fact, there is no guidance at all as to where one should look. Less still does it entail blindly adopting all that one sees. There is, in this epistemic process, no categorical difference between internal or external precedents or between a case and a law review article. It is all potential legal

---

[189] See e.g. Case C-292/10 G v. *Cornelius de Visser* (First Chamber) [2012] ECR I-0000 (para. 58).

[190] See e.g. Case C-162/96 *A Racke GmbH & Co.* v. *Hauptzollamt Mainz* [1998] ECR I-3655 (para. 24); Case C-37/00 *Herbert Weber* v. *Universal Ogden Services Ltd* (Sixth Chamber) [2002] ECR I-2013 (para. 34).

information. It 'simply helps [adjudicators] do a better job at home'.[191] A common habit when trying to make sense of something is to discriminate other things as irrelevant. That alone makes the objections of 'militant provincialism'[192] regarding eclectic precedent citation ring hollow. Such provincialism takes information to be more than it actually is (i.e. considers it a 'thing in itself') and denies any creative or imaginative effort on behalf of the decision-maker (since he or she supposedly has access to the 'thing in itself'). That may be seductive, but it fundamentally ignores the gradation between something being authoritative and it being authoritarian.

All of this does not mean that lawyering becomes a free-for-all, or free of hierarchy and ordering concepts. It remains a technicality in various important respects. For instance, the concept of something being 'binding' or 'possessing normative quality' remains significant, not least because it signals something that has currency in much legal discourse. Formal sources can continue to play a prominent role, not only as important (albeit not exclusive) vehicles of legal information, but also as vital means of allowing democratic debate to feed back into professional legal discourse. Syllogistic reasoning, often said to be a favourite of the ECJ, can also remain a feature of legal decision-making. Its reception waxes and wanes with the changing fortunes of 'formalism', an altogether ambiguous concept that is at times ridiculed and demonised yet every so often revived and celebrated, especially in intergovernmental contexts.[193] Its enduring esteem is owed to the fact that it makes something logically follow when something else is given. Even if they might not be sufficient to resolve difficult legal questions, like many other tools of formalism, syllogisms can help to weed out certain answers, for instance leaps in logic, but they properly never seek to achieve more than to detect errors consequent upon other premises.[194]

---

[191] A.-M. Slaughter, 'A Global Community of Courts', *Harvard International Law Journal*, 44 (2003), 191, 201. Note that this does not imply 'better' judgments.

[192] S. Levinson, 'Looking Abroad when Interpreting the US Constitution: Some Reflections', *Texas International Law Journal*, 39 (2004), 353, 358.

[193] More recent discussions of formalism include J. von Bernstorff, *The Public International Law Theory of Hans Kelsen: Believing in Universal Law* (Cambridge University Press, 2010), pp. 233–71; J. D'Aspremont, *Formalism and the Sources of International Law* (Oxford University Press, 2011). See also (2011–1) 30 *L'Observateur des Nations Unies*, an entire issue devoted to 'le formalisme juridique dans le droit international du XXIème siècle'.

[194] See Bengoetxea, MacCormick and Moral Soriano (n. 19 above), p. 60 (on this 'negative test'). See also H.-J. Koch and H. Rüßmann, *Juristische Begründungslehre* (C. H. Beck,

Moreover, the ECJ's judges invariably have to produce a single, coherent and authoritative answer to admissible legal disputes. A *non liquet* is widely rejected; the Court has never invoked this to refuse a ruling. But that does not require it to treat the law as determinate or a metaphysical 'thing in itself'. Given the 'bareness of logic' and 'fertility of language',[195] it is not that judges *may* make choices in adjudicating, they *have* to make choices. There is in principle no difference here between so-called hard cases and ordinary cases, and it would be a mistake to assume that one requires a fundamentally different approach from the other.[196] Of course one might say that the application of free movement jurisprudence to '*such* national regulations [as those at issue in the main proceedings]' in cases like *Mickelsson* is not as creative as staking out the fundamentals of the free movements of goods in the first place in cases like *Dassonville* or *Cassis de Dijon*.[197] Yet sufficiency rather than totality is the key. In a later situation, interpreters of law – that is to say, judges, parties and commentators alike – are satisfied simply to a specific point and stop looking further. In fact, that is a major draw of precedent. Complexity is reduced, difficult prior contestation of legal information abbreviated.

If this train of thought is broadly correct – EU law can only be known through legal information and prior cases are a type of this – the official classification of precedents as a formal source of law or not ceases to be of overriding importance. Such an alternative conception poses its own challenges. Chiefly, it destabilises the credo of a fixed boundary between the application and creation of law. How can one be bound by something that did not exist previously – that is to say, has just been made? As a purely logical problem, this charge has little bite if it resurrects the timeworn 'retrieval' view of interpretation. But there is a real substantive issue here. Accepting limited cognition, how can the alternative model

---

Munich, 1982), p. 28; D. Simon, 'Alle Quixe sind Quaxe – Aristoteles und die juristische Argumentation', *Juristenzeitung*, 66 (2011), 697, 698–9.

[195] Expressions used by J. Stone, *Precedent and Law* (Butterworths, Sydney, 1985), p. 227.

[196] See R. Dworkin, *Law's Empire* (reprint edn, Hart, Oxford, 1998 (1986)), pp. 353–4 (rejecting the 'some-things-go-without-saying' objection to this view as a pseudo-problem). For a critique see G. J. Postema, '"Protestant" Interpretation and Social Practices', *Law and Philosophy*, 6 (1987), 283, 288–9.

[197] Case C-142/05 *Åklagaren* v. *Percy Mickelsson and Joakim Roos* (Second Chamber) [2009] ECR I-4273 (paras. 44, 40; emphasis added); Case 8–74 *Procureur du Roi* v. *Benoît and Gustave Dassonville* [1974] ECR 837; Case 120/78 *Rewe-Zentral AG* v. *Bundesmonopolverwaltung für Branntwein* [1979] ECR 649. Cf. F. Müller and R. Christensen, *Juristische Methodik: Europarecht* (2nd edn, Duncker & Humblot, Berlin, 2007), p. 308.

avoid relapsing into the pragmatic view analysed above in which the ultimate arbiter reigns supreme?

(b) The imperative strikes back

The key point that sets the alternative model apart from the pragmatic one is that EU law need not be conceived solely from the ECJ's viewpoint.[198] Limited cognition has an immense emancipatory potential. It disempowers the hierarchical funnelling of information from top to bottom, such as through unquestioning invocation of precedents. Although there is ultimately little else to go by, legal information is always only a proxy; that is both its curse and salvation. Of course, assertions of control and (mis)direction attempts remain a constant feature of legal discourse just as elsewhere, and it would be naïve to deny that ECJ judges enjoy a very privileged position in this respect. But that cannot stop alternative views from forming.[199] Innovation is not the problem. It is what comes later that matters.

As will be fleshed-out later, techniques of precedent argumentation bear ample witness to this on a daily basis. While the 'thing in itself' is forever singular, information permits a plurality of views. The fact that opposing sides can be taken on points of EU law is neither a meaningless truism nor a logical flaw of sorts.[200] Closed contexts of creation – an ECJ judgment, for instance – have no stranglehold over meaning and interpretation. Leaving aside the effects on the case immediately at hand, they too generate malleable legal information. This is a creative process that can impose an argumentative burden. But just as meaning is not a fixed property of a text, it is also not the exclusive domain of the interpreter or immune from later transformation.

How then can one break out of the endless epistemic morass of limited cognition? Given the premises of the alternative model, that is in a sense the wrong question. In any event, practice has largely adopted the Kantian

---

[198]   Cf. L. H. Tribe, *American Constitutional Law* (2nd edn, Foundation Press, Mineola, 1988), p. 37 (on how this argument softens the anti-democratic barb of many critiques of adjudication).

[199]   Cf. P. Wachsmann, 'La Volonté de l'interprète', *Droits*, 28 (1998), 29, 30.

[200]   This is where the supposed paradox that only that which is in principle undecidable can be decided is, for all its subtlety, misleading. Cf. N. Luhmann, 'Die Paradoxie des Entscheidens', *Verwaltungsarchiv*, 84 (1993), 287, 289 (referencing Heinz von Foerster). Everything can always be decided. Even if one might think a question impossibly difficult or so obvious as to not even merit an answer, it can be decided. That the answer might then be thought wrong is beside the point. This allows for new solutions and thus transformation, e.g. to reflect a change in circumstances. Incidentally, the ECJ's jurisprudence concerning repeat preliminary references reflects this.

solution to his rather bleak initial diagnosis concerning cognitive limits. Once one renounces claims to absolute knowledge of law and accepts the sprawling and heterogeneous nature of legal information *qua* the 'thing in itself', the question becomes not what the 'true nature' of the law on point X is, but rather what to do in situation X. For most participants, the focus thus shifts from theoretical or pure to practical reason.[201] Action rather than belief in truth becomes central.

Proceedings at the ECJ echo this. The Court is asked *to declare* whether a Member State has infringed the treaties (TFEU Art. 258), *to annul* a supranational act (TFEU Art. 263), *to declare* that an institution has failed to act (TFEU Art. 265) or *to establish* the Union's obligation to compensate (TFEU Art. 340). These are all direct 'actions', seeking a very precise effect. Even when prompted by a request for a preliminary ruling, the ECJ pays attention to the underlying practical problem and refuses hypothetical, albeit not artificially engineered,[202] questions. Precedent reasoning also displays streaks of practical rather than pure reason. As will be extrapolated later, the practical worth of precedent-following is often at stake, for instance when a precedent's workability, age, doctrinal fit or effects are questioned. Similarly, while moving at different speeds in different places, much of recent legal scholarship is increasingly less of an oracular discipline that is obsessed with legal sources and their meaning and instead interested in problem-oriented decision-making, regulation and the preconditions, reasons and consequences of law and legal practice.[203]

What to do in a particular (legal) situation is a matter of argumentation. It depends on reasons and is, as such, a normative activity.[204] Particulars

---

[201] See e.g. R. Alexy, *A Theory of Legal Argumentation* (Clarendon Press, Oxford, 1989), pp. 211–20. But see J. Habermas, 'A Short Reply', *Ratio Juris*, 12 (1999), 445, 447. Yet there is nothing to assume that normative or doctrinal concerns would have to be sidelined. The point is to openly look forward – e.g. by revitalising the public sphere – rather than to rely on forms of legal tasseography.

[202] One such case was Case C-144/04 *Werner Mangold* v. *Rüdiger Helm* (Grand Chamber) [2005] ECR I-9981. It was engineered for a very specific practical purpose, namely to torpedo domestic employment legislation.

[203] See e.g. many of the contributions in M. Ruffert (ed.), *The Transformation of Administrative Law in Europe* (Sellier, Munich, 2007) and A. von Bogdandy, S. Cassese and P. M. Huber (eds.), *Handbuch Ius Publicum Europaeum*, 8 vols. planned (C. F. Müller, Heidelberg, 2010), III.

[204] See J. Raz, 'Interpretation without Retrieval' in A. Marmor (ed.), *Law and Interpretation* (Oxford University Press, 1995), pp. 155, 162, 174 (albeit claiming only to discuss the interpretation of art).

of claim and applications invite defences,[205] and every reply tempts a rejoinder.[206] Judges probe hypotheticals. Participants in legal discourse constantly stress what courts like the ECJ ought to do or not, partly by appealing to what is just or required, partly by appealing to concrete consequences (i.e. policy, empirical findings, utilitarian considerations); these are familiar poles that inform thinking about law – and thus legal practice – across the world.[207] Viewed through this prism, law and adjudication in the context of the EU and elsewhere are neither purely *prudentia* nor *scientia*.[208] As is developed over the course of this book, precedent is no different in this respect. Like all questions of legal method,[209] precedent points are ultimately substantive points, but they too have developed their own vocabulary and technique. Throughout this, legal reasoning remains enigmatic and difficult to predict, as any practising lawyer will not tire of telling his or her clients.

This impossibility of anything resembling a bright dividing line or logical proof is not a flaw in legal reasoning, but rather an inherent limitation on account of the richness of language, complexity of the subject matter and changing societal preferences.[210] The same applies in many other fields of human activity; the track record of complete 'proofs' in philosophy, linguistics or even the natural sciences is not exactly impressive. That is not fatal. On the contrary, it allows for innovation in social and political life; law can adapt to new challenges and demands. Good faith efforts count, rather than imaginary cognitive perfection. What commonly passes for methodological rules in law simply structures

---

[205] Cf. ECJ Rules of Procedure Art. 124(1); Civil Procedure Rules of England and Wales (April 2013) Rule 9.2(b), Part 15.

[206] Cf. ECJ Rules of Procedure Art. 126.

[207] See Kelsen (n. 57 above), pp. 20–38 (on law as both ideology and social technique); D. Kennedy, 'Theses about International Legal Discourse', *German Yearbook of International Law*, 23 (1980), 353, 362–5 (on the basic tension and movement in legal discussions between abstract ideal and concrete application); V. Heiskanen, *International Legal Topics* (Lakimiesliiton Kustannus, Helsinki, 1992), pp. 82–3 (on how international legal practice shies away both from directly normative and plainly concrete decisions); M. Koskenniemi, *From Apology to Utopia* (reissue edn, Cambridge University Press, 2005), pp. 58–60 (on 'descending' patterns of argumentation privileging normativity and 'ascending' patterns privileging concreteness).

[208] Cf. M. Kriele, 'Das demokratische Prinzip im Grundgesetz', *Veröffentlichungen der Vereinigung der deutschen Staatsrechtslehrer*, 29 (1971), 46, 51. Jurisprudence and *Rechtswissenschaft* can hence be misleading terms if read too narrowly.

[209] Cf. Müller and Christensen (n. 89 above), p. 32.

[210] See L. L. Weinreb, *Legal Reason: The Use of Analogy in Legal Argument* (Cambridge University Press, 2005), p. 6.

the generation of normative content through the exclusion of types of arguments that are currently considered less relevant. The point is not to find a 'true' answer, but to give sense to a decision so that it can be generalised, criticised and possibly remade.[211] The refusal to elide the possible into the actual sets the alternative model apart from pragmatic decisionism and history worship.

(c) Beyond optionality and finality

For the alternative model, adjudication is a creative process that is neither prearranged nor immune to being challenged. Rigid theories of sources or validity do not adequately capture precedent in the ECJ. It is at the same time both correct and wrong to say that prior cases are 'illustrative' of law.[212] They are illustrative because they point to past instantiations of law application, but they are materially the law because there is simply no way to know the law other than to know it[213] and no meaning without interpretation.[214] In this respect, precedents are no different from other sources in that they are the stuff of legal information.

It is important to note that what is not claimed here is that the making of EU law is solely the doing of a small group of judges. The present inquiry is conceptual rather than causative. Concerning causality, there would be much reason to look beyond the judges, who are (an important) part of a much longer chain. In particular the historical input of supranational and domestic institutions as well as crusading individuals, but also of pioneering law firms with a strong background in new fringe areas of law with broad but largely untested legal standards, would be of interest.

Crucially, law-making by the ECJ has to be appreciated critically. Fishing for answers in the quagmire of gelatinous wording and context serves a deeper purpose by allowing everyone a shot at implementing designs. It lubricates social interaction and enables basic coexistence and, ultimately, democratic renewal by resisting preordination and allowing for broader public participation in vital (legal) discourse.

---

[211] Cf. T. Sampaio Ferraz Junior, 'On Sense and Sensibility in Legal Interpretation', *Rechtstheorie*, 42 (2011), 139.

[212] Cf. S. Pötters and R. Christensen, 'Das Unionsrecht als Hybridform zwischen case law und Gesetzesrecht', *Juristenzeitung*, 67 (2012), 289, 293–4, 297 (recognising the limits of both case law and statute law, albeit appearing to privilege the latter in the end).

[213] Cf. Somek (n. 92 above), pp. 32–6.

[214] Which is not the same as saying only the interpreter matters; text and author are also vital components in this epistemic pluralism. On this see Christensen (n. 80 above), p. 225.

That does not mean that critiques of a decision's method or substance invariably have to drown in endless discourses on politics, history or philosophy. Law retains its own vocabulary. This allows for a realistic yet emancipatory legal discourse. Legal arguments can be utilised to mediate between law-making through the Court and distrust thereof, rather than to pretend the former did not exist or simply accept it as preordained. For instance, arguments seeking to support ECJ law-making might invoke the function of the Court, fundamental rights, sincere co-operation, implied powers, denial of justice and special delegation, for instance concerning non-contractual EU liability. In an attempt to dampen ECJ law-making, one could consider arguments based on the proper balance of powers, limited attribution of competences, subsidiarity or proportionality. To be sure, these are all non-exhaustive possibilities each meriting in-depth treatment. The main point here is that this is not a quest for a ready-made abstract line drawn somewhere, but an exploratory process whereby a series of solutions are tested and possibly rejected as uncompelling in a given situation, without a *numerus clausus* of legal tools.

This fluid yet responsible approach is preferable to several other options. First, without conceptual grandstanding, judges can distance themselves from megalomaniac master plans.[215] Charges of 'ECJ activism' alone are much too blunt. Not only do they usually fail to differentiate between the types of arguments being made, they also beg the question according to which conception this should be assessed.[216] Such accusations also tend to be either selective in what to bemoan or naïve as to the possibility of stasis. Secondly, 'progressive development' or incrementalism borrows too heavily from obsolete conceptualisations and is itself always in danger of presenting judicial work as a predestined technicality limited to conflict resolution. Thirdly, purely pragmatic approaches acknowledge judicial law-making, but they are limited to extolling the cunning of the *status quo* or can become mired in despair. Rising above these alternatives requires a combination of factual and normative

---

[215] See e.g. G. Slynn, 'Critics of the Court: A Reconsideration' in M. T. Andenæs and F. G. Jacobs (eds.), *European Community Law in the English Courts* (Clarendon Press, Oxford and New York, 1998), p. 7 (asserting that, were it all just 'federalists conspiring', a 'great deal of hard-headed discussion in thrashing out judgments within the framework of the Treaty could have been avoided'); K. Lenaerts, 'Federalism and the Rule of Law: Perspective from the European Court of Justice', *Fordham International Law Journal*, 33 (2010), 1338.

[216] See A. Rosas, 'Separation of Powers in the European Union', *The International Lawyer*, 41 (2007), 1033, 1037.

astuteness with a rejection of historical inevitability. As indicated here, alternatives exist, although a 'one-size-fits-all' master key does not.

F Dimensions of positive precedent

i Not legislation or treaty-making

Law-making through adjudication need not be equated with law-making through democratically sanctioned representation.[217] Nor is an acknowledgement tantamount to saying that EU law revolves exclusively around the ECJ.[218] In the present context, there is little point in treating the Court's precedents exactly like primary EU law or secondary legislation. As seen above, the pragmatic model makes no real differentiation in this respect between law-making by courts and tribunals and legislation.[219] That is infelicitous. Precedents have their own peculiarities; they are highly context-dependent.[220] Five points are worth mentioning.

First, unlike the respective political organs, the ECJ cannot act on its own motion; despite a steady stream, it generally has to wait for opportune cases. True, it is a permanent body and can at times send more-or-less overt signals inviting claims. In particular the curious nature of the judicial co-operation between the European and domestic level with its preliminary reference mechanism might seem suitable for such courting and winking.[221] But, at the end of the day, it is dependent on external initiative.

---

[217] Cf. H. Lauterpacht, *The Function of Law in the International Community* (Clarendon Press, Oxford, 1933), p. 307.

[218] 'It is customary to say that the law is applied and interpreted by the courts. For the most part that is false. Law is interpreted and applied to particular situations by ordinary people and ordinary officials doing roughly what they think it says and ordering their relations in some kind of accordance with its provisions': J. Waldron, *The Law* (Routledge, London, 1990), pp. 3–6. See also M. Shapiro, 'Law, Courts and Politics' in T. Ginsburg and R. A. Kagan (eds.), *Institutions and Public Law: Comparative Approaches* (Lang, New York, 2005), p. 282.

[219] Note that this is not incompatible with the idea of programming normative discourse within the respective constitutional settings. See C. Behrendt, *Le Juge constitutionnel, un législateur-cadre positif* (Bruylant, Brussels, 2006).

[220] See G. Lamond, 'Do Precedents Create Rules?', *Legal Theory*, 11 (2005), 1, 18; P. Pescatore, '*Van Gend en Loos*, 3 February 1963 – A View from Within' in M. Poiares Maduro and L. Azoulai (eds.), *The Past and Future of EU Law* (Hart, Oxford and Portland, 2010), p. 3.

[221] See J. H. H. Weiler, 'The Transformation of Europe', *Yale Law Journal*, 100 (1990–1991), 2403, 2426.

Secondly, when cases do appear in the Court's docket, they are often circumscribed by their factual and legal specificities and by the way they are pleaded. Claimants obviously use courts to get very specific results. Judges often rely on submissions and only solicit certain types of arguments.[222] They try to avoid straying *ultra petita*. Despite provisions for third-party proceedings and intervention,[223] there is normally no wider stakeholder consultation that feeds directly into ECJ decisions.[224]

Thirdly, being decision-makers that strive for solutions that convincingly dispose of specific legal problems, judges like those at the ECJ do not normally address deeper issues in a way that takes time, resources, means and other expertise. Rather, their general *modus operandi* is that of resolving a dispute in one focused judgment, even if their role often goes well beyond that.

Fourthly, as will be elaborated upon in due course, all courts and tribunals, including the ECJ, possess ample possibilities to manipulate the legal information transmitted through cases by distinguishing and overruling them.[225] At the same time, they are expected to be mindful of existing doctrine, even if they change it.

Fifthly, law-making by adjudication privileges private and particular contexts of law-creation. Adjudicating is a different sphere of social interaction from legislating.[226] A whole school of thought, often lumped together under the loose label 'discourse theory', seeks to reject not only banal determinism but also brute decisionism.[227] While the broader issue is beyond the scope of this study of ECJ precedent, there is much to support the view that law-making through courts and tribunals differs from law-making through organs of democratic representation, for which the term legislation is better reserved. Nor is the output of adjudication identical to treaties between sovereign nations, not least on account of their more intimately consensual and transactional nature. Much of this goes back to the perennial countermajoritarian problem. Courts like the

---

222 See e.g. Case C-229/05 P *Osman Ocalan, on behalf of the Kurdistan Workers' Party (PKK) and Serif Vanly, on behalf of the Kurdistan National Congress (KNK)* v. *Council* (First Chamber) [2007] ECR I-439 (para. 64).

223 See e.g. CJEU Statute Arts. 40, 42, 43; ECJ Rules of Procedure Arts. 129–31, 157.

224 Given the remit of this study, it will be assumed that traditional law-making processes are in fact adequate in this respect, a common concession that has its own share of problems.

225 Cf. J. Raz, *The Authority of Law* (2nd edn, Oxford University Press, 2009), p. 195.

226 See Habermas (n. 201 above), p. 447 (insisting on limited independence only of adjudication from legislative discourse). Cf. Schauer and Wise (n. 176 above), p. 1081.

227 See U. Neumann, *Juristische Argumentationslehre* (Wiss. Buchges., Darmstadt, 1986), p. 2.

ECJ are considered ill-placed to engage in what is ultimately an exercise that involves mobilising popular support.[228] According to the prevailing paradigm, judges' reasoning cannot be candidly political, such as along plain party-political lines. Other outlets exist for that. It is precisely this that nurtured Bentham's fears that adjudicators would always shy away from true reform and instead perpetuate existing structures.[229]

Adjudicators worldwide are keen not to appear to be legislating.[230] In *Wall*, the ECJ was pressed by a referring domestic court that the obligation of transparency which it had expounded could not ultimately give rise to liability in national law since it was 'purely judge-made' and not customary law on account of lacking prolonged and consistent usage.[231] The ECJ dryly replied that said obligation of transparency derived from 'the law of the European Union' (read: 'not the ECJ') and then invoked direct effect and necessary observance. Alas, this understandable rejection of the legislator badge is often taken as a relapse into self-defeating binary or ternary models of adjudication, as in the ICJ's *Legality* opinion just cited. But, and this is the crux, saying judges make law is perfectly compatible with saying they do not legislate. Instead, these are complementary modes of social ordering.[232]

The complementary nature of judicial law-making and legislation is plain to see in the EU. The European Parliament has become more and more of an important player in its own right. That the ECJ sees itself as paired with, rather than contrary to, other branches of power is palpable when the Court alludes to supposed gaps in effective and sufficient legal protection.[233] Famous examples again span direct effect, fundamental rights or state liability. The ECJ clearly lacks the more obvious trappings of a forum in which broader policy concerns can be addressed: it does not admit US-style class actions,[234] popular constitutional complaints

[228] Cf. W. M. Reisman, 'Judge Shigeru Oda: A Tribute to an International Treasure', *Leiden Journal of International Law*, 16 (2003), 57, 63.
[229] See G. J. Postema, *Bentham and the Common Law Tradition* (Clarendon Press, Oxford, 1986), pp. 202–4.
[230] See e.g. ICJ, *Legality of the Threat or Use of Nuclear Weapons*, Advisory Opinion of 8 Jul. 1996, ICJ Rep 1996, 226 (para. 18).
[231] Case C-91/08 *Wall AG v. Stadt Frankfurt am Main and FES GmbH* (Grand Chamber) [2010] ECR I-2815 (paras. 67–9).
[232] Cf. Burrows (n. 6 above), pp. 234, 258 (rejecting an unmixed 'oil and water' view of statute law and case law).
[233] See e.g. Case C-50/00 P *Unión de Pequeños Agricultores v. Council* [2002] ECR I-6677 (para. 40).
[234] See T. Chieu, 'Class Actions in the European Union?', *Cardozo Journal of International and Comparative Law*, 18 (2010), 123, 141 (regarding competition law).

or what are sometimes called 'Brandeis' briefs.[235] Preliminary references may occasionally be a vent for such concerns, but a filtered one at best, not least because they are often a tool wielded by national courts rather than individuals.

Not that the ECJ is particularly bashful. The Court often appears quite happy to play a game of ping-pong with other European actors. Of course it is fully aware that it is far from a legislative assembly. At the same time, it displays a keen awareness that political processes are themselves anything but perfect. Legislation can be drafted shoddily, yet nonetheless has to be rendered operable in real-life situations. This requires creativity, both in the sense of resourcefulness and making something new. Overall, the ECJ is quite willing to adopt a 'wait and see' tactic by playing its part in shaping the EU legal landscape and then waiting for any potential reaction from the Member States or EU institutions, assuming that no news is good news.[236] Deliberately or not, this exploits political disagreement, given that the last bit of legal information is often the most influential, especially when expressed in the vocabulary of *ratio* rather than *voluntas*. Prime examples of such interplay are directives on the rights of residence and corresponding ECJ decisions. Moreover, the work of the Court is reflected both positively and negatively in treaty provisions,[237] protocols,[238] annexed declarations,[239] secondary law[240] and

---

[235] See H. Schepel and E. Blankenburg, 'Mobilizing the European Court of Justice' in G. de Búrca and J. Weiler (eds.), *The European Court of Justice* (Oxford University Press, 2001), p. 41.

[236] Cf. Lenaerts and Gutiérrez-Fons (n. 43 above), p. 1668 ('called upon to address politically-charged questions left unresolved by the political process'). Likewise, other Union institutions also often bounce off of the Court's jurisprudence. See e.g. Craig (n. 165 above), pp. 4–6.

[237] See e.g. TEU Art. 6(3) on fundamental rights.

[238] See e.g. Protocol (No. 33) Concerning Article 157 of the Treaty on the Functioning of the European Union [2010] OJ C83/319, the so-called 'Barber Protocol'; Protocol (No. 35) on Article 40.3.3 of the Constitution of Ireland [2010] OJ C83/321, sometimes called the 'Irish Abortion Protocol'.

[239] See e.g. Declaration concerning primacy, Declarations annexed to the Final Act of the Intergovernmental Conference which adopted the Treaty of Lisbon [2010] OJ C83/344, No. 17.

[240] See e.g. Regulation (EEC) No. 1408/71 of the Council of 14 Jun. 1971 on the application of social security schemes to employed persons and their families moving within the Community [1971] OJ L149/2; Directive 2004/38/EC of the European Parliament and of the Council of 29 Apr. 2004 on the right of citizens of the Union and their family members to move and reside freely within the territory of the Member States [1980] OJ L158/77; Directive 2006/123/EC of the European Parliament and of the Council of 12 Dec. 2006 on services in the internal market [2006] OJ L376/36.

rules of procedure.[241] Such ping-pong makes a lot of sense for the ECJ. Whatever its detractors might suggest, it is not the only show in town. Indeed, it can get a lot more done if it involves the other players, chiefly (but not solely) its traditional ally, the Commission.[242] In the end, the Court is fed by many hands and embedded in a deep institutional structure, meaning it can be more self-confident and outspoken in this respect than international courts and tribunals which hang directly from the silken thread of consensual jurisdiction.

Finally, just as it is too simplistic to view judicial law-making as legislation or treaty-making, it is also too crude to simply contrast it with or equate it to 'common law'. While there are certainly expressions suggesting the contrary,[243] other strands of common law thought flatly refuse to equate judges with legislators.[244] The separation of powers remains a pervasive idea, if usually in the guise of a proper balance rather than a strict division. For normative and descriptive reasons, judicial law-making is frequently not considered legislation in common law legal orders. Consider the following words of Justice Scalia: 'I am not so naive (nor do I think our forebears were) as to be unaware that judges in a real sense "make" law. But they make it *as judges make it*, which is to say *as though* they were "finding" it.'[245] This is an evident recognition of law-making by adjudication that retains its own distinctive identity.

To wrap up, equating ECJ law-making with legislation or treaty-making may be a long-standing and perhaps effective scandalisation technique,[246] but it ignores the practical specificities of dispute resolution, elides important differences between political and adjudicatory discourse, bluntly suggests categorical jurisprudential distinctions along the lines of dated

---

[241] See e.g. ECJ Rules of Procedure Arts. 63–5 (measures of inquiry), 99 (replies by reasoned order to requests for preliminary references), 100 (circumstances in which the ECJ remains seised) and 129–31 (intervention).

[242] Cf. A. Vauchez, 'The Transnational Politics of Judicialization: *Van Gend en Loos* and the Making of EU Polity', *European Law Journal*, 16 (2010), 1, 1, 4, 11.

[243] See e.g. *Southern Pacific Company* v. *Jensen*, 244 US 205, 221 (1917) (Holmes J, dissenting): 'I recognize without hesitation that judges do and must legislate, but they can do so only interstitially.'

[244] See e.g. W. Geldart, W. S. Holdsworth and H. G. Hanbury, *Elements of English Law* (6th edn, Oxford University Press, London, 1959), p. 15.

[245] *James M Beam Distilling Co* v. *Georgia*, 501 US 529, 549 (1991) (Scalia J, concurring; original emphasis).

[246] See e.g. E. R. Thayer, 'Judicial Legislation: Its Legitimiate Function in the Development of the Common Law', *Harvard Law Review*, 5 (1891), 172 (pointing out the 'usurpation' and 'reproach' of the phrase).

macro-comparatist demarcations and is in constant danger of falling back into binary or ternary models of adjudication.[247]

ii Not stare decisis

Another necessary clarification is that a recognition of law-making by the ECJ is not tantamount to ascribing its precedents so-called *stare decisis* force. The latter is commonly understood as a formal legal obligation on subsequent adjudicators to treat precedents as binding. *Stare decisis* may spring from the same worry as a denial of law-making by judges, but it is historically and conceptually a different animal. It is dealt with in detail in the second half of this book when analysing negative precedent, namely the constraining aspects of prior ECJ decisions on later adjudication.[248] In brief, *stare decisis* is a (common law) doctrine that counsels against adjudicators reopening previous arguments in certain situations. The point on law-making is a more fundamental epistemic and theoretical claim that does not focus solely on the respective legal decision-maker and particular doctrinal context.

iii Individual law-making

Adjudication in a very concrete and rather unremarkable sense makes law in individual cases between the involved parties by applying governing norms with authority in a particular dispute. Once a decision is finalised, the parties are committed to something that was previously, almost by definition, contested, with next to no recourse. For instance, a Member State will or will not have infringed EU law so that it must change its domestic legislation. This form of law-making is particularly difficult to shake off, but it is also the less controversial type. Even if admissibility might be contested in specific situations, the basic willingness to participate in this system of adjudication is manifest via domestic membership in the EU or through bringing a claim and satisfying standing requirements. When push comes to shove, the parties have asked (or are taken

---

[247] It nevertheless remains popular. Cf., in a different context, B. Saul, 'Legislating from a Radical Hague: The United Nations Special Tribunal for Lebanon Invents an International Crime of Transnational Terrorism', *Leiden Journal of International Law*, 24 (2011), 677.

[248] See e.g. Ch. 8.

to have asked) for this more immediate form of judicial creativity, so that legitimacy concerns fade into the background.

iv General law-making

The more intriguing dimension of law-making through adjudication is the extent to which it reaches beyond the individual case at hand. This differs from the previous perspective in that here parties that were not involved in the prior case are affected by a precedent. This happens whenever judges make statements that allow for abstraction beyond the individual case and subsequent iteration.

The point to note here is that such prising apart of legal norms and individual cases does not depend on grand and speculative political conjecturing by judges. It happens almost automatically in the course of what can broadly be called syllogistic reasoning and crops up countless times in what may very well be considered to be 'dry', 'routine' or 'technical' lawyering that revolves around the construction and application of treaty texts or secondary EU legislation.

To give an example that deservedly failed to make the headlines, the ECJ once decided in a case involving reindeer meat that, for the purposes of the common customs tariff, game meat is meat of animals living in the wild that are hunted.[249] Without much ado, (arguably trivial) normative content was lifted from an individual decision. Almost thirty-eight years later, the Court used this to decide that imported frozen camel meat that did not come from farm-raised animals could also be considered game meat and thus paved the way for an aggrieved importer's reimbursement of import duty.[250] Precedents like those are unlikely to stoke the hotter passions of most women or men. But the technique is the same here as in cases echoing principles of dizzying constitutional importance: an abstract part and a concrete application. In fact, grasping the prevalence of such reasoning is perhaps the most powerful antidote against the worn assertion of 'judicial activism'. Figure 2.F.iv. illustrates this general law-making technique.

This capacity to reach beyond an individual case is undoubtedly what makes an adjudicatory body like the ECJ powerful and precedent

---

[249] Case 149–73 *Otto Witt KG* v. *Hauptzollamt Hamburg-Ericus* [1973] ECR 1587 (para. 3).
[250] Case C-559/10 *Deli Ostrich NV* v. *Belgische Staat* (Eighth Chamber) [2011] ECR I-10873 (paras. 27–31).

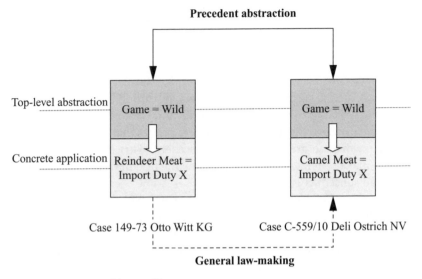

Figure 2.F.iv   General law-making

suspicious to a degree. It is here that the traditional dampeners on adjudication – jurisdiction and procedural fettering – are circumvented. Courts
thereby set standards that enable transcending individual context, regardless of any deeply reflected precedent theory.[251]

The draw of this is twofold. First, such universalisation permits progressive unfolding to cover ever more situations. For instance, concerning EU state liability, once it was established that Member State institutions in breach of European law could trigger such liability in certain
circumstances, this could first be applied to administrative and legislative organs and then also to judicial organs.[252] Likewise, Union law primacy applies vis-à-vis national legislatures, but is expanded to national
administrations.[253] Secondly, the abstracted premises or standards are
insulated from the respective application. Evidently, the more general and

---

[251] Cf. O. Lepsius, 'Die maßstabsetzende Gewalt' in M. Jestaedt *et al.* (eds.), *Das entgrenzte Gericht: Eine kritische Bilanz nach sechzig Jahren Bundesverfassungsgericht* (Suhrkamp, Berlin, 2011), pp. 165–75 (tracing the standard-setting and standard-application tech-nique with respect to the German Federal Constitutional Court).

[252] See Case C-224/01 *Gerhard Köbler* v. *Republik Österreich* (Grand Chamber) [2003] ECR 10239.

[253] See e.g. Case C-341/08 *Domnica Petersen* v. *Berufungsausschuss für Zahnärzte für den Bezirk Westfalen-Lippe* (Grand Chamber) [2010] ECR I-47 (para. 80) (with further references).

decontextualised the top layer is (i.e. the abstracted premises, standards or categories), the more likely new situations will fit under it and hence the greater the adjudicatory body's sway.[254] Contestation appears more difficult. As will be analysed later, the ECJ is very fond of this technique.[255] In fact, the top layer need not even be a case reference at all; it can be the start as well as the continuation of a chain of precedents.

---

[254] See Schauer (n. 2 above), p. 591.   [255] See Ch. 4, C.ii.

3

Determining the essence of ECJ precedents

A The inevitability of interpretation

Before examining the various uses of prior cases by the ECJ, it is important to investigate how to attribute meaning to precedents. After all, in order to make elementary precedent reasoning workable[1] – point X_2 is to be decided in manner Y because X_1 was previously decided in manner Y – one first needs to know what the earlier decision was.

Following precedent has, with good reason, been called a 'complex' idea.[2] Determining a precedent's essence or reasoning is the preliminary, and often silent, prologue to any argumentative use of prior jurisprudence and precedes more familiar questions such as what control or constricting effect a precedent might have on the Court. In fact, without at least a broad idea of the crux of a case, it is not rationally possible without external help to even single out a decision from the over 17,500 ECJ cases to date, with around an additional 600 completed cases a year in recent times.[3]

Establishing the meaning of a decided case is a delicate affair.[4] A precedent is defined by specific factual circumstances, has been channelled by procedure and party submissions and often seeks to address a particular

---

[1] On the basics see Ch. 2, A. Three possible models are discussed in L. Alexander, 'Precedential Constraint, its Scope and Strength: A Brief Survey of the Possibilities and their Merits' in T. Bustamente and C. Bernal Pulido (eds.), *On the Philosophy of Precedent* (Franz Steiner, Stuttgart, 2012), pp. 75–9.

[2] G. Marshall, 'What is Binding in a Precedent' in N. MacCormick and R. Summers (eds.), *Interpreting Precedents: A Comparative Study* (Ashgate, Aldershot, 1997), p. 503.

[3] That is more reported ECJ cases per year than disputes brought to the WTO altogether, another example of effective institutionalised dispute settlement beyond state borders (457 as of April 2013). The ICJ has seen about 160 cases since 1947 (as of 2012). See Court of Justice of the European Union, *Annual Report 2011* (Luxembourg, 2012), 116, http://curia.europa.eu/.

[4] See e.g. P. Pescatore, '*Van Gend en Loos*, 3 February 1963: A View from Within' in M. Poiares Maduro and L. Azoulai (eds.), *The Past and Future of EU Law* (Hart, Oxford and Portland 2010), p. 3 (flatly calling the habit of reading and citing prior rulings as if they were legislative texts 'a mistake').

constellation or problem, sometimes with preciously little consideration of further consequences. Language and tone tend to differ from the more abstract pronouncements commonly found in treaties and secondary legislation. It is therefore best to begin with three negatives.

First, the search for an ECJ precedent's rationale is not tantamount to a quest for the actual cause of a Court decision, but rather for a plausible rationalisation.[5] It is not the same as the judges' motivation or their actual reasoning.[6] The inquiry is rather for something that the precedent convincingly embodies, be it a standard, principle or any other basis for later decision-making.

Secondly, the essence of a precedent is not a fixed, single property. It varies according to the issue. All prior cases contain different pieces of legal information that can be adduced according to the situation, for which this then becomes the pertinent rationale. To give only one example, a decision like *Bosman* can stand for the proposition that the Court will not generally review the need for a preliminary ruling that sport is subject to EU law in so far as it constitutes an economic activity and that domestic measures which preclude or deter a national of a Member State from leaving his country of origin in order to exercise his right to free movement constitute restrictions even if they apply without regard to nationality.[7] *Bosman* can be a precedent on any or all of these points, and on others.

Thirdly, the supposed essence of a prior case is sometimes called its *ratio decidendi*, particularly – but not exclusively[8] – in common law systems, where it is traditionally considered to be the reason for deciding or the reason for a decision.[9] But as will be outlined shortly, there is no agreement as to what that in turn means. In fact, the best view may be that the *ratio decidendi* is not simply the case itself; not everything is relevant. The point of the interpretive prologue is not Latin taxonomy, as if this could somehow magically ennoble a prior statement with

---

[5] Cf. R. A. Posner, *How Judges Think* (Harvard University Press, Cambridge, MA, 2008), p. 111.

[6] See N. Duxbury, *The Nature and Authority of Precedent* (Cambridge University Press, 2008), pp. 66–8 (noting that there is often, but not inevitably, a connection between an adjudicator's reasoning and a precedent's rationale or essence).

[7] Case C-415/93 *Union royale belge des sociétés de football association ASBL* v. *Jean-Marc Bosman* [1995] ECR I-4921 (paras. 59, 73 and 96).

[8] See e.g. the use in Case C-526/08 *Commission* v. *Grand Duchy of Luxembourg* [2010] ECR I-6151 Opinion of AG Kokott (para. 38), where the AG noted in the context of a plea of *res judicata* that the *ratio decidendi* was 'inseparable' from the operative part of a judgment (with further references).

[9] See Duxbury (n. 6 above), p. 67.

universal relevance.[10] *Ratio decidendi* may be shorthand, but it can only be the result of interpretation and argumentation and not a replacement thereof. The ECJ does use the expression now and again,[11] in particular when delineating the scope of judgments annulling supranational measures.[12] The term is also popular with Advocates General.[13] But even when not explicitly mentioned, courts and tribunals inevitably employ such a concept whenever they refer to legal propositions abstracted from groups of cases. That the term is not exclusive to a particular adjudicatory body or legal system – in other words, is not doctrinal but theoretical – is further evident from the fact that it also finds expression elsewhere, such as in secondary legislation on Community trademarks in the context of decisions of the Boards of Appeal of the Office for Harmonisation in the Internal Market (OHIM).[14]

B Universalisability

The search for the meaning of an ECJ precedent is essentially the search for something that is capable of universal application.[15] Universalisability serves various needs. From a practical perspective, it allows iteration. Of course, no two situations will ever be exactly the same. If there was no possibility of abstracting beyond specific circumstances there could never be any precedent-based reasoning together with any efficiency and

---

[10] This seems to have troubled various Advocates General of the Court, as if this might predetermine the question of bindingness. See e.g. Case C-262/96 *Sema Sürül* v. *Bundesanstalt für Arbeit* [1999] ECR I-2685, Opinion of AG La Pergola (para. 36) (referring to an earlier statement of AG Roemer).

[11] Equivalents in French and German include 'les motifs de l'arrêt qui constituent le soutien nécessaire de son dispositif' and 'die Gründe des Urteils, die den Tenor tragen'.

[12] See e.g. Case C-310/97 P *Commission* v. *AssiDomän Kraft Products AB and ors* [1999] ECR I-5363 (para. 54); Case C-372/97 *Italian Republic* v. *Commission* (Sixth Chamber) [2004] ECR I-3679 (para. 36); Case C-308/07 P *Koldo Gorostiaga Atxalandabaso* v. *Parliament* (First Chamber) [2009] ECR I-1059 (para. 57). For a more general use see Case C-266/91 *Celulose Beira Industrial SA* v. *Fazenda Pública* [1993] ECR I-4337 (para. 17).

[13] See e.g. Case C-44/93 *Namur-Les Assurances du Crédit SA* v. *Office National du Ducroire and the Belgian State* [1994] ECR I-3829, Opinion of AG Lenz (para. 116); Joined Cases C-147/06 and C-148/06 *SECAP SpA and Santorso Soc. coop. arl* v. *Comune di Torino* [2008] ECR I-3565, Opinion of AG Ruiz-Jarabo Colomer (para. 27); Case C-127/08 *Blaise Baheten Metock and ors* v. *Minister for Justice, Equality and Law Reform* [2008] ECR I-6241, Opinion of AG Poiares Maduro (para. 13).

[14] Council Regulation (EC) No. 207/2009 of 26 Feb. 2009 on the Community trade mark [2009] OJ L78 (Art. 64(2)).

[15] Cf. N. MacCormick, 'Why Cases Have Rationes and What These Are' in L. Goldstein (ed.), *Precedent in Law* (Clarendon Press, Oxford, 1987), p. 162.

coherence gains this might entail. Precedents reduce complexity and isolate certain arguments from their larger environment, thus promoting manageability, which is imperative in light of the Court's vast output. From a substantive point of view, universalisability suggests regularity transcending individual decisionism and arbitrariness. It is essentially a process suffused with egalitarian ambition in which the rule of law rises above the rule of adjudicators.[16] Like should be treated alike. In this respect, case-based reasoning differs little from applying norms contained in legislation or treaties, and it is hence close to the heart of all lawyers. Finally, in logical terms, universalisability precludes a decision from condemning itself. A decision would fail on its own terms if it could not establish what it established, all other things being equal. Universalisability has both a horizontal and a vertical dimension, concerning abstraction and concretisation over a period of time.[17]

i Horizontal

Concerning the temporal dimension, through precedent-based reasoning the ECJ connects different cases at different points in time. Perhaps the more common way to think about precedents is through the backward orientation of a current legal decision-maker. Here precedents are the 'usable past'.[18]

At the same time, this also contains a forward-looking element. As one commentator observed, today is not only yesterday's tomorrow, it is also tomorrow's yesterday.[19] An awareness of this often informs reticence and cautious reasoning amongst the judges, evident in guarded language or explicit reservations in order not to trigger any unwanted development. At other times, judges might deliberately exploit this propensity by sowing seeds to bloom later, such as when the ECJ dropped the not-so-subtle hint in *Grzelczyk* that EU citizenship was 'destined to be the fundamental status' of Member State nationals, an indication that was readily picked up dozens of times since, including in *Ruiz Zambrano*.[20] Assuming that is true and perplexing though it may seem, this then means that precedent

---

[16] Cf. T. Vesting, *Rechtstheorie* (C. H. Beck, Munich, 2007), p. 26; W. Weischedel, *Die philosophische Hintertreppe* (38th edn, DTV, Munich, 2009), p. 186.

[17] See also Ch. 2, F.iv.   [18] See Duxbury (n. 6 above), ch. 1.

[19] See F. Schauer, 'Precedent', *Stanford Law Review*, 39 (1986–1987), 571, 573.

[20] Case C-184/99 *Rudy Grzelczyk* v. *Centre public d'aide sociale d'Ottignies-Louvain-la-Neuve* [2001] ECR I-6193 (para. 31); Case C-34/09 *Gerardo Ruiz Zambrano* v. *Office national de l'emploi (ONEm) (Grand Chamber)* [2011] ECR I-1177 (para. 41).

exerts an effect even where there is no prior decision.[21] Whether or not this results in sub-optimal decisions is a question that cannot be pursued here, but this feature additionally helps to explain the reluctance of many legal systems, including EU law, to acknowledge the existence of precedent or at least to sternly reject any binding effect.

ii Vertical

The vertical dimension of precedent places the Court's reasoning beyond the individual case but beneath a general norm. This allows for differentiation that can flexibly accommodate a myriad of situations and concerns; precedent as an unfinished business. It is also critical in bolstering the larger normative framework.

To give an example of such accommodating intermediate precedent abstraction, a finding of non-contractual liability of the Union generally requires a sufficiently serious breach of a rule of law designed to confer rights on an individual.[22] This prescription breaks down the abstraction of TFEU Art. 340(2) and allows for a case-by-case jurisprudence that pays attention to the degree of discretion the institutions possessed in the respective situations. It compensates the absence of an express requirement of fault in TFEU Art. 340(2) and can reign in an overly strict conception of liability. Similarly, the 'sufficiently serious breach' condition for Member State liability allowed the ECJ to limit national responsibility for decisions of domestic courts to manifest infringements, which avoids overly irritating long-standing partners.[23]

The idea of abstraction beyond the concrete case also invokes systematicity. Consider the following statement by AG Cruz Villalón in his opinion in *Lady & Kid*, where he examined a particular strand of the ECJ's jurisprudence on exceptions to the obligation to reimburse improper levies: 'Most of the cases coming before the Court of Justice to date *fit comfortably within a model*.'[24] In essence, the idea is similar to joinder of actions.

---

[21] See Schauer (n. 19 above), p. 588.

[22] See e.g. Joined Cases C-120/06 P and C-121/06 P *Fabbrica italiana accumulatori motocarri Montecchio SpA (FIAMM) and ors* v. *Council and Commission* (Grand Chamber) [2008] ECR I-6513 (para. 172).

[23] See Case C-224/01 *Gerhard Köbler* v. *Republik Österreich* (Grand Chamber) [2003] ECR 10239 (paras. 53–9); Case C-568/08 *Combinatie Spijker Infrabouw-De Jonge Konstruktie and ors* v. *Provincie Drenthe* [2010] ECR I-12655, Opinion of AG Cruz Villalón (fn. 40).

[24] Case C-398/09 *Lady & Kid A/S and ors* v. *Skatteministeriet* [2011] ECR I-7375 Opinion of AG Cruz Villalón (para. 36; emphasis added).

Whatever the abstracted reasoning of a previous ECJ case, it needs to apply equally under equal circumstances. It must be generalisable or 'rule-like'.[25] Hence in this first stage the net is cast wide. This provides a modest starting point: whatever the nub, crux, essence or *ratio* of a precedent, it is not identical to the concrete decision in the respective case.[26] It is distinct but inseparable from the operative part of a judgment.[27] The latter is the final result of the application of a more-or-less cogent process of legal reasoning to the specific situation before an adjudicatory body at that particular point in time.[28] It does not necessarily reflect all that influenced its conclusion. Rather, it merely accepts or rejects the submissions of the principal claim or, in the case of requests for preliminary rulings, provides a clipped response to a narrowly tailored reference. The ECJ formulaically states the operative part at the end after any decision on costs.[29] For the last few years, this is distinctively set in bold typeface. The so-called *dispositif* is usually prefaced by the words 'On those grounds, the Court... hereby (rules)'.[30] The first three words announce that the decision is a result of the preceding reasoning. It is even more context-specific

---

[25] For discussion of the 'rule model' of precedent see Alexander (n. 1 above), pp. 76–9.

[26] See G. Williams, *Salmond on Jurisprudence* (11th edn, Sweet & Maxwell, London, 1957), p. 223; K. Larenz and C.-W. Canaris, *Methodenlehre der Rechtswissenschaft* (3rd edn, Springer, Berlin and Heidelberg, 1995), p. 178; O. Lepsius, 'Die maßstabsetzende Gewalt' in M. Jestaedt *et al.* (eds.), *Das entgrenzte Gericht: Eine kritische Bilanz nach sechzig Jahren Bundesverfassungsgericht* (Suhrkamp, Berlin, 2011), p. 175.

[27] See e.g. Joined Cases C-442/03 P and C-471/03 P *P & O European Ferries (Vizcaya) SA and Diputación Foral de Vizcaya* v. *Commission* (Third Chamber) [2006] ECR I-4845 (para. 44).

[28] For one attempt to dissect common reasoning stages see J. Bengoetxea, N. MacCormick and L. Moral Soriano, 'Integration and Integrity in the Legal Reasoning of the European Court of Justice' in G. de Búrca and J. Weiler (eds.), *The European Court of Justice* (Oxford University Press, 2001), pp. 51–60.

[29] On the typical form of ECJ judgments see e.g. J. J. Barceló, 'Precedent in European Community Law' in N. MacCormick and R. Summers (eds.), *Interpreting Precedents: A Comparative Study* (Ashgate, Aldershot, 1997), pp. 412–15; T. C. Hartley, *The Foundations of European Union Law* (7th edn, Oxford University Press, 2010), pp. 68–9.

[30] The last word is added in preliminary rulings under TFEU Art. 267, where the ECJ does not technically settle the matter as such but rather 'enlightens' the referring court in respect of EU law. The French and German language versions are more obvious. Compare 'dit pour droit' and 'für Recht erkannt' to the more decisive 'déclare et arête' and 'für Recht erkannt und entschieden'. This difference should not however lead anyone to believe that interpretations in preliminary references are not obligatory for the national courts seized in the main proceedings. See e.g. Case 29–68 *Milch-, Fett- und Eierkontor GmbH* v. *Hauptzollamt Saarbrücken* [1969] ECR 165 (para. 3). In fact, this applies to all national authorities: Case C-453/00 *Kühne & Heitz NV* v. *Produktschap voor Pluimvee en Eieren* [2004] ECR I-837 (paras. 21–2).

than any rationale and binding on the parties involved.[31] A rationale's higher degree of abstraction on the other hand is what allows its use in other cases. Consequently, it will often be scrutinised intently by a much wider audience, which may very well be blasé about the decision as such.

Two examples from the ECJ's vast repository illustrate the difference between decisions and rationales. One of the Court's classic pronouncements, *Cassis de Dijon* is well known for its elaboration of two intertwined concepts of free movement of goods law.[32] Its potentially vast deregulation rationale ('mutual recognition') was brought to bear on a miscellany of trade barriers over the last thirty years, striking at national rules for goods as varied as certain types of vinegar, margarine, alarm systems, moth-repellent cedar blocks and motorcycle trailers.[33] The reasoning stays the same while transcending the facts, decisions and compositions of the individual cases. Secondly, *Cassis de Dijon* is frequently quoted for the principle that Member States may in the absence of harmonisation enact indistinctly applicable legislation obstructing the internal market in so far as this is necessary to satisfy so-called mandatory requirements in the public interest. This 'rule of reason' introduces a dynamic element besides the justifications listed in what is now TFEU Art. 36 and allows unwritten restrictions to be taken into account, provided they are not disproportionate. Later cases have taken this up and deliberated other potential mandatory requirements.[34]

The actual decision in *Cassis de Dijon*, while of course prompted by considerations relating to mutual recognition and mandatory requirements, was more specific, covering *a rule fixing the minimum content of alcohol for alcoholic beverages* lawfully produced and marketed in another Member State that was not saved by *consumer protection* concerns. The

---

[31] See Case 112/76 *Renato Manzoni* v. *Fonds National de Retraite des Ouvriers Mineurs* [1977] ECR 1647, Opinion of AG Warner (p. 1662) (drawing a distinction between *ratio decidendi* and the operative part).

[32] Case 120/78 *Rewe-Zentral AG* v. *Bundesmonopolverwaltung für Branntwein* [1979] ECR 649.

[33] See Case 788/79 *Criminal proceedings against Herbert Gilli and Paul Andres* [1980] ECR 2071; Case 261/81 *Walter Rau Lebensmittelwerke* v. *De Smedt PVBA* [1982] ECR 3961; Case C-14/02 *ATRAL SA* v. *État belge* [2003] ECR I-4431; Case C-443/02 *Criminal proceedings against Nicolas Schreiber* (First Chamber) [2004] ECR I-7275; Case C-110/05 *Commission* v. *Italian Republic* (Grand Chamber) [2009] ECR I-519.

[34] See e.g. Case 302/86 *Commission* v. *Kingdom of Denmark* [1988] ECR 4607 (environmental protection); Case C-368/95 *Vereinigte Familiapress Zeitungsverlags- und vertriebs GmbH* v. *Heinrich Bauer Verlag* [1997] ECR I-3689 (press diversity); Case C-531/07 *Fachverband der Buch- und Medienwirtschaft* v. *LIBRO Handelsgesellschaft mbH* (Second Chamber) [2009] ECR I-3717 (protection of books as cultural objects); Case C-110/05 *Commission* v. *Italian Republic* (Grand Chamber) [2009] ECR I-519 (road safety).

decision settled a precise dispute; its reasoning went beyond the case at hand.

At least on paper, this distinction is even more noticeable in proceedings other than preliminary rulings, which by their consultative nature blur the boundary between decisions and reasons. The point can hence be made more briefly in the second illustration, an infringement case. In *Commission v. Kingdom of Spain*, the ECJ ruled that Spain had breached its obligations by failing to transpose a directive relating to the protection of waters against agricultural pollution.[35] Specifically, Spain had neither designated certain areas of land as vulnerable zones nor drawn up all the required codes of good agricultural practice in time. What is not immediately evident from the bare decision, yet nevertheless forms an intrinsic part of the ECJ's reasoning, is that it is irrelevant that a responsible Member State fails to fulfil its obligations on account of technical difficulties. This part of the reasoning, abstracted from the immediate decision, subsequently denied other Member States recourse to such a defence in other infringement actions based on failing to abide by different pieces of EU legislation.[36]

The other side of the vertical dimension is that, at the same time as being more general than an individual ECJ decision, case rationales tend to be of a lower degree of abstraction than most treaty provisions or legislation. They render abstract norms more concrete and thus stabilise expectations.[37] All the same, abstract norms, such as treaty provisions, remain the ultimate normative vanishing point. They are 'the norm' in the sense of being the overarching, standardised case of their own application. They do not give details as to possible instantiations, but are instead satisfied only to mention a very general quality of those cases within their scope. Concerning *Cassis de Dijon*, what is now TFEU Art. 34 consists of one sentence and a mere sixteen words. It makes no mention of mutual recognition, mandatory requirements or even the breadth of 'measures having equivalent effect'. Similar considerations apply to TFEU

[35] Case C-71/97 *Commission* v. *Kingdom of Spain* (Sixth Chamber) [1998] ECR I-5991.

[36] See e.g. Case C-333/99 *Commission* v. *French Republic* (Fifth Chamber) [2001] ECR I-1025 (para. 36) (fisheries); Case C-152/98 *Commission* v. *Kingdom of the Netherlands* (Sixth Chamber) [2001] ECR I-3463 (para. 41) (water pollution); Case C-297/08 *Commission* v. *Italian Republic* (Fourth Chamber) [2010] ECR I-1749 (para. 82) (waste management).

[37] This best explains the common law tradition traceable to the likes of Blackstone, Coke and Hale, according to which precedents are not identical to 'the law', which is conceptually a distinct position from an actual denial of law-making by adjudication. See C. K. Allen, *Law in the Making* (6th edn, Clarendon Press, Oxford, 1958), p. 225. Cf. E. Schlüchter, *Mittlerfunktion der Präjudizien* (de Gruyter, Berlin, 1986), pp. 123–5; Lepsius (n. 26 above), pp. 175–7.

Art. 20 and the 'genuine enjoyment of the substance of EU citizenship rights' test shaped by the Court in cases like *Dereci*.[38]

Indeed, in many settings, constitutional considerations and democratic concerns militate against eliding case rationales and the ultimate normative layer.[39] This reflects the basic tenet of modern positivism that, for law to possess the regularity that is required to transcend arbitrariness, and thus for it to fulfil its ordering and civilising promise, it must exist independently from its concrete application. Without such a timeless and context-independent layer, there can be neither deduction from the general to the specific nor application of law to an individual case.[40] This is the driving force behind conventional syllogistic methodology and its trinity of major premise (norms), minor premise (facts) and conclusion (decision). Even for Kelsen, who dealt short shrift to simplistic declaratory theories of adjudication and the 'illusion of legal certainty', the general norm remains a superimposed point of reference for the individual decision which, in turn, is the necessary concretisation of the abstract norm.[41] Such a layering of norms according to their generality (*Stufenbau*) asserts both order and authority.

The idea of intermediate precedent abstraction is familiar to two legal traditions which are habitually – but sometimes all too readily – considered to be at odds in their treatment of prior cases, in particular as concerns the obligatory quality of precedents and their classification as sources of law.[42] The deductive mindset said to predominate in civil law systems quite naturally looks to the essence of decided cases as presumptive or hypothetical instances of norm-application in its ratiocination from abstract norm (*Rechtsnorm*) to concrete judicial decision (*Einzelakt*).[43]

---

[38] See Case C-256/11 *Murat Dereci and ors* v. *Bundesministerium für Inneres* (Grand Chamber) [2011] ECR I-11315 (paras. 62–7).

[39] See Ch. 2, F.i. on the distinction between precedents and legislation or treaties.

[40] See G. W. F. Hegel, *Outlines of the Philosophy of Right* (Oxford University Press, 2008 (1821)), paras. 13–14, 21, 211–14.

[41] H. Kelsen, *Reine Rechtslehre* (Franz Deuticke, Leipzig and Vienna, 1934), pp. 79–80, 99–100.

[42] See Schlüchter (n. 37 above), pp. 124–5; R. Schulze and U. Seif, 'Einführung' in R. Schulze and U. Seif (eds.), *Richterrecht und Rechtsfortbildung in der Europäischen Rechtsgemeinschaft* (Mohr Siebeck, Tübingen, 2003), pp. 8–9. On different approaches in general see P. S. Atiyah and R. Summers, *Form and Substance in Anglo-American Law* (Clarendon Press, Oxford, 1987), pp. 115–56; R. Cross and J. W. Harris, *Precedent in English Law* (4th edn, Clarendon Press, Oxford, 1991), pp. 10–15; S. Vogenauer, *Die Auslegung von Gesetzen in England und auf dem Kontinent*, 2 vols. (Mohr Siebeck, Tübingen 2001), I, pp. 224–6.

[43] See e.g. M. Kriele, *Theorie der Rechtsgewinnung* (2nd edn, Duncker & Humblot, Berlin, 1976), pp. 243, 248, 271–3; F. Bydlinski, *Juristische Methodenlehre und Rechtsbegriff* (2nd edn, Springer, Vienna, 1991), p. 504.

Despite the imagination of a codified system of closed rationality, the reasoning undergirding decided cases has real operational value, structures legal analysis and is hence an aid to judicial decision-making.[44] Put differently, it is valuable legal information.

Crossing the channel (or pond), in what is often thought to be predominantly inductive common law method, a precedent is only considered a precedent for what it actually stands for. Past decisions are often 'the best proof' of what the law is, as Coke once remarked.[45] In a similar vein, Hale wrote that precedents 'have a great weight and authority in expounding, declaring, and publishing what the law of this kingdom is'.[46] This was later overshadowed by a Victorian fixation with *stare decisis* and its hagiographic preference for arguments based on institutional authority.[47] But there is much to be said for the view that this was largely an aid to constructing a workable court hierarchy rather than the product of a thorough philosophy of law. While itself a characteristic overstatement, Lord Denning's extrajudicial frankness is telling: 'I refer sometimes to previous authorities – I have to do so – because I know that people are prone not to accept my views unless they have support from the books.'[48] On the whole, the obsession with *stare decisis* is a relative latecomer in the history of the common law. It is too reductionist to consider the common law method irredeemably particularistic and solely concerned with welding legal propositions to the facts of cases. It, too, pays regard to broader systemic considerations, especially in light of its persistent propensity to link and bundle the results of the institutionalised processes of adjudication in a more general fashion when faced with a specific concern.[49]

In conclusion, even though they might approach precedents from the opposite ends of the spectrum of concreteness and abstraction, both

---

[44] See F. Müller and R. Christensen, *Juristische Methodik: Grundlagen* (9th edn, Duncker & Humblot, Berlin, 2004), pp. 518–9; F. Bydlinski, *Grundzüge der Juristischen Methodenlehre* (WUV, Vienna, 2005), p. 99. On the rationality mindset of legal traditions dominated by a culture of codification see H. P. Glenn, *Legal Traditions of the World* (4th edn, Oxford University Press, 2010), pp. 145–55.

[45] E. Coke, *The First Part of the Institutes of the Laws of England: or, a Commentary upon Littleton* (15th edn, E. and R. Brooke, London, 1794), m.n. 254a. See also Allen (n. 37 above), p. 203.

[46] M. Hale, *The History of the Common Law of England* (reprint edn, Rothman, Littleton, 1987 (1713)), p. 68.

[47] It should also not be understood to demote cases to 'mere evidence' while law otherwise is a 'thing in itself'.

[48] A. T. D. Denning, *The Family Story* (Hamlyn, Feltham, 1982), p. 207.

[49] See Williams (n. 26 above), p. 222; Allen (n. 37 above), p. 213; M. A. Eisenberg, *The Nature of the Common Law* (Harvard University Press, London, 1988), pp. 154–60; E. W. Thomas, *The Judicial Process* (Cambridge University Press, 2005), p. 158.

civil law and common law thinking appreciate precedents as legal devices of medium-level abstraction. Usefulness and legitimacy are ubiquitous concerns.

C Linking cases

Arguing by precedent is at its core asserting that there is an overarching category or organising theory covering both the supposed precedent and the present situation. The cases are relevantly similar. Where this cannot be established, the earlier case is, strictly speaking, not a precedent at all. There is a certain circularity to extracting a fitting rationale from a vast body of ECJ jurisprudence, since a case can only really be considered relevant once its rationale has been grasped. Again, limited cognition rears its head.[50]

There are almost as many proposed methods for cutting this Gordian knot and distilling the reasoning of a precedent in order to link it to the current situation as there are decided cases. They range from quasi-automatic and highly formalistic rules via the moderately principled to the entirely discretionary. A selection of archetypal approaches is outlined next. The ECJ does not display a clear proclivity in this respect. On the whole, its practice intermittently hints at reconstruction approaches while relying considerably on institutional memory.

i Rules of relevance

At its most extreme, the essence of a precedent is simply dictated in an atmosphere of argumentative closure. One theorist refers to this as 'judicial reference', an approach in which the subsequent judge is largely passive and simply receives meaning defined by someone else.[51] An answer given in a preliminary reference procedure under TFEU Art. 267 might be conceived in these terms, since it is considered to determine the reasoning that directly solves a question in another case, namely the main proceedings in a national court. Evidently, this is at best of limited applicability. A recurrent formula for extracting what is relevant in a precedent that is traditionally popular in English courts is to look for the rule that was

---

[50] Cf. Ch. 2, E.ii.(a) above.
[51] See R. Siltala, *A Theory of Precedent: From Analytical Positivism to a Post-Analytical Philosophy of Law* (Hart, Oxford, 2000), pp. 78–80.

a 'necessary step' taken by the adjudicator in reaching the conclusion.[52] Various tests, most of them professing to be thoroughly mechanistic to limit arbitrariness, have been espoused over time to render this operable. For instance, one method is to take a possible rationale and then invert it.[53] If the actual decision of the precedent still fits, the rationale was wrong. The weakness of such exclusionary reasoning is that it becomes a potentially never-ending fishing expedition. Nor can alternative strands of reasoning be computed. Rival classic approaches focus on similarity or sameness of facts.[54] But sameness comes in degrees and ways: a cat might sound exactly like the other, but look slightly different.

The ECJ does not limit its precedent use to the indispensable parts of a prior case in the sense of a strict *ratio decidendi* as in some formalistic common law theories. Instead, the Court is quite happy to implicitly or expressly invoke what would be considered *obiter dicta* according to such approaches.[55] This is already borne out by its frequent phrase 'see to that effect', which signals a more generous link to an earlier case. AG Roemer put it quite bluntly half a century ago:

> The question where, in judgments, the decisive grounds of judgment end and any *obiter dicta* begin seems to me in any case to be of secondary importance. In each case everything that is said in the text of the judgment expresses the will of the Court.[56]

Overall, definitional niceties are not considered particularly significant when citing cases.[57] For instance, in *Brouwer*, a reference concerning wage discrimination, the ECJ referred to the well-known *Grzelczyk* case,

---

[52] See e.g. UK CA, *Deane* v. *Secretary of State for Work and Pensions* [2011] 1 WLR 743 (paras. 32–3) (referring to prior judicial approval of a statement to that effect in Cross and Harris (n. 42 above), p. 72).

[53] See e.g. E. Wambaugh, *The Study of Cases* (2nd edn, Little, Brown, Boston, 1894), pp. 5–8.

[54] See e.g. A. Goodheart, 'Determining the Ratio Decidendi of a Case' in A. Goodheart (ed.), *Essays in Jurisprudence and the Common Law* (Cambridge University Press, 1931), pp. 4–25.

[55] See e.g. Case C-235/09 *DHL Express France SAS* v. *Chronopost SA* [2011] ECR I-2801, Opinion of AG Cruz Villalón (para. 57).

[56] Case 9/61 *Kingdom of the Netherlands* v. *High Authority of the European Coal and Steel Community* [1962] ECR 213, Opinion of AG Roemer (p. 242).

[57] See e.g. A. G. Toth, 'The Authority of Judgments of the European Court of Justice: Bindig Force and Legal Effects', *Yearbook of European Law*, 4 (1985), 1, 36–42; T. Koopmans, 'Stare Decisis in European Law' in D. O'Keeffe and H. G. Schermers (eds.), *Essays in European Law and Integration* (Kluwer, Deventer, 1982), pp. 22–4; A. Arnull, 'Owning Up to Fallibility: Precedent and the European Court of Justice', *Common Market Law Review*, 30 (1993), 247, 249.

together with a string of other decisions, to make the point that financial consequences that might ensue for a Member State from a preliminary ruling do not themselves justify limiting its temporal effects.[58] *Grzelczyk* concerned the access of migrant students within the EU to subsistence allowance of other Member States. The essence of that case was the Court's emphatic insistence that citizenship enables those in the same situation to enjoy within the scope *ratione materiae* of the treaties the same treatment irrespective of their nationality, albeit subject to certain exceptions.[59] The temporal limitation point was not indispensable to that and was proclaimed to apply only in rare situations. In fact, the paragraph of *Grzelczyk* which *Brouwer* cited in turn simply refers to previous cases without any reasoning of its own. Ironically, the illustrious turn of phrase from *Grzelczyk* that is now frequently bandied around verbatim on the destiny of EU citizenship was – as far as the minimalistic logic of the decision on the entitlement to non-contributory social benefits is concerned – also strictly speaking irrelevant.[60]

ii Scepticism

Recognising the shortcomings of formalistic rules of relevance often triggers scepticism. According to such views, the hunt for any clearly defined and pre-existing rationale or essence of a precedent is a 'wild goose chase starting from a logical confusion' or simply illusory.[61] Given limited cognition, that is a tempting proposition, but it is important to remember that such scepticism is primarily addressed to rigid reliance on mechanistic approaches. Critiquing those is one thing, but it is quite a different thing to claim that in the absence of any such magic formulae precedent interpretation and linking is necessarily up to adjudicators' hunches or even a grand charade in the name of (false) authority or legitimacy.

What is more, for the legal worker, namely the ECJ judge, practising lawyer or legal academic, the problem remains how to justify his or

---

[58] Case C-577/08 *Rijksdienst voor Pensioenen* v. *Elisabeth Brouwer* (Fourth Chamber) [2010] ECR I-7485 (para. 34).

[59] Case C-184/99 *Rudy Grzelczyk* v. *Centre public d'aide sociale d'Ottignies-Louvain-la-Neuve* [2001] ECR I-6193 (paras. 29–33).

[60] See J. Shaw, 'A View of the Citizenship Classics: *Martinez Sala* and Subsequent Cases on Citizenship of the Union' in M. Poiares Maduro and L. Azoulai (eds.), *The Past and Future of EU Law* (Hart, Oxford and Portland, 2010), p. 359.

[61] For the former see F. S. Cohen, 'The Problems of a Functional Jurisprudence', *Modern Law Review*, 1 (1937), 5, 20. For the latter see J. Stone, *Precedent and Law* (Butterworths, Sydney, 1985), pp. 74–5.

her own precedent-based arguments. Without a means of separating the wheat from the chaff meaningful use of precedents would be difficult and most of the associated advantages eradicated.[62] Moreover, EU law can and does denote certain arguments as impermissible. Reason-giving is regularly a prerequisite,[63] and anything else is unlikely to satisfy participants spending a lot of time, money and effort on a dispute. For case-based reasoning to remain a useful type of discourse in its own right it cannot be supplanted by plain choice. As noted by Llewellyn, techniques without ideals are a menace, while ideals without technique are a mess.[64]

iii Reasoned reconstruction

A third approach proceeds from the principle of reason-giving and looks for what might be the best possible reconstruction of a point made in an earlier decision. The focus shifts to justifying a decision *ex post*.[65] Essentially, a judge starts with an intuition or hypothesis as to what the rationale or norm in a precedent might be and then seeks to confirm and explain this.[66] There is no single way to go about interpreting and linking cases, but the point is rather that the reasoning has to be traceable. In a usually more-or-less subliminal process, the legal worker looks for something that 'fits and justifies' a complex part of legal practice.[67] Factors that can be relevant in reconstructing the essence of a precedent include its wording, facts, outcome, systemic constellations, problems that were addressed at the time, prior history, subsequent development and so on. Nothing is excluded *a priori* in this eclectic methodological approach.

Precedents are then never set in stone but constantly subject to dynamic re-characterisation; again, unfinished business. Indeed, it is hard to overstate the role played by a later bench looking at an earlier case. Reasoned reconstruction means that irrelevance (i.e. *obiter dictum*) is not an inherent property of an argument.[68] Rather, it depends on argumentation and context. But despite this fluidity, there is still a notion of 'carrying grounds'

---

[62] On these see Ch. 2, B.   [63] See ECJ Rules of Procedure Arts. 32(3), 87(m), 89(c).

[64] K. N. Llewellyn, 'On What is Wrong with So-Called Legal Education', *Columbia Law Review*, 35 (1935), 651, 662.

[65] Cf. MacCormick (n. 15 above), p. 170.

[66] See Kriele (n. 43 above), p. 271. Cf. K. Langenbucher, *Die Entwicklung und Auslegung von Richterrecht* (C. H. Beck, Munich 1996), pp. 77–93.

[67] See R. Dworkin, *Law's Empire* (reprint edn, Hart, Oxford, 1998 (1986)), p. 228. This does not necessarily entail a deep commitment to a specific theory of law.

[68] Cf. Case C-262/96 *Sema Sürül v. Bundesanstalt für Arbeit* [1999] ECR I-2685, Opinion of AG La Pergola (para. 37).

in the guise of more-or-less relevant passages in past judgments. This is also evident in the ECJ's case law on appeals, which states that the Court will reject complaints directed against grounds of a GC judgment that were included 'purely for the sake of completeness'; these cannot lead to the judgment being set aside.[69]

The ECJ displays this approach hesitantly.[70] As will be shown later, detailed discussion of prior cases does not feature copiously in ECJ judgments, which instead often emphasise overarching systematicity.

iv Institutional memory

The three approaches just sketched are rarely if ever openly discussed by courts like the ECJ. In actual practice, interpreting and linking precedents tends to be an 'incompletely theorised' exercise in the sense that the actual basis for a judge's reasoning is unknown or not laid open clearly.[71] This is supported by two points. First, doctrinal (let alone theoretical or methodological) disputes are often left to the academy. AG Lagrange once said of the task of a judge of the Court of Justice of the European Coal and Steel Community that it was 'not to put forward theories but to dispense justice'.[72] Secondly, the multiplicity of judges alone coupled with the plethora of divergent views on this difficult topic militates against a single shared approach as to how to go about determining when or why a precedent is relevantly similar.

There is, however, an important crutch for the ECJ when it comes to precedent-based reasoning. In practice, finding and linking cases is an affair that revolves heavily around how the respective institutional memory is organised with respect to past cases. This is of fundamental importance since it channels the transmission of ideas about precedents. It ranges from seemingly mundane aspects such as how case data is stored and how such data can be accessed and manipulated to more rarefied

---

[69] See Case C-441/07 P *Commission* v. *Alrosa Company Ltd* (Grand Chamber) [2010] ECR I-5949 (para. 71).

[70] But see e.g. the reconstruction of a precedent on citizenship and the 'purely internal situation' in Case C-256/11 *Murat Dereci and ors* v. *Bundesministerium für Inneres* (Grand Chamber) [2011] ECR I-11315 (paras. 65–6). Advocates General at times engage in such exercises, see e.g. Case C-150/03 P *Chantal Hectors* v. *Parliament* [2004] ECR I-8691, Opinion of AG Ruiz-Jarabo Colomer (para. 37).

[71] On this concept see C. R. Sunstein, 'On Analogical Reasoning', *Harvard Law Review*, 106 (1993), 741, 745–6.

[72] Case 8–55 *Fédération Charbonnière de Belgique* v. *High Authority of the European Coal and Steel Community* [1956] ECR 245 Opinion of AG Lagrange (p. 261).

concepts such as institutional identity and individual autonomy. It is an important funnel for legal information.

To give a historical example, in the early days of the common law, beginning at the end of the twelfth century, only the skeletal results of proceedings were recorded in so-called plea rolls, formulaic documents that were shorn of factual details and the reasoning of the parties and judges. Not only were the medieval records prone to inaccuracy, judges also often plainly refused to make entries where there was substantive disagreement. Consequently, many of the assumptions and workings of the law remained within the legal community and were passed down orally or through private manuscripts. Personal memory and experience were key. Precedent consisted of what passed for 'common learning' rather than individual decisions.[73] However, over time, the written form – year books, law reports, treatises – had a profound impact. Judges were aware that their words would be taken as law in future cases. Print fortified the notion that law was being made rather than found and supported the modern notion of precedent as something existing externally from the oral tradition and collective hive mind of lawyers.[74] As the organisation of memory changed, so did the legal institutions.

The interplay between ECJ judges and the Court's institutional memory is complex. Accessing precedents is heavily dependant on personal style and experience. Much will be intuitive and particular; some judges and Advocates General have a background in EU law, others do not. Party submissions play an important role in bringing cases to the Court's attention or failing to do so. But there are institutionalised commonalities. For one, members of the ECJ can and will ask their *référendaires*, the legal secretaries that are the silent workhorses of the Court.[75] The Research and Documentation department also stands at their disposal for various tasks.

Crucially, all actors can draw upon centralised databases. It is hard to image that any modern technological innovation other than word processing has had such an effect on the practice of law as the introduction of searchable databanks. They form the backbone of many institutions'

---

[73] See J. H. Baker, *An Introduction to English Legal History* (4th edn, Butterworths, London, 2002), pp. 197–201.

[74] Cf. R. J. Ross, 'The Commoning of the Common Law: The Renaissance Debate over Printing English Law, 1520–1640', *University of Pennsylvania Law Review*, 146 (1998), 323, 325–6.

[75] Each of the currently twenty-eight judges has at least three legal secretaries. The nine Advocates General are entitled to four each.

memory. The Court has its own internal systems, some of which resemble the publicly available EUR-Lex service, albeit with more powerful search features and tailored to the Court's specific needs.[76] It would be wrong to assume that such a tool will automatically produce a seamlessly coherent approach to the treatment of precedents, not least since interpretation will always remain a necessity. Moreover, some actors will chose a different route, preferring to go straight to their textbooks or commentaries; others might plough through the databases more thoroughly than their colleagues and prefer to search through specialised queries rather than on a semantic basis. There will also likely be organisational wrinkles, such as different internal systems of document organisation or storage.

But this existence of a comprehensive, centralised and searchable database that is tended, catalogued and indexed by a permanent staff does lay the groundwork for a more mechanistic approach to the Court's own jurisprudence. First, it emphasises the importance of precedents and their more general normative nexus through perpetuating prior points of view. What is more, distinguishing becomes a real option where earlier judgments are recorded so thoroughly and easy to find. In particular, this seamless coverage promotes the appearance of uniformity. Private organisation of case law memory and hence a more personal and idiosyncratic approach are implicitly discouraged. Predefined classification and systemic grouping further suppress the need to spell out why a case is considered relevant.

Wrapping up this section on discerning a precedent's relevance and essence, quite what in the end makes an ECJ case a 'controlling' or 'leading' case is anything but obvious and as much a matter of historical developments, behavioural idiosyncrasies and institutional implications as of legal doctrine.[77] But above all, it remains a matter of argumentation. This imbues case-based reasoning at the Court both with a potential for systematisation and elasticity, but also opens up room for (external) critique.

---

[76] E.g. pending cases can be queried. Exploiting the fact that the Court's internal working language is French, faster and more precise results can also generally be elicited.

[77] Cf. I. Richardson, 'What Makes a "Leading" Case', *Victoria University of Wellington Law Review*, 41 (2010), 317.

4

Precedent application by the ECJ

This chapter closely examines the ECJ's distinct style of precedent application. It elicits that the Court's practice of invoking prior cases is a lot more varied than may appear at first glance. What further emerges is that the Court's technique is to a large extent an expedient of its particular situation and the demands it faces. Amongst other things, the findings question received approaches to judicial law-making and binding precedent.[1]

A Methodological preliminaries

i Data set

For the quantitative parts, data was collected from fifty-two recent ECJ Grand Chamber judgments and fifty-two awards, orders or decisions of international investment tribunals.[2] Both batches were delivered in 2010. The latter serve as an ideal test for the thesis that the ECJ's precedent use is highly context-sensitive by pitting permanent supranational adjudication against *ad hoc* international arbitration.[3]

Concerning ECJ decisions, the Court sits in three basic formations: as a full Court, as a Grand Chamber composed of fifteen judges or in chambers composed of three or five judges.[4] In its early days, the Court always sat in plenary session, which at the time meant seven judges. Nowadays, on account of enlargement and an ever-burgeoning case load of more than 600 new cases a year, the smaller formations are essentially the default option. For example, in 2011, almost 88 per cent of cases were dealt with in that way, the majority being chambers of five judges (just over

---

[1] Examined in Chs. 2 and 8.   [2] Annexed.
[3] *Ad hoc* in the sense of there not being a standing international investment court. The vast majority of these cases were bilateral investment treaty ('BIT') disputes arbitrated under the auspices of the International Centre for Settlement of Investment Disputes ('ICSID'). All of those decisions are in the public domain and available at: http://italaw.com.
[4] CJEU Statute Art. 16; ECJ Rules of Procedure Arts. 11, 27.

55 per cent).[5] A case is assigned to the Grand Chamber when its difficulty, importance or particular circumstances so require or if a Member State or institution of the Union that is party to the proceedings so requests.[6] This happened in more than 11 per cent of cases in 2011. Full Court sittings are now exceedingly rare, with only one or two a year, if at all. For instance, the ECJ sits in this formation in special situations stipulated by the TFEU that relate to the dismissal or compulsory retirement of certain officeholders.[7] The Court may also sit in full where a case is of exceptional importance.

A few things are worth bearing in mind regarding the design and purpose of the quantitative element of this work. First, it is observational in that it is not conceived as a true statistical experiment in which explanatory variables are manipulated with a view to extracting clear cause-and-effect relations. Confounding factors cannot be ruled out, which is why qualitative analysis remains vitally important. Secondly, while it examines a manageable number of cases, it nevertheless consists of over 2,200 individual references to precedent made in those decisions which provide a sufficiently broad basis for conclusions. Thirdly, the year 2010 was chosen as the population of interest in order to make a timely assessment of the modern practice of the ECJ. While no further control was exercised in determining exactly which cases go into the two groups,[8] strictly speaking this at best only allows for very tentative generalisations beyond the year 2010, since the data is not collected from a random sample of all respective decisions ever dispatched.[9] In particular, focusing on the Grand Chamber decisions also means that it is, again from a purely statistical point of view, not possible to make unqualified claims about the ECJ as a whole. This can in turn be taken with a grain of salt, since the Grand Chamber's output is significant for the Court as a whole on account of its representative composition and guiding function.[10] But the data set is, in order to reflect important up-to-date legal practice, deliberately imprinted with a degree

---

[5] Court of Justice of the European Union, *Annual Report 2011* (Luxembourg, 2012) 102, http://curia.europa.eu.

[6] ECJ Rules of Procedure Art. 60(1).

[7] CJEU Statute Art. 16; TFEU Arts. 228(2), 245(2), 247 and 286(6).

[8] The sample does not deliberately exclude any of the ECJ Grand Chamber judgments handed down that year. A corresponding number of investment treaty decisions were drawn randomly.

[9] Cf. D. Freedman, R. Pisani and R. Purves, *Statistics* (4th edn, W.W. Norton, New York, 2007), chs. 1–2 (on designing studies and the use and misuse of statistical methods).

[10] It routinely consists of the President, Vice-President, three senior Presidents of chambers of five judges and the number of judges needed to reach fifteen.

of selection bias, which will be pointed out where relevant. Overall, the point of the limited quantitative analysis here is not to make bold claims based on the second decimal after the point, but to gauge larger tendencies and reasonable generalisations, support hypotheses and combine it with qualitative analysis, so that these mutually inform each other with neither claiming exclusive explanatory power.

ii Caveats

In addition to the limitations imposed by the data, important methodological caveats need to be made at the outset when analysing the use of precedents by the ECJ. Not only is precedent-following difficult to conceptualise, it is also notoriously tricky to ascertain and evaluate. To begin with, what should one focus on? Whether or not precedents are applied or followed in the sense of actually drawing upon a prior solution to a legal problem cannot be established simply by pointing to the frequency of their invocation.[11] Without more, positive citation could perhaps only be non-causative window-dressing in the sense that the same decision would have been reached in any event; perhaps the prior cases adduced are considered to be 'merely illustrative' or employed out of a genuine desire to bolster jurisprudential coherence or, more cynically, to provide a veneer of rationality or legitimacy. What is more, citation alone says nothing about whether or not any adverse precedents existed that were overlooked, ignored or selectively modified without mention.[12]

On account of these shortcoming one might be tempted to concentrate solely on those instances – or the lack thereof – in which the Court makes use of past decisions despite being unconvinced of them or even in outright disagreement with them. This is occasionally considered the litmus test for 'true' precedent.[13] But compelled adherence, assuming it

---

[11] See T. Healy, 'Stare Decisis and the Consitution: Four Questions and Answers', Notre Dame Law Review, 83 (2008), 1173, 1181; T. W. Morrison, 'Stare Decisis in the Office of Legal Counsel', Columbia Law Review, 100 (2010), 101, 127.

[12] Cf. the accusations of one dissenting arbitrator: CME Czech Republic BV v. Czech Republic, Arbitration under UNCITRAL Rules, Dissenting Opinion of Arbitrator Hándl of 13 Sep. 2001 (p. 2): '[T]he two arbitrators pointed out in the Award only the "Authorities" presented by the Claimant, without mentioning that the Respondent presented also his "Authorities".'

[13] A famous expression is that of Lord Devlin in the UK House of Lords in Jones v. DPP [1962] AC 635, 711. Referring to a series of precedents, he noted: 'The principle [of stare decisis] does not apply only to good decisions; if it did, it would have neither value nor meaning.' Note however the nuancing that immediately followed: '[I]t is only if a decision

is a viable concept, may of course never become known, especially if a judgment eschews detailed discussion of the relevant jurisprudence and does not allow for individual dissenting opinions, as tends to be the case with the ECJ.

The surrogate test is to look for the opposite and to draw inferences based on whether or not the Court makes it known that it is departing from or distinguishing a precedent. Unfortunately, that invites its own problems. Non-overruling or the lack of modification of prior jurisprudence alone does not necessarily entail respect for precedent in general, for instance where there is in fact no precedent that might influence a decision-maker.[14] There is also the very real possibility that the ECJ modifies or overrules a precedent indirectly or wordlessly (i.e. *sub silentio*) or contradicts a prior assessment without acknowledging this.

To give just one example, the ECJ in *Centros* ruled that it was contrary to the freedom of establishment to refuse to register a branch of a company duly formed in another Member State, even though the company conducts no business in that other Member State and was simply set up there for the purpose of avoiding minimum share capital requirements.[15] In so doing it did not refer to – but arguably cut across or at least modified – *Daily Mail*, a less invasive decision in which the Court had previously stressed that it was permissible, on account of varying national requirements regarding the necessary connection between a company and successful incorporation in a Member State, to require that the real head office rather than just the registered office should be situated in the respective territory.[16] Reconciling these decisions is not impossible, for instance through distinguishing the situations, but it at the very least demands an effort.[17]

is doubtful that the principle has to be invoked. It is a *useful principle* and based on an essential characteristic of our law, namely, that it is developed not merely for elegance and correctitude but for use in practice. If mistakes have been made, . . . but *if the result produced is a sensible one* that has established itself in the practice of the law, let it be left alone' (emphasis added). Cf. F. Schauer, 'Precedent', *Stanford Law Review*, 39 (1986– 1987), 571, 576 ('If precedent matters, a prior decision now believed erroneous still affects the current decision simply because it is prior.').

14 See Morrison (note 11), p. 127.
15 Case C-212/97 *Centros Ltd* v. *Erhvervs- og Selskabsstyrelsen* [1999] ECR I-1459 (para. 30).
16 Case 81/87 *The Queen* v. *HM Treasury and Commissioners of Inland Revenue, ex parte Daily Mail and General Trust plc* [1988] ECR 5483 (para. 23). *Centros* on the other hand later simply held that 'the fact that company law is not completely harmonised in the Community is of little consequence' (para. 28).
17 See in this respect Case C-208/00 *Überseering BV* v. *Nordic Construction Company Baumanagement GmbH (NCC)* [2002] ECR I-9919 (paras. 58–63); Case C-210/06 *CARTESIO Oktató és Szolgáltató bt* (Grand Chamber) [2008] ECR I-9641 (para. 122); Case

Crucially, however, the point of this monograph is not an (inevitably selective and ultimately hopeless) attempt to map the entire case law of the ECJ in order to gauge its overall consistency. It is almost banal to note that it is all but impossible in practice to keep track of all potential precedents, certainly when the corpus of decided cases numbers in the hundreds and thousands and time and other resources are limited. Unannounced shifts happen frequently, not only because a more open approach might be considered unpalatable, but simply because of the near infinite possibility of linking and contrasting different points discussed in different cases. In short, negative treatment is at best a snapshot of a larger unfinished business; tracing all potential leads is a Sisyphean errand that is hostage to particular views on substantive EU law and systematicity.

The upshot of these methodological qualifications is that, short of the proverbial crystal ball, the true power of precedent will often remain obscure, not least because sophisticated legal reasoning – not only the judges', but also commentators' – ultimately retains a residue of decision-ist mystery.[18] Complex dispute settlement invariably involves different degrees of 'muddling through',[19] psychology, procedural stratagems and sometimes plain happenstance. There is thus no way to ascertain with any sufficient degree of certainty what exactly motivated or caused an ECJ judgment; its reasoning, including the precedent techniques used, may very well just be an *ex post* attempt to rationalise behaviour. Hence, one response is to focus not so much on specific causes but rather on more general reasons for a certain practice, namely the broader contextual setting. This will be addressed in Chapter 7.

Moreover, the very fact that judges consider it relevant to make visible efforts to deal with precedents can itself be revealing.[20] The focus then shifts from the *making* of decisions to the practice of *justifying* decisions. At the very least, the combined analysis of general features such as precedent frequency, precision and use together with an examination of

---

C-371/10 *National Grid Indus BV* v. *Inspecteur van de Belastingdienst Rijnmond/kantoor Rotterdam* (Grand Chamber) [2011] ECR I-12273 (paras. 26–7).

[18] For different variations of this theme that nevertheless share this basic inkling cf. K. N. Llewellyn, *The Bramble Bush* (Oceana, New York, 1930), pp. 42–3 ('Onto the green, with luck, your science takes you. But when it comes to putting you will work by art and hunch'); U. Di Fabio, *Das Recht offener Staaten. Grundlinien einer Staats- und Rechtstheorie* (Mohr Siebeck, Tübingen, 1998), p. 150; I. Augsberg, *Die Lesbarkeit des Rechts* (Velbrück, Weilerswist, 2009), ch. VII.

[19] Cf. C. E. Lindblom, 'The Science of "Muddling Through"', *Public Administration Review*, 19 (1959), 79.

[20] Cf. G. A. Caldeira, 'Legal Precedent: Structures of Communication between State Courts', *Social Networks*, 10 (1988), 29, 30.

negative treatment as undertaken here presents a starting point for deeper insights or future predictions. Importantly, it provides a basis for what might be called phronetic inquiry:[21] where is the ECJ heading; who gains and who loses; is this desirable; what can be done about it?

B Frequency

This book charts multiple ways in which precedents appear in judgments of the ECJ. A first aspect is the rate of precedent references in its justificatory practice.

i Popularity and density

The ECJ regularly invokes its own jurisprudence in deciding cases.[22] It is almost impossible nowadays to read a decision by the Court and not come across a reference to an earlier decision. This is borne out by a quantitative assessment of the outward citations (i.e. citations *from* a case) found in fifty-two Grand Chamber judgments handed down by the Court in 2010. Three points are worth noting. First, the decisions surveyed made a total of 977 references to individual precedents, a figure including repeat citations to the same precedent but excluding mentions in reported pleadings and procedural history. That amounts to almost nineteen precedents invoked per case on average, with some judgments surpassing fifty such references.[23] This will be broken down in more detail in subsequent sections, but what is immediately apparent is the

---

[21] On this see B. Flyvbjerg, *Making Social Science Matter* (Cambridge University Press, 2001), pp. 1–4, part 2 (noting the perennial tension between 'pre-Kantian shaman[s]' and 'physics envy'). See also R. M. Unger, *What Should Legal Analysis Become?* (Verso, London, 1996), pp. 129–34; D. Kennedy, *A Critique of Adjudication: Fin de Siècle* (Harvard University Press, Cambridge, MA, 1997), pp. 360–1 (on critique clearing the ground for new theory rather than being inherently opposed to it).

[22] One study indicates reliance on prior cases is the main argumentative device employed by the ECJ. See M. Dederichs, *Die Methodik des EuGH: Häufigkeit und Bedeutung methodischer Argumente in den Begründungen des Gerichtofes der Europäischen Gemeinschaften* (Nomos, Baden-Baden, 2004), p. 37.

[23] See Joined Cases C-316/07, C-358/07, C-359/07, C-360/07, C-409/07 and C-410/07 *Markus Stoß and ors* v. *Wetteraukreis* (Grand Chamber) [2010] ECR I-8069; Case C-173/09 *Georgi Ivanov Elchinov* v. *Natsionalna zdravnoosiguritelna kasa* (Grand Chamber) [2010] ECR I-8889. By way of comparison, the fifty-two investment tribunal and committee decisions collectively mentioned 1,295 precedents, leading to an average of almost twenty-five precedents per case (including repeat citations). But note that those decisions are often much longer.

considerable popularity that precedents enjoy at the ECJ as a justificatory tool. Secondly, this is further teased out by the density of references to precedents in these judgments: roughly one precedent was cited every four paragraphs.[24] While it is difficult to generalise on account of inevitable variance, the Court's notably clipped style of drafting, inspired by the French legal tradition, concentrates the punctuating effect of its precedent references.[25] A third and final figure underscores this status: only a single Grand Chamber decision in the sample declined to make any mention of other cases at all.[26]

ii Frequency: the new normativity?

The legal practice just outlined rocks the wishful perception of ECJ judges as quasi-automatons solely preoccupied with and tightly fettered by treaties and secondary legislation in their daily dealings. Of course, everyone dealing with EU law in more than just a superficial manner knows this, notwithstanding enduring fictions.[27] Hence, it might be tempting to simply leave it at this first quantitative observation. Given that ECJ judges are law-makers in the sense of generating legal information,[28] does this then obviate any useful distinction between law and legal practice in the EU?

As argued earlier in response to blunt pragmatism, it does not follow from the popularity with which precedents are cited by the ECJ that numerical superiority alone becomes the be all and end all. In other words, quantity cannot replace quality, regularity is not a rule. This matters both from an orthodox point of view that has a clear-cut concept of the founding treaties as the hierarchical pinnacle and from a critical perspective that appreciates and seeks to retain the emancipatory edge of normativity in the face of sheer facticity. What makes legal arguments, including ECJ judgments, convincing is not the number of times they are heard, but their intrinsic value – however that may ultimately be

---

[24] The fifty-two decisions totalled 4,243 paragraphs and 977 precedent references, hence amounting to over four paragraphs per precedent invoked.

[25] The spread of Grand Chamber decisions for 2010 ranged from 48 to 166 paragraphs, with the average decision being almost 82 paragraphs long.

[26] See Case C-441/07 P *Commission* v. *Alrosa Company Ltd* (Grand Chamber) [2010] ECR I-5949 (which only referred to cases in the context of the procedural history of the appeal).

[27] That is, of course, not to deny that such fictions often serve a specific purpose. Cf. H. Kelsen, *Reine Rechtslehre* (Franz Deuticke, Leipzig and Vienna, 1934), pp. 79, 94–100.

[28] See Ch. 2, E.ii.

defined.[29] Nor is there reason to believe that one should not reconsider one's views in light of subsequent developments or further arguments. Briefly put, substance cannot be replaced by mathematics. Indeed, this point is made time and again by the Court when justifying the adoption of a minority position following a comparative survey of Member State legal orders in search of general principles.[30]

This fits well with the more general observation that law is an interpretive and argumentative practice. Necessarily, this includes an epistemic angle in terms of what a judge brings to the deliberation room (*Vorverständnis*). This can and will often be coloured by particularly prominent strands of prior jurisprudence. But that alone is not a suggestion of impropriety, nor does it reduce the entire exercise to a matter of quantity, just as little as judging becomes pure ideological preference or psychology.

In sum, frequency is only the beginning, and far from the end, of any inquiry into precedent.[31] Just as the plain number of ECJ case references alone does not generate normativity, it is similarly injudicious to suppose that it is entirely without consequence. The matter lies between these two extremes. The normative dimension of ECJ precedent will be probed in more detail in Chapter 8 when examining the ever-popular question of bindingness.

C Precision

Having sketched the popularity of precedent at the ECJ, the degree of precision or granularity employed in these references is where its practice begins to show more distinctive peculiarities. Quite how precedents are introduced in a judgment is not just a vain technicality. At the very least, in order for a legal decision to be intelligible and thus legitimate, it is necessary for the references to prior cases to be traceable and reproducible. But beyond that, the precision employed when invoking precedents is relevant both in terms of what can be done with an earlier decision

---

[29] Cf. *Tidewater Inc. and ors* v. *Bolivarian Republic of Venezuela*, ICSID Case No. ARB/10/5, Decision on Claimants' Proposal to Disqualify Professor Brigitte Stern of 23 Dec. 2010 (McLachlan, Rigo Sureda) (para. 26).

[30] See e.g. Joined Cases C-120/06 P and C-121/06 P *Fabbrica italiana accumulatori motocarri Montecchio SpA (FIAMM) and ors* v. *Council and Commission* [2008] ECR I-6513, Opinion of AG Poiares Maduro (para. 55).

[31] Cf. L. M. Friedman *et al.*, 'State Supreme Courts: A Century of Style and Citation', *Stanford Law Review*, 33 (1980–1981), 773, 804 (noting that 'sheer *numbers* are only the roughest of indicators'; original emphasis).

and how this is received by the parties and the broader audience. Where they exist, internal drafting guidelines reflect an awareness of this. For instance, it is suggested at the ECJ that different keywords should be used to signify the degree of specificity employed.[32] In practice, there is of course considerable variance, with much again being down to individual preference and style. But the obvious fact that the form of citation cannot be rigidly regulated does not mean that the chosen degree of precision, haphazard though it may be at times, is not without consequences. Four types will be considered: verbatim, general, string and substantive citation.

i Verbatim reproduction: echoes and LEGO®

The most direct and precise way to incorporate previous decision-making is to faithfully repeat its wording. In earlier times the ECJ was known to echo word for word whole sentences or even paragraphs from past decisions without citation.[33] This fits with a conception that there is no need for an intermediary or conduit between the law as 'contained' in textual sources and its application to a concrete situation; the Court and its creative role do not feature in that picture, a useful stance in what were then still largely untested waters.

From the 1960s on, emboldened and induced by ever-thicker, complex and tested layers of jurisprudence, the ECJ increasingly resiled from the anonymous echo or cut-and-paste approach of yore, but what might be called the LEGO® technique of constructing legal propositions from pre-formed building blocks is still alive, albeit now usually with attribution. This is especially popular whenever limbs of a test are set out, for example the main elements of state liability for loss and damage caused to individuals as a result of breaches of EU law.[34] Accurate repetition remains key, but acknowledgement of authorship is more forthcoming given the Court's more assured and accepted place in the multilevel European legal space. Such reproduction is still far more prevalent at the ECJ than in the

---

[32] In descending order of precision, these include: 'ârret', 'voir', 'voir, notamment', 'voir, en ce sens' or 'également', 'par analogie' and like formulations and combinations.

[33] See e.g. the French versions of Joined Cases 90/63 and 91/63 Commission v. Grand Duchy of Luxembourg and Kingdom of Belgium [1964] ECR 1217, 1232 and Case 52–75 Commission v. Italian Republic [1976] ECR 277 (para. 11) on the 'ordre juridique nouveau qui règle les pouvoirs, droits et obligations'; T. C. Hartley, The Foundations of European Union Law (7th edn, Oxford University Press, 2010), p. 70.

[34] See e.g. Case C-445/06 Danske Slagterier v. Bundesrepublik Deutschland (Grand Chamber) [2009] ECR I-2119 (para. 20); Case C-118/08 Transportes Urbanos y Servicios Generales SAL v. Administración del Estado (Grand Chamber) [2010] ECR I-635 (para. 30).

usually more bespoke and prolix awards and decisions of international arbitral tribunals.

The shift away from unattributed echoes of the past strongly supports one of the theses of this study: the Court's precedent usage is not solely or mainly about efficiency, but about legitimacy and acceptance. If it were otherwise, it would be more economical to use verbatim replication more widely, or – easier still – leave out citations altogether. Rather than being solely a matter of convenience or keeping translation difficulties and costs to a minimum, the lasting purpose of the LEGO® technique is to avoid a shift in jurisprudence or the mere impression thereof. After all, the ECJ's pronouncements are keenly watched by tens of thousands of courts and potentially affect over 500 million people. Previsibility is crucial. It will also be easier to convince others, including (sometimes over a dozen) colleagues, if a point can be plucked directly from a set of pre-existing, polished and succinct phrases bearing the mark of prior approval; a strong argument is often one that fits with prior jurisprudence. This will presumably be especially attractive for newly appointed judges, who might not yet be perfectly familiar with EU law or legal French before taking up their position. After all, the ECJ has a lively rotation due to its lack of lifetime tenure and relatively short judicial term limits.

But repetition is not without its downsides. Indeed, in ancient Greek mythology, the nymph Echo's habit of repeating what others had said was a curse inflicted by Hera for her deception. Turning to the present subject, stasis would appear pre-programmed. But almost to add insult to injury, replicating verbal formulations does not in fact rule out later arguments as to what the precise meaning or legal conclusion to be derived from the chosen words are.[35] What is more, the technique implicitly replicates not only the functions but also most of the costs of *stare decisis*. Chiefly, it encourages a misguided perception of judicial pronouncements as if they were legislation or set in stone. This can lead to individual infelicities where context is disregarded.

Plus, just as they can be avoided, mistakes can also be perpetuated by replication, such as when 'ampliation' and 'amplification' are mixed up.[36] Similarly, nuances can be eroded or brushed aside, such as when

---

[35] Cf. J. Stone, *Precedent and Law* (Butterworths, Sydney, 1985), p. 32.

[36] On this particular confusion see Case 108/81 *GR Amylum* v. *Council* [1982] ECR 3107 (para. 25) ('ampliation d'un moyen énoncé antérieurement'), referred to in Case 306/81 *Constantin Verros* v. *Parliament* [1983] ECR 1755 (para. 9) ('amplification d'un moyen énoncé antérieurement'). The latter is mentioned by Case C-485/08 P *Claudia Gualtieri* v. *Commission* (First Chamber) [2010] ECR I-3009 ('amplification d'un moyen énoncé antérieurement') (para. 37). But see Joined Cases C-106/09 P and C-107/09

the ECJ appears to reduce the three-prong proportionality test to a one-stage review of appropriateness[37] or when the incorrect impression is given that direct taxation is never within the purview of the EU.[38] At the very least, this raises eyebrows and demands subsequent rationalisation to determine whether inconsistencies are intentional or not. Over time, it can stifle legal evolution by making change more costly: opposition becomes more difficult, variation appears increasingly awkward.

When the wording does change after a particular phrase has become a household mantra, this provokes the understanding that the change was deliberate and signals a meaningful change, whether or not this was in fact intended. For instance, one could argue that there is a difference between non-contractual liability of the EU requiring that damage suffered was a 'sufficiently direct consequence' of the unlawful conduct of one of its organs or that there simply had to be a 'causal link' between the two.[39] The Court does not however consider this a significant variation; both formulations accommodate remoteness as a means to limit liability.[40]

ii General mention: forest not trees

At the other end of the spectrum of granularity, it is not uncommon for the ECJ to bring up judicial developments in a very broad fashion without irredeemably tying the content of a proposition to a specific

P *Commission and Kingdom of Spain* v. *Government of Gibraltar and United Kingdom* [2011] ECR I-11113, Opinion of AG Jääskinen (para. 36) ('ampliation d'un moyen énoncé antérieurement'), which refers back to the *Amylum* case.

[37] See e.g. Case C-210/03 *The Queen, on the application of Swedish Match AB and Swedish Match UK Ltd* v. *Secretary of State for Health* (Grand Chamber) [2004] ECR I-11893 and the critique in Case C-365/08 *Agrana Zucker GmbH* v. *Bundesminister für Land- und Forstwirtschaft, Umwelt und Wasserwirtschaft* [2010] ECR I-4341 Opinion of AG Trstenjak (paras. 59–64).

[38] See e.g. Case C-42/02 *Diana Elisabeth Lindman* (Fifth Chamber) [2003] ECR I-13519 (para. 18) (with further references); Case C-512/03 *EJ Blanckaert* v. *Inspecteur van de Belastingdienst/Particulieren/Ondernemingen buitenland te Heerlen* [2005] ECR I-7685, Opinion of AG Stickx-Hackl (para. 48). Competences are in fact shared. See e.g. Case C-72/09 *Établissements Rimbaud SA* v. *Directeur général des impôts and Directeur des services fiscaux d'Aix-en-Provence* [2010] ECR I-10659 Opinion of AG Jääskinen (para. 62).

[39] For the former see Joined Cases 64 and 113/76, 167 and 239/78, 27, 28 and 45/79 *Dumortier frères SA and ors* v. *Council* [1979] ECR 3091 (para. 21); the latter is used by Joined Cases C-120/06 P and C-121/06 P *Fabbrica italiana accumulatori motocarri Montecchio SpA (FIAMM) and ors* v. *Council and Commission* (Grand Chamber) [2008] ECR I-6513 (para. 106).

[40] See e.g. Case C-419/08 P *Trubowest Handel GmbH and Viktor Makarov* v. *Council* (Fourth Chamber) [2010] ECR I-2259 (para. 53).

decided case. Typical expressions flagging this technique in the English-language reports include references to 'settled', 'established' or 'consistent' 'case(-)law' or 'jurisprudence'. Such general references look to the forest rather than the individual trees. They trade the precision of a punchy individual precedent for the pillowy normativity of broader systemic demands: the sum is considered greater than the individual pieces.

The present data set of Grand Chamber decisions shows that the ECJ mentioned its own general normative output around eleven times per judgment.[41] Contrast this with international tribunals deciding matters of investment law, which on average only made five and a half such wide-ranging mentions of arbitral practice per decision.[42] This is even more noteworthy if one is prepared to accept that ECJ decisions are on average much shorter.

This practice elicits two related points. First, the ECJ is not irredeemably wed to a particular level of granularity; its technique is variable. Secondly, general citation, too, is employed in the service of boosting the Court's legitimacy. Precedents become the 'distilled wisdom' of the adjudicatory body; the latter becomes impregnable.[43] It is a technique that can be accommodated well by legal systems that purport not to give any partic-ular decision 'true' precedential force. The attraction lies in the flexibility and robustness that more nebulous invocations afford. Rough edges can be smoothed, and – also a relevant consideration at the ECJ – sub-optimal translations masked. This is again done with a view to acceptance and compliance, but it is purchased at the cost of credibility and control. To counter this, a sprinkling of concrete examples often seeks to anchor the argument being made in legal practice and thereby prevent an exces-sive loss of authority. These cases are often appended in parentheses, for instance when those studying a judgment are encouraged to see individual cases 'to that effect', 'in particular' or 'by analogy'.[44]

---

[41] There were 582 general references in fifty-two decisions. It is not necessary to draw attention to any particular instance.

[42] A total of 287 general references were culled from the 2010 data set. For an example see e.g. *Inmaris Perestroika Sailing Maritime Services GmbH and ors v. Ukraine*, ICSID Case No. ARB/08/8, Decision on Jurisdiction of 8 Mar. 2010 (Alexandrov, Cremades, Rubins) (para. 131) (referring to 'a number of tribunals and *ad hoc* committees' that of late considered the so-called *Salini* criteria to be indicative rather than mandatory).

[43] Cf. O. Lepsius, 'Die maßstabsetzende Gewalt' in M. Jestaedt *et al.* (eds.), *Das entgrenzte Gericht: Eine kritische Bilanz nach sechzig Jahren Bundesverfassungsgericht* (Suhrkamp, Berlin, 2011), pp. 179–80 (on how the German FCC uses a 'top-heavy' technique to similar effect).

[44] Such string citations are discussed in the next section.

The Court's circumstances are particularly receptive to this technique. The ECJ is a single, permanent judicial body nestled in a layered yet integrated legal system that has produced thousands of decisions for more than a half-century affecting the everyday lives of millions of people. TEU Art. 19(1) expressly asks the Court to ensure that the singular 'law' is observed in the interpretation and application of the treaties. Against this backdrop, inconsistencies are considered particularly hurtful. Sometimes this huge body of jurisprudence can only be reigned in and rendered coherent by glossing over antagonistic angles. General recourse to 'consistently held' fundamental principles is a particularly attractive method to achieve this.[45] Consistency is thus effectuated by increasing generality. This promises evenness and certainty, again pining for external amenability. Yet there comes a point when abstraction becomes unusable or so lacking in credibility that the gains are squandered again. Moreover, a remarkably consistent jurisprudence that fails to be meaningful or respectful of individual specificities is in trouble. This will be discussed subsequently in the context of jurisprudential coherence.[46]

iii Specific mention

Between the two extremes of reproducing prior reasoning verbatim and alluding to jurisprudence at large, reference is commonly made to individual ECJ precedents. This was already documented numerically at the start of this section on precision and can in turn be divided into two further types of reference: string citations and substantive citations.[47] The distinction approximately accords to whether or not a precedent's context or reasoning is explicated. One could also call these 'strong' and 'weak' forms of citation. Given individual styles and partly overlapping functions, it will not always be easy to draw a bright line between these two kinds of specific citation, but in the large majority of cases it is possible to ascribe a precedent reference to one or the other.

---

[45] See e.g. Case C-274/10 *Commission* v. *Republic of Hungary* (Third Chamber) [2011] ECR I-7289 (para. 42) (seeking to reconcile the precedents confirming the freedom of Member States to determine the conditions for the refund of excess VAT with the precedents asserting a degree of EU law control over that matter).

[46] See Ch. 5, C.

[47] Cf. C. A. Johnson, 'Follow-up Citations in the US Supreme Court', *Western Political Quarterly*, 39 (1986), 538, 543; D. J. Walsh, 'On the Meaning and Pattern of Legal Citations: Evidence from State Wrongful Discharge Precedents', *Law & Society Review*, 31 (1997), 337, 338.

(a) String citation

Legal decisions often support a point by simply appending a string of one or more precedents to a particular statement. Those references are not discussed; there is no unpacking of their context, no substantive analysis commending or critiquing their reasoning.[48] Instead, the silent string itself affirms the precedent's correctness and applicability. It implicitly asserts the accuracy of the connection made by the referring judicial or arbitral body. Such precedent arguments do not claim respect through further explanation, but ultimately by an appeal to institutional authority, be it to that of the maker of the original or present statement.[49] The primary purpose of string citations is to bolster the weight and legitimacy of a decision and to render it more palpable to an outside audience.[50] The precedents adduced may or may not have had a causal effect on the legal decision-maker, but they depict what he or she believes is required to legitimise an exercise of authority.

While most adjudicators tend to mix string and substantive citations, quantitative analyses from quite distinct national legal systems have concluded that the non-substantive string variety of precedent citation predominates in practice.[51] It almost goes without saying that these are of course very limited studies with a specific focus and distinct methodology,[52] but this is of interest because the respective legal systems are traditionally considered to adopt rather different approaches to precedent, in particular as concerns its normative force. This gives rise to the hypothesis that most references to precedent in judgments of the ECJ are also of the non-substantive kind. That assumption is confirmed by the present study, but with conspicuously varying orders of magnitude when

---

[48]　There are innumerable examples. See e.g. Joined Cases C-379/08 and C-380/08 *Raffinerie Mediterranee (ERG) SpA and ors* v. *Ministero Ambiente e Tutela del Territorio e del Mare and ors* (Grand Chamber) [2010] ECR I-2007 (paras. 26, 80) (on the admissibility of a reference from a lower court where the appellate court's ruling might lead to a violation of EU law and on the possibility of qualifying the right to property).

[49]　Cf. J. Bell, *Judiciaries within Europe* (Cambridge University Press, 2006), pp. 73–4 (discussing the function of French judgment style).

[50]　Cf. Friedman *et al.* (note 31), p. 794.

[51]　For the US: Johnson (n. 47 above), pp. 542–3. For Austria: E. Holzleithner and V. Mayer-Schönberger, 'Das Zitat als grundloser Grund rechtlicher Legitimität' in B. Feldner and N. Forgó (eds.), *Norm und Entscheidung* (Springer, Vienna and New York, 2000), pp. 345–6.

[52]　E.g., unlike in the present study, string citations are sometimes defined to require at least two or more cases cited in a row.

contrasted to international investment arbitration.[53] Of those investment tribunal decisions scrutinised, almost exactly three-quarters were not substantive.[54] But the situation is far more pronounced concerning the ECJ's Grand Chamber judgments surveyed: the overwhelming number of precedent invocations, a staggering 97 per cent, were referential string citations.[55]

The great draw of string citations is that they relieve decision-makers from the need for lengthier elaborations while at the same time seeking to recoup the advantages of arguing by precedent with minimal effort and irritation. The effect can be leveraged even further when two or more cases are mentioned. This is particularly attractive for the ECJ and explains its penchant for this kind of citation. Not only is it faced with a considerable workload,[56] far more so than in investment arbitration the crafting of its judgments is a multiparty and multi-stage process ranging from the involvement of *référendaires* to single collegiate judgments under the shadow of the vote. The language issue also rears its head, disfavouring the nimble twisting and turning of every single word of previous judgments that is typical of more substantive precedent argumentation. In addition to that, the view that the solution resides in 'the system' – the 'law' of TEU Art. 19(1) – rather than the cases as such continues to hold much sway at the Court, as evinced by the popularity of general precedent incantations highlighted above or its famous references to the 'legal order' as a whole or to that which is 'inherent in the system' of the treaties.[57] In view of that, there are in-house recommendations at the ECJ that touch upon string citations, suggesting that no more than three cases should be cited, ideally including the first and the last precedent on point.

String citations are not without their downsides. First, in contrast to substantive references, string citations do not invest further justificatory

---

[53] String citations for these purposes are all mentions of individual precedents that are not supplemented by substantive analysis as to whether and why they should be followed, distinguished, limited or otherwise treated in a specific way.

[54] 971 out of 1,295 cases mentioned were string citations.

[55] 945 out of 977 precedents invoked were string citations.

[56] The current twenty-eight judges are expected to act as *juge rapporteur* in roughly twenty to thirty cases per year and take part in a far greater number of proceedings altogether. According to official statistics, the ECJ completed 638 cases in 2011, with 849 still pending and 688 new cases having come in. See Court of Justice of the European Union, *Annual Report 2011* (Luxembourg, 2012) 95, http://curia.europa.eu.

[57] See e.g. Opinion 1/09 *Patent Litigation System* (Full Court) [2011] ECR I-1137 (para. 65) and Case C-118/08 *Transportes Urbanos y Servicios Generales SAL* v. *Administración del Estado* (Grand Chamber) [2010] ECR I-635 (para. 29), respectively.

capital other than what can be distilled from the legal proposition that is being buttressed, giving the entire practice a circular spin. Much relies on the authority and reputation of the decision-maker. The onus is firmly placed on the audience to verify the connection and its conclusiveness. In short, convenience is traded for convincingness.

Yet the practice is quite evidently far from being watertight. Consider only the *Josemans* case, which received an unusual amount of attention for a decision by a chamber of five judges on the freedom to provide services.[58] One of the basic propositions advanced was that, as a narcotic drug, the sale of cannabis could not benefit from the fundamental freedoms.[59] This statement was bolstered by various string citations 'to that effect'. But *Horvath* involved heroin rather than cannabis and concerned the impermissible application of customs duties to smuggled drugs and not fundamental freedoms.[60] *Wolf* (heroin and cocaine) was similarly concerned with whether customs debt arose upon the importation of drugs.[61] *Vereniging Happy Family* did deal with hashish, but the case centred on liability for turnover tax.[62] Since the fundamental freedoms are not coterminous with the scope of application of secondary law on VAT or the customs tariff, there might well be matters that could come under the former but not the latter. Moreover, none of the supposed precedents tackled the idiosyncratic status ('not legal but tolerated') that cannabis enjoyed in the Netherlands at the time the *Josemans* matter arose.[63]

To be clear, none of these tentative rebuttals unavoidably entails that *Josemans* 'got it wrong'.[64] The point is more modest: the string citations employed by the Court do not insuppressibly establish the opposite, but instead leave considerable room for questions and doubts. In other

---

[58] Case C-137/09 *Marc Michel Josemans* v. *Burgemeester van Maastricht* (Second Chamber) [2010] ECR I-13019. A Dutch *coffeeshop* had been closed temporarily on account of admitting non-residents.

[59] *Ibid.* paras. 36, 41–2.

[60] Case 50/80 *Jozsef Horvath* v. *Hauptzollamt Hamburg-Jonas* [1981] ECR 385.

[61] Case 221/81 *Wilfried Wolf* v. *Hauptzollamt Düsseldorf* [1982] ECR 3681.

[62] Case 289/86 *Vereniging Happy Family Rustenburgerstraat* v. *Inspecteur der Omzetbelasting* [1988] ECR 3655.

[63] Cf. L. Haasbeek, 'Soft Drugs under Scrutiny: How "Easy Going" is the Court?', *Legal Issues of Economic Integration*, 38 (2011), 389, 395–7.

[64] E.g. one could respond that, just like VAT law and the customs tariff, the fundamental freedoms are simply a means to an end, i.e. tools employed in the creation of a space of human well-being and safety. Cf. Case C-137/09 *Marc Michel Josemans* v. *Burgemeester van Maastricht* [2010] ECR I-13019, Opinion of AG Bot (para. 92).

words, they underestimate the argumentative nature of law by skirting the difficult question of what is relevant in a precedent and whether it should hold sway in the case at bar. The ECJ partly offsets these shortcomings through verbatim repetition and broader appeals to systemic trends, but these have their own difficulties, as discussed earlier. Excessive reliance on string citations that is shorn of other perspectives omits tapping into important justificatory dimensions, above all policy and social utility. This makes the reception of a judgment more difficult for a wider audience, such as when the regulated provision of cannabis in the more-or-less orderly confines of a Dutch *coffeeshop* is equated without more with the trafficking of heroin across European borders.

A closely related but not immediately evident aspect of these 'weak' string citations is that they go hand-in-hand with positive, namely affir-matory, treatment of precedent. There is a disconnect between this lean reference technique and distinguishing and departing from cases. As will soon be set out in more detail, the ECJ is loath to cite substantively and to treat precedents negatively.[65] Investment tribunals on the other hand demonstrate a greater proclivity for substantive citation, which matches their readiness to distinguish and depart from earlier decisions.

While it would likely be an oversimplification to assert that form inevitably determines substance as concerns precedent precision and precedent-following, it seems similarly short-sighted to claim that sub-stance inescapably dominates form or that the two are completely detached. A tentative hypothesis appears warranted: form and substance subtly encourage each other. On the one hand, the more readily a judge unpicks the facts and reasoning of a prior case, that is to say the more substantive the precedent citation technique is, the more likely one will come up with differences and shortcomings. On the other hand, plain invocation of a precedent without more at the very least enjoys the bene-fit of a silent presumption that all other things are equal and hence that the rationale of the prior case is applicable in the present situation. Moreover, this would seem to be 'good law'. Although it might theoretically be pos-sible to treat a precedent negatively in a purely referential string citation, that appears dubious: at least outwardly, negative precedent treatment demands more justificatory effort than adopting prior reasoning. Rup-tures require more attention than repetition. If the ECJ eschewed that effort it would seriously jeopardise the perception that it is legitimately exercising its function.

---

[65] See, respectively, Ch. 4, C.iii.(b) and Ch. 6.

At least on the face of it, the ECJ thus treats its precedents with great reverence. Yet insistence on (surface) coherence has several injurious consequences. For one, cases can become increasingly isolated over time without clearly being abandoned.[66] Questions then arise as to whether these pronouncements can still be considered 'good law'.

Moreover, detected jurisprudential shifts appear particularly jarring or confusing when not presaged by substantive argumentation or when done silently. While particular points of substantive EU law are not the focus of this book, the following examples serve to illustrate the concern. One such instance is the well-known *Bergaderm* case, where the ECJ adopted without more the test it had developed for state liability in the context of non-contractual supranational liability and no longer mentioned the violation of a 'superior rule of law' it had previously insisted on, for instance in the *Roquette frères* matter.[67] More recent examples might include the *Förster* and *Wolzenburg* decisions, which seemed to take a less exacting approach than earlier (and later) cases to the justification of restrictions on a migrant EU citizen's rights by not insisting on an assessment of individual circumstances suggesting integration.[68] Furthermore, the *Kadi* decision has been claimed to mark a clandestine departure from the ECJ's traditional approach to the relationship between EU law and public international law.[69] A particularly notorious example is the *Mangold* case, where the Court reached a different result on horizontal direct effect than it had only shortly before in *Pfeiffer* without even mentioning that judgment.[70] This is striking since both were Grand Chamber matters.

---

[66] See e.g. the fate of the judgment Case C-383/99 P *Procter & Gamble Company* v. *OHIM* [2001] ECR I-6251, which was heavily qualified by a series of later decisions of the Court without being mentioned. Cf. Case C-408/08 *Lancôme parfums et beauté & Cie SNC* v. *OHIM* [2010] ECR I-1347 Opinion of AG Ruiz-Jarabo Colomer (para. 96).

[67] Case C-352/98 P *Laboratoires pharmaceutiques Bergaderm SA and Jean-Jacques Goupil* v. *Commission* [2000] ECR I-5291 (para. 41); Case 20/88 *SA Roquette frères* v. *Commission* [1989] ECR 1553 (para. 23). See A. Arnull, *The European Union and its Court of Justice* (2nd edn, Oxford University Press, 2006), pp. 628–9 (castigating this as a 'clumsy' approach).

[68] Case C-158/07 *Jacqueline Förster* v. *Hoofddirectie van de Informatie Beheer Groep* (Grand Chamber) [2008] ECR I-8507; Case C-123/08 *Dominic Wolzenburg* (Grand Chamber) [2009] ECR I-9621.

[69] Joined Cases C-402/05 P and C-415/05 P *Yassin Abdullah Kadi and Al Barakaat International Foundation* v. *Council and Commission* (Grand Chamber) [2008] ECR I-6351. See S. Besson, 'European Legal Pluralism after "Kadi"', *European Constitutional Law Review*, 5 (2009), 237, 249.

[70] Case C-144/04 *Werner Mangold* v. *Rüdiger Helm* (Grand Chamber) [2005] ECR I-9981; Joined Cases C-397/01 to C-403/01 *Bernhard Pfeiffer* v. *Deutsches Rotes Kreuz, Kreisverband Waldshut eV* (Grand Chamber) [2004] ECR I-8835.

Indeed, litigants are encouraged to suspect and seek to exploit supposed contradictions when judgments are known to limit or omit discussion of past cases altogether. To give just one illustration, in *Reemtsma Cigaretten-fabriken* the applicant suggested that in *Langhorst* the ECJ had effectively reversed a precedent that restricted the right to deduct tax that would otherwise not have been due, thereby ushering in a more extensive right of deduction.[71] Pointing amongst other things to different subsequent decisions, the Court and AG Sharpston however maintained that *Langhorst* had not intended to upset the principle that deductions could only apply to taxes that were actually due and not just invoiced. Still, while the Advocate General in *Langhorst* had discussed the original precedent (i.e. the supposedly reversed case), the Court there made no mention of it, thus enabling the later submission.[72]

Above all, legal certainty, which ironically is thought to be best served by this form of judicial asceticism, can be jeopardised. By way of comparison, in the system of the European Convention on Human Rights ('ECHR'), inadequately reasoned departures from well-established jurisprudence can, in specific circumstances, even lead to a failure to satisfy the requirements of a fair trial.[73] Again, the point is not that the ECJ is necessarily mistaken, but rather that it becomes more vulnerable to such criticism when the supposed fit of its rulings with prior cases remains clouded. No adjudicatory body will ever be totally consistent, but the question is to what extent this can be appreciated. What matters is reasoned reconstruction, not imaginary perfection.

(b) Substantive citation

Substantive or 'strong' citations refer to precedents in order to adopt or avoid their expounded reasoning. They allow judges and arbitrators to enter into a discussion across cases on a particular point.[74] In contrast to string citations, they demand greater justificatory exertion, with the onus on the later decision-maker rather than the addressees or audience at large

---

[71] Case C-35/05 *Reemtsma Cigarettenfabriken GmbH* v. *Ministero delle Finanze* (Second Chamber) [2007] ECR I-2425 (paras. 21–3); *Ibid.* Opinion of AG Sharpston (paras. 40–5).

[72] Case C-141/96 *Finanzamt Osnabrück-Land* v. *Bernhard Langhorst* [1997] ECR I-5073, Opinion of AG Léger (paras. 53–61).

[73] See ECtHR, *Atanasovski* v. *The Former Yugoslav Republic of Macedonia*, Application No. 36815/03, Judgment of 14 Jan. 2010 (para. 38) (while recalling that there was no right to an established jurisprudence and that scarce reasoning was in principle acceptable).

[74] See Holzleithner and Mayer-Schönberger (note 51), p. 338.

to establish and support the relationship between the present instance and the precedent. They rely on content rather than command, source or *fiat* and record the reasoning they embody.[75] Non-string citations tend to be used whenever there is a greater desire to earn acceptance.[76] The likely corollaries of substantive citations are discursiveness and length.

To give an illustration from the Court's practice, in *Real Sociedad de Fútbol SAD* the ECJ was asked by a Spanish court whether national sporting rules could permissibly place a cap on the number of non-Member State players a football team could field in national competitions.[77] The dispute in the main proceedings concerned a duly registered Turkish professional footballer who had been denied a licence of the kind granted to what were then still European Community players. The ECJ had previously in two very similar references decided that the non-discrimination provisions contained in the respective Association and Partnership Agreements had to be interpreted as preventing the limited eligibility of legally employed athletes through rules drawn up by sporting federations.[78] The Court in *Real Sociedad* described the factual and legal underpinnings of these precedents, drew attention to the close resemblance of the relevant clause in the EEC–Turkey Agreement to those directly effective provisions and their common purposes and hence concluded that the interpretation adopted before was also pertinent in the present situation. It thus expended effort to explicitly make the precedent's interpretation its own.

As to a substantive citation that leads to avoidance of precedent, in *Football Association Premier League*, the Grand Chamber held that a prohibition on the use of foreign premium TV decoding devices could not be justified simply by relying on the objective of protecting intellectual property rights. It expressly referred to a supposed precedent's context,

---

[75] Cf. D. Dyzenhaus and M. Taggart, 'Reasoned Decisions and Legal Theory' in D. E. Edlin (ed.), *Common Law Theory* (Cambridge University Press, 2007), pp. 152–3 (detecting the contrary 'command conception' of authority and its justification in Hobbes' *Leviathan*).

[76] Cf. C. A. Johnson, 'Citations to Authority in Supreme Court Opinions', *Law & Policy*, 7 (1985), 509, 511. Of course, caution in ascribing causality is once again encouraged.

[77] Case C-152/08 *Real Sociedad de Fútbol SAD and Nihat Kahveci* v. *Consejo Superior de Deportes and Real Federación Española de Fútbol* (Fifth Chamber) [2008] ECR I-6291 (paras. 21–31).

[78] Case C-438/00 *Deutscher Handballbund eV* v. *Maros Kolpak* (Fifth Chamber) [2003] ECR I-4135 (concerning a Slovakian handball player in Germany); Case C-265/03 *Igor Simutenkov* v. *Ministerio de Educación y Cultura and Real Federación Española de Fútbol* (Grand Chamber) [2005] ECR I-2579 (concerning a Russian football player in Spain).

asserting this was 'not comparable' to that of the main proceedings.[79] The earlier case, the Court reasoned, should be reconstructed so that EU law did not rule out intellectual property protection in a situation in which no remuneration had been paid to and no authorisation obtained from the right-holders in the Member State of origin. This consequently enabled the ECJ to distinguish that precedent.

Overall, however, the Court's appetite for such citations remains muted. Given the dual definition adopted here, the proportion of substantive citations is the inverse of the number of string citations. This means that just over 3 per cent of precedent mentions of the Grand Chamber judgments of 2010 that were examined were substantive. Things are very different for the corresponding international investment tribunal decisions. Roughly 25 per cent of those citations were discussed in at least some detail. Four factors need to be considered concerning the degree of scrupulousness the ECJ tends to employ when it comes to precedent citation: function, structure, style and publication.[80]

Concerning function, many of the characteristics mentioned above in connection with the ECJ's preference for general precedent references and string citations apply, such as its unifying role. Unlike most arbitral panels established in investment disputes, the Court also largely deals with questions of law rather than fact.[81] Factual disputes generally provide more fodder for narrow delineations. The Luxembourg court frequently adopts a prospective orientation on account of its large influence and responsibility, which tends to play out in programmatic statements.[82] This is particularly likely to be the case in Grand Chamber matters or preliminary references, where principles of wider application are frequently considered and broad jurisprudential courses are plotted, and it differs notably from the 'made to order' nature of arbitrations that are constituted for a specific occasion only. Even in cases of non-contractual liability of the Union under TFEU Art. 340, the ECJ does not normally award a specific sum following a successful claim for damages, but delivers an

---

[79] Joined Cases C-403/08 and C-429/08 *Football Association Premier League and ors* v. *QC Leisure* (Grand Chamber) [2011] ECR I-9083 (paras. 118–20).

[80] Additional factors are assessed when unpacking the reasons for the ECJ's technique in Ch. 7.

[81] Cf. H. G. Schermers and D. F. Waelbroeck, *Judicial Protection in the European Union* (6th edn, Kluwer Law International, The Hague, 2001), pp. 240, 295.

[82] On prospective and retrospective techniques see M. Taruffo, 'Institutional Factors Influencing Precedents' in N. MacCormick and R. Summers (eds.), *Interpreting Precedents: A Comparative Study* (Ashgate, Aldershot, 1997), p. 444.

interlocutory judgment stipulating broad compensation criteria and asks the parties to reach an agreement.[83]

As to structure, the more decision-makers that are involved, the more cumbersome and costly deciding becomes. The collective nature of ECJ judgments is again relevant here. It often stands in sharp contrast to the more argumentative and loquacious opinions of its Advocates General.[84] Given the unavailability of separate or dissenting opinions, it is more difficult for the Court to pursue particularly nuanced or tendentious views of precedents. As one former judge put it, the collegiate approach 'may simply cloak an inability to reach a clear decision'.[85] Moderate views expressed in a compromising tone have become a vital means to oil collegiate cooperation and institutional loyalty, constant features and expectations in a permanent institution like the ECJ.[86] This is all the more so since the precise interpretation and significance of prior cases will often be controversial, given that they are even more malleable than legislation on account of their discursiveness, contextual specificity, factual background, unresolved relevance and heightened propensity for reformulation through sequential reinterpretation.[87] While intra-institutional rivalry can be observed in the decidedly lukewarm citation practice between the ECJ and the GC,[88] the Court is reluctant to unpick its own cases in embarrassing detail in front of the Member States and their courts. Conflicts tend to be addressed informally and behind closed doors. Individual *ad hoc* tribunals have far fewer qualms in this respect.

Turning to matters of style, the much-described French-inspired tradition with its preference for brief, legalistic and formal reasoning over prolix substantial reasoning, conceived as an enlightened triumph of

---

[83] See e.g. Case C-152/88 *Sofrimport SARL* v. *Commission* (Fifth Chamber) [1990] ECR I-2477 (para. 30).

[84] See J. J. Barceló, 'Precedent in European Community Law' in N. MacCormick and R. Summers (eds.), *Interpreting Precedents: A Comparative Study* (Ashgate, Aldershot, 1997), p. 411.

[85] D. Edward, 'How the Court of Justice Works', *European Law Review*, 20 (1995), 539, 556.

[86] On such lubrication see N. Luhmann, 'Spontane Ordnungsbildung' in F. Morstein Marx (ed.), *Verwaltung: Eine einführende Darstellung* (Duncker & Humblot, Berlin, 1965), pp. 170, 172.

[87] Cf. J. Raz, *The Authority of Law* (2nd edn, Oxford University Press, 2009), p. 195.

[88] See e.g. Case T-85/09 *Yassin Abdullah Kadi* v. *Commission* (Seventh Chamber) [2010] ECR II-5177 (paras. 121–123). Cf. A. Rosas, 'With a Little Help from My Friends: International Case-Law as a Source of Reference for the EU Courts', *The Global Community Yearbook of International Law and Jurisprudence*, 5 (2005), 203, 207; Arnull (n. 67 above), pp. 633–7.

impersonal 'judicial function' over all-too-personal 'judicial power',[89] is detectable in the ECJ's output. But its style and method has long since become a distinctive hybrid, drawing on a mix of various national and non-national elements.[90] Certain influences are discernible, but the Court's habits are not a simple pastiche of only one particular model. One should in any event be slow to revert to a caricaturesque common law–civil law schism.[91] True, the ECJ often strives to present its judgments in clinical, commanding, artificial and anonymous language, which can be an attempt to avoid confusion or critique.[92] Unlike the myth of the organic wisdom of the common law with its heavy reliance on patchwork and charismatic decision-making, the Napoleonic ideal epitomises a single posited will through depersonalised authority.[93] Similar to the traditions in France and the Nordic countries, the judge in the scheme of the EU is more of a civil servant implementing the will of the state:[94] *effet utile*. This is quite different from the romanticised ideal that adjudicators are primarily occupied with fending off authoritarian intrusion in

---

[89] On the French tradition see M. Troper and C. Grzegorczyk, 'Precedent in France' in N. MacCormick and R. Summers (eds.), *Interpreting Precedents: A Comparative Study* (Ashgate, Aldershot, 1997), pp. 107, 112 (while noting that judges there do not explicitly cite precedents in their written decisions).

[90] See L. Coutron, 'Style des arrêts de la Cour de justice et normativité de la jurisprudence communautaire', *Revue Trimestrielle de Droit Européen*, 45 (2009), 643, 644.

[91] Writing in an academic capacity, AG Lagrange thought the main difference between French and German judgments to be precisely that of non-substantive versus substantive. The former did not bother to discuss all the arguments of the parties but rather proceeded by way of logical tracing to a seemingly natural result, whereas the latter was essentially a justificatory exercise aimed at convincing the addressees that laid bare the judges' reasoning processes, hesitations and doubts. See M. Lagrange, 'La Cour de justice des Communautés européennes', *Études et Documents du Conseil d'État*, 17 (1963), 55, 62. Corroborating the view that German judgments are deductive–legalistic but also to a considerable degree substantive–argumentative: R. Alexy and R. Dreier, 'Precedent in the Federal Republic of Germany' in N. MacCormick and R. Summers (eds.), *Interpreting Precedents* (Ashgate, Aldershot, 1997), p. 21. The latter can be a deliberate choice reacting to bad experiences with more austere formalism, as was the case in Germany. But the pendulum can also swing the other way. See e.g. BVerfG, 1 BvR 550/52, *Homosexuelle*, 1. Senate, 10 May 1957 (m.n. 167) (drawing on religious sentiments in a case on the constitutionality of the criminalisation of homosexuality).

[92] On modelling such a style and its diametrical opposite see R. Summers and M. Taruffo, 'Interpretation and Comparative Analysis' in N. MacCormick and R. Summers (eds.), *Interpreting Statutes* (Dartmouth, Aldershot, 1991), pp. 500–1.

[93] See J. Malenovský, 'L'Indépendance des juges internationaux', *Recueil des Cours/Académie de Droit International de La Haye*, 349 (2010), 9, 238–9.

[94] Cf. A. Rosas, 'The European Court of Justice in Context: Forms and Patterns of Judicial Dialogue', *European Journal of Legal Studies*, 1 (2007), 1, 2.

an apolitical space, traditionally the popular image in the common law world,[95] but probably also increasingly in modern Germany. All told, the ECJ is not particularly open about working in a frequently incremental, sometimes experimental, at times accidental, fashion. This encourages a reduced interest in explicitly unpicking the facts and context of past judgments and promotes clinical (i.e. string) citations of precedents.

Yet at other times, the ECJ gushingly invokes European destiny. As will be described in due course, it also often distinguishes earlier cases, even if not quite as readily as international investment tribunals. But again, the differences run deeper than a superficial civil law–common law split might suggest. It is true that in England prior cases have probably been scrutinised in at least some detail since the days of the Tudors.[96] But a list of the ten busiest investment arbitrators, whose habits differ notably from the ECJ in this respect, provides a salutary warning: none of these was educated exclusively in a common law environment.[97]

Crucially, the Court's style has little to do with a genuine and uniform conviction that law is simply 'revealed' rather than forged through adjudication. Such a belief is not earnestly held by the ECJ, not least due to the difficulty of deep theoretical reflection in a professionalised legal environment and the impossible fiction of anthropomorphising an adjudicatory entity with more than one hundred legal minds as a single author with a clear-cut legal philosophy.[98] Limiting rulings to prospective application is only one example of a more realistic stance.[99] This is where many well-intended accounts, for all their pioneering work, too easily buy into stark theoretical distinctions that are not always reflected to the same degree in reality.[100] The customary terseness of the ECJ is far more likely

---

[95] See M. Rosenfeld, 'Comparing Constitutional Review by the European Court of Justice and the US Supreme Court' in I. Pernice, J. Kokott and C. Saunders (eds.), *The Future of the European Judicial System in a Comparative Perspective* (Nomos, Baden-Baden, 2006), p. 46.

[96] See J. H. Baker, *An Introduction to English Legal History* (4th edn, Butterworths, London, 2002), p. 198 (who points to Fitzherbert's *New Natura Brevium* of 1534 as the first such critical exposition).

[97] See 'Top Ten Arbitrators – Arbitration Scorecard 2011' *The American Lawyer* (1 Jul. 2011), www.law.com.

[98] That of course does not preclude presenting a more passive picture to the outside world.

[99] See e.g. Case C-236/09 *Association Belge des Consommateurs Test-Achats and ors* v. *Conseil des ministres* (Grand Chamber) [2011] ECR I-773 (paras. 33–4) (on equal treatment of men and women with regard to insurance premiums).

[100] See e.g. M. Gutsche, *Die Bindungswirkung der Urteile des Europäischen Gerichtshofes* (Institut für Völkerrecht, Göttingen 1967), pp. 9, 221; Hartley (n. 33 above), p. 70 (fn. 84).

a consequence of routine and intuitive legal work that tries to appear as rational and convincing as possible while seeking to accommodate very real pressures relating to time, capacity, plurality, perception and language. From 2006 to 2010, the Court's case load grew by over 17 per cent, necessitating further structural changes in the future and posing very real practical problems.[101]

It is in this rather modest and limited sense that the ECJ's activity can be said to be rational or strategic,[102] just like that of any other body that provides a legal service. This does not necessarily or even normally connote a grand design or predefined master plan of what the European future should or should not hold. While certain individuals might harbour *une certaine idée de l'Europe*, there simply exists too little evidence other than the trusting anecdotes of yore that a few heroic (or villainous, depending on one's views) individuals decisively manipulate the Court as a whole at will in the long run.[103] The daily routine in the massive Kirchberg complex is far more bureaucratic, institutional, reactive and multipolar, and far less heroic, personal, proactive and unitary than it is often portrayed to be. In short, it is neither possible nor desirable to have 500 *Costa* v. *ENELs* a year.[104]

The Court's urge to present its legal work in a way that counters legal indeterminacy is a universal feature of adjudication.[105] Findings are made to appear almost self-evidently demanded by legal necessity, even if adjudicators in their deliberation room consider a point so open that one might just as well toss a coin. The piquant question whether a snack stall selling sausages and chips or a cinema foyer offering 'sweets and drinks, portions of popcorn and tortilla chips (nachos) in various sizes' are restaurants can hardly be settled forever and decisively by the sheer

---

[101] The GC in particular is being swamped, with a growth rate of almost 50 per cent for that period. See *Draft General budget of the European Union for the financial year 2012*, 15 Jun. 2011, IV/4 (exclaiming that '*many services have reached the limit of their capacities*'; original emphasis).

[102] On this idea and the term 'legal work' see D. Kennedy, 'A Left Phenomenological Alternative to the Hart/Kelsen Theory of Legal Interpretation' in D. Kennedy (ed.), *Legal Reasoning: Collected Essays* (Davies, Aurora, 2008), pp. 158–9.

[103] For the avoidance of doubt, this study assumes that the ECJ is honest and technically competent with regard to what it does.

[104] Case 6/64 *Flaminio Costa* v. *ENEL* [1964] ECR 585.

[105] Indeed, pure show trials are defined by their efforts to appear correct and compelling to a larger audience outside the courtroom. See J. Peterson, 'Unpacking Show Trials: Situating the Trial of Saddam Hussein', *Harvard International Law Journal*, 48 (2007), 257, 260.

force of logic or doctrinal legal reasoning.[106] Yet precisely that is usually demanded of the ECJ. At the same time, its judges must not decide arbitrarily. Nor may they refuse to decide a case. There is an expectation that they behave as if the question was perfectly answerable and come down one way or the other. Legal reasoning is in this sense an exercise of rationalising decisions *ex post* rather than divining correct answers *ex ante*. Precedents play a crucial part in this process, presenting at least an argument one way or the other and hence an indicator that a decision is not entirely random. They are a tool to deal with this imperfect reality by cutting infinite regress short. And to date, the Court has not been seriously challenged to change its economical technique.

A fourth important point informing substantial precedent citation is publication. This is not simply a technical matter but instead touches upon the wider perception, namely publicity, and hence the projected self-image of the respective adjudicator. Substantive citations are a good opportunity to showcase legal or commercial acumen. But unlike in the small and privatised market of investment arbitration with its hand-selected *intuitu personae* appointments, there is less of an incentive for politically appointed, tenured and salaried judges to establish a certain reputation. Although they are always published, it is impossible for an outsider reading an ECJ judgment to know exactly who was the driving force behind a particular legal pronouncement, despite the fact that the names of the participating judges, including the reporting judge, are invariably mentioned. It certainly need not be the latter.[107] Indeed, one of the chief concerns regarding separate and dissenting opinions is that individual judges could be singled out, thereby impacting potential reappointment and possibly courting favouritism.[108]

Of course that is not an unvarying stance. On the one hand, the ECJ nowadays occupies a uniquely assured position for a non-domestic court and is often content to let others retrace its justificatory steps and vouch for its legitimacy. But, on the other hand, the halcyon days of a smaller, more homogenous and less critical Europe, united in the face of state totalitarianism are gone. The ECJ is hence increasingly willing to render

---

[106] See Joined Cases C-497/09, C-499/09, C-501/09 and C-502/09 *Finanzamt Burgdorf* v. *Manfred Bog* (Third Chamber) [2011] ECR I-1457.

[107] The President of the Court determines who the reporting judge will be and distributes matters mindful of his colleagues' workload, experience, efficiency and nationality.

[108] According to TFEU Art. 253, judges at the ECJ are appointed for six years and may be reappointed.

more argumentative judgments fifty years down the road, especially when it is aware of likely (negative) publicity, with the *Kadi* saga being only one example.[109] This can also mean using more substantive citations. Some decisions simply require more legitimation than others, be it because they are more complex or the effects more uncertain.[110] There is no easy formula for predicting these cases in which substantive citation is more probable, but stakes are likely to be high whenever national governments are found to have violated treaty obligations or when the subject matter affects a wide variety of people in a profound manner, such as in the citizenship cases. But being faced with various doctrinal solutions that are equally (im)plausible could also be a trigger for a more substantive precedent mode. By and large, however, the ECJ has to date preferred not to tap into this legitimatory resource.

Wrapping up on precedent precision, there are conspicuous peculiarities concerning the granularity of the Court's invocation of earlier decisions. The ECJ exhibits a clear preference for verbatim repetition, general mention and string citations. This creates the appearance of a smooth network of precedent-following.[111] The Court appears worried about systemic coherence and seeks to nip discord in the bud.

D Use

This section maps the precise use of precedents by the ECJ. Such an examination is often neglected in favour of an unspoken assumption that all case references are made in the context of stating a rule-like postulate or major legal premise. But while that is indeed a common use, it is by no means exclusive.[112] This section draws out the wide variety and

---

[109] Joined Cases C-402/05 P and C-415/05 P *Yassin Abdullah Kadi and Al Barakaat International Foundation* v. *Council and Commission* (Grand Chamber) [2008] ECR I-6351 (380 paragraphs long). For background and a (positive) assessment of the Court's uneasy truce between security interests and human rights see R. Streinz, 'Does the European Court of Justice Keep the Balance Between Individual and Community Interest in *Kadi?*' in U. Fastenrath *et al.* (eds.), *From Bilateralism to Community Interest: Essays in Honour of Judge Bruno Simma* (Oxford University Press, 2011), pp. 1118–31.

[110] See P. Harris, 'Difficult Cases and the Display of Authority', *Journal of Law, Economics & Organization*, 1 (1985), 209, 210.

[111] Cf. Schermers and Waelbroeck (n. 81 above), p. 135.

[112] Even according to orthodox English views precedent is distinct from a major premise since it involves both facts and conclusions. See R. Cross and J. W. Harris, *Precedent in English Law* (4th edn, Clarendon Press, Oxford, 1991), p. 178.

specific affinities of case-based reasoning in the justificatory process[113] of the supranational court.

The following enumeration is of course neither a complete checklist nor does it claim to reflect a linear sequence all involved decision-makers will invariably go through. Indeed, the finer shadings of legal reasoning or precedent use are often difficult to categorise or communicate, and if there is one overarching theme of this book, it is to get away from an overly formalistic appreciation of precedent. So while there are many ways to cut the cake,[114] nine slices will be presented here. Moreover, it is not uncommon for types of precedent use to overlap. For instance, a precedent-based interpretation of a treaty provision or legal principle might at the same time be presented as a major premise in a syllogistic calculus, just as an elaboration of a case could equally be employed to spell out the meaning of the treaties or affirm a conclusion. Accordingly, figures will only be used sparingly to highlight certain proclivities.

i Classifying a legal issue or fact

As already alluded to above, one of the earliest steps of any decision involves classification.[115] While it may often come about instinctively, quite how a legal issue or specific fact is characterised will often predetermine the answer. This makes it a natural source of controversy. The ECJ makes use of precedents when dealing with such questions and in looking beyond the formulations of the parties.

It has for example relied on precedents to classify certain transactions as involving either the supply of services or the supply of goods, which can be relevant for VAT rates.[116] Similarly, the Court has adduced earlier judgments in order to decide whether a German national and resident is exercising the freedom of establishment or the freedom to provide services

---

[113] This partly corresponds to the 'important moments' of legal decision-making identified by J. Bengoetxea, N. MacCormick and L. Moral Soriano, 'Integration and Integrity in the Legal Reasoning of the European Court of Justice' in G. de Búrca and J. Weiler (eds.), *The European Court of Justice* (Oxford University Press, 2001), pp. 48–60.

[114] See e.g. the list in O. K. Fauchald, 'The Legal Reasoning of ICSID Tribunals: An Empirical Analysis', *European Journal of International Law*, 19 (2008), 301, 335–6.

[115] This has in particular exercised private international lawyers for more than a century, albeit with a special focus on causes of action. See e.g. E. G. Lorenzen, 'The Qualification, Classification, or Characterization Problem in Conflict of Laws', *Yale Law Journal*, 50 (1941), 743.

[116] See e.g. Joined Cases C-497/09, C-499/09, C-501/09 and C-502/09 *Finanzamt Burgdorf* v. *Manfred Bog* (Third Chamber) [2011] ECR I-1457 (para. 64).

when letting an apartment in Austria, which again has tax implications.[117] It also regularly invokes precedents to characterise products for the purpose of customs tariff classification[118] or to qualify certain commercial activities as trade mark related or not.[119]

In a more abstract manner, drawing on precedents for classification purposes is to an extent institutionalised in that the Registry transmits all requests for preliminary rulings to the in-house Research and Documentation department to undertake a preliminary analysis and amongst other things look for similar cases or useful precedents that might for instance indicate an *acte clair*.[120]

ii Identifying relevant legal provisions

Sooner rather than later the Court will have to decide which norms are relevant to a dispute. How matters are pleaded will naturally often be an important factor in this process, although this need not be determinative, in which case the parties might be asked to submit new observations once it has been indicated that other provisions may be considered relevant.[121] Precedents can be helpful in this respect.

Responding to a reference from the *Landgericht* (Regional Court) Frankfurt in a matter concerning averred improprieties in the procedure for awarding a service concession for the operation and maintenance of public lavatories, the ECJ first had to sort out the pertinent legal bases.[122] It adduced various precedents to establish that the general prohibition of nationality-based discrimination contained in what is now TFEU Art. 18 was covered by the *leges speciales* of the right of establishment (TFEU Art. 49) and the freedom to provide services (TFEU Art. 56). Moreover, it took the view that service concession contracts were not governed by any of the public procurement directives but that the primary law obligations

---

[117] See e.g. Case C-97/09 *Ingrid Schmelz v. Finanzamt Waldviertel* (Grand Chamber) [2010] ECR I-10465 (paras. 36–43).

[118] See e.g. Case C-196/10 *Paderborner Brauerei Haus Cramer KG v. Hauptzollamt Bielefeld* (Eighth Chamber) [2011] ECR I-6201 (para. 39).

[119] See e.g. Joined Cases C-236/08 to C-238/08 *Google France SARL and Google Inc. v. Louis Vuitton Malletier SA* (Grand Chamber) [2010] ECR I-2417 (paras. 70–2).

[120] Cf. C. Naômé, *Le Renvoi préjudiciel en droit européen: guide pratique* (Larcier, Brussels, 2007), p. 107.

[121] E.g. hearings could be reopened, albeit in restricted circumstances. See ECJ Rules of Procedure Art. 83.

[122] Case C-91/08 *Wall AG v. Stadt Frankfurt am Main and FES GmbH* (Grand Chamber) [2010] ECR I-2815 (paras. 32–3).

of non-discrimination and transparency applied, again backing this up with string citations.

iii Stating the law

At some stage, an applicable norm controlling a specific situation will be spelled out.[123] This sets up a major premise, which is an essential ingredient of syllogistic legal reasoning, even though this is rarely prised apart in clinical terms in judgments. It is what is often meant when law-making through adjudication is being discussed.[124] Precedents feature heavily in this function and are used to expound substantive as well as procedural norms. Induction and analogy are the habitual incubators.[125]

For the ECJ, this presented the most common use overall, with almost 38 per cent of individual precedent mentions made in this context.[126] Concerning the investment tribunal data collected, this was the third most common use of individual precedent citations at just under 14 per cent.[127] What such figures at the very least show is that whatever 'the law' is in the end taken to be, it cannot exhaustively be explained by looking only at non-adjudicatory sources but instead suggests exploring alternatives akin to those models sketched at the beginning of this study.

The ECJ is particularly fond of this use of precedent. There are innumerable examples. Consider *Kücükdeveci*.[128] The case concerned employment discrimination on the grounds of age. In the space of only three short paragraphs, the Court made eleven references to precedents to anchor the following three curt statements of law: (i) national courts have to ensure that the rules of EU law are fully effective; (ii) directives do not impose obligations on individuals; (iii) directives oblige Member States to take all appropriate steps to achieve the intended results. This is a pristine example of bootstrapping by precedent – that is to say, establishing legal

---

[123] The point that stating meaning presupposes making sense of meaning has already been made above. The rough order followed here simply traces the way in which many decisions are presented.

[124] See e.g. K. Langenbucher, *Die Entwicklung und Auslegung von Richterrecht* (C. H. Beck, Munich 1996), pp. 93–104.

[125] See e.g. Case C-409/06 *Winner Wetten GmbH* v. *Bürgermeisterin der Stadt Bergheim* (Grand Chamber) [2010] ECR I-8015 (paras. 63–6) (basing the possibility of a temporary maintenance of annulled or invalidated national rules in exceptional situations on a combination of three cases 'and case-law cited' there).

[126] 370 out of 977 individual precedent mentions.

[127] 178 out of 1,295 precedent references were used to this effect.

[128] Case C-555/07 *Seda Kücükdeveci* v. *Swedex GmbH & Co. KG* (Grand Chamber) [2010] ECR I-365 (paras. 45–7).

propositions self-referentially without the help of other legal sources. Many of the Court's most consecrated pronouncements are perpetuated through such a self-sustaining process, including direct effect and the primacy of EU law.[129] Another testament to the ECJ being very partial to making normative statements via precedents is *TNT Express*, a judgment in which the Court delineated its jurisdiction in preliminary references concerning international agreements.[130] Such citations can of course often be traced back to an initial distillation from the treaties, and that is indeed one of the main validation attempts in this context, but the customary 'convenience-not-creativity' defence of course begs the question of the originality of the initial inference.[131]

iv Interpreting the law

Just because the applicable law has been exclaimed does not mean that its meaning is plain or uncontested. As already noted several times, a strong case can be made that any statement of law presupposes interpretation.[132] Be that as it may, expounding a normative proposition is rarely the end of the matter, it being commonplace that participants in legal discourse – including EU law – constantly seek to invest this with different meanings and refine certain understandings. Interpretation demands justification,[133] which again invites reference to precedents. What this category tracks are those references to precedents that are made in the course of construing legal propositions without a specific textual provision in mind, for example general principles of law or normative statements that simply do not mention a definite legal basis.

Unsurprisingly, such precedent usage usually tails preceding statements of law. In *Transportes Urbanos*, the ECJ was asked by the *Tribunal Supremo* (the Spanish Supreme Court) whether it was compatible with the

---

[129] See e.g. Opinion 1/09 *Patent Litigation System* (Full Court) [2011] ECR I-1137 (para. 65); Case C-341/08 *Domnica Petersen* v. *Berufungsausschuss für Zahnärzte für den Bezirk Westfalen-Lippe* (Grand Chamber) [2010] ECR I-47 (para. 80).

[130] Case C-533/08 *TNT Express Nederland BV* v. *AXA Versicherung AG* (Grand Chamber) [2010] ECR I-4107 (paras. 59–62; twelve string citations).

[131] Recall the reconstruction of so-called *Francovich* liability in Joined Cases C-46/93 and C-48/93 *Brasserie du Pêcheur SA* v. *Bundesrepublik Deutschland* [1996] ECR I-1029 (paras. 27–30).

[132] No attempt is made here to defend a strict delineation between the two activities. Ultimately, the difference may well boil down to one form simply being more analytical and candid about the argumentative nature of law. The categories are only kept distinct here to separately record ostensible *ex post* refinements by the ECJ.

[133] See Holzleithner and Mayer-Schönberger (note 51), p. 326.

principles of equivalence and effectiveness that an action for damages against the state based on the incompatibility of national legislation with EU law was treated differently from an identical action based on the unconstitutionality of a national measure.[134] Only the former was subject to a prior exhaustion of remedies. The Court began by stating the general principle of state liability and the individual elements that make up an action for damages for an infringement of EU law. It then reiterated the general rule of national procedural autonomy, according to which any such claim for reparation is to be made under the respective national law, subject to such vindication not being treated less favourably than similar domestic claims and not being made practically impossible. This of course was the nub of the case. Calling upon various precedents, the ECJ interpreted the already established principle of equivalence to demand that the same rules applied to both types of action without distinction, although this was further considered not to require an extension of the most favourable rules to all actions in a specific area of law.[135] With this spin, all that was left was to point to any difference in treatment in this respect, which was not difficult given the terms of the reference.

Such examples elicit that case-based reasoning can make law more detailed in due course by successively increasing the potential for linking different nodes in an ever more complex network of precedents: a network with n nodes has a maximum $n(n-1)/2$ connecting lines. In other words, the more cases there are, the greater the number of possible cross-references. Subject to departing, the more cases there are, the more legal information exists on EU law. That alone does not support a positive assessment of the qualitative effect of adjudication over time,[136] nor does it mean that legal certainty will inevitably be increased or that breaking out of such interpretations becomes impossible. It remains up to the decision-maker whether and how to capitalise on that potential.

v Interpreting specific provisions

A stock theme of adjudication is making sense of normative text. That platitude becomes more interesting when one looks at the propensity of invoking precedents in this context.

---

[134] Case C-118/08 *Transportes Urbanos y Servicios Generales SAL* v. *Administración del Estado* (Grand Chamber) [2010] ECR I-635 (para. 31).

[135] *Ibid.* paras. 33–4.

[136] For such an argument see e.g. R. A. Posner, *Economic Analysis of Law* (7th edn, Wolters Kluwer, Austin, 2007), pp. 249–53, 560–73. But see P. H. Rubin (ed.), *The Evolution of Efficient Common Law* (Elgar, Cheltenham, 2007), parts II and III.

Given the habitual catcalls, it may come as somewhat of a surprise that the ECJ is actually very fond of this use of precedents. Almost 27 per cent of its case recitals were made in order to interpret specific provisions.[137] That number may lag behind the Court's primary use of precedents – making bare statements of law – but it is comfortably in second place, eclipsing the use of cases to tie syllogistic knots by a considerable margin. The use of precedents to interpret specific provisions is widespread, and the ECJ is no different in this respect.[138] According to the present data set, this also by far amounts to the most common use of precedents by international investment tribunals.[139] This is largely explicable on account of their bespoke treaty-based existence.

Such use will often arise in the context of a preliminary reference under TFEU Art. 267 asking for interpretation of primary or secondary EU law. For instance, the Court in *Prigge* was asked to interpret a directive on equal treatment in the context of alleged age discrimination of airline pilots where an upper limit had been introduced by collective agreement to reduce air traffic risk.[140] The Court recalled earlier decisions in asserting that one had to construe narrowly the express derogations from the basic prohibition on the grounds of general public order or where this involved a 'genuine and determining' occupational requirement. Once again backing up its reasoning by precedent, it further specified that the latter exception demanded a showing of more than simply the ground on which the difference in treatment was based; instead, a corresponding characteristic was necessary. Following that, the ECJ also mentioned two precedents to shed light on what it meant for divergent treatment to pursue a 'legitimate' aim. Examples of this practice are legion and include invoking a precedent that establishes that a specific article on provisional measures is not to be understood to determine substantive jurisdiction[141] or adducing a

---

[137] Precisely 263 out of 977 precedent citations.

[138] See e.g. Case C-285/09 *Criminal proceedings against R* (Grand Chamber) [2010] ECR I-12605 (para. 39). In domestic legal systems purporting to abide by doctrines of binding precedent, material identity of facts tends not to be a prerequisite for a decision on statutory interpretation to be considered authoritative. See Cross and Harris (n. 112 above), p. 180.

[139] Around 38 per cent of all of their individual precedent references were made in the course of interpreting specific legal provisions; to be exact, 490 out of 1,295.

[140] Case C-447/09 *Reinhard Prigge and ors* v. *Deutsche Lufthansa AG* (Grand Chamber) [2011] ECR I-8003 (paras. 56–81) (interpreting Council Directive 2000/78/EC of 27 Nov. 2000 establishing a general framework for equal treatment in employment and occupation [2000] OJ L303/16).

[141] See Case C-296/10 *Bianca Purrucker* v. *Guillermo Vallés Pérez* (Second Chamber) [2010] ECR I-11163 (para. 70) (interpreting Art. 20 of Council Regulation (EC) No. 2201/2003 of

precedent that held that a particular term found in a directive is an autonomous concept of EU law.[142]

This use of precedents is also encountered outside of preliminary references and with respect to primary law, such as when the Court in infringement proceedings interprets the treaty article on the duty to co-operate.[143] It also clearly features in the delineation of fundamental freedoms assured by the treaties.[144] A final example would be an orientation along prior decisions in order to read more narrowly the undeniable right to collective bargaining contained in CFREU Art. 28 in light of basic treaty freedoms and the principle of proportionality.[145]

Two points emerge. First, the ECJ's actual behaviour calls into question its all-too-quick stigmatisation as a 'purely teleological court' in the sense that it is suggested that the Court is exclusively forward-looking or grandly pondering the next development in European history. Of course purpose remains an important ingredient in making sense of text, and naturally this can also be encapsulated in a prior decision. Nor does the Court's practice counter suppositions as to any particular motivation. But, like any other legal worker, the ECJ very often starts from bland, often downright dull, textual provisions. Where necessary, it might then look to context and purpose. Its visible preference for drawing on precedents when interpreting legal provisions discerns it as an adjudicatory body that tries to fit any chosen meaning into the existing discourse as manifest in prior cases. Even if this were to be little more than a façade, the need to appear coherent alone has an impact on room for manoeuvre. A second and broader point is that the practice of the ECJ underscores that it is premature to conceptualise precedents and other legal materials as fundamentally opposed. Prior decisions and so-called 'written sources'[146]

---

27 Nov. 2003 concerning jurisdiction and the recognition and enforcement of judgments in matrimonial matters and the matters of parental responsibility [2003] OJ L338/1).

[142] Joined Cases C-403/08 and C-429/08 *Football Association Premier League and ors* v. *QC Leisure* (Grand Chamber) [2011] ECR I-9083 (para. 154) (interpreting the term 'reproduction' found in Directive 2001/29/EC of 22 May 2001 on the harmonisation of certain aspects of copyright and related rights in the information society [2001] OJ L167/10).

[143] See e.g. Case C-246/07 *Commission* v. *Kingdom of Sweden* (Grand Chamber) [2010] ECR I-3317 (paras. 69–71).

[144] See e.g. Case C-110/05 *Commission* v. *Italian Republic* (Grand Chamber) [2009] ECR I-519 (para. 59) (on curbing the free movement of goods).

[145] See Case C-271/08 *Commission* v. *Federal Republic of Germany* (Grand Chamber) [2010] ECR I-7091 (paras. 43–4).

[146] Of course a judicial or arbitral decision will in due course also become a 'written source' in the sense of being published in a report or made accessible otherwise.

go hand-in-hand in the broader effort of forming and disseminating legal information.

vi Interpreting prior cases

Following on from that, just like any legal text, propositions adopted in past decisions demand interpretation. The meaning of a precedent lends itself particularly well to different analyses, since its context and factual backdrop provide a rich fabric to work with. Predictably, the interpretation of a particular precedent that has been invoked by the parties or the bench can itself become an important step in the justificatory process of a court. There is a large, if not quite complete, overlap in this respect between reference to precedents in order to interpret them and substantive citation, indicating a close connection here between use and precision.[147] The interpretation of a precedent will normally demand more than just a string citation.

In fact, of those Grand Chamber decisions examined, not even 5 per cent of individual case mentions were made in the context of interpreting the precedents themselves.[148] One such example is *Stoß*, where the Court at one point expressly sought to correct a 'misreading' of an earlier judgment.[149] The difference, however, relates not only to degree, but also to kind. Not infrequently case interpretations by the ECJ resemble little more than restatements of a prior ruling. Consider *Akzo Nobel*, an appeal from the GC in which the ECJ was confronted with the question of whether a precedent's denial of legal professional privilege to in-house lawyers in the context of competition investigations by the Commission still reflected the current state of EU law.[150] The ECJ devoted several paragraphs to the rationale of that antecedent, *AM & S v. Commission*, explaining that the case had turned on the common traditions of the Member States and the fact that legal professional privilege was tied to independence, namely the absence of an employment relationship.[151] While this

---

[147] Disparities will mainly arise where substantive citations are aimed more directly at other purposes, such as stating or interpreting the law (rather than a specific case).

[148] A mere 44 out of 977 instances.

[149] Joined Cases C-316/07, C-358/07, C-359/07, C-360/07, C-409/07 and C-410/07 *Markus Stoß and ors* v. *Wetteraukreis* (Grand Chamber) [2010] ECR I-8069 (paras. 71–2).

[150] Case C-550/07 P *Akzo Nobel Chemicals Ltd and Akcros Chemicals Ltd* v. *Commission* (Grand Chamber) [2010] ECR I-8301.

[151] *Ibid.* paras. 40–3, 69–70; Case 155/79 *AM & S Europe Limited* v. *Commission* [1982] ECR 1575.

may very well have begged the question and did indeed prompt critical commentary,[152] it furnished the effective basis for the later ruling. The ECJ's overall tendency in this respect essentially mirrors its preference for string citations and lends credence to the contention that there is a nexus between substantive citation, this use of precedent and the likelihood of negative treatment, which will be examined shortly.

This habit of the Court contrasts notably with the tendency of international investment tribunals: almost 17 per cent of their precedent citations in the current sample were made in order to interpret prior cases. Unlike ECJ judges, investment arbitrators thus seem much more willing to openly take sides in a dispute concerning the nuances of past precedents and to either accept or deflect them visibly.

vii Justifying an interpretation

Once a judge settles for a particular interpretation of a legal provision, this is every so often backed up by references to earlier decisions that have held likewise. It is often difficult to draw a clear line between this use of precedent and the preceding three categories. Nevertheless, the emphasis here is not so much on a (purported) process of divining or refining meaning or the crux of a prior decision, but rather on how other cases support a selected interpretation. The main function is subsequent explanation and persuasion.

The ECJ uses precedents to this effect, albeit sporadically. In one preliminary reference involving irregular invoices, the Court interpreted the common system of VAT to afford Member States the power – within limits – to stipulate exemption conditions for the intra-EU supply of goods with a view to preventing tax evasion, a finding it later reinforced by reference to two precedents.[153] Another example of this 'piling on' technique can be found in three dismissed appeals regarding limited public access to written pleadings lodged by the Commission.[154] There the ECJ first

---

[152] See e.g. M. E. Mann, 'Schutz unternehmensinterner Anwaltskorrespondenz', *Zeitschrift für vergleichende Rechtswissenschaft/Archiv für Internationales Wirtschaftsrecht*, 110 (2011), 302, 311–12 (noting the dependence of many lawyers that are not in-house practitioners and the divergent Member State laws).

[153] See Case C-285/09 *Criminal proceedings against R* (Grand Chamber) [2010] ECR I-12605 (para. 49).

[154] Joined Cases C-514/07 P, C-528/07 P and C-532/07 P *Kingdom of Sweden v. Association de la presse internationale ASBL (API)* (Grand Chamber) [2010] ECR I-8533 (paras. 88–102).

recalled the principle of equality of arms and asserted a presumption that the disclosure of such sensitive documents would disturb court proceedings and fly in the face of the exclusion of the European courts from the transparency obligation of what is now TFEU Art. 15. Moreover, it noted that the CJEU Statute and both ECJ and GC (then still CFI) Rules of Procedure provided for procedural documents to be restricted to the parties and respective institutions. In other words, there simply was no general right of third party access to pleadings. As if that were not enough, the ECJ additionally referred to an analogous case that largely denied disclosure of the Commission's administrative file relating to procedures for reviewing state aid.

viii *Asserting facts*

Prevailing modes of legal dispute settlement tend to demand the application of the governing law to a set of circumstances. Precedents can be used to establish those facts, thereby contributing to the minor premise in a traditional legal syllogism. While this is by no means the most common use of prior cases, there are examples of this in the practice of the ECJ.

For instance, precedents have been used by the Court to hold forth on a miscellany of matters ranging from the world of sports to basic human biology to market research. In the *Olympique Lyonnais* case, which dealt with the permissibility of contractual restrictions on professional football players in light of the free movement of workers, the ECJ considered that 'it must be accepted that, as the Court has already held, the prospect of receiving training fees is likely to encourage football clubs to seek new talent and train young players'.[155] That reference to its famous *Bosman* decision was an important step in seeking to justify a prima facie impermissible scheme which provided for certain payments in the event that young players signed with other football clubs at the end of their training. Ultimately, the ECJ denied that the contractual arrangement in that specific dispute was necessary to ensure what it set out to do since it revolved around damages rather than compensation for training costs. But in assessing whether a legitimate aim was being pursued, the Court happily recycled a prior factual assertion. In other cases it has invoked precedents to assert that it was 'undeniable that physical characteristics

---

[155] Case C-325/08 *Olympique Lyonnais SASP* v. *Olivier Bernard, Newcastle United FC* (Grand Chamber) [2010] ECR I-2177 (para. 41).

diminish with age'[156] and that 'consumers, knowing that they are not permitted to use their motorcycle with a trailer specially designed for it, have practically no interest in buying such a trailer'.[157]

ix Affirming conclusions

As the foregoing illustrations have shown, precedents are used by the Court in a wide variety of ways as building blocks of broadly syllogistic argumentation, even if many decisions, in particular more discursive ones, do not stick to a particularly rigid logical structure.[158] This applies no less to (interim) conclusions, where precedents are also used to shore up legal decision-making. While there are numerous permutations, these are traditionally presented as inferences following from a major and minor premise.[159] In a legal context, this will be a consequence of a statement of law applied to a set of facts.

The ECJ is known to summon the support of precedents upon having stated a conclusion. It is often said to have a penchant for syllogistic reasoning.[160] Its jurisprudence is littered with precedents appended unceremoniously to inferences drawn from premises, such as when it holds that the publication of benefits received from various European agricultural funds on a website accessible by third parties is an interference with the right of farmers to respect for private and family life as contained in CFREU Art. 7.[161] A further example would be a case

---

[156] Case C-447/09 *Reinhard Prigge and ors* v. *Deutsche Lufthansa AG* (Grand Chamber) [2011] ECR I-8003 (para. 67) (drawing on a previous decision involving firemen).

[157] Case C-110/05 *Commission* v. *Italian Republic* (Grand Chamber) [2009] ECR I-519 (para. 57) (spotting a parallel to identical consumer behaviour regarding tinted car-window film).

[158] On this difference see A. Aarnio, 'Precedent in Finland' in N. MacCormick and R. Summers (eds.), *Interpreting Precedents: A Comparative Study* (Ashgate, Aldershot 1997), p. 72 (noting that the Finnish Supreme Court very often argues *syllogistically*, despite not normally arguing *in syllogisms*).

[159] This relationship can also be expressed as a triangle made up of three dually shared terms. For detailed elaboration of this skeletal frame consisting of three propositions see I. M. Bocheński, *Ancient Formal Logic* (North-Holland, Amsterdam, 1951), pp. 36–54; J. Bung, *Subsumtion und Interpretation* (Nomos, Baden-Baden, 2004), pp. 23–41; G. Sartor, 'Syllogism and Defeasibilty', *Northern Ireland Legal Quarterly*, 59 (2008), 21.

[160] See e.g. Barceló (n. 84 above), p. 411. Yet one should not think that its style of reasoning has not evolved over the past fifty years.

[161] Joined Cases C-92/09 and C-93/09 *Volker und Markus Schecke GbR and Hartmut Eifert* v. *Land Hessen* (Grand Chamber) [2010] ECR I-11063 (para. 58).

reference to endorse a finding that national measures requiring permits from undertakings constitute a restriction of the freedom of establishment.[162]

In fact, the sample data suggests that such use of precedent is quite popular at the ECJ, with almost 13 per cent of case references having been made in this context.[163] For the comparator, international investment tribunals, this figure dropped to just over 6 per cent. This makes the affirmation of conclusions the third most popular precedent use for the ECJ within the present sample. One cardinal reason why such broadly triangular reasoning is dear to the Court, and hence also worth backing up with past cases, is that it gives the impression of decisions flowing logically from established grounds. It dispels notions of unbridled personal power and makes further justification appear unnecessary. This use of precedent is rationalised as springing from a demand for coherence and previsibility rather than being considered a corollary of the argumentative nature of law. That narrative certainly appears more befitting to a permanent and elevated institution like the ECJ that does not always deign to make sure its pronouncements are particularly compelling, unlike – to echo a persistent taunt concerning international investment arbitration[164] – the silver-tongued efforts of a select cabal of hired guns in pursuit of further appointments.

E Interim conclusion

What emerges from this analysis of the ECJ's general precedent treatment is that, despite appearances to the contrary, the Court's technique is a lot more varied than its recognisable justification-through-coherence-through-parsimony style would suggest or the simple employment of prior cases as major premises would admit. Particularly popular uses of precedent are summarised in Figure 4.E. below. Three points stand out.

First, this questions the received debate on judicial law-making while at the same time stressing the importance of paying closer attention to the Court's actual use of cases. Secondly, the relevance of the abiding bindingness debate is shaken when precedents can be a lot more than

---

[162] See e.g. Joined Cases C-570/07 and C-571/07 *José Manuel Blanco Pérez and María del Pilar Chao Gómez* v. *Consejería de Salud y Servicios Sanitarios and Principado de Asturias* (Grand Chamber) [2010] ECR I-4629 (paras. 54–5).

[163] 122 out of 977 precedent mentions.

[164] See M. Sornarajah, *The International Law on Foreign Investment* (3rd edn, Cambridge University Press, 2010), p. 8.

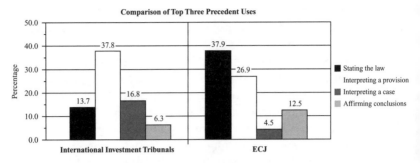

Figure 4.E   Comparison of top three precedent uses

rule-like statements.[165] Thirdly, the findings sustain the hypothesis that the ECJ's precedent technique is not so much rooted in methodological conviction or theoretical reflection. Rather, it is a function of inbound contextual constraints and outbound contextual demands. The Court draws heavily on its privileged position within its respective regime, which allows it to state the law by reference to its own output without possibility of revision. At the same time, the Court remains ever mindful of its role as a lightning rod for much of EU law. Precedents are very important in pre-empting potential responses to its work. This need not be cynical; in fact, the current set-up expects this. For instance, the Court makes use of case-based reasoning to place meaning into legal text. It also employs precedents to assert facts. Another popular use lies in affirming its own conclusions. This is also manifest in the granularity employed. The ECJ is very fond of referring to past jurisprudence in a general manner. It tends to anchor the premises of its decision-making in referential string citations. Only exceptionally does it consider it necessary to discuss the substance of an earlier decision in greater detail.

All of this can give rise to a sense of dictation by precedent. Yet there are chinks that can be exposed. The following sections further unfold the flexibility of case-based reasoning by analysing the Court's avoidance techniques.

---

[165]   Analysed in Ch. 8.

5

Avoiding ECJ precedents I

Distinguishing

One of the themes of this book is that case-based reasoning is a powerful instrument for adjudicators. A lot of this has to do with its elasticity, which is the subject of the following two chapters. They underscore that the ECJ is neither a passive mouthpiece of EU law, nor an unbridled dictator. The Court is aware of the shadow that it casts, but there remains room for improvement. The danger is that the tools, namely the precedents, become more than they are.

A Technique

Distinguishing goes to the heart of legal reasoning.[1] Applied to cases, it is a process of reverse analogy whereby a putative precedent is declared not to bear on the present situation. A successfully distinguished precedent is thus, strictly speaking, not a precedent at all, which is why distinguishing is treated as an avoidance technique here. Several points are worth noting.

First, distinguishing does not attempt to directly impugn an alleged precedent. The main claim is that the cases do not match. Important aspects informing the prior case's reasoning are materially different in the later situation, thus denying any guidance or authority. The immediate attraction of 'explaining away' cases is that one does not challenge a previous decision outright, which might be a dim prospect, undesirable for reasons of deference or comity, or inimical to the appearance of systemic unity and coherence.[2] This makes it immediately attractive for

---

[1] See C. Perelman, *Logique juridique: Nouvelle rhétorique* (2nd edn, Dalloz, Paris, 1999), p. 9.

[2] It is for instance often said that the ICJ is loath to confront inconsistencies in its own jurisprudence head on. See M. Sørensen, *Les Sources du droit international: étude sur la jurisprudence de la Cour Permanente de Justice Internationale* (Einar Munksgaard, Copenhagen, 1946), p. 166 (on its predecessor, the Permanent Court of International Justice ('PCIJ')); M. Shahabuddeen, *Precedent in the World Court* (Cambridge University Press, 1996), p. 110; S. Rosenne, *The Law and Practice of the International Court 1920–2005*, 4 vols. (4th edn, Martinus Nijhoff, Leiden, 2006), III, p. 1555.

the ECJ. It does not however mean that distinguishing will never affect a prior case, as will be shown shortly. At the very least, the more frequently and profoundly a case is distinguished, the less confidence it tends to inspire in the future.[3]

Secondly, the averred difference must be relevant. The point is not so much that the cases are different, but that there is no relevant similarity. It is of course always possible, albeit largely meaningless, to distinguish two cases on account of a minor contextual triviality. Analogy, which grounds case-based reasoning, never claims complete congruence, but rather shared participation in one type of existence, albeit in different guises.[4] Just as in the reverse process of finding similarity, there is no watertight process here that guarantees eliminating the accidental and non-representative,[5] thus again opening up the field for wider argument. The narrower the relevant part of a prior case is argued to be, the easier it is to come up with a meaningful difference; conversely, broad-brush statements make avoidance more involved.[6] Such considerations underpin much of the reticence and parsimony (or, if desired, boldness) employed in crafting decisions in the first place. It also means that the ECJ's penchant for broadness that was scrutinised above has a delayed cost.

Thirdly, it follows from the foregoing that where a difference exists but is held to be irrelevant the ambit of the prior case is extended to the degree of its later application. If it is considered immaterial in the context of liability on the part of a state causing damage to individuals as a result of a breach of EU law that the entity committing the breach is a legislative body in one case[7] and a judicial authority in a later case,[8] the prior decision's reasoning and reach is automatically adapted to accommodate the latter situation. The fact that adjudicators will often expressly present this as a logical extrapolation of the original precedent's reasoning does not diminish the point,[9] since the difference might very well have been

---

[3] See R. W. M. Dias, *Jurisprudence* (3rd edn, Butterworths, London, 1970), p. 75.

[4] See A. Kaufmann, *Analogie und "Natur der Sache"* (2nd edn, R. v. Decker & C. F. Müller, Heidelberg, 1982), p. 22.

[5] Cf. Perelman (n. 1 above), p. 129.

[6] See N. Duxbury, *The Nature and Authority of Precedent* (Cambridge University Press, 2008), pp. 113–14.

[7] Joined Cases C-46/93 and C-48/93 *Brasserie du Pêcheur SA* v. *Bundesrepublik Deutschland* [1996] ECR I-1029 (para. 36).

[8] Case C-224/01 *Gerhard Köbler* v. *Republik Österreich* (Grand Chamber) [2003] ECR 10239 (paras. 32–6).

[9] *Ibid.* para. 31.

a relevant dissimilarity that was not formerly anticipated or meant to be covered.[10] This technique is a firm favourite of the Court since it allows silent expansion.

Fourthly, distinguishing comes in varying levels of intrusiveness concerning what has already been settled. This is due to the fact that a distinction can be made either by focusing on the present case ($C_2 \neq C_1$) or by focusing on the past decision ($C_1 \neq C_2$). The less disruptive type is the former, where the relevant elements of a new case are plainly said not to match those of an older case. This is often expressed by saying that the precedent is simply not of assistance or not useful.

But distinguishing as an avoidance technique can go beyond what might be considered purely static comparison by manipulating the legal information contained in the original decision and thus influencing the argumentative burden it imposes. Sometimes it might have been possible to argue that the present situation is within the ambit of the precedent, but its rationale is instead retrospectively reformulated to the exclusion of the case at hand. Essentially, the argument is then that the precedent did not establish what it is being cited for, which is often a possibility since cases lack an irredeemably fixed rationale.

One common method is to add an aspect to the precedent that is absent in the present case. So for instance, in *TWD Textilwerke Deggendorf*, a state aid case concerning time bars and the proper sequence of remedial responses, the Court was at pains to distinguish a precedent according to which the mere possibility of bringing a direct action against a Commission decision did not prevent contesting the validity of the measure in question in national proceedings.[11] The material difference was said to be that in the earlier case the aggrieved parties had first brought an annulment action. It hence did not deal with the time bar issue, the ECJ opined. Be that as it may, it is possible to detect a shift here in the attitude towards decentralised judicial co-operation.[12]

Another technique could be called retrospective *obitering*, whereby a supposedly relevant part of the former decision is later relegated to

---

[10] This was in fact argued in particular by the French government in the example concerning EU law state liability for judicial acts. *Ibid.* Opinion of AG Léger (para. 20).

[11] Case C-188/92 *TWD Textilwerke Deggendorf GmbH* v. *Bundesrepublik Deutschland* [1994] ECR I-833 (paras. 19–20). The precedent was Joined Cases 133 to 136/85 *Walter Rau Lebensmittelwerke and ors* v. *Bundesanstalt für landwirtschaftliche Marktordnung* [1987] ECR 2289 (paras. 9–12).

[12] Cf. L. Coutron, *La Contestation incidente des actes de l'Union européenne* (Bruylant, Brussels, 2008), pp. 220–1 and fn. 746.

immateriality.[13] A different method is to argue that subsequent developments impose qualifications on an unmitigated application of the prior
case's essence. The general point is always that the more specific or narrow the prior reasoning is taken to be, the more leeway there is for
avoidance. This can go so far that a potential precedent is isolated to
the point of practical ineffectuality, confined to being a prisoner of its
own special circumstances. In practice this can have very similar effects
to overruling or departing from a precedent without actually saying so,
which can have deleterious consequences for legal certainty and credibility. But even in the more placid version, distinguishing is an act of further
specification and detailing of the network of legal information. It can
be understood as an instance of systemic elaboration and a law-making
tool.[14]

B Practice: frequent evasion

The ECJ routinely makes use of distinguishing as an avoidance
technique.[15] The idea of the *cas particulier* is a household contrivance,
even though the extent of this might come as a surprise. Of those Grand
Chamber matters decided in 2010, over 21 per cent of judgments explicitly endeavoured at one point or another to shake off an argumentative burden that was allegedly imposed by a precedent without purporting to diminish the respective point as such, namely overrule the
case.[16] In terms of techniques, the Court employs a range of distinguishing methods. Three will be sketched here in ascending order of
intrusiveness.[17]

---

[13] See Marshall, 'What is Binding in a Precedent' in N. MacCormick and R. Summers (eds.),
       Interpreting Precedents: A Comparative Study (Ashgate, Aldershot, 1997), p. 516.
[14] See C. K. Allen, *Law in the Making* (6th edn, Clarendon Press, Oxford, 1958), p. 294
       ('A man who chops a tree into logs has in a sense "made" the logs.'). But see Duxbury
       (n. 6 above), p. 115 (who only appears to treat the more invasive forms of distinguishing
       as development of the law).
[15] Cf. J. J. Barceló, 'Precedent in European Community Law' in N. MacCormick and R.
       Summers (eds.), *Interpreting Precedents: A Comparative Study* (Ashgate, Aldershot, 1997),
       p. 430; P. Wattel, '*Köbler, CILFIT* and *Welthgrove*: We Can't Go On Meeting Like This',
       Common Market Law Review, 41 (2004), 177, 179.
[16] Eleven out of fifty-two decisions openly distinguished at least one precedent.
[17] Note that the boundaries are rather fluid since it is often possible to conceptualise an act
       of distinguishing in more than one way.

i Type 1: disapplication

The plainest form is to deny that all the requirements of the precedent, which are not modified, have been met.[18] The technique is so bare it borders on circularity: the precedent is not applied because it is not applicable. One might even choose not to speak of distinguishing at all here.[19] The precedent is accepted to be C_1: A, B, C → X, but the case at hand only happens to be C_2: a, b, so that X does not follow.[20] Evidently this requires a perception and evaluation of the relevant properties.

A typical illustration that is unlikely to garner much attention outside the select groups of pre-litigation procedure enthusiasts and bird conservation activists is *Commission v. Romania*.[21] EU law mandates that Member States take conservation measures concerning the habitat of certain species of wild birds.[22] This involves the designation of special protection areas. The Commission brought infringement proceedings against Romania in this context. Romania contended the action was inadmissible because of an irregularity in the pre-litigation procedure: the Commission's reasoned opinion was not based on the same complaints as its original formal notice, essentially changing the subject matter from a failure to communicate the special areas or transpose the directive at all (i.e. presumed non-implementation) to deficient implementation. The Commission maintained that Romania could not object to this because a complaint concerning incomplete implementation was in any event part of a complaint about a total failure to transpose a directive. In so doing, it referred to an earlier statement of the Court.[23]

The ECJ in its judgment however rejected that invocation of precedent on the basis that the situation which had given rise to the prior decision was 'clearly distinguishable'.[24] Unlike Romania in the present case, the

---

[18] Raz calls this the 'tame' view of distinguishing. See J. Raz, *The Authority of Law* (2nd edn, Oxford University Press, 2009), p. 185.

[19] See e.g. Case C-548/09 P *Bank Melli Iran* v. *Council* (Grand Chamber) [2011] ECR I-11381 (paras. 89, 116) (dismissing cited case law of the ECtHR on the absolute prohibition of torture as 'not transposable' and 'not relevant' in a case concerning the non-absolute right to property).

[20] Where A, B, C are general properties of a precedent and a, b, c potential instances thereof.

[21] Case C-522/09 *Commission* v. *Romania* (Fourth Chamber) [2011] ECR I-2963.

[22] Council Directive 79/409/EEC of 2 April 1979 on the conservation of wild birds [1979] OLJ L103/1.

[23] Case C-32/05 *Commission* v. *Grand Duchy of Luxemburg* (Third Chamber) [2006] ECR I-11323 (para. 56).

[24] Case C-522/09 *Commission* v. *Romania* (Fourth Chamber) [2011] ECR I-2963 (para. 19).

recalcitrant Member State in the (supposed) precedent had not made any attempt at all to assert that it had complied with its obligations until proceedings had been initiated, that is to say after the pre-litigation procedure. Although the Court did not quite put it this way, this was a *relevant* difference: the pre-litigation procedure and its insistence on congruence between the Commission's notice and its reply are designed to protect the defence rights of the Member State in question. Here, Romania might have had a good answer before finding itself in court as to why its implementation measures should in fact be considered adequate, but it was denied that opportunity. Only in the situation where the Member State's defence rights are not prejudiced, for instance when it is reluctant to lay its cards on the table, can the subject matter of the action be changed.[25] In other words, the precedent was taken to be C_1: A (complaint about failure to transpose), B (response asserting transposition), C (opportunity to submit response in pre-litigation phase wasted) → X (permissible action for deficient transposition). But the current case was simply C_2: a, b.

Three points are worth noting regarding this example. First, the Court plainly acknowledges distinguishing as a technique, employing a reverse analogy to deny an argumentative burden allegedly imposed by a former case while keeping that decision's reasoning intact. This is a basic recognition that the prior reasoning must be respected, regardless of any elaborate doctrine or theory of binding precedent. The Court is mindful to ensure the compatibility of its jurisprudence, and just as coherence demands treating like case alike, it also necessitates treating dissimilar points dissimilarly.

Secondly, the Court displays sensitivity to context here, which is a mainstay of distinguishing. The key phrases that allude to specific states of affairs demanding individual treatment are 'Such a situation' and 'in such circumstances'.[26] Examples of equivalent indicators that serve to differentiate cases on account of contextual particularities include 'In contrast to the situation concerned in',[27] 'Unlike . . . in the case giving rise to the judgment in',[28] 'However, such reasoning does not in any way prejudge

---

[25] Cf. Case C-456/03 *Commission* v. *Italian Republic* (Third Chamber) [2005] ECR 5335 (paras. 41–2).

[26] Case C-522/09 *Commission* v. *Romania* (Fourth Chamber) [2011] ECR I-2963 (para. 19).

[27] Case C-555/07 *Seda Kücükdeveci* v. *Swedex GmbH & Co. KG* (Grand Chamber) [2010] ECR I-365 (para. 24) ('à la différence de l'affaire ayant donné lieu à l'arrêt').

[28] Case C-135/08 *Janko Rottmann* v. *Freistaat Bayern* (Grand Chamber) [2010] ECR I-1449 (para. 49) ('Contrairement . . . dans l'affaire ayant donné lieu à l'arrêt').

the separate question, specific to the present case, of'[29] and 'However, that is not the case in this instance.'[30] Such emphasis on specificity has a clear function. The narrower a point is, the easier it becomes to avoid.[31]

There is a connection between the argumentative burden imposed by a precedent and the generality employed. The degree of abstraction chosen by the Court – the contextual granularity – becomes an important device to regulate jurisprudential coherence, since distinguishing gives the impression of compatibility by avoiding direct confrontation. This is the opposite technique of increasing abstraction to the point where the legal landscape might be profoundly shaped by a bold statement, yet the practical application thereof remains difficult to predict in individual cases, so that the Court retains a considerable degree of latitude. That scenario is perhaps the more familiar one, exemplified by broad declarations of legal principles derived from the nature of the system of the treaties. But the Court's toolbox also includes this inverse instrument to ensure jurisprudential elasticity. Indeed, it would otherwise quickly deprive itself of its flexibility, especially in light of its proclivity for wide statements. The alternative to increasing specificity is to depart openly or silently in order to remain flexible, but this entails up-front or delayed costs.

Thirdly, the discussion of the (supposed) precedent, *Commission* v. *Luxembourg*, brief though it may be, nevertheless goes beyond purely referential citation. As seen, this remains a fairly rare occurrence in the Court's overall use of precedent. Most of its citations are not 'strong' in the sense that they do not discuss the reasoning of the cited precedent but simply appear to rely on the plain authority of once having decided a point without spelling out why that should be relevant or applicable in the present case. This hints at another factor that is relevant to precedent-following: discursiveness. The relationship is intricate. A first observation is that brief and focused judgments generally exert a certain attraction on judges, not least because they invite fewer sticking points for subsequent litigants to latch onto in unexpected and undesired ways.[32] They put less

---

[29] Case C-271/08 *Commission* v. *Federal Republic of Germany* (Grand Chamber) [2010] ECR I-7091 (para. 46) ('Toutefois, un tel raisonnement ne préjuge aucunement de la question distincte, propre à la présente affaire, du...').

[30] Case C-285/09 *Criminal proceedings against R* (Grand Chamber) [2010] ECR I-12605 (para. 33) ('Or, tel n'est pas le cas dans la présente affaire.').

[31] Cf. F. Schauer, 'Precedent', *Stanford Law Review*, 39 (1986–1987), 591 (albeit focusing on the ambit of a premise rather than the degree of abstraction).

[32] See A. von Bogdandy and M. Jacob, 'The Judge as Law-Maker: Thoughts on Bruno Simma's Declaration in the Kosovo Opinion' in U. Fastenrath *et al.* (eds.), *From Bilateralism to*

legal information out in the open. The more responsibility an adjudicator has to shoulder, the more cautiously she will often want to express herself. In particular appellate and inter- or supranational judges deciding cases that could potentially affect many other judges and millions of individuals – the ECJ being a prime example – will be keenly aware of this and thus extremely wary of planting any 'time bombs' in their judgments.

Another illustration of these features of classic distinguishing is *Finanzamt Burgdorf* v. *Manfred Bog*, in which the ECJ distinguished the sale of food from snack stalls from ordinary restaurant dining.[33] The latter was held to be a supply of services for VAT purposes, while the former was considered to involve a supply of goods. The Court went into almost extravagant detail in setting apart these gastronomic activities, noting amongst other things that, unlike in restaurants, at snack bars 'there are no waiters, no real advice to customers, no service properly speaking consisting in particular in transmitting orders to the kitchen and then presenting and serving dishes to customers at tables, no enclosed spaces at an appropriate temperature dedicated to the consumption of the food served, no cloakrooms or lavatories, and essentially no crockery, furniture or place settings'. The ECJ also held, again with remarkable specificity, that a party catering business would in most cases involve a supply of services.[34]

This process of denying the application of a precedent is essentially the same as the regular application of a proposition of law to a factual situation, the reverse result being the peculiarity. But despite the existence of major and minor premises it would be an oversimplification to exclusively think of this as a mechanistic process, since the norm contained in a precedent and the present factual situation have to interact meaningfully in order to see whether or not they fit.[35] The former is a conceptual postulate expressed through a string of letters and the latter an empirical fact. Their interrelation requires a cognitive act of 'translation': analogising in the Aristotelian sense, that is to say searching for shared abstraction, in

---

Community Interest: Essays in Honour of Judge Bruno Simma (Oxford University Press, 2011), p. 819.

[33] Joined Cases C-497/09, C-499/09, C-501/09 and C-502/09 *Finanzamt Burgdorf* v. *Manfred Bog* (Third Chamber) [2011] ECR I-1457 (paras. 64–74).

[34] *Ibid.* paras. 77–80.

[35] Cf. J. Bung, *Subsumtion und Interpretation* (Nomos, Baden-Baden, 2004), p. 29 on the deductive element in such reasoning.

order to ascertain possible similarity.[36] This will often be a subconsciously teleological process.[37] The following case illustrates the point.

In *Paul Miles*, the ECJ was faced with the question of whether it had jurisdiction to entertain a request for a preliminary ruling by the Complaints Board of the European Schools, educational institutions set up by international conventions that are formally distinct from the EU and the Member States.[38] Is the Complaints Board a 'court or tribunal of a Member State' for the purposes of what is now TFEU Art. 267? The applicants in the main proceedings relied among other things on *Parfums Christian Dior*, where the Court had previously held that the Benelux Court of Justice, a judicial body common to a number of Member States, could make references to the ECJ.[39] The European Schools submitted that *Parfums Christian Dior* was distinguishable because litigation in the Benelux Court had originated in a national court.[40] Declining jurisdiction, the ECJ took the same view and rejected the resemblance between the Complaints Board and the Benelux Court. The latter could be equated with the situations covered by TFEU Art. 267 since it had close ties to the national legal systems: not only is it a step in Member State proceedings, its task is to ensure that the law is applied uniformly in those states. The independent and international Complaints Board lacked such a link. Hence the Court decided neither to assimilate it to those situations covered by TFEU Art. 267 nor to the Benelux Court. This can also be expressed by saying *Paul Miles* distinguished *Parfums Christian Dior*.

It is apparent that the 'true nature' of premises such as 'court or tribunal of a Member State' of TFEU Art. 267 and its scope of application cannot be gleaned from the wording alone and that certain cases can be helpful pointers.[41] Any understanding of that provision is dependent on interpretation, rather than being antecedent to it.[42] All interpreters, and

---

[36] See T. Heller, *Logik und Axiologie der analogen Rechtsanwendung* (De Gruyter, Berlin and Cologne, 1961), p. 87; Kaufmann (n. 4 above), p. 37.

[37] See G. Radbruch, 'Die Natur der Sache als juristische Denkform' in G. C. Hernmarck (ed.), *Festschrift zu Ehren von Rudolf Laun* (Toth, Hamburg, 1948), p. 33; J. Esser, *Grundsatz und Norm in der richterlichen Fortbildung des Privatrechts* (Mohr, Tübingen, 1956), p. 253.

[38] Case C-196/09 *Paul Miles and ors* v. *Écoles européennes* (Grand Chamber) [2011] ECR I-5105.

[39] Case C-337/95 *Parfums Christian Dior SA and Parfums Christian Dior BV* v. *Evora BV* [1997] ECR I-6013 (para. 21).

[40] Para. 35.   [41] See Ch. 3 on different ways to link cases.

[42] Cf. F. Müller, R. Christensen and M. Sokolowski, *Rechtstext und Textarbeit* (Duncker & Humblot, Berlin, 1997), p. 132.

hence all adjudicatory bodies, including the ECJ, turn to forms of reasoning that try to make sense of legal text, an exercise that is in a very basic sense teleological but straddles a wide range of possible considerations. Distinguishing, just like any act of norm application,[43] is an evaluative process.

That in itself takes a lot of the sting out of the familiar yet tired accusation that the ECJ is a 'teleological' decision-maker, as if that were an altogether exceptional, unnecessary and ruinous thing.[44] Such reasoning is inescapable and is plain to see in the *Paul Miles* judgment: the Complaints Board was considered different – this was the nub – because it neither contributed to the uniform application of the legal rules of the Member State nor exercised any other meaningful function with respect to the latter.

It pays dissecting this in more detail. Although this was not set out as such by the Court itself, like all legal interpreters considering whether or not to follow a precedent on a particular point, the ECJ effectively had to consider three sets of analogical relations. For one, the Court was obviously asked to assess whether the current circumstances came within TFEU Art. 267. In so doing it then compared the situation in *Paul Miles* to that in *Parfums Christian Dior*. Perhaps less evidently, this further entailed reassessing whether that precedent itself fit TFEU Art. 267.[45] Despite superficial appearance to the contrary, precedent-following and -distinguishing are triadic rather than dyadic reasoning processes. In a legal context, the interpreter commonly constructs a triangle between the relevant norm[46] and the two cases in question: Figure 5.B.i.

The three sides represent assimilations. The parties will be most interested in the relationship between the norm and the current case

---

[43]   Cf. Kaufmann (n. 4 above), pp. 39–42; A. Somek, *Rechtliches Wissen* (Suhrkamp, Frankfurt am Main, 2006), pp. 56–7.

[44]   See I. Augsberg, 'Methoden des europäischen Verwaltungsrechts' in J. P. Terhechte (ed.), *Verwaltungsrecht der Europäischen Union* (Nomos, Baden-Baden, 2011), m.nn. 22–3 (while noting the slope from *effet utile* to *effet maximal*).

[45]   Case C-196/09 *Paul Miles and ors* v. *Écoles européennes* (Grand Chamber) [2011] ECR I-5105 (para. 41).

[46]   This need not necessarily be a written rule of law, let alone a single paragraph in a treaty, law or piece of secondary legislation. Rather, a 'norm' in this context provides the instruction needed to solve the legal problem at hand one way or another. It can be reconstructed from acknowledged positive sources, unwritten principles, cases, deontological or consequentialist considerations or a mixture thereof, i.e. from all possible legal information. See W. Fikentscher, *Methoden des Rechts in vergleichender Darstellung*, 5 vols. (Mohr, Tübingen, 1977), IV, pp. 186, 202; F. Müller and R. Christensen, *Juristische Methodik: Europarecht* (2nd edn, Duncker & Humblot, Berlin, 2007), p. 293.

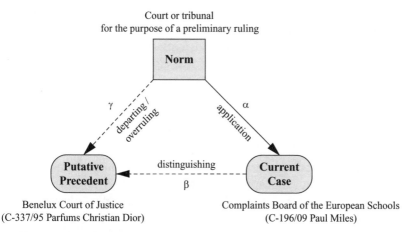

Figure 5.B.i   The (dis)application triangle

(side α), with one side battling for correlation and the other opposing it. The association between the current case and the putative precedent (side β) might influence this, depending on how the precedent itself relates to the norm (side γ). Denying a meaningful connection between the two cases (side β) is commonly called *distinguishing* and is the subject of this chapter. Refuting a proper assimilation of the precedent and the norm (side γ) is the theme of *departing* or *overruling*, which will be dealt with in the next chapter.

Any invocation of precedent inevitably, if largely implicitly, creates this triadic situation. A dyadic conception of precedent, whereby only two points of reference are brought into an analogous relation is incomplete to the point of being useless. It is literally one-dimensional. Such depictions leave out a crucial angle. Focusing only on side β – the common law caricature – turns a blind eye to the fact that decided cases cannot as such be brought into a meaningful relation without an overarching concept, namely their relation to a norm.[47] Cases are not cited in complete abstraction, but in order to make or refute a point. This is a cognitive process and thus subject to debate and competing opinions. Insisting solely on side α – an illusion of archetypal civilian approaches – ignores the futility of pure rational deduction[48] and the need for assimilation in every

---

[47] It is thus imprecise to speak of 'extracting' a norm from a decision. What is extracted is a rationale or essence, which in turn serves to specify normative instruction.

[48] On this see H. Kelsen, *Reine Rechtslehre* (Franz Deuticke, Leipzig and Vienna, 1934), p. 96; A. Peczenik, 'Jumps and Logic in the Law', *Artificial Intelligence and Law*, 4 (1996),

application of norms to facts. Text is not a substitute for meaning, with law being an inevitably argumentative practice. This helps to account for the universality of reasoning by precedents: they cast some light into the void between norms and facts. The ECJ also uses them as such, which once again defuses many charges of dictation, but also takes the Court down a notch.

ii Type 2: manipulation

A second form of distinguishing involves modifying the precedent to some extent so that it does not apply to the present case. This is plainly a creative exercise.[49] For instance, the ECJ at times creates a disparity by increasing the specificity of a precedent, for example by adding to its relevant facts or considerations, thus driving a wedge between it and the present situation. Whereas the original view of the precedent might have been C_1: A, B, C → X, following the new reading it is in fact said to be C_{1*}: A, B, C, D → X. For example, in *Dereci*, the Court distinguished an earlier pronouncement through specification by adding to the 'deprivation of genuine enjoyment' test on residence rights resulting from EU citizenship a lack of alternative options and more than just temporal deprivation.[50] This is just one example where the ECJ not only makes law but also avoids its own past output.

Sometimes, the rationale of a precedent is manipulated more directly. C_1: A, B, C → X then becomes C_{1*}: A*, B, C → X. To give an example, in *Commission* v. *Portuguese Republic*, the Commission claimed that Portugal had failed to fulfil its obligations under what are now TFEU Arts. 63 and 49, which prohibit restrictions on the right of establishment and the movement of capital between Member States.[51] The Portuguese state and other public bodies had in the course of the privatisation of Portugal

---

297; U. Neumann, *Recht als Struktur und Argumentation* (Nomos, Baden-Baden, 2008), pp. 85–7.

[49] '[T]the power to distinguish is a power to develop the law even when deciding regulated cases and even by courts which have no power to overrule': Raz (n. 18 above), p. 185.

[50] Case C-256/11 *Murat Dereci and ors* v. *Bundesministerium für Inneres* (Grand Chamber) [2011] ECR I-11315 (paras. 66–7) (emphasising the exceptional nature of the precedent in question). For the inverse technique where the present situation is elaborated in more detail to effectively narrow the precedent see e.g. Case T-203/96 *Embassy Limousines & Services* v. *Parliament* [1998] ECR II-4239 (para. 80), where an encouragement was considered by the (then still) CFI to take the situation outside the remit of the precedents on simple errors and wrongful acts.

[51] Case C-171/08 *Commission* v. *Portuguese Republic* (First Chamber) [2010] ECR I-6817.

Telecom retained 'golden' shares in the company's share capital. The defendant Republic denied any infringement, arguing *inter alia* that the legislative measures concerning these privileged shares granting special rights were simply non-discriminatory rules on the management of the shareholdings and not rules for their acquisition. It thus submitted that the well-known rationale of *Keck and Mithouard*,[52] which distinguishes between (generally impermissible) product requirements and (generally permissible) selling arrangements, ought to be applied to the present case, that is it to say transplanted from the free movement of goods context to freedom of capital and establishment. The Court followed AG Mengozzi in declining this. It distinguished *Keck and Mithouard* on the basis that the selling arrangement exception was held to be inapplicable where the measures concerned constituted an impediment to market access, a refinement of the binary formula the Court had developed over time. Investors from other Member States would be deterred from taking an interest in the company. After all, the Portuguese Republic could exercise influence over management decisions via its privileged shares. Ergo, the *Keck and Mithouard* escape route was blocked by re-interpreting one of its limbs.

Another example in this vein is *Commission* v. *Spain*, in which the Grand Chamber held that so-called *Vanbraekel* reimbursement of cross-border healthcare costs did not apply to unforeseen (as opposed to planned) treatment.[53] This was a highly controversial issue with potentially vast financial ramifications that had previously been considered capable of going either way, not least because such unforeseeability had not yet been addressed by the Court.[54] In its judgment, the ECJ expressly claimed to distinguish the precedent on precisely that ground. Whatever the merits of that decision, what is of interest here is the precedent technique employed. If one takes the argument seriously that the point was left open by and after *Vanbraekel*, distinguishing would seem paradoxical for exactly that reason. The ECJ's reasoning makes more sense however if one reconstructs the precedent to have solely concerned scheduled treatment, which is what the Court evidently did. Arguments can certainly be marshalled in support

---

[52] Joined Cases C-267/91 and C-268/91 *Criminal proceedings against Bernard Keck and Daniel Mithouard* [1993] ECR I-6097.

[53] Case C-211/08 *Commission* v. *Kingdom of Spain* (Grand Chamber) [2010] ECR I-5267; Case C-368/98 *Abdon Vanbraekel and ors* v. *Alliance nationale des mutualités chrétiennes (ANMC)* [2001] ECR I-5363.

[54] See A. P. van der Mei, 'Cross-Border Access to Healthcare and Entitlement to Complementary "*Vanbraekel* Reimbursement"', *European Law Review*, 36 (2011), 431, 434.

of such a restrictive view, for instance the negligible chilling effect on the internal market or the unpredictable costs. But only after having made up one's mind about the relevant differences can they be asserted. It would also be short-sighted to consider this form of distinguishing to be nothing more than a mere disapplication of a prior case, since the judgment has a real effect on how the precedent is understood. *Vanbraekel* and what it stands for was not overturned, but it was not left completely untouched either.

iii Type 3: obitering

Thirdly, and most disruptively, the ECJ is no stranger to consigning a precedent to inconsequence by continuously moulding and chipping away at its rationale, a technique that could politely be called wholesale *obitering*. In the end, what was once C_1: A, B, C → X effectively becomes C_{1^*}: A*, B*, C* → X. One of the most conspicuous episodes relates to remedies for breaches of EU obligations and concerns the fate of the judgment in *Emmott*.[55] Guided by the loadstar of decentral application, national procedural autonomy has always been an important concept in EU law, provided certain basic requirements are met.[56] *Emmott* at the time caused a stir when it boldly held that a Member State in breach of its obligations under secondary EU law was precluded from relying on national time limits in situations involving deficiently transposed equal treatment directives: time could only run from the date of proper implementation, when the concerned individual was able to ascertain the full extent of her rights. The reception of the decision was uneven, but the critics prevailed over time, arguing that the judgment was an untenable restriction of national autonomy and unworkable in practice because legal certainty would be vastly undermined and Member States might be rendered liable on an unforeseeable scale, given the landmark *Francovich* judgment.[57]

---

[55] Case C-208/90 *Theresa Emmott* v. *Minister for Social Welfare and Attorney General* [1991] ECR I-4269.

[56] Chiefly equivalence and effectiveness: Case C-445/06 *Danske Slagterier* v. *Bundesrepublik Deutschland* (Grand Chamber) [2009] ECR I-2119 (paras. 31, 69); Case C-118/08 *Transportes Urbanos y Servicios Generales SAL* v. *Administración del Estado* (Grand Chamber) [2010] ECR I-635 (para. 31).

[57] See e.g. J. Gundel, 'Keine Durchbrechung nationaler Verfahrensfristen zugunsten von Rechten aus nicht umgesetzten EG-Richtlinien', *Neue Zeitschrift für Verwaltungsrecht*, 17 (1998), 910, 912–13; M. Horspool and M. Humphreys, *European Union Law* (6th edn, Oxford University Press, 2010), pp. 221, 586.

Later ECJ decisions in which submissions were based on *Emmott* took this to heart and successively distanced themselves from that judgment. *Steenhorst-Neerings* distinguished the case on the basis that *Emmott* concerned a total bar to bringing a claim, whereas the Dutch provision in question only permissibly restricted the retroactive effect of benefit claims to one year before the claim was brought.[58] While this might at first blush appear to be a conservative form of distinguishing by asserting relevant differences (here: time limits do not equal rules on the scope of incapacity benefits), *Steenhorst-Neerings* manipulated the rationale of *Emmott* more directly by cutting back the full extent of the claimant's rights in the interests of 'sound administration' and financial equilibrium.[59] Being able to ascertain one's rights, a precept of *Emmott*, no longer played a cardinal role.

This crossing-over from ostensible distinguishing to effective overruling was continued in *Johnson*, another decision concerning sex equality and benefit arrears.[60] The Court again reconsidered the essence of the worrisome precedent, this time relegating *Emmott* to the 'particular circumstances of that case' by confining its logic to the preclusion of outright deprivation of the applicant's claim by the respective authorities.[61] In so doing *Johnson* built upon and expressly declined to distinguish *Steenhorst-Neerings*, but the ECJ was more direct in re-moulding *Emmott*, visibly content not to preoccupy itself specifically with distinguishing between time limits and rules on the scope of incapacity benefits.

What is more, subsequent decisions which could have invoked *Emmott* analogously outside the context of gender-based discrimination refused to utilise the case as a trump in the context of a national failure to implement a directive, instead treating it like an interchangeable authority for the general principle that national measures must not be less advantageous.[62] The ECJ dealt another blow to the precedent when it briskly declined to apply its rationale to obligations stemming from primary law.[63] Given that, *ceteris paribus*, the effectiveness of EU law and the

---

[58] Case C-338/91 *H. Steenhorst-Neerings* v. *Bestuur van de Bedrijfsvereniging voor Detailhandel, Ambachten en Huisvrouwen* [1993] ECR I-5475 (para. 21).

[59] *Ibid.* para. 23.

[60] Case C-410/92 *Elsie Rita Johnson* v. *Chief Adjudication Officer* [1994] ECR I-5483 (paras. 26–7).

[61] *Ibid.* paras. 26–30.

[62] See e.g. Case C-62/93 *BP Soupergaz Anonimos Etairia Geniki Emporiki-Viomichaniki kai Antiprossopeion* v. *Greek State* (Sixth Chamber) [1995] ECR I-1883 (para. 41).

[63] See Joined Cases C-114/95 and C-115/95 *Texaco A/S* v. *Middelfart Havn and ors and Olieselskabet Danmark amba* v. *Trafikministeriet and ors* (Sixth Chamber) [1997] ECR I-4263 (paras. 47–9).

protection of rights afforded thereby would have suggested an analogous application, this blunt refusal strongly suggests disapproval of the precedent rather that plain distinguishing. But the Court could again not bring itself to unambiguously abandon the original case, despite the resentment expressed by AG Jacobs and his persistent efforts to qualify the decision notwithstanding its general language.[64]

Fantask finally is widely understood to have marked the completion of the ECJ's elongated U-turn.[65] The Court allowed a Danish limitation period to run from the date on which charges that had erroneously been levied became payable, irrespective of the date of transposition of the directive in question, so long as the provision was not discriminatory and did not render the exercise of EU rights virtually impossible. While nominally distinguishing *Emmott* once again on the basis that the individual in the alleged precedent was deprived of any opportunity whatsoever to rely on her rights, this effectively amounted to an overruling of *Emmott* in all but name.[66] This new 'settled case-law following *Emmott*'[67] has now almost completely unsettled the former precedent, demonstrating the mercurial nature of legal information and claims about law, even when proposed by a single institution. It is no exaggeration to say that the original gist[68] was 'distinguished' beyond recognition, surviving only in those exceptional situations when Member States cause a delay by their own conduct or mislead an applicant. Other than that it is massaged into the general consensus on the outer limits of national procedural autonomy.

Whether or not it was proper to abandon *Emmott*, the technique employed comes with strings attached. Its attraction lies in aiming both for consistency and change. On the face of it, the ECJ is a dutiful

---

[64] *Ibid.* Opinion of AG Jacobs (para. 167); Case C-2/94 *Denkavit International BV and ors* v. *Kamer van Koophandel en Fabrieken voor Midden-Gelderland and ors* [1996] ECR I-2827, Opinion of AG Jacobs (paras. 71–8).

[65] Case C-188/95 *Fantask A/S e.a.* v. *Industriministeriet (Erhvervministeriet)* [1997] ECR I-6783 (para. 42); N. Notaro, 'Case C-188/95, Fantask A/S and Others v. Industriministeriet (Erhvervsministeriet): Annotation', *Common Market Law Review*, 35 (1998), 1385, 1390 (referring to *Fantask* as the 'final stage in what could be called a step-by-step overruling of the *Emmott* judgment').

[66] For recent affirmation of this approach see Case C-452/09 *Tonina Enza Iaia and ors* v. *Ministero dell'Istruzione, dell'Università e della Ricerca and ors* (First Chamber) [2011] ECR I-4043 (para. 19–21); Joined Cases C-89/10 and C-96/10 *Q-Beef NV* v. *Belgian State* (Fourth Chamber) [2011] ECR I-7819 (para. 50) ('justified by the circumstances particular to that case').

[67] *Ibid.*

[68] Arguably, the Irish authorities' mistake was never the essence of *Emmott*, but instead the effective vindication of individual rights.

automaton; under the surface, it constantly reshapes the European legal order on a case-by-case basis. Yet the price of not wanting to be seen to overrule past jurisprudence is twofold. First, it becomes very difficult to keep track of subtle shifts.[69] Clear cuts are easier to follow. Through such creeping retreats, the Court sends mixed signals to the national courts and commentators, some of the former of which indeed continued to apply *Emmott* for some time.[70] Alternatively, national courts might take this as an invitation to jump the gun and hastily dispense with what was said altogether.[71] Such confusion is precisely what the Court wants to avoid. The second point is that attempting to save face can also backfire. Perhaps *Emmott* was not working. But it is questionable to what extent an honest reversal harms the overall perception of the ECJ more than a sluggish, largely clandestine about-face. There is no hard-and-fast answer to this, but the Court puts its reputation on the line when its very real, if often unspoken, precedent technique acquires an air of pretence. This is regrettable, since it swamps the often very ordinary fact-based and sys-temically minded work of the Court and nurtures naïve and overstated anti-teleology and anti-judicial law-making witch hunts. Moreover, the post-*Emmott* technique is particularly perilous in combination with the ECJ's regular habit of not elaborating in more detail what troubled it about a case and what it hence proposes to do about this. More substan-tive argumentation in this respect can provide not only a tool for greater clarity but also for more legitimacy.

Conclusively, the ECJ acknowledges distinguishing as a useful prece-dent technique. This allows for valuable dissemination of legal informa-tion and can contribute to the clarity and systematicity of its adjudication. It is certainly not an entirely passive activity. But the concept still poses difficulties for the ECJ at times, mostly in the form of what are effec-tively *sub silentio* departures. These are rooted in an extreme eagerness to appear coherent and find sustenance in the Court's terse style of reason-ing, the general or referential precedent citations and its dislike for open overruling and separate or concurring opinions.

By way of a brief comparison, distinguishing is also an abundantly common precedent technique of international investment tribunals. This

---

[69] See M. J. Gerhardt, *The Power of Precedent* (Oxford University Press, 2008), p. 35 (regarding the US Supreme Court).
[70] See Gundel (n. 57 above), pp. 914–15 (on disparities in French and Italian jurisprudence).
[71] Cf. R. Gordon, *EC Law in Judicial Review* (Oxford University Press, 2007), pp. 94–6 (on the general tendency of English courts to curtail *Emmott*).

is corroborated by the present data set: almost half the cases thus examined distinguished one or more precedents.[72] That is more than double the rate of the ECJ's Grand Chamber judgments for the same year, which was itself not insignificant. What is telling in this context is the far greater willingness of those tribunals to make substantive citations, namely to elaborate why exactly a precedent is or is not on point. Roughly a quarter of citations analysed was more than just referential.[73] While this cannot be fleshed out here due to constraints of space and focus, in drawing on prior cases investment tribunals display the full gamut of distinguishing techniques just surveyed with respect to the ECJ, ranging from more-or-less neutral disapplication to direct manipulation of a precedent's rationale.

Contrasting that practice to that of the ECJ, the first point to note is the popularity of this avoidance technique in both regimes. As already mentioned, the fact that a case is distinguished rather than rejected outright is an unspoken admission that the precedent is taken seriously. Despite being an avoidance technique, distinguishing is hence also a crucial tool for consistency and systemic evolution, interests that are dear to most systems of adjudication. Distinguishing allows for a degree of volatility and refinement while encouraging adjustments that fit into what already exists. This curbs particularistic and personal views since the precedent is usually not erased. At the very least, this gives the impression of respecting different circumstances rather than promoting individual whims. Such an appearance of self-limitation is fundamentally important for courts and tribunals that rely so heavily on cases in their decision-making as do the ECJ and investment tribunals. Another draw lies in the possibility of provisional solutions.[74] The technique can presage a bigger change and be a useful outlet when an adjudicator does not consider the situation at hand to be suitable for a more fundamental change.

Concerning the lower willingness of the ECJ to openly distinguish precedents (when compared to investment tribunals), this can to a large extent be explained by the more unitary nature of EU law, be it in terms of temporal institutional existence, rival interpretive authorities and specific legal bases. Another reason lies in the often very fact-driven nature of investment disputes, which provides a wider range of materials to draw

---

[72] Precisely twenty-four out of fifty-two (i.e. just over 46 per cent).
[73] To be exact, 324 out of 1,295 individual mentions.
[74] Cf. M. A. Eisenberg, *The Nature of the Common Law* (Harvard University Press, London, 1988), p. 139.

distinctions.[75] The Court's habitual *modus operandi* is far less fact-centric. Moreover, the less discursive reasoning style and compulsory collegiate opinions further discourage being distinctive about different contexts. In sum, the centripetal pull is much stronger at the ECJ, and one thing that forces this almost as much as not discussing differences at all is distinguishing them.

C Coherence: the new normativity?

Albeit perhaps counterintuitive at first for an avoidance technique, distinguishing by the ECJ is a characteristic attempt at demonstrating systemic coherence by refusing to rework patterns in EU law simply because certain aspects differ. Unlike in overruling or departing, old legal information is not invariably overwritten; instead, something new tends to be added to this. By declaring that dissimilar cases should be treated dissimilarly, the Court implies that like should be treated alike. This explains the attraction even in those situations where judges do not consider themselves under any actual obligation to follow precedents, as at the ECJ, or when they think of themselves as simply settling disputes rather than engaging in any systemic work at all.

Such is the allure of coherence that it at times appears to become the principal determinant of legal decision-making. Undoubtedly, the epistemic limitations discussed earlier cause palpable unease.[76] Since it is practically[77] impossible to come up with a complete and accurate mapping of 'the law', a surrogate for 'right' decisions is a tantalising proposition. Coherence seems the perfect candidate.[78] For one, it promises previsibility and legal certainty through repetition. 'A judicial decision is right', a young Carl Schmitt concluded, 'when it is foreseeable and predictable.'[79]

---

[75] To give an example, one tribunal refused to rely on prior decisions dealing with indirect investments by virtue of chain corporate ownership in a situation involving a network of contractual arrangements: *Inmaris Perestroika Sailing Maritime Services GmbH and ors v. Ukraine*, ICSID Case No. ARB/08/8, Decision on Jurisdiction of 8.3.2010 (Alexandrov, Cremades, Rubins) (para. 97).

[76] See Neumann (n. 48 above), p. 84.

[77] This is not the place to discuss the all-time classic whether it might ever be possible or necessary to achieve such a Herculean feat. Cf. R. Dworkin, *A Matter of Principle* (Oxford University Press, 1985), ch. 7.

[78] See A. Amaya, 'Legal Justification by Optimal Coherence', *Ratio Juris*, 24 (2011), 304, 305.

[79] C. Schmitt, *Gesetz und Urteil: Eine Untersuchung zum Problem der Rechtspraxis* (Liebmann, Berlin, 1912), p. 111.

Previsibility thereby becomes the pragmatic proxy for the original exhortation that a judicial decision is right if it is provided for by law. It rings of regularity and therefore, ultimately, norm-compliance.

Of course there is something missing: the compulsion that separates it from habit or proclivity. But coherence is more than previsibility and legal certainty. It approaches law from an internal standpoint, rather than from the external perspective of the potentially affected. It provides a structure within which pointillist decisions blend into a larger backdrop. The legal interpreter thereby disempowers herself in favour of the impersonal system. Its salvation lies in its repeatability. Coherence between two cases suggests that they are both iterable instances of an overarching normative structure. Shorn of unnecessary fluff (normally certain facts or whatever might be considered *obiter dicta*), they are materially the same as evinced by a shared medium level of abstraction. Coherence implies that – all other things being equal – the decision was correct, because it fits the former decision, which has not been upset. It suggests that there is essentially nothing new to a decision; the latter simply repeats the application of an existing body of norms to a novel factual situation.[80] The unruly horse of legal decision-making is seemingly subdued by embedding it into a larger normative milieu.

The ECJ is particularly tempted to make coherence the leitmotif of its interaction with its own precedents. Article 19(1) of the TEU ambiguously asks the Court to ensure that 'the [singular] law is observed' in the interpretation and application of the treaties. The way this extremely liberal mandate is phrased lends strong support to approaches that cultivate a preference for systematic consistency over particularistic formalism and static textualism. It injects an overarching yet hazy sense of 'doing justice' into the modern and technical world of professionalised legal dispute settlement, an almost archaic moral ideal.[81] The ECJ has at various critical junctions relied on the centripetal thrust of this idea of substantive unity and systemic completeness of EU law.[82] As a supranational

---

[80] See I. Augsberg, *Die Lesbarkeit des Rechts* (Velbrück, Weilerswist, 2009), pp. 87–8.

[81] See F. C. Mayer, 'Art. 19 EUV' in E. Grabitz, M. Hilf and M. Nettesheim (eds.), *Das Recht der Europäischen Union* (C. H. Beck, Munich, 2010), m.nn. 23–5.

[82] See only Case 44/79 *Liselotte Hauer* v. *Land Rheinland-Pfalz* [1979] ECR 3727 (para. 14); Joined Cases C-402/05 P and C-415/05 P *Yassin Abdullah Kadi and Al Barakaat International Foundation* v. *Council and Commission* (Grand Chamber) [2008] ECR I-6351 (para. 281). See also J. Bengoetxea, N. MacCormick and L. Moral Soriano, 'Integration and Integrity in the Legal Reasoning of the European Court of Justice' in G. de Búrca and J. Weiler (eds.), *The European Court of Justice* (Oxford University Press, 2001), pp. 64–81 (on different balancing tests employed to establish systemic coherence).

construct interacting with almost thirty sovereign states on a daily basis, it is difficult to imagine that the Court will ever entirely shake off its existential uneasiness, and reliance on systematicity buttresses its subsistence and legitimacy. There is little to suggest this should be any different in seemingly routine treatments of its case law. In fact, various factors indicate and reinforce such an inclination. For instance, the clipped collegiate judgments promote a reduction of complexity to what are considered essential expressions of systemic points, which can readily be gleaned from other cases and are subsequently themselves drawn upon, often word for word.[83] It can be more difficult to connect lengthy discursive pronouncements than the abstract nodes of legal information favoured by the ECJ.

To give an illustration from its jurisprudence, *McCarthy* is another case about deriving rights for non-EU nationals from the rights of Union citizens.[84] What is relevant for present purposes is that only two months earlier, the Grand Chamber in *Ruiz Zambrano* decided that the citizenship provisions in the TFEU preclude national measures which effectively deprive EU citizens of the enjoyment of their corresponding rights.[85] Third-state nationals can indirectly benefit from the rights EU nationals are afforded though Union citizenship; in that case, their dependent children's right of residence. Mrs McCarthy sought to extend her own unquestionable right of residence and free movement as a citizen of the EU[86] to her husband, a Jamaican national. In vain, the Court held. The national measure she was challenging – she had, resourcefully but unsuccessfully, applied for a residence permit in the UK after having additionally obtained Irish citizenship in addition to her original British citizenship following her marriage – did not deprive her of the genuine enjoyment of her right to move and reside freely in the EU: she would in any event not have to leave the UK or EU.[87] This was held to be unlike *Ruiz Zambrano*, where expulsion of the respective third-state nationals would have

---

[83] On co-ordinating expectations through networks of abstraction see K.-H. Ladeur, 'Der "Eigenwert" des Rechts – Die Selbstorganisationsfähigkeit der Gesellschaft und die relationale Rationalität des Rechts' in C. J. Meier-Schatz (ed.), *Die Zukunft des Rechts* (Helbing & Lichtenhahn, Basel, Geneva and Munich 1999), pp. 41–3.

[84] Case C-434/09 *Shirley McCarthy* v. *Secretary of State for the Home Department* (Third Chamber) [2011] ECR I-3375.

[85] Case C-34/09 *Gerardo Ruiz Zambrano* v. *Office national de l'emploi (ONEm)* *(Grand Chamber)* [2011] ECR I-1177 (para. 42).

[86] Case C-434/09 *Shirley McCarthy* v. *Secretary of State for the Home Department* (Third Chamber) [2011] ECR I-3375 (para. 48).

[87] *Ibid.* para. 49.

seriously prejudiced the enjoyment of the Union citizenship rights in question: young children depend on their parents.

So while the cases are superficially similar in that they both concern the right of abode of family members of EU citizens, they are different on account of one situation (*Ruiz Zambrano*) involving ascendants of dependent minors and the other (*McCarthy*) involving an adult spouse. In other words, the Zambrano's Belgian children, Diego and Jessica, made all the difference on this point.[88] The Court considered this dissimilarity relevant, since only in that situation was there substantial prejudice to the rights afforded to EU citizens. That is the consistent connector; it hence does not matter that the individual cases fall on either side of the line. *McCarthy* seeks to maintain systemic coherence *by*, rather than *despite*, distinguishing *Ruiz Zambrano*.

Turning to the consequences, coherence as a sop to limited cognition comes at a cost. First, it strongly reinforces a form of deductive reasoning, only this time not based on letters and text, but on a comforting conception of what 'the system' entails. Insisting on coherence places the system on a pedestal and continuously reinforces it. The practice suggests that while matters come before the Court in infinite variety, the system itself is approached *as if* it were meaningful and logically complete.[89] Reasoning by precedent supports this notion in its unspoken disjunctive obligation that cases that are considered in the course of adjudication are either applied or avoided in some way.[90] Whichever option is chosen, the system not only always has an answer, it also invariably reaffirms itself, regardless of the actual decision. Rather attractively, anything resembling a *non liquet* becomes doubtful.

Secondly, this leads to interdependence or, to use a popular if slightly artificial catchword, 'path-dependency'.[91] The idea is that, at the very

---

[88] *Ibid.* para. 50. The same might be said of baby Catherine in Case C-200/02 *Kunqian Catherine Zhu and Man Lavette Chen* v. *Secretary of State for the Home Department* (Full Court) [2004] ECR I-9925 (paras. 45–56).

[89] Cf. T. Vesting, *Rechtstheorie* (C. H. Beck, Munich, 2007), p. 49.

[90] See G. Lamond, 'Precedent and Analogy in Legal Reasoning' Stanford Encyclopedia of Philosophy, http://plato.stanford.edu/, para. 2.1.2.

[91] See e.g. O. A. Hathaway, 'Path Dependence in the Law: The Course and Pattern of Legal Change in a Common Law System', *Iowa Law Review*, 86 (2001), 101, 104; M. Shapiro and A. Stone Sweet, *On Law, Politics, and Judicialization* (Oxford University Press, 2002), pp. 112–35; V. Fon, F. Parisi and B. Depoorter, 'Litigation, Judicial Path-Dependence, and Legal Change', *European Journal of Law and Economics*, 20 (2005), 43; S. K. Schmidt, 'Gefangen im "lock in"? Zur Pfadabhängigkeit der Rechtsprechung des Europäischen Gerichtshofs', *Der Moderne Staat*, 2 (2010), 455.

least, there is no longer a blank slate to proceed from if a similar question arises later in time.[92] By insisting on coherence, judges effectively build a chain of dominos. If one case topples, chances are that those decisions standing in the same line will also fall. A 'path-breaking' case[93] sets a new tone for decisions to come, for instance when it becomes more efficient to continue down a particular road.[94]

Thirdly and closely related, this is a strong disincentive for proclaiming errors in the case law. The more decisions that are connected, the more dominoes standing in a chain, the less willing one might be to tip one over, in particularly if the troublesome precedent cements the start of a long row of cases. It is a proclivity that is self-reinforcing: the cost of departing from cases increases as the chain lengthens. This is an important consideration to bear in mind when assessing the ECJ's aversion to unconcealed departures and when contrasting it with the willingness of investment tribunals to do this.[95] Moreover, the assumption of logical perfection inherent in many approaches to systematicity easily breeds a belief in substantial perfection, which again stifles intra-systemic critique.

Fourthly, the move from correctness to coherence fosters a case law culture in which the critical gaze wanders from decision to decision; whatever the final verdict, be it application, distinguishing or overruling of a precedent, the court or tribunal will emerge triumphant in this closed contest between two or more products of adjudication. The impersonality of the system turns out to be a fiction. As the jurisprudence becomes thicker and thicker, it not only becomes possible but indeed imperative to answer sophisticated legal questions with reference to cases. There comes a point where precedents are no longer seriously questioned; think only of EU law primacy, fundamental rights or state liability. True, other actors can seek to regain their voice by reclaiming such innovations through treaty amendments or legislation. But the everyday supervision of the

---

[92] See Gerhardt (n. 69 above), p. 79 ('[T]he 81st justice to consider an issue previously decided by the Court will not write about that issues as if he were writing on a blank slate and ignore what the previous 80 justices have said – or the next 80 may say – about the issue before him.').

[93] Cf. K. Alter and S. Meunier-Aitsahalia, 'Judicial Politics in the European Community: European Integration and the Pathbreaking Cassis de Dijon Decision', *Comparative Political Studies*, 26 (1994), 535, 545 (emphasising the responses to a decision rather than its originality).

[94] Hathaway refers to this as 'increasing returns path dependence': Hathaway (n. 91 above), pp. 106–13.

[95] Cf. Ch. 6, B.

system is largely left to judges, a role that is by no means entirely self-assumed.

But there are several flies in the ointment that suggest that coherence ultimately remains a crutch rather than a replacement for normativity. It may be a useful fiction, but it remains a fiction.[96] From a legal perspective, consistency is important, but neither approaches which privilege formal validity nor ones which favour integrity put coherence at their apex, given that this would deprive law of its edge over facticity.[97] Insisting on coherence with 'wrong' decisions – however that may be established – would hardly be considered an appropriate exercise of the ECJ's function. The EU lays claim to being a 'community of law' informed by the principle of legality.[98] Indeed, the ECJ itself does not purport to subscribe to a doctrine of *stare decisis*.[99] It almost goes without saying that complete uniformity is impossible and undesirable, but coherence itself adds nothing to the adjudicator's toolbox to indicate when it ought to be overridden.

Furthermore, coherence alone does not provide any means to distinguish it from what might be called surface coherence. From a logical point of view, it is possible to be consistently and coherently wrong. Coherence is not sufficient for 'correct' adjudication, since the coherence of two legal decisions is consistent with the 'falsity' of both. Rather, the concept of coherence presupposes that a precedent is apposite. The upshot is that unsupported assertions of coherence demand a lot of trust. The ECJ is a particularly likely candidate in this respect, given its habitual lack of discursive reasoning and its many string citations.[100]

The following example concerning derogations in the field of direct taxation illustrates the point. EU law famously guarantees the mobility of 'factors of production', namely the free movement of workers, services, capital and the right of establishment in other Member States without

---

[96] Cf. G. Jellinek, *Allgemeine Staatslehre* (3rd edn, Springer, Berlin, 1922), p. 353.

[97] On the difference between consistency and integrity see R. Dworkin, *Law's Empire* (reprint edn, Hart, Oxford, 1998 (1986)), pp. 227–8.

[98] On the latter see A. von Bogdandy, 'Founding Principles' in A. von Bogdandy and J. Bast (eds.), *Principles of European Constitutional Law* (2nd edn, Hart & C. H. Beck, Oxford and Munich 2010), pp. 33–5.

[99] And even systems that do have ways of sidestepping unquestioning obedience, including the *per incuriam* doctrine (i.e. that judicial oversights do not bind) or reconceptualisation in the form of *obitering* unwelcome points.

[100] See Ch. 4, C.iii.(a).

hindrance and on equal grounds.[101] As it happens, national tax regimes can pose a serious constraint on these pan-European freedoms. But the rights are not absolute. They can, given overriding concerns relating to the public interest, be subject to restrictions. In fact, limits on cross-border mobility can be permissible where this is necessary to ensure the unity of a national tax system, which is a matter for each Member State. That was the nub of a series of cases that demonstrate the fickleness of coherence.

In *Bachmann*, Belgian revenue law made the deductibility of certain supplementary sickness and pension contributions for income tax purposes conditional upon these being paid in Belgium.[102] The ECJ had little difficulty in detecting indirect discrimination, since nationals of other Member States would most likely have concluded such arrangements outside of Belgium. But it decided that the measures at stake were justified as they were necessary to ensure the unity of the Belgian tax system, which offset such losses of revenue through the taxation of sums payable by the respective insurers.[103] In the Court's view, this may well have been impossible or at least fraught with difficulties in that case, with foreign enforcement actions, deposits and bilateral conventions all providing inadequate or speculative recovery options. Hence the only way to ensure tax cohesion was to deny deductibility, which accordingly was compatible with EU law.

When the point came up again in *Société Papillon*, the ECJ came down on the other side of the fence and refused to consider the restriction in question justified by the need to ensure the cohesion a national system of taxation.[104] The Court took care at the outset to point out the existence of that general rule of medium abstraction by express reference to *Bachmann*.[105] But it held that less restrictive measures existed for that purpose. The particular rules in question made an advantageous French group tax regime unavailable to parent companies where resident sub-subsidiaries were held through subsidiaries with registered offices in other Member States. The Court noted that such a cross-border structure could

---

[101] The basic primary law norms are TFEU Arts. 45, 56, 63, 49. For a general overview see C. Barnard, *The Substantive Law of the EU: The Four Freedoms* (3rd edn, Oxford University Press, 2010), chs. 8–11, 15.

[102] Case C-204/09 *Hanns-Martin Bachmann* v. *Belgian State* [1992] ECR I-249.

[103] *Ibid.* paras. 21–8.

[104] Case C-418/07 *Société Papillon* v. *Ministère du Budget, des Comptes publics et de la Fonction publique* (Fourth Chamber) [2008] ECR I-8947 (para. 62).

[105] *Ibid.* para. 43.

in fact affect the unity of the tax regime, since intra-group neutralisation would be upset. However, double counting of losses could be avoided by less restrictive means, such as by requesting the necessary information from the authorities of the other Member State or by permitting the company chain itself to provide such information in order to properly assess tax liability.[106] Hence the measure in question impermissibly infringed the right of establishment.

Société Papillon clearly sought to maintain the systemic coherence of EU law. It did so by iterating the possibility of justifying a fetter on the freedom of establishment in order to preserve the cohesion of a domestic tax regime. The different result does not matter as such: on the face of it, the result in *Bachmann* does not preclude that in *Société Papillon* and vice versa.

But such consistency, constructed by linking cases via a test of intermediate abstraction alone is only skin-deep. It is a negative analytical device and only rules out what is incoherent. It is tempting to treat selective juxtapositions as part of a deep-rooted rationality, but a negative coherence test alone cannot serve to that effect. The Court's habit of expressing itself curtly and eschewing broader explanations, both generally and specifically when it comes to derogations of the freedom of establishment,[107] does little to change this.

Close reading shows that *Bachmann* was noticeably more lenient vis-à-vis national restrictions and seemed prepared to rule out alternative measures if they were less likely to succeed; the fact that they were available 'in principle' did not automatically foil the national legislation if they were likely to be frustrated in practice.[108] *Société Papillon* conversely took a far more exacting approach concerning the justification of restrictions, asserting that practical difficulties alone were not a good reason for an inhibition of a freedom guaranteed by the treaties.[109]

Not only that, just a month earlier the same chamber as in *Société Papillon* – albeit with a different reporting judge – handed down the *Wannsee* judgment.[110] That case concerned German tax rules which

---

[106]   *Ibid.* paras. 55–61.
[107]   Cf. U. Forsthoff, *Niederlassungsfreiheit für Gesellschaften* (Nomos, Baden-Baden, 2006), p. 75.
[108]   Case C-204/09 *Hanns-Martin Bachmann* v. *Belgian State* [1992] ECR I-249 (para. 25).
[109]   Case C-418/07 *Société Papillon* v. *Ministère du Budget, des Comptes publics et de la Fonction publique* (Fourth Chamber) [2008] ECR I-8947 (para. 54).
[110]   Case C-157/07 *Finanzamt für Körperschaften III in Berlin* v. *Krankenheim Ruhesitz am Wannsee-Seniorenheimstatt GmbH* (Fourth Chamber) [2008] ECR I-8061.

in effect restricted the analogous right of establishment contained in Art. 31 of the EEA Agreement by catching German companies with permanent establishments in a Member State of the EEA (Austria, at the time) between a rock and a hard place.[111] Turning to the existence of a justification, the ECJ was of the opinion that the detrimental tax provision was perfectly logical and symmetrical and therefore validated by the need to guarantee the unity of the German tax regime.[112] The combined effects of different interacting tax systems that led to the unfavourable situation were considered insufficient to shake this assessment: Member States could not be asked to design their tax regime with foreign systems in mind; besides, any restriction was ultimately imputable to the other Member State.[113]

Again, the test for justifying inhibitions based on the cohesion of a national system of tax features prominently, thereby giving the impression of systemic coherence. And once more, the approach taken by the ECJ seems, by itself, quite plausible, with the subtext being 'sue in Austria!' But one can make a strong argument that it sits very uneasily with *Société Papillon* since it completely countermands the latter's enthusiasm for fiscal Europeanisation. Such disparities do not of course automatically suggest that one or the other case was wrongly decided, but they draw attention to the very real possibility of cracks being papered over by an overly heavy reliance on the coherence proxy. In other words, repeating a common test does not by itself ensure genuine coherence.

Despite reaching the opposed result in cases that revolve around the same point, *Société Papillon* distinguished neither *Bachmann* nor *Wannsee* explicitly.[114] It may very well have been that the Court did in fact consider (and discard) these precedents in its research or deliberations, that they were thought to be sufficiently addressed by the parties in their submissions or by the Advocate General, or that the ECJ was of the opinion that other cases expressed the salient points better. Nor is it of course a flaw per se not to mention all potentially pertinent cases, which will usually be impossible, impractical or simply unnecessary. But in a situation in which a legal decision-maker exercises public authority and is obliged to state the grounds for its judgments, it cannot rely on iteration alone to

---

[111] *Ibid.* paras. 36–9. Essentially, German law rescinded an earlier tax advantage by reintegrating the losses of the foreign establishment when assessing the principal's liability, but offsetting had been denied in Austria.

[112] *Ibid.* paras. 42–3, 54.   [113] *Ibid.* paras. 46–51.

[114] *Wannsee* also did not refer to *Bachmann*.

shore up its legitimacy, not least since it alone proclaims what is legal and what is illegal, which is the hallmark of its authority.[115]

In conclusion, distinguishing as a means to ensure coherence is a popular device at the Court. But like deductive reasoning in general and syllogisms in particular, coherence is best thought of as a supplementary test of negative control. It can flag decisions that might have to be revisited. But it alone cannot guarantee adequate adjudication. It is a 'good argument', presupposing all other things to be equal, nothing more. An argument is never truly dispositive,[116] but the ECJ generally seems tempted to treat coherence as such in a very Schmittian sense,[117] nurturing misguided views on dictation by precedent.

---

[115] Cf. N. Luhmann, *Das Recht der Gesellschaft* (5th edn, Suhrkamp, Frankfurt am Main, 1995), p. 69.

[116] See Neumann (n. 48 above), p. 85.

[117] See Schmitt (n. 79 above), pp. 112–13 ('Soweit das positive Recht die Rechtsbestimmtheit zu garantieren imstande ist und eine eindeutige Praxis hervorruft, ist die "Gesetzmäßigkeit" der Entscheidung ein Beweis ihrer Richtigkeit').

6

Avoiding ECJ precedents II

Departing

A Technique

Overruling a prior case is an exercise in walking the tightrope between stability and change in law.[1] Unlike distinguishing, the argumentative burden is not avoided by holding it inapplicable in the present context through more-or-less subtle manipulation, but by challenging the intrinsic rationale of the precedent outright. The dividing line between distinguishing and departing from a precedent is not always obvious or firm, since the former comes in varying degrees of intrusiveness. But legal practice in general has developed a fairly universal view of overruling or departing from a precedent, which revolves around abandoning the pertinent point of an earlier case.[2] It is perhaps best expressed by Llewellyn's laconic formulation of 'killing the precedent'.[3]

Overruling is not the same thing as reversing on appeal, which concerns changing the decision of a lower court in the same case and is an independent concept. Given the lack of appeals from the ECJ this is not focal here. Overruling refers to departing from a precedent, namely a prior case that normally has no procedural connection but appears instructive on account of relevant similarity. It is an act of refuting an earlier legal argument, and not necessarily a rejection of the outcome of a prior case.[4]

---

[1] No special meaning will be attached to any distinction between 'overruling' and 'departing from' a precedent. The former tends to be used in a hierarchical context or with reference to an adjudicatory body's own precedents.

[2] In distinguishing, the core idea of a precedent is preserved. On this view, the divergence between the two negative techniques is one of degree rather than type. See J. Raz, *The Authority of Law* (2nd edn, Oxford University Press, 2009), pp. 188–9.

[3] K. N. Llewellyn, *The Common Law Tradition: Deciding Appeals* (4th edn, Little, Brown, Boston, 1960), p. 87.

[4] This is sometimes expressed by saying the *ratio* rather than the decision is overruled. Cf. R. Cross and J. W. Harris, *Precedent in English Law* (4th edn, Clarendon Press, Oxford, 1991), pp. 131–2.

There is a temptation to consider overruling as a simple mirror image of the discussion on bindingness of precedent.[5] That would be imprecise. One might assume that *no* binding decision can be departed from. But at least according to formal precedent doctrines, *only* binding decisions can be overruled, since the others do not even exert compulsive force; they do not matter anyway. That, however, simultaneously overplays the bindingness point and neglects the burden imposed by earlier decisions in the argumentative practice of law. The position taken here is that, since all relevantly similar decisions allow for the borrowing of ideas to solve legal problems, *all* decisions can in principle be overruled. Besides its theoretical merits, this view also better explains actual practice, which will be examined shortly.

The precise technique of overruling or departing is rarely discussed in detail in legal systems that do not purport to be based on 'binding' precedent, such as EU law or public international law. The 'blank slate' premise is translated into an entitlement to normally depart freely as one sees fit. But the situation on the ground is more complex, with concepts such as legitimate expectations or requirements as to reason-giving weighing in on the exercise of departing from precedents.

In common law systems, overruling or departing tends to be discussed more watchfully, since too much leeway would make a mockery of the *stare decisis* postulate, which is conceived as an antidote to more-or-less openly acknowledged judicial law-making. The power to overrule is hence limited, but not entirely dismissed. All independent courts in a *Rechtsstaat*, common law or not, ultimately consider it their overriding objective to 'administer justice fairly and in accordance with the law'.[6]

Such a limitation is usually expressed in a set of rules on precedent, albeit ones that are derived from the common law, that is to say the courts themselves, and rarely if ever formalised.[7] In essence, only courts higher up the judicial ladder can overrule precedents. What is particularly important is that legal decision-makers from which there is no further appeal are afforded considerable leeway to depart from their own precedents. This

---

[5] On ECJ precedents' binding force see Ch. 8.

[6] These are the words of Lord Nichols in the House of Lords in *National Westminster Bank plc* v. *Spectrum Plus Ltd and ors* [2005] 2 AC 680 (para. 40) (in the context of prospective overruling). He further stated in his speech (para. 41): 'Rigidity in the operation of a legal system is a sign of weakness, not strength. It deprives a legal system of necessary elasticity.'

[7] *Ibid.* para. 39: 'In this country the established practice of judicial precedent derives from the common law. Constitutionally the judges have power to modify this practice.'

is the position of the Supreme Courts both in the US[8] and the UK.[9] They will overrule their own precedents, albeit not lightly. That instances of last resort claim the power to depart from their own precedents is as much, if not more, a matter of self-deprecation than self-aggrandisement.

All of this gives rise to the assumption that the ECJ will similarly not shy away from overruling its precedents. Not only is it situated in a system that does not officially recognise precedents as binding, it is also an instance of last resort. The ECJ can hear appeals from the GC on points of law under TFEU Art. 256, but its own decisions cannot be appealed. The absence of direct judicial correction is compounded by the fact that in this particular supranational context the alternative routes for adjusting jurisprudential developments, in other words the equivalent of legislative or constitutional amendment in a domestic setting, are often cumbersome or politically naïve. That should not be taken to mean that the political and judicial processes in the EU are ignorant of each other. Far from it. But it does hint at a possibility of different ways of adjusting unwanted developments and remedying adjudicatory sclerosis.

When and how to depart is a difficult question. The concept of binding-ness disappoints, since it either precludes or replaces any nuanced inquiry. Probably the most prominent discussions by legal decision-makers in more recent times are the ruminations of the US Supreme Court. They provide a good starting point. The Supreme Court expressly confronted departing from precedents in *Casey*, a key case on abortion in which it was once again asked to overrule its famous *Roe* decision.[10] Its judgment was deeply divided, with a narrow plurality upholding the core of *Roe*.

---

[8] See US SC, *United States* v. *Scott* 437 US 82, 101 (1978), quoting from US SC, *Burnet* v. *Coronado Oil & Gas Co* 285 US 393, 406–8 (1932) (Brandeis J, dissenting): '[I]n cases involving the Federal Constitution, where correction through legislative action is practically impossible, this Court has often overruled its earlier decisions. The Court bows to the lessons of experience and the force of better reasoning, recognizing that the process of trial and error, so fruitful in the physical sciences, is appropriate also in the judicial function.'; US SC, *Garcia* v. *San Antonio Metropolitan Transit Authority* 469 US 528, 557 (1985); R. H. Fallon, '*Stare Decisis* and the Constitution', *New York University Law Review*, 76 (2001), 570, 572 (with further examples). Note that overruling is of course also an option in non-constitutional (i.e. 'statutory') cases, even if it tends to be met with more hesitancy there.

[9] The practice of what is now the UK Supreme Court reverted back to this original flexible stance following the House of Lords' famed Practice Statement (Judicial Precedent) [1966] 1 WLR 1234 after it had temporarily adopted a 'pretention to infallibility' at the beginning of the twentieth century. See UK HL, *R* v. *Shivpuri* [1987] AC 1 (Lord Bridge, p. 14).

[10] US SC, *Planned Parenthood of Southeastern Pennsylvania* v. *Casey* 505 US 833 (1992); *Roe* v. *Wade* 410 US 113 (1973).

Channelling Cardozo, it drew attention to potentially conflicting requirements of society concerning normativity, continuity and feasibility, and listed a non-exhaustive catalogue of situations when it might overrule its precedents.[11] These are united by the need for a 'special reason over and above the belief that a prior case was wrongly decided'[12] and 'notwithstanding an individual Justice's concerns about the merits',[13] thus evincing some traits of a 'true' doctrine of precedent that affords decided cases a degree of durability. At the same time, the plurality suggested a 'prudential and pragmatic' calculus, 'designed to test the consistency of overruling a prior decision with the ideal of the rule of law, and to gauge the respective costs of reaffirming and overruling a prior case'.[14]

Once again the argumentative nature of legal discourse shines through. There is no hard-and-fast rule or commitment when to overrule. Rather, this has to be argued for by invoking normativity (i.e. what is just or otherwise required) and by appealing to concrete consequences (i.e. policy, empirical points, social utility). The *Casey* plurality's approach by no means meets everyone's approval,[15] but it has proved very influential if one considers more recent decisions.[16] In *Citizens United*, a 2010 decision permitting 'big money' corporate spending in electoral campaigns by way of free speech, the US Supreme Court overruled ('reconsidered') a precedent that allowed for the restriction of certain corporate expenditures, thus reverting to its prior position.[17] Without explicitly referring to *Casey*, very similar considerations were mentioned, such as workability, general developments and changing factual circumstances since the precedent was decided ('experience') and the reliance interests at stake.

The Chief Justice in particular devoted several pages to the methodology of overruling and how it applied to the case at hand.[18] His exposition drips with flexible, non-absolutist language: how much 'weight to give to

---

[11] *Ibid.* pp. 854–5. For a similar enumeration in a German context see L. Kähler, *Strukturen und Methoden der Rechtsprechungsänderung* (2nd edn, Nomos, Baden-Baden, 2011), pp. 83–94.

[12] *Ibid.* p. 864.   [13] Stevens J, concurring in part and dissenting in part (p. 912).

[14] *Ibid.* p. 854.

[15] See e.g. M. S. Paulsen, 'The Worst Constitutional Decision of All Time', *Notre Dame Law Review*, 78 (2003), 995, 998, 1035 (expressing bewilderment that it took the court 203 years to come up with a 'Grand Theory of Egregious Error Entrenchment').

[16] See e.g. US SC, *Lakhdar Boumediene* v. *George W Bush* 553 US 723 (2008) (Scalia J, dissenting) (p. 17).

[17] US SC, *Citizens United* v. *Federal Election Committee* 558 US 310 (2010) (pp. 20, 47–50).

[18] US SC, *Citizens United* v. *Federal Election Committee* 558 US 310 (2010) (Roberts CJ, concurring) (pp. 5–14).

stare decisis'? What was the 'preferred course'? Was there a 'special justification' for abandoning the precedent? What did a 'sober appraisal of disadvantages' reveal? Which 'considerations weighed against retaining' the precedent? In the end, after 'conducting this balancing', he agreed that '*stare decisis* is not an end in itself' and not an 'inexorable command'. Just as the majority had held, it was a 'principle of policy and not a mechanical formula'.[19] One had to 'balance the importance of having constitutional questions *decided* against the importance of having them *decided right*'.[20] Coming from the head of the judicial branch of a prominent common law system, this is remarkable.

Three points are worth bearing in mind before turning to the ECJ. First, even in systems formally purporting to abide by precedents this practice is argumentative, the question being whether or not there is a convincing interest that justifies repeating the prior case's essence. That will often involve an assessment of repudiation costs but can also include non-consequentialist (e.g. doctrinal) considerations. Secondly, regardless of the difficulty of doing so, the very fact that at least some argumentation is required implies that the burden is on whoever subsequently seeks to come to a different conclusion on a particular point.[21] Thirdly, departing from precedents too can be an act of system maintenance. Earlier cases are weeded out because of an impression that the overarching circumstances, be they legal, factual or otherwise, demand a different solution. The difference with respect to distinguishing is that prior legal information is replaced rather than supplemented.

B Practice: faux infallibility

While the ECJ is quite willing to distinguish cases, it is loath to openly depart from precedents. To use the words of a former Advocate General, express departures from earlier cases are 'as few as they are celebrated'.[22]

---

[19] This was a quote from US SC, *Helvering* v. *Hallock* 309 US 106, 119 (1940).

[20] US SC, *Citizens United* v. *Federal Election Committee* 558 US 310 (2010) (Roberts CJ, concurring), p. 6 (original emphasis).

[21] See US SC, *Citizens United* v. *Federal Election Committee* 558 US 310 (2010) ('Our precedent is to be respected *unless* the most convincing of reasons demonstrates that adherence to it puts us on a course that is sure error.' p. 47; emphasis added).

[22] Case C-262/96 *Sema Sürül* v. *Bundesanstalt für Arbeit* [1999] ECR I-2685, Opinion of AG La Pergola (fn. 35). See also P. Demaret, 'Le Juge et le jugement dans l'Europe d'aujourd'hui: la Cour de justice des Communautés européennes' in R. Jacob (ed.), *Le Juge et le jugement dans les traditions juridiques européennes* (Libr. Générale de Droit et le Jurisprudence, Paris, 1996), p. 342.

This is corroborated by fact that there was no explicit departure from prior jurisprudence in the fifty-two Grand Chamber decisions of 2010. This is not only remarkable in light of the vast body of existing decisions and the close to 1,000 citations thereto made by those judgments surveyed, but also because one would expect such a *revirement*, if anywhere, to be undertaken by the Grand Chamber, given its general guiding function.

Nonetheless, it would be hasty to elevate this tendency befitting of the Court's general style to a fundamental tenet. There is no objection in principle to departing from prior jurisprudence. Despite its insistence on legal certainty and predictability, the ECJ has since its inception generally preferred a dynamic and evolutionary methodology.[23] This also applies to its treatment of past decisions.

To give an example, the Court in 2010 openly considered overruling itself in *Akzo Nobel*.[24] One consistently delicate matter in competition investigations is whether access to documents between an undertaking and its in-house lawyers can be demanded. In *Akzo Nobel*, the ECJ dismissed an appeal against a GC judgment that denied legal professional privilege to internal communications between parties and their employed counsel. In so doing, it chose to follow a restrictive 1982 precedent.[25] Drawing on an evaluative review of Member States laws, that judgment had held that one fundamental condition warranting privilege was independence, which was lacking in a situation of salaried employment. Irrespective of whether or not this was a correct application of the precedent, the appellants in *Akzo Nobel* argued in the alternative that the Court should 'reinterpret' (i.e. overrule) it in light of changes 'in the legal landscape' since that case had been decided roughly thirty years ago.[26] The ECJ refused, but due to specifics rather than in principle. It considered there to have been insufficient evolution in the legal systems of the Member States to afford in-house counsel the same status as external lawyers in private practice concerning legal professional privilege. Four points can be gleaned from this episode.

First, as has already been alluded to, the ECJ is certainly alive to the possibility of changing its jurisprudence, notwithstanding its general reluctance. Neither the judges, nor the Advocate General in her opinion, nor

---

[23] See R. Mehdi, 'Le Revirement jurisprudentiel en droit communautaire' in J. Bourrinet (ed.), *L'Intégration européenne au XXIe siècle: en hommage à Jacques Bourrinet* (La Documentation Française, Paris, 2004), p. 114.

[24] Case C-550/07 P *Akzo Nobel Chemicals Ltd and Akcros Chemicals Ltd* v. *Commission* (Grand Chamber) [2010] ECR I-8301.

[25] Case 155/79 *AM & S Europe Limited* v. *Commission* [1982] ECR 1575.

[26] *Ibid.* para. 65.

the Commission appeared in principle to have a problem with the Court reversing its precedents; they were simply not persuaded that a qualitative survey of the Member State laws supported the appellants' contention, hence considering a departure unwarranted. This further fits with the recurrent assertion that the Court is not bound by its precedents, which will be addressed later.

Secondly, this possibility of revisiting precedents is of course not lost on other participants in the Union legal system. Not only do litigants challenge existing decisions, as *Akzo Nobel* exemplifies, but national courts, the crucial collaborators in the decentralised system of the EU,[27] regularly seek to provoke departures from precedents or novel judicial developments through requests for preliminary rulings under what is now TFEU Art. 267.[28] The Court will often respond to this defensively by 'clarifying' its case law.[29]

A recent case in this respect is *Lady & Kid*, a reference from the Danish *Østre Landsret* (Eastern Division of the High Court).[30] The applicants were denied reimbursements by the tax authorities for charges levied contrary to EU law because they had been spared employer contributions for that period according to the prevailing legislation at the time. The general right to a refund is well-established, but its qualifications long remained contentious. In *Hans Just* and a string of subsequent decisions, the ECJ had held that restitution by Member States of charges levied contrary to EU tax provisions was subject to the prohibition of unjust enrichment of the entitled party.[31] This would be the case where the improper burden was passed on to consumers or traders, in other words incorporated into

---

[27] See J. H. H. Weiler, 'The Transformation of Europe', *Yale Law Journal*, 100 (1990–1991), 2403, 2420–1; Editorial, 'The Court of Justice as the Guardian of National Courts – Or Not?', *European Law Review*, 36 (2011), 319 ('truism verging on banality'); R. Baratta, 'National Courts as "Guardians" and "Ordinary Courts" of EU Law: Opinion 1/09 of the ECJ', *Legal Issues of Economic Integration*, 38 (2011), 297, 307–9.

[28] See e.g. Joined Cases C-145/08 and C-149/08 *Club Hotel Loutraki AE and ors* v. *Ethnico Symvoulio Radiotileorasis* [2010] ECR I-4165, Opinion of AG Sharpston (para. 95).

[29] See e.g. Case C-17/05 *BF Cadman* v. *Health & Safety Executive* (Grand Chamber) [2006] ECR I-9583 (paras. 23, 43). Cf. U. Everling, 'On the Judge-Made Law of the European Community's Courts' in D. O'Keeffe and A. Bavasso (eds.), *Judicial Review in European Union Law: Liber Amicorum in Honour of Lord Slynn of Hadley*, 2 vols. (Kluwer Law International, The Hague, London & Boston, 2000), I, p. 40 (with further examples of 'corrections').

[30] Case C-398/09 *Lady & Kid A/S and ors* v. *Skatteministeriet* (Grand Chamber) [2011] ECR I-7375.

[31] Case 68/79 *Hans Just I/S* v. *Danish Ministry for Fiscal Affairs* [1980] ECR 501 (para. 26); Joined Cases C-192/95 to C-218/95 *Société Comateb and ors* v. *Directeur général des douanes et droits indirects* [1997] ECR I-165 (paras. 21–31).

the price. Almost thirty years later, the referring court in *Lady & Kid* now wanted to know whether such 'passing on' might also take the form of or be equivalent to an attendant elimination of employer contributions as provided for by Danish law. Given that *Hans Just* and its descendants are not infrequently read categorically in the sense of establishing a clearly defined and limited exception,[32] the reference effectively probed a reconsideration of the ECJ's precedents on this point by inviting the Court to actively shape the law on the repayment of improper charges and unjust enrichment with sizeable financial consequences either way. The Court replied with a clear signal, affirming the narrow interpretation and limiting unjust enrichment arguments to the circumstance of an increase in the price of goods to customers to accommodate the tax charge; unjust enrichment could not follow from savings made but only from direct 'passing on'.[33]

This irritation through national courts, genuine European courts in their own right, is vital, since cases might otherwise become so entrenched as to verge on the irremediable and thus sooner or later lead to anachronisms, especially in areas in which the workload of the Court is fairly light.[34] Anachronisms put at risk the Court's acceptance. This also explains why even after the relaxation of the reference requirement through the ECJ and its Rules of Procedure there remains the possibility for national courts to make references even if matters appear clear enough.

Thirdly, there is a parallel here with the Court's preference for string citations and the comparative dearth of in-depth case discussion. Reconsidering precedents demands argumentation. Even if one does not vest decided cases with any formal authority, replacing earlier solutions with new ones demands explanation since it implies that the past decision was either incorrect or otherwise considered undesirable. Departures that are not justified or made plain cause mistrust, suggesting adjudicatory *fiat* rather than reasoned decision-making.

Fourthly, as with all precedent techniques, the rate of departing from precedents varies according to the specific context. For instance, of the present study's data set, eleven of the fifty-two decisions of international

---

[32] Cf. Case C-398/09 *Lady & Kid A/S and ors* v. *Skatteministeriet* [2011] ECR I-7375, Opinion of AG Cruz Villalón (para. 37, fn. 24). Note that the AG however did not share such a narrow interpretation (paras. 38–42).

[33] *Ibid.* paras. 20, 25 ('sole exception').

[34] Cf. Joined Cases C-94/04 and C-202/04 *Federico Cipolla* v. *Rosaria Fazari (née Portolese)* [2006] ECR I-11421, Opinion of AG Poiares Maduro (paras. 28–9, fn. 17) (noting further that 'stability is not and should not be an absolute value').

investment tribunals that were scrutinised qualify as having departed from at least one otherwise pertinent decision at one point, putting the overall rate at just over 21 per cent. This greater flexibility is rooted in far looser institutional ties and keen interpretative rivalry. On the other hand, the corresponding percentages of the Warren and Burger courts of the US Supreme Court are said to have hovered somewhere between 2.5 and 2 per cent.[35] Studies concerning the practice of select higher courts in Germany have also come to percentages below 3 per cent.[36] The more homogenous, domestic setting is evident. The reasons underpinning the ECJ's apparent infallibility will be unravelled following an examination of the grounds for departing from its precedents.

C Grounds

i Precedent was incorrectly decided

It is every so often assumed that 'true' respect for precedent cannot allow for departures from past cases simply because they were decided incorrectly.[37] 'What is *stare decisis* if not a duty to repeat errors?', the argument goes. A first observation here would be that all non-domestic legal systems, including EU law, disclaim such a doctrine, as do most national systems.[38] But leaving that aside for a moment, while the 'true' view may have the benefit of lucidity, historical evidence suggests that in practice the matter was rarely that straightforward or pedantic. Even during what is traditionally considered to be the most stern period of precedent, the Victorian age in England, nonsensical, impeachable or unreasonable precedents were regularly ignored.[39] The need for certainty never did away with rival concerns. Indeed, it is hard to deny that an extreme take on fixity rests awkwardly with a judge's principal function to apply the law, rather than individual cases, and do justice, whatever

---

[35] See C. P. Banks, 'The Supreme Court and Precedent: An Analysis of Natural Courts and Reversal Trends', *Judicature*, 75 (1992), 262, 264. It is hard to pin down an accurate figure, given the different ways of going about quantitative assessment. What matters is the larger order of magnitude. For discussion of further studies concerning the US Supreme Court see Kähler (n. 11 above), pp. 246–52.

[36] See Kähler (n. 11 above), pp. 107–10.

[37] See F. Schauer, 'Precedent', *Stanford Law Review*, 39 (1986–1987), 575.

[38] For more detail see Ch. 8.

[39] See T. F. T. Plucknett, *A Concise History of the Common Law* (5th edn, Little, Brown, Boston, 1956), p. 350; J. H. Baker, *An Introduction to English Legal History* (4th edn, Butterworths, London, 2002), pp. 199–200.

that may ultimately entail. It was also always the view of the orthodox English doctrine of precedent that *rationes decidendi* bind, rather than cases as such; and the former are forever subject to being shaped through (re)interpretation. The rule of standing by things decided was hence often treated as a matter of degree – softer somewhere, more rigid elsewhere, such as in property law or constitutional matters – rather than a question of kind.

In short, the supposed litmus test of the common law thus becomes a common sense rule of thumb. That one needs a 'special reason over and above' the belief that a prior case was wrongly decided in order to depart is perfectly compatible with a general rule about sticking to past decisions. It is a conservative expression of the view that precedent is not an absolutely rigid command.[40] That view is readily transferrable. No rational decision-maker likes erratic behaviour, which can lie both in accepting a flawed argument and in rejecting one that makes sense.

The ECJ will readily if cautiously reconsider a previous decision if it thinks that it was wholly or partially decided wrongly.[41] This is apparent from the fact that it ensures that 'the law' is observed under TEU Art. 19(1) and that it does not prohibit repeat preliminary references on the same point under TFEU Art. 267, which signals a continuous readiness to be persuaded otherwise.[42]

One of the most prominent instances in recent years is *Metock*, a case on intra-European migration involving non-EU family members.[43] The case is intriguing not only on account of being one of the select instances of an explicit departure, but also because of the various grounds hinted at by the Court for departing from a precedent. Since it features several types of overruling, it bears sketching out the antecedents to that litigation.

In *Akrich*, the ECJ had held that leave to enter and remain in the territory of a spouse that is a citizen of the EU as granted by a particular regulation was contingent upon a non-Member State national's prior lawful residence in the Union.[44] The ruling sought to preclude inhibition of the

---

[40] See *Planned Parenthood of Southeastern Pennsylvania* v. *Casey* 505 US 833, 864 (1992).

[41] Cf. Joined Cases C-267/95 and C-268/95 *Merck & Co. Inc. and ors* v. *Europharm of Worthing Ltd* [1996] ECR I-6285, Opinion of AG Fennelly (para. 143).

[42] Although it may then afford them short shrift according to ECJ Rules of Procedure Art. 99, which stipulates that the ECJ may give its decision by reasoned order.

[43] Case C-127/08 *Blaise Baheten Metock and ors* v. *Minister for Justice, Equality and Law Reform* (Grand Chamber) [2008] ECR I-6241.

[44] Case C-109/01 *Secretary of State for the Home Department* v. *Hacene Akrich* [2003] ECR I-9607 (para. 50).

free movement of workers where these would be prevented from lawfully living together with their spouses. At the same time, the Court was clearly anxious not to sanction a circumvention of national immigration laws. After all, migration is traditionally hotly debated and touches upon sensitive matters close to the heart of national sovereignty and self-identity.[45] Precisely what influence EU law has on the all-important right of first entry of non-Member State family members was however left in doubt even after subsequent litigation. Enter an intricate 2004 directive that sought to redress this.[46] Every so often national legislation transposing that instrument however continued to reiterate the prior lawful residence restriction that had featured in *Akrich*. The question thus came up in *Metock* whether the directive precluded Member States from requiring prior lawful residence in order to benefit from its provisions. The Court held it could not and expressly 'reconsidered' the conclusion in *Akrich*.[47] The ECJ acknowledged the precedent's argumentative pull ('It is true that'), but did not seek to distinguish the case.[48]

While *Metock* can certainly also be understood as an illustration of the ECJ fixing a practically unworkable situation or getting rid of a doctrinal anachronism, it can also be seen as an instance in which the precedent, *Akrich*, was held to have been decided wrongly in the first place. The Court alluded to this by drawing attention to the reasoning of an earlier and a later judgment. They suggest that the benefits in question could – *contra Akrich* – not have been made dependent on the requirements as stipulated by said precedent.[49] Viewed in that light, even at the time *Akrich* was decided, Member States could not deny entry to third-country

---

[45] Cf. R. Hofmann and P. B. Donath, 'Die Asylverfahrensrichtlinie unter besonderer Berücksichtigung völkerrechtlicher Standards' in R. Hofmann (ed.), *Europäisches Flüchtlings- und Einwanderungsrecht* (Nomos, Baden-Baden, 2008), p. 19; J. Bast, *Aufenthaltsrecht und Migrationssteuerung* (Mohr Siebeck, Tübingen, 2011), pp. 6–23.

[46] Directive 2004/38/EC of the European Parliament and of the Council of 29 April 2004 on the right of citizens of the Union and their family members to move and reside freely within the territory of the Member States [1980] OJ L158/77.

[47] Case C-127/08 *Blaise Baheten Metock and ors v. Minister for Justice, Equality and Law Reform* [2008] ECR I-6241, para. 58. The German version is less diplomatic: 'Hieran ist jedoch nicht festzuhalten.'

[48] AG Poiares Maduro on the other hand seemed prepared to accept the more common route of distinguishing the precedent by limiting it to the specific situation of illicitly evading national immigration laws: '*Akrich* cannot have the general scope that the Member States ascribe to it.' *Ibid*. Opinion of AG Poiares Maduro (paras. 11–13).

[49] These are Case C-459/99 *Mouvement contre le racisme, l'antisémitisme et la xénophobie ASBL (MRAX) v. Belgian State* [2002] ECR I-6591 (para. 59) (decided previously and holding that 'the exercise of that right may be conditional on possession of a visa'); Case

family members that move with their EU spouses on the basis of lacking prior lawful residence. In other words, *Akrich* got it wrong. This change of mind is further apparent in the subsequent order in *Sahin*, which affirmed *Metock* and made no mention of the now defunct precedent.[50]

These adverse judgments are however not quite as conclusive as *Metock* might seem to indicate, with the Court couching its references in a guarded 'see, to that effect'.[51] True, those decisions had insisted that the right of entry of third-country spouses derived under European law from the respective family ties. But they left room for certain qualifications, albeit chiefly with visa and documentary requirements (i.e. evidentiary or declaratory matters) in mind. The issue hence ultimately turns on an interpretation of the relevant secondary legislation, which of course begs the question. Unlike *Akrich*, *Metock* saw no room for prior residence requirements, neither under the old legislation nor according to the present directive.[52]

This condition of interpretive uncertainty should not however be thought to be entirely unwelcome for the ECJ. That *Akrich* was at least arguable and not scolded as manifestly off the mark[53] does less damage to the overarching perception of continuity and previsibility of the Court's work. At the same time, saying that *Akrich* was decided wrongly (instead of simply unwisely or impractically) reinforces another cardinal theme, namely that of judicial passivity and impersonal law-application that does not illegitimately usurp political processes. By 'reconsidering' *Akrich*, the Court shows deference to 'the law' as mentioned in TEU Art. 19(1). The fact that the ECJ in *Metock* referred to two of its own cases to hold that *Akrich* was decided wrongly was the icing on the cake, quietly asserting the Court's authority just as it would seem to be slipping.

It should be apparent from this that saying that something is incorrect demands a degree of argumentative effort beyond simply saying something else is arguable.[54] The mere existence of an alternative view is not

---

C-157/03 *Commission* v. *Kingdom of Spain* (Second Chamber) [2005] ECR I-2911 (para. 28) (decided subsequently and stressing 'the family relationship alone').

[50] Case C-551/07 *Deniz Sahin* v. *Bundesminister für Inneres* [2008] ECR I-10453. See also Case C-34/09 *Gerardo Ruiz Zambrano* v. *Office national de l'emploi (ONEm)* [2011] ECR I-1177, Opinion of AG Sharpston (para. 138).

[51] Case C-127/08 *Blaise Baheten Metock and ors* v. *Minister for Justice, Equality and Law Reform* [2008] ECR I-6241, para. 58.

[52] *Ibid.* paras. 59–70.

[53] The *a fortiori* argument adopted *ibid.* para. 59 is particularly telling.

[54] Unconvinced that a departure was necessary, AG Sharpston once noted in a case that the criticisms submitted were at most 'an alternative analysis which is not without attraction

sufficient. While this can be conceptualised as a pure matter of persuasion, it is in fact not too dissimilar from the common law exhortation noted earlier that a 'special reason over and above the belief that a prior case was wrongly decided' needs to be adduced, for example by showing that the new solution is in the interest of uniformity of legal protection.[55] This introduces an important degree of inertia and thus stability into EU law, checking the pace of legal change. Without it, it would be hard to imagine pronouncements of the Court having much weight at all beyond individual disputes.

ii Precedent is unworkable in practice

Sometimes the cost of continuing a certain strand of jurisprudence is considered to outweigh the harm resulting from abandoning it. In other words, the precedent is no longer considered feasible or workable. *Metock* is again a good example.[56] Quite how *Akrich* and its requirement of prior lawful residence fit with the subsequent secondary legislation had caused considerable hesitation and insecurity both among national courts and affected families.[57] Clearly, the ECJ considered the state of affairs untenable. One indication is the swiftness with which the precedent was reassessed. Not only was *Akrich* not even five years old at the time, but the President of the Court also saw it fit to order accelerated procedure.[58] The Court in *Metock* was of the view that Member State reaction to *Akrich* had disrupted 'normal family life' and frustrated the exercise of guaranteed freedoms.[59]

Viewed in this light, *Metock* did not only impugn the accuracy of *Akrich* but also the workability of the decision in practice. To be sure, the Member States could have understood and used *Akrich* differently. But they did not, so that the Court considered it necessary to put its foot

---

but which is by no means... the sole and inescapable interpretation of the legislation': Case C-460/07 *Sandra Puffer* v. *Unabhängiger Finanzsenat, Außenstelle Linz* [2009] ECR I-3251, Opinion of AG Sharpston (para. 56).

[55] Cf. Mehdi (n. 23 above), pp. 120–4.

[56] Case C-127/08 *Blaise Baheten Metock and ors* v. *Minister for Justice, Equality and Law Reform* (Grand Chamber) [2008] ECR I-6241.

[57] See e.g. C. Costello, 'Metock: Free Movement and "Normal Family Life" in the Union', *Common Market Law Review*, 46 (2009), 587, 595–6 (speaking of deleterious 'legal limbo' and 'contradictory, erroneous rulings').

[58] See D. Chalmers, 'The Secret Delivery of Justice', *European Law Review*, 33 (2008), 773.

[59] Case C-127/08 *Blaise Baheten Metock and ors* v. *Minister for Justice, Equality and Law Reform* [2008] ECR I-6241, paras. 62, 64.

down quickly in what had become a rather messy situation. This stance is not fundamentally different from the English position, where wrongness is not necessary for the Supreme Court to depart from its precedents.[60] It is effectively the inverse of refusing to overrule where this would cause a great deal of hardship or even chaos, such as if the ECJ were to consider abandoning its direct effect, primacy or state liability jurisprudence.

iii Legal anachronism I: incompatibility with subsequent decisions

In a perfectly rational and orderly world, relevantly similar cases would be decided with complete cognisance and consideration of each other. But information, including information about EU law, is not always generated and distributed hierarchically and certainly not in uniform and streamlined ways. Law built up through a mesh of cases tends to be muddled – or, perhaps more euphemistically, organic, as in Tennyson's familiar lines about the 'codeless myriad of precedent, that wilderness of single instances, through which a few, by wit or fortune led, may beat a pathway'.[61] That fertility is not necessarily down to design, but rather due to the banal fact that different people decide different points at different points in time. It presents a powerful motivation to reconsider and revise precedents.

A case from the ECJ in this mould is *HAG II*, a preliminary ruling on the relation between the free movement of goods and trade mark protection.[62] The dispute arose from the curious incident that the identical brand of decaffeinated coffee ('HAG') was owned by different parties in different Member States on account of the post-war expropriation of a wholly owned Benelux subsidiary of a German company together with its marks. When the German company sought to import coffee to Luxembourg in the early 1970s, litigation ensued in which the ECJ ruled by way of reference that a prohibition based solely on identical marks having the same origin would be incompatible with the free circulation of goods.[63] That was *HAG I* and its so-called doctrine of common origin, which was rooted in a fear of dividing markets through territorialist national provisions on

---

[60] Cf. Cross and Harris (n. 4 above), p. 138 (on its immediate predecessor).

[61] A. Tennyson, *Aylmer's Field* (Macmillan, London & New York 1891), p. 14. His lines are both datedly romantic and revealing in their description of the 'lawless science' of law. Cf. D. Hunter, 'No Wilderness of Single Instances: Inductive Inference in Law', *Journal of Legal Education*, 48 (1998), 365.

[62] Case C-10/89 *SA CNL-SUCAL NV* v. *HAG GF AG ('HAG II')* [1990] ECR I-3711.

[63] Case 192–73 *Van Zuylen frères* v. *Hag ('HAG I')* [1974] ECR 731.

intellectual property.[64] *HAG II* was concerned with the contrary situation. This time, the owner of the Benelux mark imported coffee to Germany. An injunction swiftly followed, as did another request for a preliminary ruling, in which the *Bundesgerichtshof* (the German Federal Court of Justice) this time essentially invited the ECJ to reconsider its doctrine of common origin where this might confuse consumers. The Court largely acceded, buoyed by a punchy opinion of its Advocate General that tackled the overruling point head-on with considerable detail.[65] Amongst other things, he drew attention to several judgments that the ECJ had handed down in the intervening sixteen years between *HAG I* and *HAG II*. In his view these had chipped away at the former's rationale by evincing an increasing appreciation of intangible property rights in general and a better understanding of the consumer protection function of trade marks in particular.

This evidently struck a chord with the Court, which considered it necessary to reconsider *HAG I* 'in the light of the case-law which has developed'.[66] Emphasising consumer protection and a lack of consent in the present situation, it concluded that – despite the common origin of the brands – each of the trade mark proprietors had the right to oppose importation and marketing in so far as this would likely cause confusion.

Three things are worth noting. First, although questions remained as to the precise scope of this (over)ruling, it amounted to a plain reversal of an applicable precedent by the ECJ that was justified by reference to its own intermediary output. Secondly, while the plausibility of that argument is open to doubt,[67] the Court once again presented its conclusion as 'necessary'. Thirdly, the doctrinal anachronism reasoning rests alongside other grounds for overruling *HAG I*, including that the precedent was erroneously decided in the first place[68] or that it was guilty of unsettling

---

[64] *Ibid.* paras. 11–13.

[65] Case C-10/89 *SA CNL-SUCAL NV* v. *HAG GF AG* (*'HAG II'*) [1990] ECR I-3711, Opinion of AG Jacobs (paras. 22–50, 67). Note that neither party had an interest in completely demolishing the precedent, given that one had originally benefited from it and the other now wanted to rely on it in this mirror situation.

[66] *Ibid.* para. 10.

[67] See e.g. R. Joliet and D. T. Keeling, 'Trade Mark Law and the Free Movement of Goods: The Overruling of the Judgment in Hag I', *International Review of Industrial Property and Copyright Law*, (1991), 303, 309 (arguing that the cases adduced did not really presage such a change).

[68] As demonstrated by using the treaties as the ultimate yardstick. The Advocate General had suggested this angle when submitting that the doctrine of common origin was 'not a legitimate creature of Community law', presumably anticipating that the Court was most

a delicate balance between competing principles, namely free movement of goods and trade mark protection.[69]

Another example of a precedent being overruled for being incompatible with a subsequent decision of the Court is again *Akrich*, which was superseded by *Commission* v. *Spain* as interpreted by *Metock*.[70] In the later case the ECJ held that while certain formalities remained to be observed, the right of entry into the territory of a Member State granted to a non-European national who was the spouse of an EU national derived from the family relationship alone. It is difficult, if not impossible, to square this with the prior case. While *Commission* v. *Spain* itself made no mention of *Akrich*, the *Metock* judgment picked up on that later case in putting *Akrich* to rest.[71]

iv Legal anachronism II: incompatibility with other changes in the law

Sometimes doctrinal changes outside case law developments upset the recognition and application of an ECJ precedent. Like most law, EU law springs from various materials. Once more, *Metock* overruling *Akrich* is on point. The latter and its progeny imposed a requirement of prior lawful residence. In *Metock*, the Court noted that no provision of a post-dating directive made its application conditional on family members of a Union citizen having previously resided in a Member State.[72] In a similar vein, in *Grzelczyk* and *Bidar*, the ECJ noted that since it had decided its earlier more restrictive cases on student maintenance and training assistance, the TEU had introduced Union citizenship and added provisions on education and vocational training, necessitating a different appreciation of the situation.[73] In another case, a Member State being sued in an infringement action challenged the ECJ's case law on account of international law

---

likely to be persuaded by this least adventurous of grounds: Case C-10/89 *SA CNL-SUCAL NV* v. *HAG GF AG ('HAG II')* [1990] ECR I-3711, Opinion of AG Jacobs (para. 26).

[69] As shown by the repeated references to the essential function of trade marks (paras. 14–18).

[70] Case C-157/03 *Commission* v. *Kingdom of Spain* (Second Chamber) [2005] ECR I-2911; Case C-127/08 *Blaise Baheten Metock and ors* v. *Minister for Justice, Equality and Law Reform* (Grand Chamber) [2008] ECR I-6241.

[71] *Ibid.* paras. 56–8.

[72] Case C-127/08 *Blaise Baheten Metock and ors* v. *Minister for Justice, Equality and Law Reform* (Grand Chamber) [2008] ECR I-6241 (paras. 49–50). Indeed, the Advocate General had urged the Court to take changes brought about by the new directive into account: *Ibid.* Opinion of AG Poiares Maduro (para. 13).

[73] Case C-184/99 *Rudy Grzelczyk* v. *Centre public d'aide sociale d'Ottignies-Louvain-la-Neuve* [2001] ECR I-6193 (para. 35); Case C-209/03 *The Queen, on the application of Dany*

developments, specifically the WHO Framework Convention on Tobacco Control of 2003.[74] This, it was argued amongst other things, warranted a departure from the prior restrictive approach that forbade the imposition of minimum retail prices for cigarettes and other tobacco products. The Court followed the Advocate General in interpreting the WHO Convention not to conflict with its prior stance, but it is worth noting that it did not categorically dismiss the argument.

v Imbalance between principles

In a well-known episode that has been hailed as a 'milestone' and a 'momentous judgment' by some[75] and pilloried as ignorant of nothing less than that 'which is fundamental to the Western concept of law' by others,[76] the ECJ in *Les Verts* ruled that it could review the legality of acts of the European Parliament.[77] The bone of contention was the plainly missing treaty wording that had only recently been affirmed in the Single European Act of 1986. Whatever the merits of that interpretation, the Parliament could henceforth be a defendant in an action for annulment. With capacity to be sued out of the way, the Parliament then tackled its real objective, namely the right to bring proceedings itself.[78] However, standing was denied somewhat surprisingly and against the view of the Advocate General in the *Comitology* case, where the Court rejected any necessary parallel between the ability to defend and apply for judicial review.[79] In essence, it considered the system of the treaties to demand no more than judicial protection against institutional acts that are capable of

---

Bidar v. *London Borough of Ealing and Secretary of State for Education and Skills* (Grand Chamber) [2005] ECR I-2119 (paras. 38–9).

[74] Case C-197/08 *Commission* v. *French Republic* (Third Chamber) [2010] ECR I-1599.

[75] K. Lenaerts, 'The Basic Constitutional Charter of a Community Based on the Rule of Law' in M. Poiares Maduro and L. Azoulai (eds.), *The Past and Future of EU Law* (Hart, Oxford and Portland, 2010), pp. 295, 315.

[76] T. C. Hartley, *The Foundations of European Union Law* (7th edn, Oxford University Press, 2010), p. 73.

[77] Case 294/83 *Parti écologiste "Les Verts"* v. *Parliament* [1986] ECR 1339 (paras. 23–5). Ever since the Maastricht Treaty, what is now Art. 263 TFEU expressly extends to legislative acts, making this another example of the interplay between legislative and judicial actors in the EU.

[78] On this strategic sacrifice see the comments by one of the agents representing the Parliament in that case: J.-P. Jacqué, '*Les Verts v The European Parliament*' in M. Poiares Maduro and L. Azoulai (eds.), *The Past and Future of EU Law* (Hart, Oxford and Portland 2010), p. 317 ('just as Saint Sebastian opened himself up to the archers' arrows').

[79] Case 302/87 *Parliament* v. *Council ('Comitology')* [1988] ECR 5615 (paras. 19–21).

having legal effect. Various devices other than *locus standi* could achieve this, the ECJ opined, such as actions brought by the Commission or individuals.

Not even twenty months later, yet with new arrivals on the bench, the departure came in *Chernobyl*.[80] The Court now based its opposing approach on the preservation of institutional equilibrium, a theme familiar from *Les Verts*. The European institutions had to have due regard to each other in exercising their powers. Using the language of balancing competing concerns, the Court reasoned that the absence of treaty wording could not prevail over this 'fundamental interest'.[81] So while the departure from *Comitology* in *Chernobyl* could also be read as a case in which the precedent was incorrectly decided[82] or practically unworkable,[83] it further stands as an example of a reversal of jurisprudence that seeks to realign important principles in a more general sense. In *Comitology*, the Court had rejected an over-broad notion of the Parliament as an all-purpose 'defender of [Union] law',[84] but as *Chernobyl* insisted this could not lead to the other extreme of emaciating the defence of its own prerogatives or the effective and coherent system of legal protection established by the treaties.

A brief return to *Keck and Mithouard* is merited.[85] The case shows two things. Not only is it another instance in which the Court departed from a precedent to redress a perceived imbalance, it also proves that a departure from earlier jurisprudence does not have to amount to an across-the-board abandonment or wholesale epistemic eradication of a precedent. In this it demonstrates on a small scale the increasing intricacy of sequential reasoning with cases, which can be both a boon by showing individual concern when tailoring specific solutions to particular situations or a bane by escalating complexity and artificiality.

To recall, in one of the most famous lines of case law on the free movement of goods – the traditional meat and potatoes of EU law[86] – the ECJ in

---

[80] Case C-70/88 *Parliament* v. *Council ('Chernobyl')* [1988] ECR I-2041 (para. 27).

[81] *Ibid.* para. 26.

[82] Because the treaties had set up a system in which the standing of its institutions in actions for annulment was implicit.

[83] Because the alternative routes for preserving the Parliament's prerogatives were uncertain and inadequate.

[84] Case C-70/88 *Parliament* v. *Council ('Chernobyl')* [1988] ECR I-2041, Opinion of AG Van Gerven (para. 2).

[85] Joined Cases C-267/91 and C-268/91 *Criminal proceedings against Bernard Keck and Daniel Mithouard* [1993] ECR I-6097.

[86] In actual fact, surprisingly, often alcoholic beverages.

Keck and Mithouard rejected its celebrated *Cassis de Dijon* 'mutual recognition' rationale in so far as it was supposed to apply to 'selling arrangements' (e.g. rules on sales promotion, sale outlets, opening hours, resale at a loss) rather than 'product requirements' (e.g. rules on name, form, composition, packaging).[87] Provided they are non-discriminatory, the former were not even caught by the prohibition on quantitative restrictions on imports and all measures having equivalent effect between Member States found in what is now TFEU Art. 28.[88] The merits of this modification continue to be hotly debated, largely because of its seemingly naked assumption that such measures simply do not hinder trade and because of the difficulties of applying these categories in practice. But there can be little doubt that this marks a partial overruling of an otherwise applicable precedent. For one, the Court itself seemed to think so, deliberately ruling 'contrary to what has previously been decided'.[89] Moreover, as argued earlier, there is little point in denying that such jurisprudential innovation is an act of law-making or in rehearsing supposedly more polite synonyms such as 'refining', 'particularising' or 'rendering concrete' the law.[90] But while the establishment of this privileged first category marked a departure from precedent, *Keck and Mithouard* confirmed and followed *Cassis de Dijon* in respect of the latter category.[91] Product requirements, even if applicable indiscriminately to foreign and domestic products, were again held to come within the general treaty proscription.

This revisiting of *Cassis de Dijon* sprang from a desire to ensure market access and avoid economic protectionism while steering clear of excessive use of the treaties to torpedo any and all regulatory policies of the Member States as soon as they are commercially inconvenient to a trader.[92] Liberalisation of trade should not come at all costs.

In a similar vein, what was arguably at the heart in *Metock*, and hence led to a disapproval of *Akrich*, was a schism between the Court's

---

[87] Case 120/78 *Rewe-Zentral AG* v. *Bundesmonopolverwaltung für Branntwein* [1979] ECR 649.

[88] Joined Cases C-267/91 and C-268/91 *Criminal proceedings against Bernard Keck and Daniel Mithouard* [1993] ECR I-6097, para. 16.

[89] *Ibid.*

[90] Legislation can still be differentiated. See Ch. 2, F.i. Cf. F. Picod, 'La Nouvelle Approche de la Cour de justice en matière d'entraves aux échanges', *Revue Trimestrielle de Droit Européen*, 34 (1998), 169.

[91] Cf. the assessment in Case C-110/05 *Commission* v. *Italian Republic* [2009] ECR I-519, Opinion of AG Bot (paras. 65, 70).

[92] Joined Cases C-267/91 and C-268/91 *Criminal proceedings against Bernard Keck and Daniel Mithouard* [1993] ECR I-6097, para. 14.

preference for a rights-based take on immigration control and the more orthodox governmental-discretion approach that places a greater emphasis on sovereign autonomy.[93] Here, too, different principles were adjusted so that the latter did not swamp the former.

Ruiz Zambrano is yet another example.[94] The entire drama played out in one Member State: Belgium. There was no immediate cross-border element, which had until that time often been considered an essential ingredient in the determination of whether EU law was applicable in the first place. Whether or not Mr Zambrano's victory truly marked a paradigm shift, as the Advocate General seemed to suggest in her opinion, or just an isolated incident designed to redress particular hardship in cases involving dependent minors, as the unadorned reasoning of the ECJ and subsequent jurisprudence indicate,[95] the Court seemed content to define the position of third-country family members by looking to the fundamental status of Union citizenship. There is much force in the argument that the simple binary border-crossing test as a proxy for market activity is not what necessarily makes or breaks EU constitutional law. The right of EU citizens to reside freely in the Union is a question of EU law. Instead of obsessing with one (often artificially engineered) factual specificity, the Court was more concerned with the actual effect a national measure might have on rights afforded by the treaties. Viewed in this light, the ECJ did not fling open the floodgates, but it rebalanced EU citizenship and Member State regulatory autonomy where the latter threatened to completely cloud out the former.[96] This is a forever delicate and shifting, but never unilateral, exercise.

This ground for departing from precedents evidently has a strong substantive flavour and might at times seem to come close to more direct policy-making, such as when the ECJ rebalances the free movement of goods and the protection of intellectual and commercial property.[97] But there are of course constraints, not least that these principles are rooted in the respective treaties and have to be argued for convincingly in a legal setting. For example, purely ethical considerations in the absence of a

---

[93] See Costello (n. 57 above).

[94] Case C-34/09 *Gerardo Ruiz Zambrano* v. *Office national de l'emploi (ONEm) (Grand Chamber)* [2011] ECR I-1177.

[95] See Case C-256/11 *Murat Dereci and ors* v. *Bundesministerium für Inneres* (Grand Chamber) [2011] ECR I-11315.

[96] See P. van Elsuwege, 'Shifting the Boundaries? European Union Citizenship and the Scope of Application of EU Law', *Legal Issues of Economic Integration*, 38 (2011), 263, 272–6.

[97] See Case C-10/89 *SA CNL-SUCAL NV* v. *HAG GF AG ('HAG II')* [1990] ECR I-3711.

legal obligation were not considered a valid basis for derogating from a rule laid down in a prior case.[98]

vi Changed factual or societal premises

Occasionally a non-legal change might render the nub of a precedent irrelevant or unjustifiable. One of the most celebrated instances hereof in domestic legal systems, albeit one that is also very much suffused with heroic assumptions, is the unanimous overruling of the infamous *Plessy* precedent by the US Supreme Court in *Brown* when it rejected the 'separate but equal' doctrine.[99] Another well-known example is when the UK House of Lords in 1991 abolished the barbaric and anachronistic 'implied consent' common law fiction that served as a defence in cases of marital rape.[100]

There are no such dramatic examples in EU law. But the ECJ in *Akzo Nobel* considered whether the broader factual context had changed as concerns in-house legal professional privilege with a view to departing from one if its precedents, which it denied.[101] *Keck and Mithouard* also arguably fits this ground, since rules on selling arrangements had been excessively challenged by shrewd retailers exploiting the internal market rationale, necessitating a correction.[102] Furthermore, as AG La Pergola observed in *Sema Sürül*, 'new matters' may generally lead to different decisions compared to earlier answers given in preliminary references.[103]

In any event, the contextual change must of course still be relevant. In *Merck*, the patent holders argued that patent protection had in the meanwhile become the norm, whereas it had previously been the exception. The Court bluntly replied that this was true, but that it did not mean that the underlying rule was superseded.[104] The danger of a patent

---

[98] See Joined Cases C-267/95 and C-268/95 *Merck & Co. Inc. and ors* v. *Primecrown Ltd and ors* [1996] ECR I-6285 (para. 53).

[99] US SC, *Brown* v. *Board of Education of Topeka*, 347 US 483 (1954); US SC, *Plessy* v. *Ferguson*, 163 US 537 (1896).

[100] UK HL, *R* v. *R* [1992] 1 AC 599.

[101] Case C-550/07 P *Akzo Nobel Chemicals Ltd and Akcros Chemicals Ltd* v. *Commission* (Grand Chamber) [2010] ECR I-8301.

[102] Joined Cases C-267/91 and C-268/91 *Criminal proceedings against Bernard Keck and Daniel Mithouard* [1993] ECR I-6097.

[103] Case C-262/96 *Sema Sürül* v. *Bundesanstalt für Arbeit* [1999] ECR I-2685, Opinion of AG La Pergola (para. 36).

[104] Joined Cases C-267/95 and C-268/95 *Merck & Co. Inc. and ors* v. *Primecrown Ltd and ors* [1996] ECR I-6285 (para. 34).

holder restricting trade and splitting markets was still present. If a patent holder put a product on the market in a Member State where it is was not patentable, he would have to accept the consequences of his choice as regards the possibility of parallel imports. Patent protection was hence not expanded accordingly.

D Factors

i Precedent weight: the threshold

Just as elsewhere, in ECJ litigation precedent departures ultimately occur when the respective decision-makers are convinced that there is a better decision than the earlier one. What is at stake is essentially the rationality of rule-following. This can be conceptualised as a broad cost–benefit assessment, but it need not in fact be an exercise in precise 'social mathematics' and can naturally involve considerations that are typically considered to be 'classical' legal arguments. Nevertheless, this examination of the quality of prior reasoning in the widest sense is not limited to doctrinal arguments.[105] It can be rephrased as a question concerning a precedent's weight. At the end of the day, this requires a specific assessment of the particular prior and current legal and factual situation, which is why it is impossible to generalise as to when a departure will occur. Without demeaning the entire enterprise as a pure matter of personal ideology, questions of legal method are, ultimately, questions of substance; precedent logic is case-by-case reasoning in the truest sense.

Various factors play into this step, none of which can on account of the argumentative nature of precedent and law in general be excluded *a priori*. Nor can any of these claim for itself to be guaranteed to exclusively and decisively regulate the matter.

Quite how difficult it is to try to permanently ascribe a precise effect to one of these factors can be teased out by a brief consideration of the age of precedents that were later reconsidered. One might think the ECJ more eager to overrule old precedents, but at the same time age can suggest a tried and tested solution or heavy reliance, which militates against a departure.

---

[105] Cf. L. Coutron, 'Style des arrêts de la Cour de justice et normativité de la jurisprudence communautaire', *Revue Trimestrielle de Droit Européen*, 45 (2009), 643, 665 (referring to the ECJ's rejection of the departure proposed by its Advocate General in the interest of legal certainty in Case C-461/03 *Gaston Schul Douane-expediteur BV v. Minister van Landbouw, Natuur en Voedselkwaliteit* (Grand Chamber) [2005] ECR I-10513).

When the ECJ is confronted with precedents that have seen quite a few years since their handing down, this is not infrequently alluded to in a disapproving way by aggrieved parties, often by reference to the generally accepted notion that the EU is a dynamic legal order. For example, the precedent sought to be dislodged by the appellants in *Akzo Nobel* dated from 1982.[106] Nevertheless, the ECJ was not swayed by this. Similarly, in *Urszula Ruhr*, Advocate General Alber noted that the salient case law which was called into question had been established twenty-five years ago.[107] Yet in the end he also did not consider this alone decisive, but rather concentrated on a more substantive argument. On the other hand, in *Metock* the Court did not hesitate to revisit a case that was not even five years old.[108] And if one considers *Dereci* to have qualified the previous leading case on Union citizenship in the sense of not simply distinguishing it without modification, which is highly arguable, only thirty-six weeks had passed between those two decisions, with the earlier case not even having been published in the official series of reports at the time.[109]

In short, precedent age is by itself neither here nor there, at least given the current constellation of the decisions available to the Court. It may well be that, going forward, open acts of overruling will increase on account of the greater likelihood of changed factual or societal premises.[110] The vast majority of precedents are presently only a few decades old. But in principle, a case may have engendered considerable justifiable reliance over time, just as it may have caused considerable confusion. The ECJ is not extraordinary in this respect. In its prior incarnation as the House of Lords, the UK Supreme Court explicitly overruled a case for the first time following its change of precedent practice in the mid-twentieth century just one year and six days after handing down the impugned judgment.[111]

---

[106] See e.g. Case C-550/07 P *Akzo Nobel Chemicals Ltd and Akcros Chemicals Ltd* v. *Commission* (Grand Chamber) [2010] ECR I-8301 (para. 62).

[107] Case C-189/00 *Urszula Ruhr* v. *Bundesanstalt für Arbeit* [2001] ECR I-8225, Opinion of AG Alber (paras. 53–6)

[108] Case C-127/08 *Blaise Baheten Metock and ors* v. *Minister for Justice, Equality and Law Reform* (Grand Chamber) [2008] ECR I-6241 (para. 58).

[109] Case C-256/11 *Murat Dereci and ors* v. *Bundesministerium für Inneres* (Grand Chamber) [2011] ECR I-11315 (paras. 64–8).

[110] Cf. S. Brenner and H. J. Spaeth, *Stare Indecisis: The Alteration of Precedent on the Supreme Court, 1946–1992* (Cambridge University Press, 1995), p. 29 (noting that US Supreme Court cases that were older than ninety years were particularly likely to being overruled).

[111] The ill-fated precedent was UK HL, *Anderton* v. *Ryan* [1985] AC 560, a case on the law of criminal attempts. As Lord Bridge put it in UK HL, *R* v. *Shivpuri* [1987] AC 1 (p. 14): 'First, I am undeterred by the consideration that the decision in *Anderton* v. *Ryan* was so

Besides a precedent's age, a non-exhaustive enumeration of aspects that can further factor into such a calculus includes the nature of the underlying legal basis;[112] the specific area of law;[113] the composition of the previous adjudicatory body;[114] the overall degree of reliance placed on the decision in the meanwhile;[115] Member State and EU institutional acceptance; acceptance by other judges and Advocates General (including the amount of prior distinguishing); academic reception; serious unfairness or financial consequences stemming from the decision; and the capacity of the subsequent decision-maker to properly exercise its function and protect the integrity of its respective role.[116]

As elsewhere, there is no algorithm that determines when the ECJ should overrule a case.[117] Probably the closest one can get to describing this exercise without being infelicitous to the perplexing array of potentially unlimited influences and thus giving a skewed account is to note that the ECJ and those using it are not solely obsessed with hermeneutics but instead engage in a broader application of context-sensitive practical reasoning that assesses the salience of a prior case.[118]

---

recent... If a serious error embodied in a decision of this House has distorted the law, the sooner it is corrected the better.'

[112] E.g. the US Supreme Court is traditionally said to be more flexible when dealing with 'constitutional' rather than 'statutory' precedents. See W. N. Eskridge Jr, 'Overruling Statutory Precedents', *Georgetown Law Journal*, 76 (1987–1988), 1361, 1362 (the idea being that amending the US Constitution is a very difficult process compared to amending an ordinary statute, hence demanding a safety valve to deal with obsolete doctrine). Similarly, a reading of the treaties might be more malleable than the gloss on an arcane provision of secondary law.

[113] E.g. it is unlikely that the ECJ would readily overthrow fundamental constitutional building blocks such as primacy, direct effect and Member State liability.

[114] Concerning the ECJ, a chamber of three or five judges will be slow to confront a Grand Chamber decision.

[115] E.g. think of the effect EU free movement of persons and rights of residence have on household structures and family ties. Indeed, the UK Supreme Court in its prior incarnation has made it known over time that it takes into account novel reasons and the absence of justified reliance in situations where a relevant improvement of the law is attainable. See Cross and Harris (n. 4 above), pp. 138–43.

[116] Cf. T. W. Morrison, '*Stare Decisis* in the Office of Legal Counsel', *Columbia Law Review*, 100 (2010), 101, 161.

[117] Cf. L. Alexander, 'Precedential Constraint, its Scope and Strength: A Brief Survey of the Possibilities and their Merits' in T. Bustamante and C. Bernal Pulido (eds.), *On the Philosophy of Precedent* (Franz Steiner, Stuttgart, 2012), pp. 81–2.

[118] Cf. Case C-110/05 *Commission* v. *Italian Republic* [2009] ECR I-519 Opinion of AG Bot (para. 102) (stating that he saw 'no reason for departing from [the current] analytical approach').

Two tentative frameworks with three steps each are sketched next by way of example, not in order to gauge whether they impose 'strict' bindingness, but rather as possible avenues to explore when considering whether or not to follow a precedent of the Court. At the end of the day, such considerations are at best rough frameworks to channel thoughts; they neither impose mandatory decisional exclusivity nor are they guaranteed to lead to 'proper' precedent-following. What they can do is help to structure legal discourse on the issue and point out the more egregious jumps and leaps by way of a supplementary negative check.

ii Equality and non-discrimination: a tentative test

Precedent draws heavily on the intuitive appeal of treating like cases alike. The underlying idea finds expression in most legal systems. Equal treatment is an important tenet of EU law, expressed or contained in numerous treaty provisions and often given special expression in particular secondary legislation. But even absent an explicit clause it applies as a general principle of EU law.[119]

Three important caveats need to be made at the outset. First, the idea is not to use this model to directly assess the exercise of the judicial function. The idea is rather to inform precedent-handling. Secondly, such commitments do not demand complete equality. Evidently, the ECJ's loadstar is that the law of the EU is observed. This might, of course, demand unequal treatment. The German FCC, for instance, has repeatedly considered the administration of justice to necessarily be 'constitutionally uneven'.[120] That conclusion also flows from the independence of the judges. Thirdly, equal treatment demands parity at the moment a norm is applied, not over time. That is another reason why the concept is ill-suited as a basis for 'strict' *stare decisis* as it is commonly understood.

What equality and non-discrimination demand is that comparable situations be treated similarly, and non-identical situations not be treated identically. Different treatment alone is not sufficient, since it might either be warranted on account of different situations or be justifiable in similar

---

[119] See e.g. Case C-236/09 *Association Belge des Consommateurs Test-Achats and ors* v. *Conseil des ministres* (Grand Chamber) [2011] ECR I-773 (para. 28). For a plethora of older case law see K. P. E. Lasok and T. Millett, *Judicial Control in the EU: Procedures and Principles* (Richmond Law & Tax, Richmond, 2004), m.nn. 589–94.

[120] See e.g. BVerfG, 1 BvR 1911/06, *Schuldenbereinigungsversuch*, 1. Senate, 4 Sep. 2006 (m.n. 14) ('konstitutionell uneinheitlich').

or identical situations. Applying this idea to precedent departures would suggest a scheme like the following to overruling or discarding prior pronouncements. First, are the cases relatively similar? Secondly, what is the reason for (hypothetical) different treatment? Thirdly, is this justifiable?

Difficulties concerning the first step have already been noted.[121] Things to look out for at the second stage would be the typical 'alarm bell' considerations, including fundamental rights aspects, nationality, place of establishment and the like. At the same time, countervailing factors might include different treatment resulting from differently worded legal text,[122] doctrinal anachronisms, changed factual premises or the precedent's incorrectness. The last step essentially forces an open explanation as to whether the break in continuity can be argued convincingly. In substantive terms, it becomes a question whether the detriment suffered by a change in jurisprudence is a burden that is justly borne by those upon whom it is imposed. It is partly, but not exclusively, an effects-based test. In a *Brown* or *R* v. *R* type of situation, this might seem straightforward.[123] But concerning the minutiae of much of EU law this will be far more difficult; for a case to make it to the ECJ the normative and concrete considerations are rarely obviously one-sided.

iii Legitimate expectations: another tentative test

Another candidate for framing precedent departures is the need for the exercise of public authority, including law and adjudication, to be foreseeable. As noted above, a precedent's weight can be influenced by the degree of reliance that has been placed on it in the meantime. One way to formulate this is through a demand that legitimate expectations be respected. This is a prominent element in EU law, where it resurfaces as a general principle and corollary of legal certainty.[124] Again, the point is neither to establish 'strict' bindingness nor to seek to paint judges' behaviour as wrongful should they nevertheless consider a departure warranted. Moreover, where legitimate expectations are unsettled,

---

[121] See Ch. 3.

[122] See e.g. Case C-331/88 *The Queen* v. *Minister of Agriculture, Fisheries and Food and Secretary of State for Health, ex parte Fedesa and ors* (Fifth Chamber) [1990] ECR I-4023 (para. 20).

[123] US SC, *Brown* v. *Board of Education of Topeka*, 347 US 483 (1954) (racial segregation); UK HL, *R* v. *R* [1992] 1 AC 599 (spousal rape).

[124] See e.g. Case C-352/09 P *ThyssenKrupp Nirosta GmbH* v. *Commission* (Grand Chamber) [2011] ECR I-2359 (para. 79).

ameliorating arrangements could be made, such as limiting the effect of a precedent departure *ex nunc*.[125]

The principle behind the concept is that reasonable (i.e. justifiable) expectations and hopes should not be disappointed in respect of matters falling within an entity's decision-makers power, subject to appropriate warning and the opportunity to make transitional arrangements. Three steps can be carved out. First, a prior ECJ decision creates an expectation. Secondly, this gives rise to reliance and a change of position. Thirdly, it was reasonable to expect that the prior position espoused by the Court would remain unchanged.

Given the oracular quality of many ECJ judgments, let alone the fact that not even specialised legal practitioners are usually aware of the entirety of the Court's vast adjudicatory output, the first step would already appear to be a stumbling block in many respects. But there could certainly be exceptions. For instance, hardly anyone would consider the ECJ to overrule its direct effect, primacy or state-liability jurisprudence anytime soon.

In many ways this also presages the second stage. A past decision alone does not create a reliance interest that deserves protection; what is required is a change of position occasioned by confidence in a precedent.[126] Again, in many cases this will not militate against a departure, but in areas such as corporate law or tax law it is not at all far-fetched to assume that legal persons will structure their relations according to advice received on important decisions. Moreover, Member States are prone to react to EU law, which is keenly watched in various European government ministries. Nonetheless, specifically in the European context, it is hardly a secret that the concept of *effet utile* plays an important role in the Court's jurisprudence and instils a fluctuating dynamic into its adjudication.

The third stage is again likely to cause a lot of head-scratching. On the one hand, it is hard to see what the point of a lot of adjudication is, certainly when it comes to permanent bodies such as the ECJ and in particular its answers to preliminary references, if this does not clarify fundamental positions beyond the immediate case at hand.[127] This is a strong argument in a constitutional context. But repetition seems uncalled for where there have been important changes in factual or societal premises,

---

[125] See only Case C-163/09 *Repertoire Culinaire Ltd* v. *The Commissioners of Her Majesty's Revenue & Customs* [2010] ECR I-12717, Opinion of AG Kokott (para. 62).

[126] For a discussion of this in a German context see Kähler (n. 11 above), pp. 346–60.

[127] Cf. B.-O. Bryde, *Verfassungsentwicklung: Stabilität und Dynamik im Verfassungsrecht der Bundesrepublik Deutschland* (Nomos, Baden-Baden, 1982), p. 421.

or whenever a precedent is simply considered practically unworkable or wrong. In the end, this is again likely to result in a broader cost–benefit calculus as noted above. Like in so many legal tests, including the vaunted proportionality exercise, the ultimate stage cannot completely dispense with the decisionist residue that remains in 'reasonableness', 'justifiability' or 'balancing' elements. Little else can be expected in light of limited cognition and in the absence of a clear preference that is voiced to cut that very last stretch short.

7

ECJ precedents in context

The preceding analysis shows that the ECJ utilises its own past pronouncements in many different ways. On the face of it, the Court seems
to have mastered the art of coherent and predictable jurisprudence.
Dinguishing cases fits with this as a popular maintenance technique.
While rare, the ECJ also overrules itself *because of* rather than *despite* an
insistence on continuity and coherence. This links to the earlier break-
down of its general precedent use. The Court's abstract reference practice
and relative scarcity of 'strong' citations correlates with its preference for
distinguishing precedents and avoiding express overruling of its cases.
The deeper reasons for the ECJ's precedent practice will be tackled next.

One of the theses of this book is that precedent use is highly context-
dependant. It is ubiquitous but customised. It is not shackled to a particular legal family or tradition. One has to be sensitive to the organisational,
contextual and perhaps downright accidental without overplaying a single
point. Of course it is difficult to separate the 'merely practical or periph-
eral' from the 'material and real'. The position taken here is to neither
elide the two completely nor pretend that they are wholly divorced. What
this chapter draws out is that the ECJ's precedent-handling is not so much
owed to a carefully devised legal methodology or clearly defined ambition,
but that it is to a large extent rooted in the specific constellation in which
the Court operates and the demands it has to satisfy. This situation-sense
and contextuality, coupled with the basic impulse of any judicial body –
including the ECJ – to come across as a rational decision-maker, better
explains the Court's precedent technique than simplistic conjectures as to
its political motivation ('the judges are always pro-integration') or asper-
sions regarding its legal reasoning ('the Court simply does what it wants').

A Asymmetry

To begin with, the precedent methodology of the ECJ is informed by
an asymmetry between the Court's adjudicatory power and the available

correctives. This emboldens it and fosters a habit of making statements about law by reference to its own output. At the same time, this encourages distinguishing cases, which the ECJ is often prone to do, and leaves the door open for departing from prior decisions, albeit without compelling this.

i Effectiveness

On the one hand, the adjudication of the ECJ has proved to be remarkably effective. The Court is a very successful dispute settlement body. Compulsory jurisdiction plays a large part. Ordinarily, consent goes to the heart of legal proceedings beyond the nation state.[1] The ECJ however is a highly evolved specimen of such activity – indeed, at least in part an entirely novel form. It takes a different approach to what might be considered the 'golden rule' of consent-based non-domestic adjudication, barring select international human rights courts.[2] The Court's jurisdiction is obligatory. There is no optional clause in the EU treaties. Given the EU's famous decentralised constellation and robust co-operative mechanisms, the Court benefits from a remarkable degree of inter-penetration and efficacy.[3] Primacy and self-determined direct effect further set it apart from dispute settlement according to traditional international law. There is no evidence that Member States routinely ignore the Court's decisions.

ii Lack of appellate review and ready political corrective

On the other hand, the ECJ is not an adjudicatory body of inferior jurisdiction in a ranked system of dispute settlement where a higher tier could always revise its decisions if need be. This is unlike the basic position within the WTO, where the Understanding on Rules and Procedures Governing the Settlement of Disputes provides for the possibility of

---

[1] See e.g. E. Lauterpacht, 'Principles of Procedure in International Law', *Recueil des Cours/ Académie de Droit International de La Haye*, 345 (2009), 391, 444–5, 453–4; A. M. Steingruber, *Consent in International Arbitration* (Oxford University Press, 2012), p. 12.

[2] Cf. J. G. Merrills, *International Dispute Settlement* (3rd edn, Cambridge University Press, 1998) 122; A. Bleckmann, *Völkerrecht* (Nomos, Baden-Baden, 2001), p. 357.

[3] See e.g. R. Schütze, *From Dual to Cooperative Federalism: The Changing Structure of European Law* (Oxford University Press, 2009), pp. 241–65.

internal review in the form of a standing body that hears appeals from panel cases.[4] In this respect the Court's situation does not differ a lot from domestic courts of last resort, with the exception that the majority of the ECJ's cases are not appellate cases. Even when 'true' precedent doctrines are accepted, such courts regularly reserve the right to change their case law, with the Supreme Courts of the US and UK being prime examples.

What is more, political correctives are not readily available. While there are particularities, treaty amendment is by and large cumbersome and political opposition either likely to be unsuccessful or very costly.[5] This again differs in a specific respect from WTO dispute resolution. While the 'negative consensus' rule of DSU Arts. 16(4) and 17(14) is likely to lead to automatic adoption in virtually all cases, it is inherent in the very concept of adoption that a stamp of political approval in the form of Dispute Settlement Body acquiescence is required. At the very least, this gives the relationship between adjudication and other forms of decision-making a different spin by nominally taking the former down a peg.

The consequence of this position of strength coupled with the associated responsibility is that the ECJ takes it upon itself to authoritatively stake out what it believes to be the law, which encourages recurrently referencing its own respective output in broad and steadfast terms, not least because this also suggests remaining within established bounds.[6] Distinguishing does no harm to this but rather furthers any system-fortification efforts by adding surplus legal information to what are otherwise often skeletal frames. In a similar vein, precedent citations that vest legal provisions with meaning are popular. The lack of a readily accessible external 'pressure valve' in the form of adjudicatory or politico-legislative control leads to the facility of overruling or departing from precedent being kept alive, although tempered in light of the above.[7]

---

[4] Final Act Embodying the Results of the Uruguay Round of Multilateral Trade Negotiations of 15 Sep. 1994, Annex 2, Understanding on Rules and Procedures Governing the Settlement of Disputes ('DSU') Art. 17.

[5] The very real practical difficulties surrounding treaty amendment could be witnessed only recently in light of efforts to bolster the single currency.

[6] See A. Stone Sweet, 'Conclusion' in A. Stone Sweet (ed.), *The Judicial Construction of Europe* (Oxford University Press, 2004), p. 10.

[7] Cf. J. Hillmann, 'An Emerging International Rule of Law? The WTO Dispute Settlement System's Role in its Evolution', *Ottawa Law Review*, 42 (2010–2011), 269, 283 (on how the lack of a convenient political corrective in the WTO leads to 'conservative' judgments that 'fear to branch out very far').

B Function of the Court

i Depoliticisation

Just as in law and adjudication in general, depoliticisation plays an important role in the surveyed milieu. Although the EU is a project that is with growing maturity all the more focused on substance rather than processes, the European endeavour at times resembles a functionalist venture to 'roll back' excesses of the nation state while at the same time remaining respectful of individual specificities.[8] It, too, is an elite-led project that has largely been accomplished on the back of adjudication, which is however – and this is crucial – not the same thing as saying purely by adjudicators. Rather, regulatory ideas and market concepts are deliberately exported through channels other than what might be considered more traditional political discourse.

Of course 'depoliticised' in this sense does not equate to 'apolitical'; the project effectuates powerful agendas. But the case law of the ECJ is implicitly sanctioned by this larger effort to offload difficult or unpopular decisions to such a forum. While frequently heckled for 'undemocratically' meddling with other directly or indirectly affected concerns, the ECJ clearly benefits from such an arrangement. The Court constantly acknowledges this transfer when it intones Member State legal traditions or falls back on the 'absence of harmonisation' narrative.

What this means for precedent use is that statements of law can acceptably be grounded in past pronouncements, even though this might at first appear a circuitous act of self-promotion. Moreover, critical disputes as to the meaning of treaty provisions are also entrusted to the principal adjudicatory body. Finally, distinguishing as an act of incrementally expanding the scope of adjudicatory coverage over time is stimulated.

ii Different roles

At its most basic and as such unremarkably, the ECJ settles disputes between involved parties. On a deeper level, it affects private organisation and the structures and principles that underpin the operation of (non-)domestic public order. Indeed, co-operative regime maintenance is an important role of many adjudicators.[9] This is all the more so for the

---

[8] See e.g. TEU Art. 4(2); Case C-208/09 *Ilonka Sayn-Wittgenstein* v. *Landeshauptmann von Wien* (Second Chamber) [2010] ECR I-13693 (paras. 83–4) (factoring 'an element of national identity' into a proportionality test).

[9] Cf. Y. Shany, 'No Longer a Weak Department of Power? Reflections on the Emergence of a New International Judiciary', *European Journal of International Law*, 20 (2009), 73, 81–2.

Court. In doing so it softens up national boundaries, incidentally upsetting received thinking on supposedly distinct planes of organisation, the perfect separation of powers and readily definable law-making.

A closer look reveals that the ECJ wears different hats at different times. At least four can be discerned. First, it plays the role of a constitutional court when it is asked to strike down EU legislation, when it rules on fundamental rights and freedoms,[10] when it renders opinions on whether international agreements between the Union and third countries or international organisations are compatible with the treaties[11] or when it decides questions of inter-institutional design.[12] Secondly, it acts as a supreme court when hearing appeals from the GC and specialised courts. Thirdly, it is routinely an administrative court or regulatory complaints board when it considers actions against EU institutions such as reviewing the legality of the Union's enormous 'regulatory machine',[13] for instance in actions against penalties imposed by EU institutions or when determining failures to act or deciding claims for compensation. Fourthly, it resembles an international court when the Commission or a Member State brings another Member State before the ECJ for failing to fulfil its treaty obligations or when it settles arguments between Member States on the subject matter of the treaties that were submitted to it by special agreement. In more general terms, its functions can roughly be divided into traditional dispute settlement between litigants at loggerheads and indirect legal supervision in the form of opinions and preliminary rulings.[14]

Yet importantly, all of these are emanations of the ECJ's broader function as the – albeit non-exclusive, certainly very prominent – guarantor of 'a particular legal order', tasked with contributing to its subsistence and

---

[10] Cf. C. N. Kakouris, 'La Cour de Justice des Communautés européennes comme Cour Constitutionnelle: trois observations' in O. Due, M. Lutter and J. Schwarze (eds.), *Festschrift für Ulrich Everling*, 2 vols. (Nomos, Baden-Baden, 1995), I, p. 634; A. Rosas, 'The European Union and Fundamental Rights/Human Rights' in C. Krause and M. Scheinin (eds.), *International Protection of Human Rights: A Textbook* (Åbo Akademi University Institute for Human Rights, Turku, 2009), p. 444.

[11] For an equally classic and determined defence of the integrity of the European legal order in a time of considerable flux see Opinion 1/91 *Draft Agreement Between the Community and the Countries of the European Free Trade Association Relating to the Creation of the European Economic Area* [1991] ECR I-6079.

[12] Cf. J. A. Frowein, 'Die Verfassung der Europäischen Union aus der Sicht der Mitgliedstaaten', *Europarecht*, 30 (1995), 315.

[13] H. Schepel and E. Blankenburg, 'Mobilizing the European Court of Justice' in G. de Búrca and J. Weiler (eds.), *The European Court of Justice* (Oxford University Press, 2001), p. 21.

[14] Cf. R. H. Lauwaars, 'Institutional Structure' in P. J. G. Kapteyn and P. VerLoren van Themaat (eds.), *The Law of the European Union and the European Communities* (4th edn, Kluwer Law International, Alphen aan den Rijn, 2008), pp. 238–40.

development.[15] TEU Art. 19(1) is habitually read to the effect that the Court is an appointed custodian of EU law, a mission it readily embraces.[16] This emancipation beyond what might be considered 'pure' dispute settlement traditionally enjoys staunch support amongst the cognoscenti.[17] The Court considers itself to be more than a bespoke problem-solver equipped with a narrow mandate to get a very particular job done. The basis of its jurisdiction is not simply a (bilateral) transactional treaty, that is to say a classic inter-state bargain, the sole legitimacy and need for legitimation of which rests on a supposedly keenly assessed *quid pro quo* agreement.[18] Its mindset differs from that of typical international adjudicators, who generally consider themselves to simply afford what is due, which is mostly – so the underpinning fiction goes – not something a larger order warrants, but rather what the parties themselves agreed but perhaps either forgot or chose to forget in the spur of the moment.[19] The ECJ is not paid to resolve disputes on a *pro rata* basis. It is not limited to granting monetary relief and is not simply used to cut losses, but rather to engineer the system in a way that Member States, Union institutions and private individuals consider desirable.

Given that it constantly has the long-term interests of the Union as a whole in the back of its mind, the Court therefore gravitates towards more assertive and definitive forms of reasoning. This manifests itself in a precedent practice that stresses basic commonalities rather than individual particularities that might foster fragmentation. Coherence becomes key.

---

[15] Opinion 1/91 *Draft Agreement Between the Community and the Countries of the European Free Trade Association Relating to the Creation of the European Economic Area* [1991] ECR I-6079 (para. 50).

[16] Cf. Opinion 1/09 *Patent Litigation System* (Full Court) [2011] ECR I-1137 (para. 66).

[17] See e.g. M. Cappelletti, 'Is the European Court of Justice "Running Wild"?', *European Law Review*, 12 (1987), 3, 6–10; K.-D. Borchardt, 'Richterrecht durch den Gerichtshof der Europäischen Gemeinschaften' in A. Randelzhofer, R. Scholz and D. Wilke (eds.), *Gedächtnisschrift für Eberhard Grabitz* (C. H. Beck, Munich, 1995), pp. 30–1; A. Albors-Llorens, 'The European Court of Justice: More than a Teleological Court', *The Cambridge Yearbook of European Legal Studies*, 2 (1999), 373; M. Zuleeg, 'The Advantages of the European Constitution' in A. von Bogdandy and J. Bast (eds.), *Principles of European Constitutional Law* (Hart and C. H. Beck, Oxford and Munich, 2010), pp. 768, 775, 777; M. Poiares Maduro and L. Azoulai, 'Introduction' in M. Poiares Maduro and L. Azoulai (eds.), *The Past and Future of EU Law* (Hart, Oxford and Portland, 2010), p. xvi (asserting that the Court also acts as a limit to supranational power).

[18] On the thin line between contractarianism and governance see J. H. H. Weiler, 'The Geology of International Law: Governance, Democracy and Legitimacy', *Zeitschrift für ausländisches öffentliches Recht und Völkerrecht*, 64 (2004), 547, 553–4.

[19] To be sure, international courts and tribunals also indubitably exercise an important public function. But that is still an underdeveloped angle that has difficulties asserting its emancipation.

First up are general invocations of broader strands of case law and frequent string citations, all of which emphasise systematicity over substantive specificity.[20] Fidelity is ultimately owed to the nebulous and impersonal 'whole', rather than to special manifestations of individual consent. There is little to no fear of general precedent use being an underhand short-cut that does violence to the individual bargains contained in specific treaties. Spelling out the factual context of prior cases and prying into their substantive reasoning processes also becomes less focal. Secondly, this invites a heavier emphasis on presenting the results of adjudication as flowing naturally from the larger system, which finds common expression in the ECJ's increased use of precedents to affirm *ex post* the conclusions of its legal reasoning. The Court does not seek legitimacy in exhaustive argumentative efforts, but mainly in consistency and systematicity, which further encourages bald statements of law via precedents. Not only the decision, but the legal order as such is thereby vindicated. Thirdly, while distinguishing implicitly affirms the system, open departures are seen as a tear within the larger fabric, engendering considerable cost and carrying heavily symbolic overtones.[21] They are hence rare. All the same, given that the cardinal determinant is the efficacy and realisation of the ever-closer union, the Court will, if need be, consign precedents to the dustbin of history, albeit reluctantly given its guarantor status.

C Supranational aspects

Although it has in the past not always been easy for international law(yers) to let go, it is now widely accepted that the EU with its supranational legal system is a different animal than just a regular international organisation devoted to regional economic co-operation.[22] The special supranational context bears on the ECJ's precedent technique in a variety of ways.

i Institutional embedding

A cardinal aspect that influences how cases are treated is that the ECJ is firmly embedded in the EU, a legal community that is backed by a fully fledged and in certain respects uniform political system. Even the briefest perusal of its EUR-Lex portal bears witness to its gargantuan governance

---

[20] Outside of precedent practice, this is also reflected in its fondness of general principles.

[21] E.g. according to TFEU Art. 256, the key concept mediating the relationship between the ECJ and the GC is that of 'serious risk of the unity or consistency of Union law'.

[22] See e.g. W. Graf Vitzthum, 'Begriff, Geschichte und Rechtsquellen des Völkerrechts' in W. Graf Vitzthum (ed.), *Völkerrecht* (5th edn, De Gruyter, Berlin, 2010), p. 20.

apparatus,[23] which is bolstered by doctrines such as primacy, direct effect and horizontal as well as vertical constitutional compatibility.[24] The EU has a legislature of an increasingly parliamentary nature. It is more complex than a unitary supra-statist assembly, yet far more developed than the closest approximations of public international law. This means that the ECJ can be bolder than if it was operating on its own, which is reflected in its precedent practice, for instance by using past cases to make naked statements of law. Quite how this ping-pong works can be seen in the endorsement of its pronouncements on direct effect, primacy and fundamental rights in primary law and in secondary law.[25]

Where wider normative patronage and collaborative institutionalised law-makers exist, as in the EU, the need to explain rulings in detail can seem less acute. Being cushioned in an overarching project also acts as a natural disincentive to jurisprudential zigzagging. At the same time, this allows the Court to present unflinchingly its past reasoning as the essential condensation of the wisdom of the surrounding deliberative space, be it in affirmatory syllogisms or in broader (i.e. less fact-specific) terms. It almost goes without saying that the existence of a highly active legislative machinery also boosts the use of precedent to make sense of specific written provisions. And where there is strong structural support there is also more constraint: the compulsion to abide by precedents increases whenever the judge is not a lone wolf.

ii Permanence

Turning to the temporal dimension, the ECJ is a permanent body. Unlike *ad hoc* tribunals, it is locked in a constant dialogue with the same states and institutions and under the same daily glare of public opinion. This has advantages and disadvantages. The Court has the luxury of awaiting a response by the Member States and then correcting what it considers misinterpretations of its precedents or 'clarifying' what is for all intents and purposes plainly a bad previous judgment. At the same time, the ECJ knows very well that an error or a lingering gripe in one of its judgments will come back to haunt it in a few years time.[26] If it is too specific on

---

[23] Available at http://eur-lex.europa.eu.   [24] See e.g. TEU Arts. 2, 7, 48.

[25] See e.g. TFEU Art. 6(2) (fundamental rights); TEU 34(2)(b) (direct effect); Declaration concerning primacy, Declarations annexed to the Final Act of the Intergovernmental Conference which adopted the Treaty of Lisbon [2010] OJ C83/344, no. 17.

[26] See e.g. Case C-2/06 *Willy Kempter KG v. Hauptzollamt Hamburg-Jonas* (Grand Chamber) [2008] ECR I-411 (para. 1).

a particular point or if it upsets an established series of precedents inadvertently, this will cause more than just a ripple. Cases can boomerang. This courts a natural reticence as concerns precedent-handling. Loquacious expositions of precedents can trigger impressions that might not be desirable, making general references a safer bet. What is more, being seen to change one's position could, if not reasoned adequately, be taken as a sign of weakness.

There is another angle to this. The Court's judges are tenured and occupy full-time positions.[27] Their legal reasoning on display is not necessarily their calling card, as is the case with most arbitrators. While they can be re-elected, the judges are, if anything, considered too independent (and 'activist'), rather than too dependent.[28] Without seeking to reduce comprehensive and explanatory precedent-handling to bootlicking, the Court can in many respects still get away with being less 'user friendly' or persuasive. Short of a seismic constitutional shift or an outright rebellion of the Member States or their courts, there is less to fear in this respect, not least since its overall precedent technique is hardly ever the focus of more intensive scrutiny, unlike its final holdings. The Court is often blasé about upsetting entire industries with the stroke of a pen.[29] On the contrary, most international courts and tribunals have to ensure a much higher degree of pragmatic realism that 'future-proofs' their decisions. While generalisations are necessarily crude, investment tribunals for instance are tempted not to err on the side of re-imagination of present conditions. This often means adding detail to potentially unpleasant decisions, including the precedents used to arrive at them, and generally making decisions as exhaustive and 'life-like' as can be.

iii (De)centralisation

Despite the patent importance of its supranational core, the EU legal system is famously complex, one important aspect of which is decentralisation. Different forces pull both inwards and outwards. National

---

[27] See TFEU Art. 253.

[28] See A. Rosas, 'Separation of Powers in the European Union', *The International Lawyer*, 41 (2007), 1033, 1045. The Court is, of course, also independent from the Commission's legal service.

[29] See e.g. Case C-415/93 *Union royale belge des sociétés de football association ASBL v. Jean-Marc Bosman* [1995] ECR I-4921 (professional football); Case C-236/09 *Association Belge des Consommateurs Test-Achats and ors v. Conseil des ministres* (Grand Chamber) [2011] ECR I-773 (insurance); Joined Cases C-403/08 and C-429/08 *Football Association Premier League and ors v. QC Leisure* (Grand Chamber) [2011] ECR I-9083 (broadcasting rights).

enforcement remains key in this arrangement, but the idea can also be traced in matters ranging from subsidiarity to diversity of representation in EU institutions. Without this outward vector, the European project would become practically unworkable and impossible to legitimise.

But as each federal system of political organisation knows, there comes a tipping point where decentralisation leads to disintegration. What this does is to provoke the main judicial organ to make greater centripetal efforts in the name of 'cohesion, uniformity and legal certainty'.[30] The EU is a real quantum leap beyond the age-old, loose multilateral co-ordination of nation states. Sweeping references to precedents underpin a strongly unificatory jurisprudence, as does their bundling in clusters composed of cases that are of equal worth in terms of the legal information that can be milked from them. Individual features of precedents on the other hand can be irritants. Broader tendencies rationalise earlier adjudication and make it appear harmonious and respectable, unless the Court wishes to visibly imprint systemic development at a particular moment. Frequent self-correction by the ECJ and open rifts in its jurisprudence are likely to be considered obstacles to centralisation.

In many respects, such self-reinforcement is hard-wired into legal systems like the EU that seek to exert their own authority rather than depend on external authority.[31] Invoking a precedent is an obvious expression of a belief in a legal order as an antagonist to blunter forms of individualistic, clientele-driven or functionalistic decision-making. Not only can the Court thereby assert a point that might contradict the stance of the Council, Commission, Parliament, Member States or others, this also has a strong reinforcing potential, since it suggests that the system is replicating itself in its application. It is an old and powerful fiction. '[O]ur positive law', Savigny wrote in 1840, 'is complemented from within, as we assume an organic constructivist vigour in the very same.'[32]

Indeed, the TEU speaks of the illustrious 'ever closer union' in its Preamble and in Art. 1. A common response to charges of 'judicial activism' has thus been that all the ECJ is doing is giving effect to written provisions that are premised on the very idea of integration and

---

[30] Joined Cases C-94/04 and C-202/04 *Federico Cipolla* v. *Rosaria Fazari (née Portolese)* [2006] ECR I-11421, Opinion of AG Poiares Maduro (para. 28).

[31] Arguably, the very concept of a 'system' necessitates an integrated whole that separates it from its surrounding environment. Note that this does not seek to doubt the familiar wisdom that adjudicators control neither purse strings nor armies.

[32] F. C. von Savigny, *System des heutigen Römischen Rechts*, 9 vols. (Veit, Berlin, 1840), I, pp. 290–291 (author's translation).

have this as their core purpose: how could the Court *not* put integration at the core of its reasoning?[33] This self-sustaining tendency, which can also be observed with respect to the international protection of human rights, need not amount to disparagement of the individual decision-makers operating within the system, who can of course still go about their business in a professional manner. Saying that a system is endowed with the capacity to create broader desired results is not tantamount to behavioural or attitudinal cynicism according to which lawyers' familiar materials such as norms, statutes, cases and doctrines are ultimately of negligible explanatory power and resemble formalistic props used, if not as part of a larger ideological masquerade, then at least in a self-delusional way.[34] The point is not that the background, experience and ambition of ECJ judges overshadow everything else,[35] but that certain patterns of thinking and arguing are routinely nurtured.

This self-reinforcing drive of EU law is reflected in a shared approach to sources that has by and large abandoned the strict deductivism of classical legal thought that presupposes a logically perfect tree-structure[36] in favour of pragmatism combined with intermittent normative reconstruction and the ubiquitous balancing tests of the age of adjudication. Two important pillars of this self-sustaining practice are referring to prior jurisprudence in expounding law and the practice of distinguishing precedents, especially when this leaves much of the past pronouncement intact.

iv Potential impact

The ECJ effectively partakes in shaping the law for half a billion people and thousands of courts. Its pronouncements vitally affect what at the end of the first decade of the new millennium was the largest economy

[33] See V. Skouris, 'Self-Conception, Challenges and Perspectives of the EU Courts' in I. Pernice, J. Kokott and C. Saunders (eds.), *The Future of the European Judicial System in a Comparative Perspective* (Nomos, Baden-Baden, 2006), p. 25. To deflect hostility such candidness is then again often couched in 'gap-filling' terminology and images of passively mirroring external processes.

[34] Cf. L. Kalman, *The Strange Career of Legal Liberalism* (Yale University Press, New Haven and London 1996), p. 47; N. Maveety, 'The Study of Judicial Behaviour and the Discipline of Political Science' in N. Maveety (ed.), *The Pioneers of Judicial Behaviour* (University of Michigan Press, Ann Arbor, 2003), p. 5.

[35] For such an approach in the context of international arbitration see D. Schneiderman, 'Judicial Politics and International Investment Arbitration: Seeking an Explanation for Conflicting Outcomes', *Northwestern Journal of International Law & Business*, 30 (2010), 383, 395–8.

[36] Such modes are mainly revived for defensive purposes. Cf. Ch. 2, D.

worldwide.[37] It needs to respect not one but almost thirty legal systems in addition to autonomous supranational law, many of which most members of the Court will naturally not be experts in. All courts and tribunals dislike littering the sands of time with jurisprudential landmines, but the ECJ is particularly wary of this. Not only are the stakes particularly high, in the complex multilevel system and distinctive supranational legal regime in which it operates potential knock-on effects can be especially hard to gauge. Following the Court's jurisprudence is stressful and expensive for national governments. Consensus and consistency are always on its mind, both writ large as concerns its perception as legitimate by sovereign and self-confident nation states and other political entities as well as internally when it comes to decision-making and precedent treatment. This caution breeds argumentative parsimony.

Is this frugality meaningful? Many elements of the ECJ's imposing premises on the city of Luxembourg's Kirchberg reflect a golden hue – supposedly a nod to the colour of justice. Sometimes, the Court's silence is indeed golden and not purely a matter of economy. At its best, it can be a device to foster pluralist discourse by leaving room for potentially affected actors to hash out specifics.[38] More mundanely, with the EU past its age of innocence, 'il faut être prudent' increasingly supplants the more carefree 'il faut construire un système' of yore in the Court's adjudication.[39] While it is not a sure-fire success, such hesitant caution partly explains the frequently pilloried style of its judgments.[40] Sometimes, however, this silence is less precious, resembling instead a tin foil hat, that is to say an unfounded hope to be impervious to manipulation and critique.

Most likely, the Court's sparse argumentation is at least partly a genuine desire to be consistent. Recycling past phases that have not (yet) caused a ruckus is reassuring and is often a signal that no change in law is intended. Ironically, it is however exactly this verbal frugality and stylistic broadness

---

[37] Both in GDP at purchasing power parity and by nominal GDP. See IMF, *World Economic Outlook (September 2011): Slowing Growth, Rising Risks* (IMF, Washington, 2011). Statistics available at: www.imf.org/external/datamapper/index.php.

[38] See D. Sarmiento, 'The Silent Lamb and the Deaf Wolves' in M. Avbelj and J. Komarek (eds.), *Constitutional Pluralism in the European Union and Beyond* (Hart, Oxford, 2012), pp. 310–11.

[39] Of course, the ECJ still has its frontiers and 'new toys' to play with, at the moment chiefly EU citizenship. The point cannot be pursued in more detail here, but the basic building blocks are firmly in place by now.

[40] A familiar complaint is that its abrupt 'Cartesian' style makes it authoritarian rather than authoritative. See J. H. H. Weiler, 'Epilogue: The Judicial Après Nice' in G. de Búrca and J. Weiler (eds.), *The European Court of Justice* (Oxford University Press, 2001), p. 225.

that can backfire and give rise to speculation and protean interpretation, as the citizenship saga amply demonstrates. The Court finds itself in a difficult position. It does not want to say too much, but by doing so it leaves the door wide open for creative lawyering, including of course its own. Therefore, limiting phrases can be found in many judgments seeking to confine the effect of a pronouncement to the present case. These are direct attempts to reconcile the need for certainty and direction with the fertility of language and the necessary breathing space for the development of EU law. That the ECJ is watchful of the reception and impact of its decisions is evinced by *Metock*'s castigation of what the Court considered a misleading isolation of certain statements in *Akrich*. Overall, the shadow cast by the ECJ's vast influence disfavours express and frequent precedent departures and supports a more minimal and mechanistic approach to its own jurisprudence.

D Internal arrangements

i Special formations

Several internal factors condition the Court's precedent treatment. First, established since the Treaty of Nice and successor of the *petit plenum*, the Grand Chamber is a special formation for legal decision-making that makes its influence felt at the ECJ.[41] It is the master gardener of the Palais at the Niedergrünewald. Besides planting seeds and watering the EU legal landscape in both *grands arrêts* and everyday cases, it seeks to preserve jurisprudential coherence and intra-institutional continuity, transplanting and pruning the wild growth of a voluminous and sprouting case law.[42] Its motto is quality control, and hence legitimacy, through carefully sculpted consistency rather than fickle discursiveness – something that it considers akin to playing with fire or simply not very helpful.

Fittingly, its methods of achieving this are more cloistered and serene than the open squabbling of judicial egos. It strives for constancy on an interpersonal level through the participation of a certain nucleus of senior people, including the President, Vice-President and three Presidents of chambers of five judges. This is designed to let consistency percolate through the chambers of five, which bear the brunt of the daily work of

---

[41] The days of the Court routinely sitting in plenary session are long gone, not least because of the vastly increased workload and successive enlargements.

[42] Cf. Skouris (n. 33 above), p. 23.

the Court at just over 55 per cent of cases being heard there.[43] At the same time, this arrangement allows for greater rotation and thus broader participation than in the past. Even if this involvement is unlikely to promote shared views as such – indeed, antagonisms might become just as entrenched through ritualised forms of collaboration – it is nevertheless not unlikely to increase the familiarity and collegiality of those present and thus gel communication and enhance basic efficiency in the long run.[44] As a result, outward discussion of precedents can be kept to a minimum, which is reflected in the low number of substantive citations and proclivity for referring to the Court's output in a general and anonymised manner. Moreover, given its numerical superiority and high-powered participation, the Grand Chamber can most easily afford to make bald statements of law, far more so that a chamber of five or three judges, which helps to explain why this use of precedent came out on top.

This also leads to a dislike of open disagreement with past pronouncements as reflected in its low overruling rates and preference for skirting around potential conflicts, a fact that is accentuated by the following consideration. If there is going to be an express departure, it will most certainly be a Grand Chamber matter. Should a judge or Advocate General consider a point to be particularly important, new or worthy of a departure, he or she will likely make efforts to get a case into the Grand Chamber in the weekly meeting of all members of the Court and the Registrar, the *réunion générale*.[45] Questions that have essentially already been dealt with in past cases will most likely be sent to a chamber of three.[46] Again, precedent plays a prominent role, but again largely out of sight. The Grand Chamber is mainly reserved for institutional or sensitive matters, such as fundamental rights, citizenship, important fiscal questions, matters of national procedural law and, what is of particular interest here, for matters directly concerning the Court's precedents.[47] Accordingly, the

---

[43] See Court of Justice of the European Union, *Annual Report 2011* (Luxembourg, 2012) 102, http://curia.europa.eu.

[44] Cf. N. Luhmann, 'Spontane Ordnungsbildung' in F. Morstein Marx (ed.), *Verwaltung: Eine einführende Darstellung* (Duncker & Humblot, Berlin, 1965), pp. 170–3, 181–2.

[45] The general meeting is mentioned in ECJ Rules of Procedure Arts. 9(2), 25, 59, 63(1). The Court will have the benefit of the reporting judge's confidential *rapport préalable*. See generally C. Naômé, *Le Renvoi préjudiciel en droit européen: guide pratique* (Larcier, Brussels, 2007), pp. 112–13.

[46] Often cases that turn on highly specific technical points, e.g. agricultural or customs matters. See D. Edward, 'How the Court of Justice Works', *European Law Review*, 20 (1995), 539, 552.

[47] See further CJEU Statute Art. 16(3) (concerning requests by a Member State or Union institution).

already pathologically low figures for open departures of precedent are likely to be even lower if one considers the practice of the ECJ as a whole, that is to say also outside the Grand Chamber.

It is unclear if the Grand Chamber is fighting a winning war. For one, there is the issue of overload for those judges involved in different formations. Secondly, even if there is no impression of a cadre monopolising the big cases and thus undermining the much-vaunted collegiality, a higher degree of consistency could arguably be achieved through greater rotation. This was partly addressed in the 2012 composition change, which also introduced the office of Vice-President, although the significance of that particular position remains to be seen. Given that the Court only regularly gets together as a whole during the weekly reunion, another possibility might be to introduce circulars sent by the President's chamber to ensure the Court as a whole is aware of jurisprudential developments.

Dwelling on special formations, the ECJ's rotating chambers are not set up to concentrate particular expertise, with the basic rule still being that the judges are generalists rather than specialists.[48] This de-personalises judgments by routinely breaking up joint interpretive experience and hence fosters recourse to broader systematicity; the voice making a particular pronouncement, together with all its idiosyncrasies and the weight it places on certain aspects of a dispute, fades into the background. It becomes less memorable for later usage, which encourages exchangeable string citations.

ii Assistance

A peculiarity for a non-domestic court are the ECJ's Advocates General. As is well known, the office is based on the *commissaires du gouvernement* of the French *Conseil d'État*,[49] while the designation harks back to other senior legal officers, the *advocats généraux*, who act as public prosecutors or represent the public interest, for example at the *Court de Cassation* (Supreme Court of Judicature). This historical parentage is epitomised

---

[48] See A. Rosas, 'Justice in Haste, Justice Denied? The European Court of Justice and the Area of Freedom, Security and Justice', *The Cambridge Yearbook of European Legal Studies*, 11 (2009), 1, 6. But note that to a degree expertise can and is taken into account by the President when allotting a *juge rapporteur* to a case. All the same, this is different from the situation at e.g. the German FCC.

[49] See K. Borgsmidt, 'The Advocate General at the European Court of Justice: A Comparative Study', *European Law Review*, 13 (1988), 106 (citing the official report of the French delegation, which considered it 'l'homologue des commissaires'); T. Tridimas, 'The Role of the Advocate General in the Development of Community Law: Some Reflections', *Common Market Law Review*, 34 (1997), 1349, 1350 ('analogue').

in the person of Maurice Lagrange, who in 1952 was the first Advocate
General following the inception of the Union's precursor and who had
previously been such a *commissaire* in his native France. Still, the institution has its own distinctive Unional traits. Unlike the *commissaires*,
Advocates General do not retire with the judges to deliberate in closed
session, yet their opinions are published. They are equal in status to judges
and not partisan advocates.[50]

According to TFEU Art. 252, the Advocates General 'assist' the Court.
They do so by suggesting decisions, namely proposing legal solutions, by
way of 'reasoned submissions'. The possibility of augmenting the Court's
reasoning is hence hard-wired into the treaty system. One important
feature of the opinions rendered by the Advocates General is the contex-
tualisation of disputes.[51] Matters brought before the Court often appear
rather specific or arcane at first glance, especially if packaged in a concise and technical preliminary reference. Consider *van Gend*.[52] A dispute
arising from the charging of an 8 per cent duty instead of 3 per cent
on the importation of 'aqueous emulsion of ureaformaldehyde' does not
have the whiff of a cataclysmic 'new legal order' to it, even when worded
as a question as to whether an express prohibition of customs duties
contained in a treaty has 'direct application within the territory' of a
state party. Of course those directly involved – namely the parties, the
members of the ECJ and any national court seized, the institutions of
the EU and the Member States – will often be aware of the height of the
stakes. While there is much to suggest that the decision in *van Gend* was
hardly a surprise to the legally versed insiders, who strategically made the
most of this golden opportunity, the perception of the case's importance
owes much to subsequent talking up of the decision.[53] For non-experts
and the public at large it can be difficult to spot the potentially vast

---

[50] The moniker is hence mildly misleading, same as modern *commissaires* do not represent
the government. Indeed, on his retirement, AG Lagrange took the opportunity to reflect
on these offices, noting amongst other things that the name *commissaire du gouvernement*
was 'sans doute critiquable': *Discours prononcé par M. l'Avocat général Maurice Lagrange,
à l'audience solennelle de la Cour, le 8 octobre 1964,* www.cvce.eu.

[51] Their potential for providing something akin to a separate or dissenting opinion is
discussed in the following subsection.

[52] Case 26–62 *NV Algemene Transport- en Expeditie Onderneming van Gend & Loos* v.
Netherlands Inland Revenue Administration [1963] ECR 1.

[53] See A. Vauchez, 'The Transnational Politics of Judicialization. *Van Gend en Loos* and the
Making of EU Polity', *European Law Journal*, 16 (2010), 1, 9 ('Far from being a thunderbolt
in a calm judicial sky, *Van Gend en Loos* had been awaited for a couple of years within the
then still restricted circles of Euro-implicated lawyers'), 13–4 ('ventriloquism').

practical significance of what appears like an innocuous and isolated legal dispute.

This is where the Advocates General can play a role. To begin with, given that not all cases are pleaded particularly well, they filter and focus submissions. They further assist in procedural matters. They can draw attention to important facts. Importantly given the present context, they often select, summarise and assess relevant strands of precedents, together with potential complications. Through this they can explore new angles of law, which might also include assessing the merits and demerits of a possible decision instead of treating it as pre-imposed.[54] In this spirit of supplementing potentially relevant legal information, the Advocates General also often explicitly refer to, discuss and rely on legal literature in the course of their opinions.[55] This is a real possibility since they write in their own or a very familiar language. As a single author and freed from the requirements of judicial diplomacy, the Advocate General can canvass her legal opinion in a more nuanced and punchier manner than a collegiate judgment will usually allow. Such fuller reasoning can better satisfy 'users' demands.[56] Overall, their opinions are reminiscent of the more exhaustive style of reasoning found in investment tribunals, at times even sparking a competition for good solutions.[57]

The actual effect of the Advocates General on the reasoning processes of the Court is difficult to measure. The necessity of maintaining the office is certainly not beyond doubt.[58] If the French blueprint is anything to go by,

---

[54] See e.g. Case C-302/04 *Ynos kft* v. *János Varga* [2006] ECR I-371, Opinion of AG Tizzano (paras. 49–50).

[55] See e.g. Case C-64/05 P *Kingdom of Sweden* v. *Commission and ors* [2007] ECR I-11389, Opinion of AG Poiares Maduro (paras. 31, 34, fns. 18–21, 26); Case C-436/03 *Parliament* v. *Council* [2006] ECR I-3733, Opinion of AG Stix-Hackl (para. 91, fns. 20–6, 28–36); Case C-137/08 *VB Pénzügyi Lízing Zrt* v. *Ferenc Schneider* [2010] ECR I-10847, Opinion of AG Trstenjak (para. 79, fns. 29–32); Case C-434/09 *Shirley McCarthy* v. *Secretary of State for the Home Department* [2011] ECR I-3375, Opinion of AG Kokott (para. 41, fn. 38). As is to be expected, there is a degree of variation here depending on individual preference.

[56] See E. Sharpston, 'The Changing Role of the Advocate General' in A. Arnull, P. Eeckhout and T. Tridimas (eds.), *Continuity and Change in EU Law* (Oxford University Press, 2008), p. 23.

[57] On the latter idea see C. O. Lenz, 'Das Amt des Generalanwalts am Europäischen Gerichtshof' in O. Due, M. Lutter and J. Schwarze (eds.), *Festschrift für Ulrich Everling*, 2 vols. (Nomos, Baden-Baden, 1995), I, p. 725.

[58] See N. Burrows and R. Greaves, *The Advocate General and EC Law* (Oxford University Press, 2007), p. 298; K. Schiemann, 'The Functioning of the Court of Justice in an Enlarged Union and the Future of the Court' in A. Arnull, P. Eeckhout and T. Tridimas (eds.), *Continuity and Change in EU Law* (Oxford University Press, 2008), p. 14 (arguing that the reporting judge's first draft could fulfil that role).

they can be influential, depending on their charisma and persuasiveness. Nevertheless, their submissions can be dispensed with by the Court.[59] A quick scan shows that the ECJ adopts some, none or all of their opinions. Since the 1990s, all of this has been done explicitly.

But what is particularly pertinent in the context of the present study is that this institution provides a foil for the ECJ in the sense of an institutionalised *amicus curiae* brief or an (instantly appealed) first instance judgment. The present arrangement takes a lot of weight off the Court's shoulders, permitting or even inducing terse reasoning. This will most likely extend to precedent treatment, with the need to summarise or even mention various strands of case law, be it approvingly or critically, ostensibly lessened. Past jurisprudence can then be invoked in more general terms, little substantive precedent reference appears necessary.

A large adjudicatory machine like the ECJ could not function without further support infrastructure. Another institutional feature designed to ensure coherence at the Court are the in-house *lecteurs d'arrêts* and proofreaders assisting the judges.[60] The former report directly to the President and are usually native French-speakers with legal training who support the largely non-native francophone judges in matters of drafting before and after deliberations. While the ultimate responsibility of course remains with the reporting judge, the *lecteurs* will sometimes make suggestions that transcend purely stylistic matters, including which precedents are cited. What is more, at the very start of a case, even before the President has appointed a *juge rapporteur*, a new matter will routinely be analysed by the Court's Research and Documentation department, which will amongst other things scour the case law for comparable cases. These arrangements compel a certain degree of standardisation and homogeneity that sustain the Court's more general citation practice.

Moreover, *référendaires* (i.e. legal secretaries) are a substantial pillar of the Court. Habits vary, but besides conducting legal research and bouncing ideas around with their judge, they frequently draft not only pre-hearing reports but also, following conclusion of oral proceedings, the *projets de motifs*, namely the draft judgments.[61] Farming out drafting work has been criticised in various contexts, not least as an inroad for missing

---

[59] See TFEU Art. 252; CJEU Statute Art. 20.   [60] Cf. Naômé (n. 45 above), pp. 19–20.

[61] See S. J. Kenney, 'Beyond Principals and Agents: Seeing Courts as Organizations by Comparing Référendaires at the European Court of Justice and Law Clerks at the US Supreme Court', *Comparative Political Studies*, 33 (2000), 593, 610–11. For the individual steps in a typical case see Naômé (n. 45 above), pp. 107–19. Note that Advocates General also have their *référendaires*.

or mischaracterising precedents.[62] The point here is not to speculate on the degree of work that is delegated (ir)reponsibly to assistants, not least since there is little evidence that this will inevitably result in a poorer decision. Rather, the point is that the extensive, routine and uniform support infrastructure at the ECJ is another piece in the mosaic that makes up its comparably routine and standardised precedent practice.

In this respect, the technical process after decision-making, that is to say the route from decision to case report, also matters. A precedent cannot effectively become legal information if it is not known. History is replete with examples of proprietary struggles not only over the meaning of law, but also over its presentation, access and cabining.[63] The ECJ's reports are produced in an in-house process involving the Research and Documentation department, which assists the reporting judge in coming up with keywords for a judgment. It also catalogues a decision systematically for the case law digest of the Court, which is accessible online. All of this is essentially done with a view to fitting the cases into a larger legal cosmos. It is another subtle inlet for homogenisation and fosters either a practice or at least the appearance of more streamlined and harmonious reason-giving through cases. Overall, a formulaic and canonical precedent technique is fused into the ECJ's working routine.

Another important point to consider with respect to the internal organisation of adjudicatory bodies and how it relates to precedent treatment is the organisation of the respective institutional memory.[64] The complex, multi-stage process encountered at the ECJ further supports the findings indicating a large degree of generalisation and abstraction.

iii Composite judgments

A prominent aspect of the ECJ's preference for stern coherence over exploratory discursiveness that also bears on its precedent method is the composite nature of its judgments. As is well known, the Court produces

---

[62] Concerning US Supreme Court clerks see N. J. Wichern, 'A Court of Clerks, Not of Men: Serving Justice in the Media Age', *DePaul Law Review*, 49 (1999), 621, 662. But cf. A. Ward and D. L. Weiden, *Sorcerers' Apprentices: 100 Years of Law Clerks at the United States Supreme Court* (New York University Press, 2006), p. 241 (suggesting that 'traditional factors' were more decisive in judicial decision-making).

[63] See R. J. Ross, 'The Commoning of the Common Law: The Renaissance Debate over Printing English Law, 1520-1640', *University of Pennsylvania Law Review*, 146 (1998), 323, 361–73, 453–61 (on the use of publicity and printing both to oppose and support the 'educator father-king owning the law' in Renaissance England).

[64] See Ch. 3, C.iv.

a single, unsigned opinion reached by a majority.[65] There are no dissents or concurring opinions and its deliberations and splits of opinion remain secret.[66] The recurrent debate over whether and when separate opinions are appropriate cannot satisfactorily be answered globally or purely by reference to historical pedigree.[67] Viewed in clinical isolation, there is much to be said for the proposition that the whole 'separate opinion or not' debate has become rather fusty. At the same time, the practice evinces a specific method of dealing with uncertainty in law that bears on the respective practice concerning precedents. Regardless of one's particular preferences, collegiality has consequences for judicial opinion-writing.[68]

At the ECJ, the internal view has traditionally been set against judges writing separately.[69] The predominant take is that this would undermine the Court's coherence and credibility. In other words, this is a necessary sacrifice in order not to weaken the institutional impact of the Court and make it look fractious and indecisive, given that it faces not only a rival executive and legislature, but in fact more than two dozen Member State orders that are hardly ever entirely happy about all the rulings coming out of Luxembourg. They regularly take opposing views on matters of EU law and will readily seek to exploit jurisprudential ambiguities, so that dissents would be easy prey and detract from the effectiveness and efficiency of the current arrangement, especially if allowed in preliminary rulings. The ECJ is particularly cagey about its authority, a protectiveness cemented in its deterministic 'new legal order' founding myth and constant insistence that this is still a fragile construct.

Further concerns besides additional translation burdens that support this practice include the relatively short terms of the judges, coupled with the possibility of re-election,[70] and the traditional lack of screening

[65] See e.g. ECJ Rules of Procedure Art. 88.
[66] See CJEU Statute Arts. 2, 10, 13, 35; ECJ Rules of Procedure Arts. 4, 32(1).
[67] A simple common law/civil law explanation is again too crude; e.g. the German Federal Constitutional Court has allowed dissenting opinions since 1970. The practices of the UK and US Supreme Court are also not identical. The former normally still states all involved judges' reasons separately and sequentially, while the latter announces judgments of the court, albeit with the possibility for each judge to write individually.
[68] See e.g. D. Landa and J. R. Lax, 'Legal Doctrine on Collegial Courts', *Journal of Politics*, 71 (2009), 946, 960.
[69] See e.g. D. Edward, 'How the Court of Justice Works', *European Law Review*, 20 (1995), 539, 557. Cf. J. Azizi, 'Unveiling the EU Courts' Internal Decision-Making Process: A Case for Dissenting Opinions?', *ERA Forum*, 12 (2011), 49. The following analysis leaves aside the technical legal point of amending the CJEU Statute.
[70] Similarly, Advocates General tend not to be assigned to cases concerning 'their' Member State.

procedure for new appointments. Moreover, it is thought that the unavailability of dissents gives rise to more democratic and accommodating judgments that can garner broader support in the Member States and provide clearer guidance for the future.[71] Even if no harm is seen in concurring opinions that show alternative routes to the same result, dissents are at times not considered to fulfil any meaningful purpose since the ECJ can, as a court of last resort, always push for a change in the law. According to that view, dissents are only really useful for courts of inferior jurisdiction, with any commentary or critique here best left to external participants, namely academics. Rather than egotistically raising their own profile and putting their personal view over that of the collective, the individual judges should refrain from driving a wedge between their own position and that of a majority with a nonchalant 'je peux vivre avec ça'. This is yet another facet of the impersonal collegiality that is reflected in the Court's fairly unspecific precedent use.

Four corollaries of this practice are immediately relevant. First, it reinforces the reluctance to cite substantively. For one, there appears on the surface to be less need to explore and reconcile prior conflicting views. The practice also forces coalition-building and possibly brinkmanship in the deliberation room, which is likely to result in a compromise of sorts.[72] Even accepting that judges with a minority view will do their best to make a judgment as solid as possible, something not everyone might be prepared to assume,[73] it is plainly more difficult to make finer points

---

[71] See D. Edward, 'How the Court of Justice Works', *European Law Review*, 20 (1995), 539, 737–8.

[72] On judicial deliberations at the ECJ see D. Edward, 'How the Court of Justice Works', *European Law Review*, 20 (1995), 539, 556 ('open discussion, often vigorous and sometimes heated, which goes on until a consensus or a clear difference of opinion emerges. If there is a clear difference of opinion, the President will take a vote'; footnote omitted). Besides being genuinely convinced of a solution, possible reasons for coalitions at the Court could, as elsewhere, also be down to the fact that the respective judges have internalised norms of loyalty and solidarity; want to advance their careers; or can be effectively disciplined.

[73] Jefferson's stinging critique of the Marshall court could unkindly be alluded to here: 'An opinion is huddled up in conclave, perhaps by a majority of one, delivered as if unanimous, and with the silent acquiescence of lazy and timid associates, by a crafty chief judge, who sophisticates the law to his mind, by the turn of his own reasoning.' He therefore proposed 'every one's giving his opinion *seriatim* and publicly on the case he decides. Let him prove by his reasoning that he has read the papers, that he has considered the case, that in the application of the law to it, he uses his own judgment; independently... The very idea of cooking up opinions in conclave begets suspicions that something passes which fears the public ear.' Quoted in B. W. Palmer, 'Judicial Review: Usurpation or Abdication?', *ABA Journal*, 46 (1960), 881, 887.

when in large numbers. Hence general citations become more palatable. Secondly, this helps to explain the low occurrence of departing; there is far less 'usable past' to work with, be it for the Court, future litigants or commentators. Consequently, distinguishing receives an uplift. Thirdly, when there are express *revirements*, they appear more dramatic and generate more astounded coverage, partly because it is not that easy to point to an alternative strand of thought that is already out in the open but simply failed to carry a majority in the past. Fourthly, there is the risk of making the jurisprudence look so smooth that it appears unfeasibly glib, failing to convince at large and relying essentially on the Court's privileged position to compensate for the lack of persuasiveness, which in turn entrenches the current precedent practice and does little overall to warm the sometimes rather frosty reception. In sum, it fits with the ECJ's penchant for terseness and consistency rather than persuasion and discursiveness.[74]

It could be thought that the Advocates General step into the breach and fulfil the same function as separate opinions. But that would be simplistic. Since the Treaty of Nice, their opinions are not even a necessity where no new points of law are raised. More often than not, the Court and the Advocate General will also reach a similar conclusion, although that statistic can be deceiving.[75] But while they can also in the long run be considered a means of quality control, they are essentially a one man (or woman) show lacking the Court's numerical and legitimatory capital. They are not the responsible decision-makers. As a modern day *buffon de la cour*, the job of an Advocate General is to highlight problems, uncover ambiguous lines of case law and recommend solutions. They can speak their mind without the eternal need to compromise, but they stand outside the collegiate decision-making process. Their strength is hence also their weakness. They have to be tactically astute and write persuasively to convince the Court, which often involves drawing on the 'development' or 'refinement' narrative or daring it, in particular when in a smaller

---

[74] Cf. J. Komárek, 'Judicial Lawmaking and Precedent in Supreme Courts', *LSE Law, Society and Economy Working Papers 4/2011* (2011), p. 37.

[75] Sometimes an Advocate General will want to add something despite the fact that the reporting judge's *rapport préalable* has already set out a fairly clear-cut answer to what appears to be a relatively straightforward matter and does not recommend the involvement of an Advocate General. In more complex matters, the reporting judge might be more cautious in expressing a preliminary view, in which case there is a higher likelihood of the Court's and Advocate General's approaches diverging.

formation, to depart from precedents.[76] In this respect their opinions resemble a party's pleadings rather than the *ex cathedra* statements of the ECJ. There are of course plenty of examples where the opinions of Advocates General have been tapped into explicitly or impliedly at a later point in time,[77] but these have more to do with the argumentative nature of law and dispute settlement than with their likeness to separate opinions.[78]

Leaving the point whether or not separate opinions would truly undermine the Court's overall authority for later,[79] it is important to remember that such multifaceted discursiveness is considered a double-edged sword in systems where separate opinions are available. The possibility of writing separately should not be equated with a need to do so. It is a tool to be employed judiciously. The main point is to set conditions whereby the majority opinion will be improved, since all adjudicators have to be more precise when plausible contrary views can also be published[80] and individual colleagues appeal to 'the intelligence of a future day'.[81] Indeed, one could argue that credibility and reputation not only survives but is also increased when courts openly reflect conflicting views. This reputation will make the reception of difficult decisions easier later in time since the decision-makers are not perceived as puppets or fiddlers.

Indeed, despite their availability, concurring opinions and dissents are far from ubiquitous elsewhere (e.g. in international investment arbitration or at the German FCC), reflecting a pragmatic acumen. Of course, regard must be had to the fact that few courts and tribunals are as large and diverse as the ECJ. The Court has become particularly diverse since the 2004 enlargement. Be that as it may, the mere possibility of dissents

---

[76] See e.g. Case C-380/05 *Centro Europa 7 Srl* v. *Ministero delle Comunicazioni e Autorità per le Garanzie nelle Comunicazioni* [2008] ECR I-349, Opinion of AG Poiares Maduro (para. 17); Case C-339/07 *Christopher Seagon* v. *Deko Marty Belgium NV* [2009] ECR I-767, Opinion of AG Ruiz-Jarabo Colomer (para. 72).

[77] See only Case C-408/08 *Lancôme parfums et beauté & Cie SNC* v. *OHIM* [2010] ECR I-1347, Opinion of AG Ruiz-Jarabo Colomer (para. 94).

[78] Cf. I. Solanke, '"Stop the ECJ"? An Empirical Analysis of Activism at the Court', *European Law Journal*, 17 (2011), 764, 783 (arguing that it is not readily possible to link the institution of Advocates General and ECJ 'activism').

[79] See Ch. 9.

[80] See R. Bader Ginsburg, 'The Role of Dissenting Opinions', *Minnesota Law Review*, 95 (2010), 1, 3.

[81] A phrase used by C. E. Hughes, *The Supreme Court of the United States* (4th print edn, Columbia University Press, New York, 1947), p. 68.

would have consequences for its precedent technique. At the ECJ, there is no vent for when negotiations between adjudicators fail. Writing – and hence perceptible reasoning, including case-based argumentation – cannot be as pointed. Dilution and homogeneity are again ingrained systemically. Sharp differences of opinion are not a real possibility, not only vis-à-vis different benches in time, but also within the same bench. This is closely allied to a culture of string precedent references and in particular to avoiding open (as opposed to silent) departures. Hairs can only be split where there is sufficient precision and arguing by precedent is often the fine art of splitting hairs.

iv Language

The EU is a multilingual area. The more than twenty different language versions of the treaties are equally authentic.[82] The Union's institutions have an equal number of official and working languages.[83] But as often there comes a point in practice where diversity has to make way for feasibility. Only few working documents are in fact translated into all languages given the constraints of time and cost. The Commission for instance employs English, French and German as its procedural languages.

The Court pursues a similar line on account of its special exemption from more exacting multilingualism requirements.[84] The rules are fairly detailed.[85] Internally, and for its own working purposes, the language at the Court is French, which can be attributed to the fact that French is spoken in three of the founding Member States of the EC and since other Member States were historically not in a position to make such demands at the time. This internal arrangement differs from the 'language of the case', which is the language in which proceedings are conducted.[86] The latter must be used for written statements. Supporting documents in other languages must be translated accordingly. It is interpreted simultaneously

---

[82] TEU Art. 55(1); TFEU Art. 358.

[83] TFEU Art. 342; EEC Council: Regulation No. 1 determining the languages to be used by the European Economic Community 15 Apr. 1958[1958] OJ 17/385.

[84] CJEU Statute Art. 64; TFEU Art. 342.

[85] See K. P. E. Lasok and T. Millett, *Judicial Control in the EU: Procedures and Principles* (Richmond Law & Tax, Richmond, 2004), m.nn. 414–19.

[86] Chosen by the applicant, save where the defendant is a Member State or a natural or legal person. In preliminary rulings the language of the case is that of the referring court.

during oral pleadings, but the judges deliberate in French without the aid of an interpreter. Governments are entitled to intervene in their official language.

It is not hard to fathom that this language diversity has an impact on legal argumentation and hence also precedent use.[87] Even the best interpretation or translation can erode or change nuances of meaning, especially if a concept is not readily familiar elsewhere, such as the idea of an English legal trust or the German distinction between *formelle* and *materielle Rechtskraft*. Some have even suggested the current arrangement at the ECJ privileges 'French legal thinking',[88] which might imply a reduced desire to be exhaustive and substantive as concerns precedent treatment. While the point can certainly be overplayed, not least since most judges and advocates are not native francophones, the present arrangement likely promotes greater abstraction and depersonalisation.[89] Astute participants will be aware that linguistic pirouettes on the point of a needle, popular in precedent-handling, are probably going to come undone. Broad principles and general case law statements are more likely to have an impact. And the larger the categorical umbrellas become, the less falls by the wayside, suggesting coherence and fit that dissuades departures.

---

[87] It is both a platitude and profound insight that law and language are intimately entangled. Law materialises in words, which make up treaties, legislation and decisions. Words express ideas and enable communication. They allow for inferences, e.g. a ball is round. Some inferences appear less prone to controversy, often those keyed closely to experience. In one preliminary reference, the ECJ had little ostensible trouble determining that poultry meant all those birds farmed for their eggs or their meat, including quails, partridges and pigeons: Case C-473/07 *Association Nationale pour la Protection des Eaux et Rivières-TOS and Association OABA* v. *Ministère de l'Ecologie, du Développement et de l'Aménagement durables* (Second Chamber) [2009] ECR I-319 (para. 23). Other inferences are more abstract. This is where things get messy in legal practice. Is a cinema a place where an audience of more than one person pays in advance to watch the same film at the same time? This is what the Belgian tax authorities had argued in Case C-3/09 *Erotic Center BVBA* v. *Belgische Staat* (Eighth Chamber) [2010] ECR I-2361 (paras. 16–19). The Court agreed. Drawing on the 'usual meaning', it held that coin-operated cubicles in which individuals could watch pornographic movies on their own were not 'cinemas'. The applicant was thus not entitled to the exceptional VAT reduction for cultural events and facilities contained in Annex H to Sixth Council Directive 77/388/EEC of 17 May 1977 on the harmonisation of the laws of the Member States relating to turnover taxes [1977] OJ L145/1.

[88] See T. C. Hartley, *The Foundations of European Union Law* (7th edn, Oxford University Press, 2010), p. 67.

[89] See Schiemann (n. 58 above), p. 10 (also noting use of the passive voice).

E Mode and style of justification

It is chiefly institutional factors rather than open discursiveness or argumentative allure that the ECJ draws on for legitimacy.[90] Process and purpose, not persuasion, are key. For instance, under the new Rules of Procedure of September 2012, the Court may decide not to hold a hearing at all if it thinks that it has sufficient information to give a ruling.[91] The overall impression appears to be that, given the workload, an intensive exchange of ideas of the involved parties by way of a contested oral hearing can be sidelined.[92] Moreover, the judicial decision should not be the sole focus, and less still the individual decision-maker. Rather, judgments must be seen in light of the larger framework in which they are embedded, including the diligent officialdom in the preparation of decisions, the frank deliberations behind closed doors, the equal spread of judicial appointments and the interaction with other important players, including the European legislature and executive as well as national institutions and courts.

All of this is reflected in the style and tone of ECJ judgments. While progressively opening up more in recent years, they are still considered arid and bureaucratic by most standards.[93] Judgments are short.[94] The structure is rigid, with the abstracted legal background set out in an established formula beforehand. Personal opinion is avoided. The

---

[90] For an argument that this is the typical – and simply different rather than inferior – French way of doing things see M. Lasser, 'The European Pasteurization of French Law', *Cornell Law Review*, 90 (2005), 995, 1005–15. This has however been questioned as buying too heavily into the original utopia of the French Revolution and depicting too little of the decidedly less ideal reality: K. Lemmens, 'But Pasteur was French: Comments on Mitchel Lasser's *The European Pasteurization of French Law*' in N. Huls, M. Adams and J. Bomhoff (eds.), *The Legitimacy of Highest Courts' Rulings: Judicial Deliberations and Beyond* (TMC Asser Press, The Hague, 2009), pp. 154–62.

[91] ECJ Rules of Procedure Art. 76(2).

[92] Cf. G. M. Berrisch, 'Die neue Verfahrensordnung des EuGH – Verfahrensbeschleunigung auf Kosten des Anhörungsrechts', *Europäische Zeitschrift für Wirtschaftsrecht*, (2012), 881, 882.

[93] See also Ch. 4, C.iii.(b) above on what is considered a French-inspired tradition and its oversimplification.

[94] Standardising at 4,000 symbols per page without spaces (and omitting citations in what follows for readability), much maligned *Mangold* barely makes more than ten pages of reading and reasoning, its progeny *Kücükdeveci* not even a slender eight pages. The bane of antisocial dumping activists, twins *Viking* and *Laval*, just about edge twelve and eighteen pages, respectively. Even a modern-day behemoth of constitutional significance like *Kadi* weighs in at just under forty-two pages, clearly surpassing the foundational evergreens *van Gend* (less than four pages) and *Costa* v. *ENEL* (five and a half pages).

Court favours 'shorthand slogans that do little more than cut debate short with a false sense of necessity' without sufficient 'interpretative trust'.[95] While certainly French-inspired, the Court's style has in the meantime acquired its own Unional flavour.[96] More than fifty years down the line and after several waves of significant and diverse enlargement, the ECJ is hardly a perfect replica of the Revolutionary prototype. The famous *Kadi* judgment for instance is comparatively long and discursive, seeking to set out arguments and concerns in some detail.[97] Yet overall, the general tone can still be considered officious and lacking in vigour.

This, too, is part of the self-disempowerment narrative. Populism and judicial ego should be kept in check.[98] A decision is not considered an appropriate forum to vent professional frustrations or air private views. While it is hard to deny that it is shielded from more direct control,[99] the Court's habits are rooted in a distinctive diplomatic sensitivity that stems from operating in a delicate non-domestic context with lingering intergovernmental overtones. Not that a shared *ésprit de corps* and elitism of senior officialdom cannot be detected, but that is more an on-the-job development than the product of a shared domestic experience or ideological outlook.

The evocative quality that the ECJ's broader mode of justification might lack is partly made up by the Advocates General, acting at times as a foil for the Court. Known for his flamboyant opinions, AG Ruiz-Jarabo Colomer in an action for infringement through suspension of customs duties incurred on the importation of defence equipment for example once referred to Beethoven's Symphony No. 9 in D major, 'the legendary song "Imagine" by John Lennon', 'a burlesque slip of the tongue from

---

[95] M. Lasser, *Judicial Deliberations: A Comparative Analysis of Judicial Transparency and Legitimacy* (Oxford University Press, 2004), p. 359.

[96] Cf. T. von Danwitz, *Verwaltungsrechtliches System und europäische Integration* (Mohr, Tübingen, 1996), pp. 150–4. Again, it would be too simple to attribute this to a civil law/common law split. Some of the more recent pronouncements of the German FCC seem downright garrulous. See e.g. BVerfG, 2 BvE 2/08, *Lissabon*, 2nd Senate, 30 Jun. 2009, which weighs in at over eighty standardised pages.

[97] Joined Cases C-402/05 P and C-415/05 P *Yassin Abdullah Kadi and Al Barakaat International Foundation v. Council and Commission* (Grand Chamber) [2008] ECR I-6351.

[98] Cf. H. Sendler, 'Über sog. humoristische Urteile', *Neue Juristische Wochenschrift* (1995), 847, 848.

[99] See J. Komárek, 'Questioning Judicial Deliberations', *Oxford Journal of Legal Studies*, 29 (2009), 805, 818.

the mouth of Don Quixote' as well as philosopher and penal reformer Beccaria, all within the space of four consecutive footnotes.[100] Seeking to provoke a departure from precedent, he once also compared the insistence of *Foto-Frost* that national courts need to make a reference before invalidating supranational legislation to the 'absurd hero' Sisyphus and his eternal condemnation and 'gruelling task'.[101] In another case on survivors' pensions and same-sex partnerships he quoted a Woody Allen movie to the effect that 'there are homosexual people, heterosexual people and people who are not interested in sex at all and become lawyers'.[102]

Yet the judgments themselves are often conceptualised as a stark preference for arguments from authority over arguments from reason.[103] It is tempting to view the ECJ's precedent practice through this prism; its heavy reliance on string citations is certainly indicative. Nonetheless, an all too schematic 'argument from authority' versus 'argument from reason' dichotomy is better avoided. It can be artificial because relying on authority is also an appeal to a particular reason and since reasons provided in legal discourse also claim authority. It is rudimentary since the Court's practice can shift, depending on what it considers appropriate in a particular situation:[104] 'authority' where a certain result is imperative, 'reason' where the spotlight is particularly intense. Contrast only a *van Gend*-like situation with a decision in a *Kadi*-esque saga. Of course there are differences of degree and general proclivities; but it is easy to overstate the importance of such categories. More concrete observations like those just offered relating to the extent of depersonalisation, systemic trajectories, institutional backing and the like appear more rewarding in the long run.

---

[100] Case C-284/05 *Commission* v. *Republic of Finland* [2009] ECR I-11705, Opinion of AG Ruiz-Jarabo Colomer (fns. 6–9).

[101] Case C-461/03 *Gaston Schul Douane-expediteur BV* v. *Minister van Landbouw, Natuur en Voedselkwaliteit* [2005] ECR I-10513, Opinion of AG Ruiz-Jarabo Colomer (paras. 2–4, 89).

[102] Case C-267/06 *Tadao Maruko* v. *Versorgungsanstalt der deutschen Bühnen* [2008] ECR I-1757, Opinion of AG Ruiz-Jarabo Colomer (fn. 86).

[103] See e.g. V. Perju, 'Reason and Authority in the European Court of Justice', *Virginia Journal of International Law*, 49 (2009), 307, 338–69 (arguing that the Court should adapt its old recipe for success and become more discursive).

[104] Cf. L. Coutron, 'Style des arrêts de la Cour de justice et normativité de la jurisprudence communautaire', *Revue Trimestrielle de Droit Européen*, 45 (2009), 643, 648 (on the ECJ).

A minimalistic inclination is further evident in the ECJ's relinquishing of broader legitimatory sources such as academic commentary or other auxiliary materials in its judgments. Of course the Court is not blind or fundamentally opposed to scholarly offerings, as officially demonstrated by the published *notes de doctrine*, which list relevant case comments.[105] But they are conspicuously absent in its expressed reasoning. The short answer is that it is simply not feasible to include them. Advocates General habitually engage with scholarly discourse in their opinions, but they have the privilege of writing in their mother tongue or a similarly familiar language. That is not possible in a court with a plurality of members that are deliberately drawn from different countries; translation costs alone are prohibitive, the argument goes. But besides practical exigencies, the legitimacy of the Court's pronouncements is also considered to lie solely and sufficiently in the fact that their spark can be traced through any secondary legislation to the primary materials, namely the treaties, and thus to democratic consent. That this might very well beg the question is neglected, with the views of academics or other considerations becoming at best a sideshow.

This minimalism resonates in precedent use. Interested observers are welcome to read up on the details of a case being adduced for a particular purpose, but the Court will not normally explain why it considers it relevant. In line with this, a parenthetical appendage is all that is required to justify a breathtakingly short summary of decades of jurisprudential creation and development. The ECJ does not see itself as in the business of digging up inconsistencies. Necessity rather than possibility is the yardstick of its persuasive efforts. Focusing on persuasiveness would mean directing decisions at the loser, but the Court rarely 'look[s] him or his advocate in the eye' in an effort to convince him that he had to lose the case.[106] Instead, it often employs a top-down mode of justification that relies on para-statal symbolism and a broader normative framework, rather than a more horizontal form of interaction in which not the last word but the better argument – however that may be defined – is considered to be the hurdle a decision-maker has to cross.

---

[105] More informally, but in keeping with the spirit of supplementing theoretical plausibility with empiricism, a quick look at the desk or bookshelf of many a judge or *référendaire* would yield similar conclusions.

[106] K. Schiemann, *Vom Richter des Common Law zum Richter des Europäischen Rechts* (Vorträge und Berichte Nr 145, Zentrum für Europäisches Wirtschaftsrecht, Rheinische Friedrich-Wilhelms-Universität, Bonn, 2005), p. 3 (on persuasive judgments).

F Case-load

i Age and volume of precedents

Citation patterns vary over time according to the number of relevant precedents available. Outward citations generally increase with more legal material to choose from, while inward citations (i.e. citations *to* a case) tend to take a dip with respect to newer cases, which – all other things being equal – have not been around for long enough to have a wide impact.[107] The jurisprudence of the ECJ spans a period of around sixty years.[108] In the course of this, the Court has built up a body of over 17,500 cases.

Accordingly, there are certain points of EU law that have been repeated so many times over the course of innumerable decisions and continually gone unchallenged by the Member States that precedent citation seems almost superfluous. Once again, this might be the case for primacy, direct effect, fundamental rights or state liability. Many of these have over time been officially recognised by primary or secondary law. They are such an entrenched part of the *acquis communautaire* that any precedent citation appears ornamental, since they are practically immune to being overturned.[109] Indeed, any elaboration beyond general mention or string citation would likely be considered eccentric or an attempt to dislodge certain fundamental aspects. Unsurprisingly, this discourages not only subsequent fluctuation but also discussion of the merits or finer points of precedents unless they are specifically called into question during proceedings. Of course departures are still an option, but the price is likely to be higher. Most international courts and tribunals on the other hand are nowhere near as encumbered by similarly copious and repetitive precedents, which fosters a more flexible practice.

Another point to bear in mind is that the older a legal text becomes and the more litigation is has spawned, the more interpretative gloss it accumulates. This makes precedents not only more important, it also

---

[107] See Y. Lupu and E. Voeten, 'Precedent in International Courts: A Network Analysis of Case Citations by the European Court of Human Rights', *British Journal of Political Science*, 42 (2012), 413, 426 (with figures on the ECtHR and US Supreme Court).

[108] The first case available in the official EUR-Lex database is Case 1–54 *French Republic* v. *High Authority of the European Coal and Steel Community*, delivered by the Court of Justice of the European Coal and Steel Community on 21 Dec. 1954 together with a judgment in an action brought by the Italian government.

[109] In particular US commentators like to refer to such decisions as 'super precedents' see e.g. M. J. Gerhardt, *The Power of Precedent* (Oxford University Press, 2008), pp. 177–98.

requires a considerable effort to consolidate and synthesise past jurisprudence in order to keep things manageable. This encourages quick bullet references, preferably formulated as statements of law, rather than an involved discussion of the context of the cases.

Moreover, resources are constrained at the Court. It is a publicly funded institution. Around half of its budget is spent on translation alone. This helps to explain why in the past it cut the *rapport d'audience* from the published reports and why it tends to relay parties' arguments sporadically. Generally, the Court strives for parsimonious judgments, ever keen to balance efficiency and visibility.[110] Conversely, at least in international arbitration, costs besides lawyers' fees and expenses include administrative fees and arbitrators' fees and expenses. This enables tribunals to explore various different avenues, including those suggested by past cases.

The Court's workload must also be factored into an analysis of its precedent treatment. In 2011, the ECJ completed 638 cases, with 849 still pending.[111] By way of comparison, the UK Supreme Court handed down sixty judgments in 2011.[112] Roughly speaking, the ECJ produces ten times as many judgments with just over double the number of judges. The judges do not have the luxury of absolute control over their docket. This again contributes to less lavish treatment of precedents.

ii Subject matter diversity and abstraction

The EU was always a broad political project, with regulation playing a powerful role in its market vision.[113] Its technocratic governance and lawmaking ranges from cavils about safety standards for bicycles to grand views on citizenship. Fittingly, the ECJ is vested with ample competences. Its rulings span subject matters ranging from the purely commercial and technical via fundamental market freedoms, social issues, fundamental rights and police and judicial co-operation[114] to questions of larger institutional design. While a market economy and free competition coupled with interventionist economy policies are close to the core of EU law as

---

[110] See Skouris (n. 33 above), pp. 24–5 (insisting that the primary aim is not to save translation time, but to make judgments more concise and readable).
[111] See Ch. 4, n. 56.   [112] They are available at www.bailii.org/uk/cases/UKSC/.
[113] See D. Kennedy, *The Dark Sides of Virtue* (Princeton University Press, 2004), pp. 180–1.
[114] What was formerly the so-called 'third pillar' was brought into the fold of the TFEU following the Treaty of Lisbon, which also abolished the former TEU Art. 35 that limited the ECJ's jurisdiction in this respect.

the 'engine' of European integration,[115] the economy was at all times a means rather than an end.[116] The EU pursues a diverse range of broader socio-political objectives. To give just a sprinkling of more recent examples, the jurisprudence of the Court has demonstrated that non-economic rationales carried the day in cases concerning the sale of 'soft' drugs in licensed premises,[117] competition between pharmacies[118] or the patentability of certain uses of human embryos for the purposes of scientific research.[119]

Essentially, the treaties are an unfinished and co-operative project.[120] They lack the relative closure and focus of most international treaties. In many respects they are better seen as an open-ended constitution than a concluded bargain. The EU's 'soul', writes one commentator, remains 'uncertain' beyond the rudimentary basics, just as the voice of its central judicial organ rarely if ever proclaims a particular philosophy of society.[121] What it means for something to be 'European' is an open-ended question, for good reason.[122] The ECJ needs to be mindful of the multifaceted needs of a European polity. Its reasoning generally seeks to be inclusive and embracing. Like the larger polity, it rests in the ideal of union rather than perfect unity.[123] While not a necessity, as many domestic judicial opinions show, being diffuse can contribute to this. One way to do so is to water down precedent references to bare essentials, that is case names and citations, without stressing the substantive angles of particular cases. And

---

[115] On the 'economic constitution' that lies at the junction of EU law and its economy see A. Hatje, 'The Economic Constitution within the Internal Market' in A. von Bogdandy and J. Bast (eds.), *Principles of European Constitutional Law* (2nd edn, Hart and C. H. Beck, Oxford and Munich, 2010), pp. 590–3.

[116] Cf. Opinion 1/91 *Draft Agreement Between the Community and the Countries of the European Free Trade Association Relating to the Creation of the European Economic Area* [1991] ECR I-6079 (para. 50) ('[L]e libre-échange et la concurrence ne constituent que des moyens destinés à atteindre ces objectifs').

[117] Case C-137/09 *Marc Michel Josemans v. Burgemeester van Maastricht* (Second Chamber) [2010] ECR I-13019.

[118] Joined Cases C-171/07 and C-172/07 *Apothekerkammer des Saarlandes and ors v. Saarland and Ministerium für Justiz, Gesundheit und Soziales* (Grand Chamber) [2009] ECR I-4171.

[119] Case C-34/10 *Oliver Brüstle v. Greenpeace eV* (Grand Chamber) [2011] ECR I-9821.

[120] See especially TEU Arts. 3, 4; Komárek (n. 74 above), p. 29.

[121] Cf. A. Williams, *The Ethos of Europe: Values, Law and Justice in the EU* (Cambridge University Press, 2010), pp. 1–2, 254–5.

[122] See F. Hanschmann, *Der Begriff der Homogenität in der Verfassungslehre und Europarechtswissenschaft* (Springer, Berlin and Heidelberg, 2008), pp. 284–95.

[123] Cf. J. H. H. Weiler, 'The Transformation of Europe', *Yale Law Journal*, 100 (1990–1991), 2403 (juxtaposing, at the time, community and unity).

while distinguishing can suitably accommodate the many different functional logics operating within the pluralistic Union, an express departure usually amounts to a clear admission that the Court is willing to take sides in existing internal conflicts at the cost of others. This is unavoidable at times, but the ECJ seems loath to force this itself.

Overall, the Court often operates at a high level of abstraction that can seem unusual even to seasoned appellate judges. After all, it ensures that 'the law is observed'.[124] By the time a case makes it to the Grand Chamber, various legal minds will have considered a matter to involve a legal problem of relevance. The Court is then very much in the business of setting standards rather than policing them. It does more than close a case file. In fact, the precise nature of the applicant's grievance largely remains in the background. In particular preliminary references not concerning validity, that emblematic mouthpiece of the ECJ, provide an almost infinite scope for being very general about the law or the facts of a request,[125] not least since the national courts will themselves often have abstracted a problem. Generalisation reflects the split desire to harmonise without saying too much. Such broadly conceptual rather than dispute-centric thinking goes hand in hand with the Court's practice of citing wider case law developments and making statements of law through what often appears to be apodictic use of precedents.

Ultimately, abstraction and specificity can both be ways to resolve conflicts resulting from clashing interests. One can make a point so general that it allows for many different understandings or one can classify a matter so narrowly that one can count the proverbial angels dancing on the head of a pin. All decision-makers employ a mix of these techniques. The ECJ, too, has its *arrêts d'espèce*,[126] but the point is that, without a substantive argumentation culture or possibility of rebuttal, broad arguments tend to favour consensus and multiple functional logics.

---

[124] TEU Art. 19(1).

[125] See e.g. Case C-461/03 *Gaston Schul Douane-expediteur BV* v. *Minister van Landbouw, Natuur en Voedselkwaliteit* [2005] ECR I-10513, Opinion of AG Ruiz-Jarabo Colomer (para. 7) ('The facts are of minor importance with regard to the answers to be given to the questions referred for a preliminary ruling').

[126] For a good example where the ECJ was very specific in a preliminary reference see Case C-14/08 *Roda Golf & Beach Resort SL* [2009] ECR I-5439 (para. 58). The Court resisted the temptation to define an 'extrajudicial' act and responded to the request squarely on its facts. It thereby avoided the potentially huge ramifications of a sweeping definition, which would have been audacious indeed for a chamber of five.

G Oubliettes and guillotines

As others have noted and as this work confirms, the ECJ very rarely overrules its precedents openly. At the same time, and despite the best efforts of the Court to be as tight-lipped as possible as concerns stray language and reasoning, it is implausible to assume that it is perfectly consistent in all cases, not least given its vast output and because of the existence of several examples that indicate the contrary.[127] What happens to those episodes?

Given both its permanence and the need to be consistent, the Court would appear to be in a sticky situation. All legal systems need both stability and change to survive. EU law being no different in that respect, the ECJ has over time found its own way of dealing with precedents that have fallen out of favour. The process relies on silent disappearance rather than noisy beheading, which is why it might be likened to an oubliette.

The starting point is the Research and Documentation department, which will find it difficult to impossible to meaningfully prepare and categorise a precedent that makes little sense no matter which way it is turned or twisted. Keywords might be unintuitive or misleading and access via EUR-Lex through 'subject matter' or 'digest' searches will often fail to spot such a case. Even if Member States and commentators register the decision, they too will find it difficult to capitalise on its reasoning. Academic papers might avoid the case altogether or hide it behind a perfunctory and evasive 'but see' footnote with little commentary. Judges and litigators will find it hard to make good use of the case, given its inconclusiveness or downright illogicality.[128] In short, such cases fail to make a mark as useful legal information, fading unceremoniously from the system of 'collective learning' that precedent comprises. This explains the low departure rate of the ECJ despite being a lively and dynamic adjudicatory body at the same time.

While this mechanism achieves a comparable result to open overruling in terms of mediating between stability and change, it has different strings attached, just as an oubliette and a guillotine are different techniques for achieving similar results concerning unwanted persons. The latter is more obvious, meaning that legitimacy costs are paid up front. The ECJ's method on the other hand accumulates these over time. The danger

---

[127] See e.g. the examples in Ch. 4, C.iii.(a) and Ch. 5, C.

[128] See e.g. one Advocate General's suggestion that a troublesome precedent suggesting horizontal direct effect 'need not be clarified' while stating that in the absence of transposition a directive may not of itself impose obligations on an individual: Case C-418/04 *Commission v. Ireland* [2007] ECR I-10947, Opinion of AG Kokott (para. 89, fn. 58).

with this is that, in the long run, the relationship between the Court and the other participants in the European legal space becomes progressively more complicated and irritable the more the impression gains currency that the Court is not always equally thorough or open when it comes to its past decisions.

8

The normativity of ECJ precedents

A Conceptual approaches

As seen in Chapter 6, the Court departs from precedents, although it rarely does so explicitly. Its hesitancy to do so was unfolded Chapter 7. Its entitlement to depart is usually conceptualised by way of a denial of the binding force of its pronouncements outside the same set of proceedings. The point is rarely theorised in much detail. It forms the subject of this chapter.

Normativity continues to vex legal theory.[1] It is often taken to denote a metaphysical concept connecting command and obedience. Stripped of this 'ought', rules would at best be habit, possibly preference or – most ordinarily – coincidence. In this conception, a norm is a rule for behaviour, departure from which renders one liable for some form of censure. Confusion in particular surrounds the strength of any obligation to comply, that is to say the question whether or how it can be offset. This is compounded by terminological insecurity.

Purists insist that normativity is essentially bindingness and that to be bound (by precedents or otherwise) means that it is not possible to resist an obligation simply on account of what might be considered a better countervailing reason or preferable choice of action.[2] Bindingness here creates a context of decisional exclusivity. Any other reasoning, even if superior in quality, is by definition futile. Authority and argumentation are kept separate. Terms to describe this conception include 'true', 'real',

---

[1] See e.g. R. Christensen, *Was heißt Gesetzesbindung?* (Duncker & Humblot, Berlin, 1989), pp. 64–5 (claiming that (German) courts do not do what they say and do not say what they do); M. Goldmann, 'Inside Relative Normativity: From Sources to Standard Instruments for the Exercise of International Public Authority' in A. von Bogdandy, P. Dann and M. Goldmann (eds.), *The Exercise of Public Authority by International Institutions* (Springer, Heidelberg, 2010), pp. 671–9.

[2] Cf. F. Müller and R. Christensen, *Juristische Methodik: Europarecht* (2nd edn, Duncker & Humblot, Berlin, 2007), p. 304.

'pure', 'actual', 'strict', 'formal', 'legal', 'de jure', 'technical', 'authoritative', 'strong', 'theoretical' or 'binding' precedent or *stare decisis*.[3]

However, despite its internal lucidity, that approach can be criticised for its artificiality. Contexts of actual decisional exclusivity are prone to circularity and by design ignorant of other forms of normativity. Besides, any 'ought' does not per se require exclusivity (let alone actual compulsion), as exemplified by important phenomena such as 'soft law' or best practice guidelines. Indeed, one might rest one's general understanding of law on the stabilisation of normative expectations. Authority can then feature as one factor in legal argumentation.[4] Such or similar considerations resonate in expressions of 'de facto', 'persuasive', 'soft', 'weak', 'practical' or 'non-binding' precedent or in rejections of *stare decisis*.[5]

The position taken here is that it is appropriate to say that ECJ precedents are normative in the sense of forming part of EU law. Departure would, without more, cause dissatisfaction. All other things being equal, decided cases are legal information (i.e. form part of one's understanding of EU law) and demand respect if legality and systematicity are taken seriously. They at the very least impose a burden on whoever seeks a divergent solution. Denying normativity altogether neglects the dual nature of law and legal practice that oscillates between abstract ideal and concreteness.[6] At the same time, it is not wrong – albeit largely meaningless – to insist that ECJ precedents do not bind in the sense that countervailing through better reasoning is impossible. To hold otherwise could not explain practical reality, take an even stricter stance on precedent than many common law courts do, stifle emancipatory potential and again neglect the argumentative nature of law and legal practice. In other words, there is more to normativity than decisional exclusivity.

---

[3] Sometimes, this is simply considered to be 'precedent' without more. That is infelicitous since it rides roughshod over many different nuances, not least that bindingness does not exhaust precedent. The special case of *stare decisis* will be examined shortly.

[4] Cf. S. Besson, 'Theorizing the Sources of International Law' in S. Besson and J. Tasioulas (eds.), *The Philosophy of International Law* (Oxford University Press, Oxford 2010), pp. 173–4 (who speaks of 'exclusionary albeit *prima facie* reasons for action' and degrees of normativity).

[5] At times, this is also expressed by a supposed absence of 'precedent' altogether. Again, this is too crude.

[6] See H. Kelsen, *Reine Rechtslehre* (Franz Deuticke, Leipzig and Vienna, 1934), pp. 20–38; D. Kennedy, 'Theses about International Legal Discourse', *German Yearbook of International Law*, 23 (1980), 353, 362–5; V. Heiskanen, *International Legal Topics* (Lakimiesliiton Kustannus, Helsinki, 1992), pp. 82–3; M. Koskenniemi, *From Apology to Utopia* (reissue edn, Cambridge University Press, 2005), pp. 58–60.

What follows next is an overview of familiar ways of dealing with the normative force of precedents. It is not intended to be exhaustive or prescriptive,[7] but instead sets apart the traditional vantage points to prepare the ground for a closer look at the ECJ's situation.

B Archetypes

Domestic paradigms are almost invariably used in the context of discussing the binding force of precedents in inter- and supranational settings and when arguing from 'first principles'. This reflects the instinctive grounding of most lawyers, who are still primarily trained with national law in mind.

i Civil law systems

Even when they do not subscribe to mechanistic cognitivism ('law is out there and adjudicators simply have to apply it'), so-called civil law or Continental legal systems[8] consider it one of their defining hallmarks that precedents are not 'legally binding' – at least 'in theory'.[9] The train of thought usually proceeds in three steps.

(a) Codes and rational deduction

Civil law systems are, by and large, profoundly influenced by a tradition of 'rationality in law' and a particular variant of positivism.[10] Refuting the binding force of the output of adjudication is grounded in Justinian's clipped credo: 'cum non exemplis, sed legibus iudicandum sit'

---

[7] Cf. G. Frankenberg, 'Stranger than Paradise: Identity and Politics in Comparative Law', *Utah Law Review* (1997), 259, 262 (on the temptations and dangers of abusing macroscopic comparative law).

[8] Throughout this section the term 'system' is used without pretending to resolve the eternal debate as to whether legal 'family', 'tradition', 'culture' or 'circle' might not be the more appropriate concept. Cf. L. A. Luts, 'Typologies of Modern Legal Systems of the World', *Journal of Comparative Law*, 5 (2010), 28.

[9] H. G. Schermers and D. F. Waelbroeck, *Judicial Protection in the European Union* (6th edn, Kluwer Law International, The Hague, 2001), p. 134.

[10] It is a variant because positivism as such is of course not opposed to affording cases binding normative quality, as the well-known brand of common law positivism of Jeremy Bentham exemplifies, which combines a zealous appetite for codification with a defence of *stare decisis*.

('adjudication should be based not on examples but on legislation').[11] It finds its clearest expression in efforts of systemic codification around the time of the French Revolution or thereafter.[12] They form the bedrock of the opposition towards affording cases binding force. Various factors were responsible for the codification phenomenon. Many codes were an expression of the patriotism that had gripped Europe, a *ius patrium* as the crowning achievement of rekindled national pride and nascent unitary nation states.[13] But the movement was also deeply suffused with the philosophy of enlightenment and political and economic liberalism. Of course the 'sovereign will of the people' was rarely articulated directly without authoritarian intermediaries, namely ministerial bureaucracies.[14] These stood to gain a lot from wiping the slate clean. It would, however, equally be an oversimplification to say that the likes of Savigny and the disciples of the historical school of jurists, often thought of as the bogeymen of the codification movement on account of their conservative historicism, were entirely opposed to the idea of legal development.[15]

In spite of a discernible hegemonic streak, codification can certainly be conceived with emancipatory aims in mind.[16] Classical liberalism, the driving intellectual force behind much of the positivist project, seeks to

[11] Codex Iustinianus 7, 45, 13. On the lack of a system of case law in ancient Rome see E. Metzger, 'Roman Judges, Case Law, and Principles of Procedure', *Law and History Review*, 22 (2004), 243, 250–60 (while noting that precedents remained an important fixture).

[12] See H. P. Glenn, *Legal Traditions of the World* (4th edn, Oxford University Press, 2010), pp. 143, 151–5. Cf. J. Vanderlinden, *Le Concept de code en Europe occidentale du XIII. au XIX. siècle* (Editions de l'Institut de Sociologie, Université Libre de Bruxelles, Brussels, 1967), pp. 22–46.

[13] There are obviously historical and cultural differences. Some codes, such as the French *Code civil*, are cherished as glowing expressions of national identity, whereas others seem to garner mostly professional and cerebral admiration, e.g. the German *Bürgerliches Gesetzbuch*.

[14] See F. Wieacker, *Privatrechtsgeschichte der Neuzeit* (2nd edn, Vandenhoeck & Ruprecht, Göttingen, 1967), pp. 459–60. Cf. J. Isensee, *Das Volk als Grund der Verfassung: Mythos und Relevanz der Lehre von der verfassunggebenden Gewalt* (Westdeutscher Verlag, Opladen, 1995), p. 73 (on the mythologisation of the *pouvoir constituant* through enlightenment ideology).

[15] See e.g. F. C. von Savigny, *Vom Beruf unsrer Zeit für Gesetzgebung und Rechtswissenschaft* (2nd edn, J. C. B. Mohr, Heidelberg, 1828), p. 11 ('So wie für [die Sprache], gibt es auch für das Recht keinen Augenblick eines absoluten Stillstandes'). The historicists' ambivalent attitude towards codification is perhaps best evidenced in the person of Windscheid. Generally speaking, the differences concerned the *who* and the *how* of legal change, rather than the *if*.

[16] On this see U. Mattei, 'The Issue of European Civil Codification and Legal Scholarship', *Hastings International & Comparative Law Review*, 21 (1998), 883, 885.

limit authoritarian interference and demands that the individual order his affairs with the largest possible degree of autonomy and foreseeability. Private law was the field where the minimal baselines should be drawn and codes presented the perfect instrument to put this philosophy into practice.[17] The stated goal was both simple and complicated: 'réduire le droit à la loi'.[18]

Codes were also designed to order the chaos caused by a Byzantine labyrinth of different layers of Roman law, canon law, natural law as well as regional, indigenous and mercantile custom, all of which had been fashioned over time by judicial opinions and lawyers' interpretations into a Continental *ius commune*.[19] This disarray had been further exacerbated by the lack of a centralised judiciary. Codification hence presented a chance to scrupulously trim the wild growth of this *usus modernus* in the pursuit of legal certainty and efficiency, something piecemeal statutory enactments could not achieve. This posed certain demands on the chosen form of regulation. The codes had to be comprehensive, permanent, well-structured, easily navigable and free from internal logical contradiction. Haphazard on-the-spot regulation, let alone authoritative pronouncements issued by individual judges, would not be tolerated. Abstraction and generalisation were called for.

Prime examples are the German criminal and civil code, with their general parts laying down basic concepts applicable to the remainder and preceding the special parts that regulate individual situations, reminiscent of the way mathematical parentheses impose operational priority and logical coherence. Although they have been amended numerous times and are relative newcomers as far as European codes are concerned, they are still going strong at around 140 and 110 years of age, respectively. The ideal is law as a science (not tradition); the main legal technique is deduction from a coherent and autonomous entirety. Induction from decided cases jars with this mindset.

This thirst for individual liberty and perfect rationality coalesces into another central tenet of civil law systems: impersonality. Rooted in rec-ollections of the often unsavoury role judges played during the *Ancien*

---

[17] See D. Kennedy, 'Two Globalizations of Law & Legal Thought: 1850–1968', *Suffolk University Law Review*, 36 (2003), 631, 632–3.

[18] See C. Perelman, *Logique juridique: Nouvelle rhétorique* (2nd edn, Dalloz, Paris, 1999), p. 23.

[19] See H. Coing, *Europäisches Privatrecht*, 2 vols. (C. H. Beck, Munich, 1985), I, pp. 25–26, 34–42; R. Zimmermann, 'Codification: History and Present Significance of an Idea', *European Review of Private Law*, 3 (1995), 95, 98.

Régime and the French Revolution, the message seems clear: the law is to govern, not the magistrate.[20] Codification epitomises this attempted clean break with the past by putting certain premises beyond the reach of the individual participants of the legal system. Its theoretical underpinning rests on a conception of the proper relationship between legislative and judicial branches. Putting law on a positive footing is one prong of this philosophy; the other is emaciating other exponents of the law, namely lawyers and the judiciary.[21] Ideally, the individual is interchangeable in this process, as evinced by the commonality of collegiate judgments. Nor are adjudicators to be constrained by what others might have said in the past regarding a point of law. Courts must not only be allowed to deviate from their own past jurisprudence or that of other courts, even if hierarchically superior, they are even obliged to do so pursuant to their fidelity to the impersonal law. Following 'wrong' precedents could even lead to criminal charges of perverting the course of justice.

In its pursuit of impersonal law and through its dispassionate and rational opposition to what is often rather crude organic reality, this mindset creates its own brave new world with its own intrinsic rules and meticulous method.[22] In the wake of this the ontological 'rule of law' becomes the synthetic 'state of law' (*Rechtsstaat*).[23] This artificiality serves the purpose of purposely structuring relations and reigning in unencumbered discretion. To give an example from international law, the criteria of statehood are legal criteria.[24] Such an approach can be taken to extremes, for instance when a 'human' becomes a matter of legal definition. To be sure, absolutist forms of conceptualism, so-called *Begriffsjurisprudenz*, are easy to lampoon and quick to demask once one recognises that a difference exists between norms and concepts.[25] Concepts are in many ways necessary but not sufficient for law to exist. Crucially, unless they rely on circular logic, they are always liable to construal and cannot constitute

---

[20] See H. Coing, *Europäisches Privatrecht*, 2 vols. (C. H. Beck, Munich, 1989), II, p. 9. Perhaps ironically, the power thus syphoned from the judiciary privileged another group of legal drafters and exponents: university professors. See Glenn (n. 12 above), p. 148.

[21] Cf. G. Hager, *Rechtsmethoden in Europa* (Mohr Siebeck, Tübingen, 2009), p. 28 ('Die Liebe zum Gesetz wurzelte im Hass gegen die Juristen').

[22] See A. Somek, *Rechtliches Wissen* (Suhrkamp, Frankfurt am Main 2006), pp. 56–7 (on 'methodological world creation').

[23] See Glenn (n. 12 above), p. 154.

[24] For a definition see Montevideo Convention on the Rights and Duties of States of 26 Dec. 1933, 165 LNTS 19, Art. 1.

[25] See G. Jellinek, *Allgemeine Staatslehre* (3rd edn, Springer, Berlin, 1922), p. 162 ('Den Rechtsbegriffen als solchen entspricht keine Realität außer uns.').

an unshakable and completely interpretation-proof – often casually yet misleadingly expressed as 'objective' – idea.

Of course Continental jurists were neither categorically blind to the significance of adjudication nor removed from practical concerns.[26] Clearly not all situations could be anticipated. The emphasis was hence often on the *spirit* of the code; but the spirit of the *code*, nonetheless. This encouraged the ternary model examined earlier. But another upshot of this interpretive understanding is that the centre of gravity of legal agency unwittingly shifts from the drafters of codes and treaties to judges and litigants.[27] Such was the case in civil law systems,[28] such is the case for many international regimes[29] and such is the case for the EU. In all of this legal text remains focal, but not exclusive.

(b) Entrenched negation

Sometimes this article of faith resisting precedents' binding force – *quieta movere* – is expressly codified or entrenched in a constitutional proviso in addition to the pre-emptive technique just outlined. Such stipulations are further materialisations of the general positivistic thrust. They come in varying degrees of granularity, ranging from the rather precise instruction of Art. 5 of the French Civil Code to the near-unfathomable depths of Art. 20(3) of the German Basic Law.[30]

Article 5 of the French Civil Code is taken to be a countermand to the *arrêts de règlement* of the *parlements* of old, that is to say a disavowal of the generally applicable regulatory decrees of institutions that historically combined both adjudicative and legislative functions and had very much fallen into disfavour.[31] Legislation through democratic representation

---

[26] Cf. M. Lasser, *Judicial Deliberations: A Comparative Analysis of Judicial Transparency and Legitimacy* (Oxford University Press, 2004), pp. 169–71; H.-P. Haferkamp, *Georg Friedrich Puchta und die "Begriffsjurisprudenz"* (Klostermann, Frankfurt am Main, 2004).

[27] Cf. Kennedy (n. 17 above), pp. 632–3.

[28] See U. Steiner, 'Richterliche Rechtsfortbildung und Grundgesetz' in G. Müller, E. Osterloh and T. Stein (eds.), *Festschrift für Günter Hirsch zum 65. Geburtstag* (C. H. Beck, Munich, 2008), p. 611.

[29] See P. Sands, 'Introduction and Acknowledgments' in R. Mackenzie, C. Romano and Y. Shany (eds.), *Manual on International Courts and Tribunals* (2nd edn, Oxford University Press, 2010), pp. ix–x.

[30] The provisions read, respectively: 'Il est défendu aux juges de prononcer par voie de disposition générale et réglementaire sur les causes qui leur sont soumises' and 'Die Gesetzgebung ist an die verfassungsmäßige Ordnung, die vollziehende Gewalt und die Rechtsprechung sind an Gesetz und Recht gebunden.'

[31] Cf. J. P. Dawson, *The Oracles of the Law* (University of Michigan Press, Ann Arbor, 1968), pp. 301, 350.

is afforded pride of place. Judicial elites are not to impose their own designs through their decisions, even if they consider the law unwise or unjust. As such, this is an explicit prohibition of judicial legislation. From this it is then surmised that judgments cannot have binding force *stricto sensu* outside of current proceedings vis-à-vis others or a court itself.[32] The argument would seem to be that if a judge cannot make generally applicable pronouncements on the law, he likewise remains at liberty to deviate from earlier jurisprudence. The flip side is that this imposes a certain responsibility on behalf of the individual judge to base his decision on his own reasoning. The subordination of the judiciary in this scheme explains the classical methodological preference of the *école de l'exégèse*, which unsurprisingly and firmly roots interpretive efforts in the wording of the code, either by looking for the subjective will of the legislator or by trying to situate a norm objectively within the larger system, which is assumed to constitute a coherent and rational totality.[33] Or, to quote Aubry, 'Toute la loi . . . mais rien que la loi'.[34]

Turning to another provision arguably refuting 'true' (i.e. 'binding') precedent, Art. 20(3) of the German Basic Law binds the judiciary with apparent simplicity to *Gesetz* and *Recht*. For that stipulation to be a bar to constrained decision-making, both *Gesetz* and *Recht* would have to be understood to exclude judicial pronouncements. Much has been made of such juxtaposition of concrete and abstract law, which features prominently in most Continental European languages and legal orders – *loi* and *droit*, *ley* and *derecho*, *legge* and *diritto*, *lex* and *ius*, *Gesetz* and *Recht*. In English, the closest approximation that encapsulates this idea of law as distinct rules and law as a systemic whole might be the difference between laws of England and English law.[35] It has also been argued that this combination is what TEU Art. 19(1) has in mind when stating that the ECJ shall ensure that 'the law' is observed in the interpretation and application of the treaties.[36]

However, quite what is meant by such supposed opposition is a matter of perpetual controversy. It transports opposing notions of substance and

---

[32] See C. K. Allen, *Law in the Making* (6th edn, Clarendon Press, 1958), pp. 176–82.
[33] See P. Malaurie and P. Morvan, *Droit civil: introduction générale* (3rd edn, Defrénois, Paris, 2009), nos. 389–412.
[34] See J.-L. Bergel, *Théorie générale du droit* (4th edn, Dalloz, Paris, 2003), nos. 231–2.
[35] See W. Geldart, W. S. Holdsworth and H. G. Hanbury, *Elements of English Law* (6th edn, Oxford University Press, London, 1959), pp. 1–2.
[36] See e.g. F. C. Mayer, 'Art. 19 EUV' in E. Grabitz, M. Hilf and M. Nettesheim (eds.), *Das Recht der Europäischen Union* (C.H. Beck, München 2010), m.n. 23.

form as well as subjective and objective legal dimensions. But in the end these remain synthetic concepts, open to different understandings.[37] The judge is bound to something, but to what exactly?

As a starting point, it would seem that a difference between the two is allowed for; pure duplication would mean redundancy. *Gesetz* is further unproblematic in this respect, evidently referring to a manifestation of law that is the purview of a particular procedure of parliamentary law-making, be it primary legislation or the various forms of delegated legislation.

The meaning of *Recht* in the context of Art. 20(3) of the German Basic Law on the other hand is hotly contested.[38] At first glance, its additional inclusion would appear to signal a tension between positive and non-positive (read: natural) law. Indeed, insertion of *Recht* besides *Gesetz* as the yardstick for the executive and judiciary was a conscious reaction of the drafters of the Basic Law to the experiences of National Socialism.[39] Not all law is positive law (i.e. *Gesetz*) the argument goes. No longer would positivist perversions be tolerated. The imprint of the likes of Gustav Radbruch is patent in this approach[40] which the traditional English doctrine of parliamentary sovereignty rejects, classical English positivism refuses to accept and the English language even struggles to convey: laws (*Gesetze*) can be unlawful (*rechtswidrig*). *Recht* is then a reservoir for legitimation that can be tapped into in those cases where positive law does not satisfy expectations of what is considered proper adjudication.

The natural law-esque reading, historically explicable though it may be, faces several difficulties, most of which could also be brought to bear to an analogous reading of TEU Art. 19(1). The less sophisticated riposte decries the vagueness that would seep into the legal process and the categorical antagonism of natural law to the positivistic heritage and its ideal of complete and coherent systematicity. The critique becomes

---

[37] For correlations but also overlap in modern Russian legal terminology see R. A. Romashov, 'The Concepts of "Jus" and "Lex": Historical and Legal Linguistic Aspects', *Journal of Comparative Law*, 5 (2010), 145.

[38] See only H. Schulze-Fielitz, 'Art 20' in H. Dreier (ed.), *Grundgesetz Kommentar*, 3 vols. (Mohr Siebeck, Tübingen, 2006), II, m.n. 94 (discerning at least four possible interpretations: duplication, natural law, unwritten law, constitutional legal order).

[39] See B. Hoffmann, *Das Verhältnis von Gesetz und Recht* (Duncker & Humblot, Berlin 2003), pp. 32–60.

[40] Cf. M. Stolleis, *The Law under the Swastika* (University of Chicago Press, Chicago and London, 1998), pp. 158–9, 178–80. Note however that formalism was also a target of less savoury views on 'living law': W. Sauer, *Juristische Methodenlehre: Zugleich eine Einleitung in die Methodik der Geisteswissenschaften* (Enke, Stuttgart, 1940), p. 401.

more refined following the interpretative turn and the acceptance of positive law as inevitably requiring further exposition and elaboration. This stance seeks to pull away from divorcing legitimacy from legality. According to this Dworkinian train of thought, the legal order already offers ample opportunity to let such considerations flow into the process of legal reasoning and justification, even without resort to grand natural law theorising, for example via the concepts of human dignity, fundamental rights and proportionality, all of which are expressly contained in the Basic Law[41] or the primary law of the EU.[42] This fits with the civil law mindset of perceiving the legal order as a 'rational whole' (*Sinnganzes*).[43]

Recht is then understood to refer to the constitutional legal order in its entirety, which includes all law that is not parliamentary legislation, namely the Basic Law, both primary and secondary EU law, public international law – in particular the Universal Declaration of Human Rights, ECHR, and the other important human rights treaties – and what might remain of customary law.[44]

Two points follow. For one, the jurisprudence of the courts can go beyond and even contradict law as it is posited, but despite the noticeable whiff of natural law any activity of that kind that is completely independent of all laws in terms of their spirit and purpose would remain off-limits.[45] Secondly, while the law cannot be reduced to written sources alone, there is no need for recourse to other sources of legitimation, particularly precedents. *Gesetz* and *Recht* are considered to comprehensively quench the thirst for appropriate adjudication. They are the sole loadstars. Nothing exists 'outside' of this. Ergo, judicial pronouncements cannot fulfil this function and cannot be considered 'formally' or 'legally' binding. Questions of what is right or just are to be decided collectively, such as through parliamentary majorities. So while the deliberate dichotomy of Art. 20(3) enhances the role of judges in a certain respect by granting them a degree of flexibility when it comes to interpreting sources and

---

[41] See B. Grzeszick, 'Art 20 VI' in R. Herzog *et al.* (eds.), *(Maunz/Dürig) Grundgesetz Kommentar* (C. H. Beck, Munich, 2007), m.nn. 66–7; Steiner (n. 28 above), p. 616.

[42] Specifically, the TEU in combination with the CFREU.

[43] See BVerfG, 1 BvR 112/65, *Soraya*, 1st Senate, 14 Feb. 1973 (m.n. 38).

[44] See K.-P. Sommermann, 'Art 20 Abs 3' in C. Starck (ed.), *(Mangoldt/Klein) Kommentar zum Grundgesetz*, 3 vols. (5th edn, C. H. Beck, Munich, 2005), II, m.n. 265.

[45] Cf. Schulze-Fielitz (n. 38 above), m.n. 94; P. Kirchhof, 'Recht Sprechen ist Sprechen über das Gesetz' in G. Müller, E. Osterloh and T. Stein (eds.), *Festschrift für Günter Hirsch zum 65. Geburtstag* (C. H. Beck, Munich, 2008), pp. 583–4.

thus shaping the law, it at the same time takes the judiciary down a notch by denying their pronouncements conclusive force.

(c) Express exceptions

This absence of formally binding precedent can be reinforced by way of an *argumentum e contrario* that is premised on occasional provisions that explicitly break away from this general paradigm, rare instances when previous decisions are 'legally' binding on other adjudicators.[46]

In German law, for example, para. 31(1) of the *Bundesverfassungs-gerichtsgesetz* (Federal Constitutional Court Act) provides that decisions of the FCC bind all constitutional organs, courts and agencies.[47] In some cases, its decisions are even afforded the status of statutes, for instance when norms are invalidated (para. 32(2)). The FCC has understood this binding quality to extend not only to the operative part of its judgments, but also to the supporting reasons.[48] This is not considered antagonistic to judicial independence as guaranteed by Art. 97(1) of the German Basic Law, which is widely understood to protect judges from non-judicial or external pressures, rather than from judicial influence.[49]

Yet one crucial caveat to this exception is that the FCC principally does not consider itself bound by its own decisions.[50] In this it echoes the Supreme Courts of the US and UK. That defiance is not shaken by the FCC's clear penchant in practice for continuity and decisional harmony, which is borne out by two statistics. For one, the FCC only rarely

---

[46] For select historical examples see Coing (n. 20 above), p. 252. For other examples from Germany see e.g. L. Kähler, *Strukturen und Methoden der Rechtsprechungsänderung* (2nd edn, Nomos, Baden-Baden, 2011), pp. 342–59.

[47] The original reads: 'Die Entscheidungen des Bundesverfassungsgerichts binden die Ver-fassungsorgane des Bundes und der Länder sowie alle Gerichte und Behörden.'

[48] See e.g. BVerfG, 1 BvR 140/62, *Berliner Sache*, 1st Senate, 20 Jan. 1966 (m.n. 40); BVerfG, 2 BvR 1018/74, *Führerschein*, 2nd Senate, 10 Jun. 1975 (m.n. 13). The exact ambit of that extension of binding force remains contested. See e.g. K. Stern, *Das Staatsrecht der Bundesrepublik Deutschland*, 5 vols. (C. H. Beck, Munich 1980), II, pp. 1038–9.

[49] See M. Kau, *United States Supreme Court und Bundesverfassungsgericht* (Springer, Berlin and Heidelberg, 2007), p. 403.

[50] See e.g. BVerfG, 2 BvK 2/54, *Sperrklausel*, 2nd Senate, 11 Aug. 1954 (m.n. 32); BVerfG, 1 BvR 1086/82 *Arbeitnehmerüberlassung*, 1st Senate, 6 Oct. 1987 (m.n. 69). The preponder-ance of commentators appears to be in agreement. See e.g. T. Lundmark, '*Stare decisis* vor dem Bundesverfassungsgericht', *Rechtstheorie*, 28 (1997), 315, 327; E. Benda and E. Klein, *Verfassungsprozessrecht* (2nd edn, C. F. Müller, Heidelberg, 2001), p. 554. Cf. M. Sachs, *Die Bindung des Bundesverfassungsgerichts an seine Entscheidungen* (Vahlen, Munich, 1977), p. 117.

deviates from its precedents. One study put the figure at just over a dozen instances of express overruling in around 3,500 published decisions.[51] This impression of horizontal homogeneity is corroborated by the low incidence of dissenting opinions.[52] Secondly, a different study found that around 97 per cent of the FCC's decisions refer to precedents, even if this is rarely done with much elaboration or precise methodological analysis.[53] Parallels to the almost universal use of precedents by the ECJ are apparent. Likewise, an advantage of this self-referential mode of argumentation is that the FCC becomes increasingly less dependent on external sources of justification and support.[54]

Constitutional law is perhaps a special case, given the unique combination of symbolism and vastly influential decisions that have to be made. At any rate, there is a correlation between the height of the stakes involved and the willingness to tie decision-makers' hands, which can be expressed as an asymmetry between adjudicatory power and available correctives. This is confirmed when scouring other areas of German law, where indicia of binding precedent are few and far between.

One potential instance can be found in civil procedure.[55] Albeit less sweeping in effect since confined to the same set of proceedings at different stages of appeal, pursuant to para. 563(2) of the *Zivilprozessordnung* (Civil Procedure Rules) the legal findings of an appellate court that set aside a judgment are binding on the court from which the appeal originated when the case is remanded for determination.[56] The holding is binding in the sense that the lower court has to apply it in spite of any constitutional or statutory misgivings it might itself harbour, but not where it considers the decision to be incompatible with EU law. This form of bindingness has been interpreted to extend only to those legal reasons that actually led

---

[51] Lundmark (n. 50 above), p. 330. The study scrutinised FCC decisions from its inception up until 1997.

[52] Between 1971 and 2009, the FCC's judges issued dissenting opinions in just over 7 per cent of cases. Official statistics available at: www.bundesverfassungsgericht.de/en/organization.html.

[53] R. Alexy and R. Dreier, 'Precedent in the Federal Republic of Germany' in N. MacCormick and R. Summers (eds.), *Interpreting Precedents* (Ashgate, Aldershot, 1997), pp. 23–4.

[54] See R. Grawert, 'Das Grundgesetz im Lichte seiner Grundrechte. Eine judikative Entwicklungsgeschichte', *Der Staat*, 49 (2010), 507, 513 (noting that the FCC is now often capable of dispensing with a lot of legal literature since it has already expressed itself on so many matters).

[55] For further examples of exceptions see Kähler (n. 46 above), pp. 342–59.

[56] In German: 'Das Berufungsgericht hat die rechtliche Beurteilung, die der Aufhebung zugrunde gelegt ist, auch seiner Entscheidung zugrunde zu legen.'

the appellate court to set aside the judgment, expressed by some in terms of 'decisional causality' or even an exclusion of *obiter dicta*.[57] What is more, the binding force is also considered to extend to the appellate court itself, by way of logical corollary and in order to steer clear of a case being bounced back and forth endlessly between different jurisdictional tiers.[58] But it would be simplistic to treat this as an explicit acknowledgement of formally binding precedent, given that the binding force is limited to a specific case that stands to be decided. Rather than constituting a genuine rule on precedent, this provision is better understood as a procedural rule against contradiction, and thus more akin to *res judicata*.

That assessment is not unsettled by rules as to how to proceed in case of inconsistent prior judgments, such as para. 132(2) *Gerichtsverfassungsgesetz* (Courts Constitution Act). According to that provision, a Grand Panel of the *Bundesgerichtshof* (Federal Court of Justice) is to decide in the event that an individual panel wishes to deviate from the decision of another panel on a point of law. While this stipulation – neglect of which can potentially trigger a constitutional complaint[59] – is clearly intended to create decisional coherence, it does not oblige the Grand Panel to reach a particular conclusion on a previously litigated question. It lays down the procedure that is to be followed in specific divisions of judicial opinion rather than stipulating binding precedential force. In other words, it is one thing to say an earlier opposing view must be taken into account, yet quite another to assert that it has to be abided by no matter what.

To round up the civil law archetype, it is both worn fact and received opinion that Continental lawyers, including adjudicators, ceaselessly avail themselves of precedents in their everyday work.[60] Countless references to prior cases in pleadings, judgments and law review articles demonstrate that precedents obviously play an immensely important role in civil law systems. Legal terminology has long since cottoned on to this practical occurrence: *jurisprudence constante* and *ständige Rechtsprechung* comfort advocates and judges alike in making decisions that are have one foot planted in concreteness while at the same time remaining mindful of

---

[57] See J. Wenzel, '§ 563' in T. Rauscher, P. Wax and J. Wenzel (eds.), *Münchener Kommentar zur Zivilprozessordnung* (3rd edn, C. H. Beck, Munich, 2007), m.nn. 9, 12.

[58] See *ibid.* m.n. 18.

[59] See BVerfG, 1 BvR 864/03, *Revisionszulassung*, 1st Senate, 8 Jan. 2004 (para. 25).

[60] See only K. Langenbucher, *Die Entwicklung und Auslegung von Richterrecht* (C. H. Beck, Munich 1996), p. 65; F. Bydlinski, *Grundzüge der Juristischen Methodenlehre* (WUV, Vienna, 2005), p. 98.

the normative angle of law. There is not even a particularly ahistorical feel to this, given that the civilian tradition of Continental legal systems has its roots in Roman law, which itself was casuistic. French administrative law[61] and German labour law, in particular the law on industrial action,[62] are only two examples of modern Continental case law. Just as elsewhere, lawyers that are not up to speed on the relevant cases are liable to professional negligence suits; judges ignoring what their colleagues have previously said very likely increase the chances of having their judgments reversed on appeal.[63] In short, it would be mistaken to assume that the civil law archetype is entirely inconsiderate as concerns prior cases.[64]

Yet all of this stands in stark contrast to those statements just outlined to the effect that precedents are not binding. Opposing views are expected to marshal innovative and ambitious arguments and unorthodox theoretical approaches.[65] More often than not, the tension springs from an understandable reluctance to have normativity surrender in the face of facticity, in other words to have haphazard adjudication dominate externally coded rationality.[66] This leads to precedents often being denied the coveted *de jure* badge; instead, they are relegated to (ostensibly secondary) *de facto* importance, essentially little more than psychological or sociological fluff.[67] At best, related considerations such as foreseeability or equal treatment might indirectly trigger equivalent effects. However, if one takes the implications of limited cognition and the importance of concreteness or facticity in law and legal practice seriously, this archetype comes under incredible strain. The obsession with rejecting 'strict' or 'legal' bindingness is in danger of missing the forest for the (particularly rare species of) trees.

---

[61] See J. Bell, *French Legal Cultures* (Butterworths, London, 2001), p. 256.

[62] See Steiner (n. 28 above), p. 611.

[63] See S. Vogenauer, *Die Auslegung von Gesetzen in England und auf dem Kontinent,* 2 vols. (Mohr Siebeck, Tübingen 2001), I, p. 225.

[64] See G. F. Mancini and D. T. Keeling, 'Language, Culture and Politics in the Life of the European Court of Justice', *Columbia Journal of European Law,* 1 (1995), 397, 402.

[65] Cf. J. Esser, *Grundsatz und Norm in der richterlichen Fortbildung des Privatrechts* (Mohr, Tübingen 1956), pp. 161–82, 275–89; M. Kriele, *Theorie der Rechtsgewinnung* (2nd edn, Duncker & Humblot, Berlin, 1976), pp. 247–68, 290–309; W. Fikentscher, *Methoden des Rechts in vergleichender Darstellung,* 5 vols. (Mohr, Tübingen, 1977), IV, pp. 336–43.

[66] Cf. Müller and Christensen (n. 2 above), pp. 518–21.

[67] See e.g. W. Flume, *Gewohnheitsrecht und Römisches Recht* (Westdeutscher Verlag, Opladen, 1975), p. 38; Bydlinski (n. 60 above), p. 99.

ii Common law systems

Common law is the other archetype that is regularly posited in almost diametrical opposition to the one just examined. It is an archetype since the question of bindingness of precedent elicits varying responses in different systems, districts and fora.[68]

(a) Stare (in)decisis

A well-known feature and indeed one of the main reasons for its juxtaposition vis-à-vis civil law systems is that precedents are usually said to possess a special quality, either by imposing a strict obligation ('true' or 'authoritative' precedent) or by presenting a good reason for reaching the same decision ('persuasive' precedent). The former is particularly emblematic and tends to feature in nearly all comparative precedent discussions under the term *stare decisis*. Albeit subject to the particular prevailing doctrine, it generally requires the respective reasoning to issue from a superior court or, in some situations, from the same court. Cases are thus linked 'in a chain of influence and causation'.[69] While a very large amount of the law of traditional common law legal orders is nowadays put on a statutory footing, this cascading arrangement compensates for the disorderly formlessness of the common law itself by providing a degree of decisional stability while at the same time leaving open the possibility for adaptation. *Stare decisis* is the antibody injected into the common law bloodstream in an attempt to suppress virulent outbreaks. It is precisely for this reason that Bentham was strongly in favour of such a doctrine, despite being a radical reformer who believed in the emancipatory potential of positive law and notwithstanding his fervent opposition to the conservatism of the unmanageable common law.[70]

Nevertheless, it will only be expected of adjudicators to stand by things decided if a corrective facility is provided for, be it through the appellate

---

[68] On the stricter handling in England than in the US see G. Calabresi, *A Common Law for the Age of Statutes* (Harvard University Press, Cambridge, MA, 1982) 4; P. S. Atiyah and R. Summers, *Form and Substance in Anglo-American Law* (Clarendon Press, Oxford, 1987), p. 119. Cf. R. H. Kreindler, *Transnational Litigation: A Basic Primer* (Oceana, New York, 1998), p. 17.

[69] L. M. Friedman *et al.*, 'State Supreme Courts: A Century of Style and Citation', *Stanford Law Review*, 33 (1980–1981), 773.

[70] For a scornful critique of the legal establishment of the England of his day see J. Bentham, 'Truth versus Ashhurst' in J. Bowring (ed.), *The Works of Jeremy Bentham* (William Tait, Edinburgh, 1843), pp. 235–6.

hierarchy or a political aperture.[71] While this might seem paradoxical at first, it is ultimately the emanation of a constitutional insistence that consistency and predictability are not the sole goals or values of a legal system. There are many other facets to legal decision-making, not least appeals to what might be considered individual or collective justice and the repugnance of being ruled by the 'death grip' from the grave.[72] While these considerations are often suppressed by agreement in the interest of systemic operability, it would be a mistake to think that such reflections were ever completely eradicated from common law thinking. Critiques of *stare decisis* are anything but new.[73] Moreover, two of the main streams of common law jurisprudence of the twentieth century, interwar legal realism and Dworkinian supra-positivism, made legal conservatism and its love for technical justification their main target, albeit from rather different angles.[74]

Moreover, as hinted at by a well-informed Advocate General of the ECJ some time ago,[75] the doctrine of *stare decisis* is more elastic than is often assumed. The purist's view of bindingness – absolute compulsion occasioned by decisional exclusivity – borders on an epistemic fiction that serves to lubricate legal discourse rather than to actually limit legal decision-making. Limitations do of course exist, almost out of necessity to not make a mockery of the whole concept of precedent.[76] The baseline remains valid: one cannot blow hot and cold at the same time. But the boundaries are blurred.

For one, it would be imprecise to say that once something is part of a prior *ratio decidendi* it is automatically binding by virtue of that occurrence. Where a point of law enunciated by a superior court – even

---

[71] This was already referred to in the context of departing. In brief, the US Supreme Court is not above constitutional amendment just as the UK Supreme Court is not resistant to parliamentary sovereignty. Since these are ponderous processes, overruling is the alternative.

[72] R. A. Posner, *How Judges Think* (Harvard University Press, Cambridge, MA, 2008), p. 111.

[73] See e.g. H. P. Monaghan, 'Stare Decisis and Constitutional Adjudication', *Columbia Law Review*, 88 (1988), 723, 741.

[74] On the liberalism of the former see S. Brenner and H. J. Spaeth, *Stare Indecisis: The Alteration of Precedent on the Supreme Court, 1946–1992* (Cambridge University Press, 1995), p. xi. Cf. K. N. Llewellyn, *The Common Law Tradition: Deciding Appeals* (4th edn, Little, Brown, Boston, 1960), p. 62 ('I know of no phase of our law so misunderstood as our system of precedent').

[75] Case 112/76 *Renato Manzoni* v. *Fonds National de Retraite des Ouvriers Mineurs* [1977] ECR 1647, Opinion of AG Warner (p. 1663) ('C'est là, nous semble-t-il, que la doctrine du *stare decisis* doit entrer en jeu. Cette doctrine est évidemment flexible par nature').

[76] See J. Raz, *The Authority of Law* (2nd edn, Oxford University Press, 2009), pp. 189–90.

if it is essential to that court's findings – is merely *assumed* to be correct, a subsequent judge is not bound to hold that the law is settled in that respect.[77] For *stare decisis* to come into play in the first place it is necessary that there actually was proper argumentation and consideration of the issue.[78]

More importantly, not only is there usually a lot of room for manoeuvre to skirt around the compulsion issue, for example by distinguishing an irritation, many common law systems evince a fairly broadminded approach to *stare decisis*. 'Absolutist' views of *stare decisis* are routinely avoided by the US Supreme Court,[79] and despite exclamations that the doctrine 'is not a noodle' (i.e. squashy and offering little to no resistance),[80] its operation is invariably linked to malleable normative concepts such as stability and previsibility. This shifts the centre of attention from negative or exclusionary rules to positive reasons supporting a particular conclusion.[81] Smudging the line between 'authoritative' and 'persuasive' decisions, 'precedent binds absent a showing of substantial countervailing reasons'.[82] Brandeis even famously relegated *stare decisis* to little more than 'wise policy, because, in most matters, it is more important that the applicable rule of law be settled than that it be settled right'.[83] This is not a purely American stance. Indian law, too takes a more relaxed approach to the 'stranglehold' of *stare decisis*, treating it as an emanation of certain ideologies rather than a mechanistic fetter.[84] Even throughout the history of adjudication in England various judges have insisted that there is no magic to the citation of precedent.[85]

Viewed from this perspective, bindingness melds with a demand for a 'compelling reason' to adopt a different solution, thus essentially becoming a matter of argumentation, much to the dismay of the purist.

---

[77] See e.g. UK HC, *In Re Hetherington, Decd* [1990] ch. 1, 10; UK CA, *R (Kadhim) v. Brent London Borough Council Housing Benefit Review Board* [2001] QB 955 (paras. 33, 38).

[78] See UK CA, *Deane v. Secretary of State for Work and Pensions* (CA) [2011] 1 WLR 743 (paras. 29, 31).

[79] See US SC, *Citizens United v. Federal Election Committee* 558 US 310 (2010) (Stevens J, concurring in part and dissenting in part) (p. 17).

[80] US CA, *Bethesda Lutheran Homes and Services and ors v. Gerald Born and ors* 238 F3d 853, 858 (7th Cir. 2001).

[81] Cf. S. R. Perry, 'Judicial Obligation, Precedent and the Common Law', *Oxford Journal of Legal Studies*, 7 (1987), 215, 229–36.

[82] Monaghan (n. 73 above), p. 757.

[83] US SC, *Burnet v. Coronado Oil & Gas Co.* 285 US 393, 406 (1932) (Brandeis J, dissenting).

[84] See A. Lakshminath, *Precedent in Indian Law* (3rd edn, Eastern Book, Lucknow, 2009), pp. 14–30.

[85] See Allen (n. 32 above), pp. 212–15.

Authority itself becomes a reason in a larger calculus. Indeed, it is often hard to escape the impression that common law adjudicators and advocates bend over backwards to make *stare decisis* fit their reconstructed solutions rather than accept it submissively as their methodological master, up to the point where it is demoted to an admission that no better argument was found to resist the conclusions of a previous case. Quite where to draw the line remains a lasting challenge for many systems, in particular more liberal ones. But in many parts of the world, precedents are ultimately manifestations of a local tradition of how to engage with important limiting principles.[86] The point to take away from this is that, even in the common law world, bindingness is not invariably defined by a complete impossibility of departure, but rather by the quality of the arguments necessary to achieve this.

(b) Historical exceptionalism

Despite its supposed Latin pedigree, *stare decisis* is a relatively new phenomenon in the common law, which is much older than and logically independent from any notion of binding precedent. No formal concept of *stare decisis* – and certainly no uniformly strict version thereof – existed throughout most of the history of the common law. What is now often considered to be its classic form is largely a product of the nineteenth century. For the most part, earlier decisions were referred to in what might be described as a process of collective reasoning.[87] One can infer from the practice book attributed to Bracton and other writings of the thirteenth century that drawing on former cases in legal disputes was common in England long before any doctrine of 'strictly' binding precedents came to full fruition, which did not happen for another few hundred years. Baron Parke's formulation in *Mirehouse* v. *Rennell* is often considered the high watermark.[88]

---

[86] Cf. T. R. S. Allan, 'Judicial Deference and Judicial Review: Legal Doctrine and Legal Theory', *Law Quarterly Review*, 127 (2011), 96, 101, 113–15.

[87] See J. Evans, 'Change in the Doctrine of Precedent during the Nineteenth Century' in L. Goldstein (ed.), *Precedent in Law* (Clarendon Press, Oxford, 1987), pp. 35–72; D. Lieberman, *The Province of Legislation Determined* (Cambridge University Press, 1989), ch. 6; H. J. Berman, *Law and Revolution, II: The Impact of the Protestant Reformations on the Western Legal Tradition* (Harvard University Press, Cambridge, MA, 2006), pp. 273–5.

[88] *Mirehouse* v. *Rennell* (1833) 1 Cl & F 527, 546. See Allen (n. 32 above), pp. 227–8. Cf. T. E. Holland, *The Elements of Jurisprudence* (13th edn, Oxford University Press, 1924), p. 69 (dating the duty of a judge to abide by former precedents to Blackstone's time, i.e. the eighteenth century, but the argumentative use of cases in court to the reign of Edward I, i.e. the thirteenth century); R. W. M. Dias, *Jurisprudence* (3rd edn, Butterworths, London,

The medieval English concept of precedent was quite different from what it is now sometimes thought to be, resembling a more nebulous notion of 'common learning' with judges even refusing to record judgments, in other words to consider them suitable precedents, if they raised unclear novel points.[89] Put differently, precedent revolved around the idea of long, shared usage rather than a single authoritative expression. Even when it was more widely propagated in the late seventeenth century, *stare decisis* was not yet the yoke on legal decision-making it was considered to be in Victorian times.

In brief, 'strictly' binding precedent is not indispensable to common law systems. Many different attempts have been made to pinpoint the essence of the latter without reference to *stare decisis*. They range from classic views according to which cases are formal sources of law, via accounts that consider the common law to be whatever the application of the institutional principles of adjudication would yield,[90] to approaches that stress the 'ethic of adjudication'.[91] The common law archetype too struggles with the normative status of precedents, finding it hard to preserve it in the face of sheer facticity.

There is much to be said that the real differences between the two archetypes rather originate at a higher level of abstraction. If the civil law archetype favours the impersonal and formal, common law privileges the personal and substantive. This trickles down to the perception of adjudication, one potential consequence of which is *stare decisis*.

But arguably, cultural aspects play just as large a role as methodological points. It might be expected that the impact of decided cases is officially smaller in legal systems where judges are more likely to be thought of as a particular caste of career civil servants – at best diligent administrators, at worst potential autocrats – rather than romanticised as learned and wise champions of justice, equality and liberty, as in many Anglo-American (and in particular, English) accounts.[92] In the traditional common law

---

1970), p. 46 ('The doctrine of precedent in English law is of considerable antiquity, while that of *stare decisis* is relatively modern').

[89] See J. H. Baker, *An Introduction to English Legal History* (4th edn, Butterworths, London, 2002), pp. 197–8 (stressing that 'there could have been no suggestion that a court was bound by a previous decision' and noting how this encouraged an early declaratory view of law).

[90] See M. A. Eisenberg, *The Nature of the Common Law* (Harvard University Press, London, 1988), p. 154.

[91] This being the title of Glenn (n. 12 above), ch. 7.

[92] See e.g. F. Pollock, *The Genius of the Common Law* (Lawbook Exchange, Union, 2000, (1912)), pp. 123–5 (gushing that '[t]here is no more arduous enterprise for lawful men,

version the judge is, if not directly opposed to it, then not inherently part of 'the system', unlike in much of the civilian tradition. He is an umpire. Although the establishment of the UK Supreme Court in 2009 perhaps signals a shifting attitude, the senior judiciary in England is still ennobled, whereas in France the revolution brought an end to the *noblesse de robe*. In the Continental tradition, the cult of the 'hero judge' is a lot weaker.[93] The job is a career choice for recent graduates. An adjudicator is theoretically a personification of the system, for which reverence is retained. It is not unusual to find at the helms of the highest courts of the land judges who, for all their glittering professional accomplishments, may never have practiced law before. The belief rests in the system rather than the individuals. If you master it, you master judging. Even if such perceptions are difficult to verify scientifically and liable to derision as clichés, they feed into explanations concerning the way different legal systems grapple with similar problems, ranging from the appointment of judges (e.g. career or reward) via the basic conduct of proceedings (e.g. investigative or adversarial) to the treatment of prior cases.

Summing up the two archetypes, there is a remarkable degree of convergence when it comes to fidelity to precedent that continues to be overshadowed by extreme caricatures.[94] The archetypes may start from different premises – one reasoning towards constraints, the other reasoning towards freedom to depart – but upon closer examination, 'strict' bindingness is very much the exception in both. In any event, it has to be argued for; even if the common law accepts such a doctrine, it remains for the legal worker to convince a court or tribunal not only that the present case is relevantly similar, but also that a departure is not warranted.

This has two corollaries. First, it would not appear unusual for the ECJ to follow similar lines, with the question of bindingness morphing into a broader context of argumentation. Secondly, the utility of overly broad macro-comparatist invocations of the two archetypes is cast into doubt.

---

and none more noble, than the perpetual quest of justice laid upon all of us who are pledged to serve our lady the Common Law' after defending 'her' against charges of arbitrariness and capriciousness).

[93] This, too, is of course a generalisation and as such liable to specific contradiction. For instance, sixty years down the line, the FCC enjoys considerable popularity in Germany as far as state institutions go.

[94] On the tendency to overrate discrepancies in general see e.g. H. Kötz, 'Contract Law in Europe and the United States: Legal Unification in the Civil Law and Common Law', *The Tulane European and Civil Law Forum*, 27 (2012), 1, 14.

Before tackling the pull of the ECJ's precedents, it bears considering a third legal order that might serve as a blueprint.

iii International law

It is a platitude that there is no *stare decisis* doctrine in international law.[95] At the same time, the precise point and position of precedents elicits unease.[96] Decisions of the ICJ are said to lack *extra partes* binding force, with only the parties to a case bound by a particular decision. Any other authority is not 'real' but at best 'persuasive' in the sense of alluding to underlying justifications or providing good reasons for believing a decision to be correct in law.

This is usually based on a specific understanding of ICJ Statute Art. 59, in other words largely a doctrinal argument. Said article reads: 'The decision of the [ICJ] has no binding force except between the parties and in respect of that particular case.'[97] There is room for interpretation on that particular point, not least on account of the rather curious fact that the provision is nestled in chapter III of the ICJ Statute, which is not devoted to the court's competence but instead to matters of procedure.[98] Waldock for instance thought that Art. 59 does not so much represent a 'victory of the continental system', but rather gives expression to a widely shared anxiety to give a 'wholly new and untried tribunal explicit authority to lay down binding law' for all states in the absence of a centralised

---

[95] See R. Bernhardt, 'Article 59' in A. Zimmermann, K. Oellers-Frahm and C. Tomuschat (eds.), *The Statute of the International Court of Justice: A Commentary* (Oxford University Press, 2006), pp. 1232, 1244; W. Graf Vitzthum, 'Begriff, Geschichte und Rechtsquellen des Völkerrechts' in W. Graf Vitzthum (ed.), *Völkerrecht* (5th edn, De Gruyter, Berlin, 2010), p. 66.

[96] See only Y. Lupu and E. Voeten, 'Precedent in International Courts: A Network Analysis of Case Citations by the European Court of Human Rights', *British Journal of Political Science*, 42 (2012), 413, 416.

[97] See also the mimicking by the United Nations Conventions on the Law of the Sea of 10 Dec. 1982, 1833 UNTS 397, Art. 296(2): 'Any such decision shall have no binding force except between the parties and in respect of that particular dispute.'

[98] See W. E. Beckett, 'Les Questions d'intérêt général au point de vue juridique dans la jurisprudence de la Cour Permanente de Justice Internationale', *Recueil des Cours/Académie de Droit International de La Haye*, 39 (1932), 135, 141 (suggesting this deals with the operative part only of a past case, but not its essence or rationale); H. Lauterpacht, *The Development of International Law by the International Court* (Stevens, London, 1958), p. 8 (contesting that the 'somewhat wide' Art. 59 deals with precedent and arguing it states directly what Art. 63 expresses indirectly regarding third state intervention and the bindingness of treaty interpretations by the ICJ, i.e. an 'an altogether minor point').

international legislature.[99] The preponderance of views expressed on such matters suggests that what was bothering the original drafting committee was indeed the idea of adjudication forgetting its place in the international legal order and instituting something akin to the purist's version of *stare decisis*.[100]

Unsurprisingly, the ICJ and its predecessor have not felt the need to engage such quandaries head on in a systemic and penetrating fashion. Dispute resolution, not 'science for the sake of science' or 'abstract controversy', is again the leading and self-reinforcing credo.[101] Discussions of this supposedly self-denying provision habitually amount to what the PCIJ stated in 1926 in the matter concerning *Certain German Interests in Polish Upper Silesia (Merits)*: 'The object of [Art. 59] is simply to prevent legal principles accepted by the Court in a particular case from being binding upon other States or in other disputes.'[102] Each particular case must be decided individually. Quite plausibly, the reasoning and obligations of one case cannot blindly be transplanted to another situation without more. That is something the common law archetype would also claim for itself.

The other side of the coin was stated more recently by the ICJ when it interpreted the essence of Art. 59 to be 'the positive statement that the parties are bound by the decision of the Court in respect of a particular case', hence viewing Art. 59 through the narrower prism of *res judicata*.[103] Central to this is the idea of finality, that is to say that the parties to a case cannot reopen a matter that has been determined save by exceptional procedures. This *autorité de la chose jugée* generally only applies where there is an identity of proceedings, parties and issues. While this could be understood as laying down a general rule of relativity (i.e. categorical *inter partes* effect), it appears more plausible that this minimalistic construction

---

[99] H. M. Waldock, 'General Course on Public International Law', *Recueil des Cours/Académie de Droit International de La Haye*, 106 (1962), 1, 91.

[100] See M. Sørensen, *Les Sources du droit international: étude sur la jurisprudence de la Cour Permanente de Justice Internationale* (Einar Munksgaard, Copenhagen, 1946), p. 161; M. O. Hudson, *The Permanent Court of International Justice 1920–1942* (Macmillan, New York, 1943), p. 207.

[101] Expressions used by Professor de Lapradelle in his speech before the PCIJ in *Nationality Decrees Issued in Tunis and Morocco* (1923), Series C, No. 2, 58.

[102] PCIJ, *Certain German Interests in Polish Upper Silesia (Merits)* (1926), Series A, No. 7, 19.

[103] ICJ, *Case concerning the Application of the Convention on the Prevention and Punishment of the Crime of Genocide (Bosnia and Herzegovina v. Serbia and Montenegro)*, Judgment of 26 Feb. 2007, ICJ Rep 2007, 44 (para. 115).

is driven by thoroughly pragmatic concerns, akin to what the common law calls estoppel, and is not an exercise in pontificating on negative or constraining precedent as such. If anything, it is a consequence of declaratory cognitivism, but without more it seems difficult to turn this procedural rule into a sweeping jurisprudential postulate. This procedural take is in line with the understanding that there is a distinction between the operative part of a decision and the reasoning or essence upon which a judgment is based.[104] It also fits with keeping negative precedent and in particular bindingness separate from other more general legal effects of adjudication.

Be that as it may, Art. 59 is widely taken to be an abrogation of a formal doctrine of precedent and more than just a statement recalling *res judicata*, permitting the very same point to be decided completely differently by the ICJ later in time. Read in conjunction with Art. 38(1)(d) of the ICJ Statute, this leads to the predominant mantra of mainstream international law, namely that previous decisions are 'not binding, but subsidiary means' ('NBSM') only.

Drawing heavily on these observations regarding general international law, the overwhelming view thus held in international investment law and arbitration for instance is that there is no 'strictly' binding doctrine of precedent that could constrain tribunals in the sense of ruling out all countervailing reasons in the context of relevantly similar matters that have already been decided by previous tribunals.[105] NBSM is the motto,

---

[104] See Beckett (n. 98 above), p. 141. Cf. ICJ, *Case concerning the Barcelona Traction, Light and Power Company Limited (Belgium v. Spain)*, Judgment of 5 Feb. 1970, Separate Opinion of Judge Jessup, ICJ Rep 1970, 163 (para. 9): '[T]he influence of the Court's decisions is wider than their binding force.'

[105] See G. Kaufmann-Kohler, 'Arbitral Precedent: Dream, Necessity or Excuse?', *Arbitration International*, 23 (2007), 357, 368; C. McLachlan, L. Shore and M. Weiniger, *International Investment Arbitration: Substantive Principles* (Oxford University Press, 2007), p. 18; R. Dolzer and C. Schreuer, *Principles of International Investment Law* (Oxford University Press, 2008), p. 36; C. Schreuer and M. Weiniger, 'Conversations across Cases: Is There a Doctrine of Precedent in Investment Arbitration?', *Transnational Dispute Management*, 5 (2008), 1; C. Schreuer, *The ICSID Convention: A Commentary* (2nd edn, Cambridge University Press, 2009), pp. 1101–2; J. W. Salacuse, *The Law of Investment Treaties* (Oxford University Press, 2010), p. 155; G. Guillaume, 'Le Précédent dans la justice et l'arbitrage international', *Journal du Droit International*, 137 (2010), 685, 703 (invoking Justinian's maxim and exhorting that '[le précédent] ne saurait être un instrument du gouvernement des juges: il n'est qu'un auxiliaire dans la détermination du droit'); L. Reed, J. Paulsson and N. Blackaby, *Guide to ICSID Arbitration* (2nd edn, Kluwer Law International, Alphen aan den Rijn, 2011), p. 181.

stare decisis disavowed.[106] Obligations are grounded in inter-state conventions, namely specific transactional bargains. Sufficiently reassured, departing from precedents becomes a highly viable option.

More specifically, this general consensus found in international investment arbitration is based on three interlocking considerations. First, most investment treaties are silent on the matter, refusing to mention such an effect. Secondly, in almost all investment disputes 'the applicable rules of international law' will be part of the governing law, which includes Arts. 38 and 59 of the ICJ Statute, together with their precedent thinking.[107] Thirdly, different provisions echo variants of the latter provision. For example, NAFTA Art. 1136(1) declares that '[a]n award made by a Tribunal shall have no binding force except between the disputing parties and in respect of the particular case'.[108] Turning to procedural frameworks, ICSID Convention Art. 53(1) denotes inversely that '[t]he award shall be binding on the parties'.[109] This formulation is arguably less conclusive than the statement contained in the ICJ Statute or NAFTA, as it does not directly rule out any such effect; nor is any such denial to be found in the *travaux préparatoires*. The absence of an exceptional doctrine supports the exclusion of any 'knockout' binding legal effect.

What undoubtedly plays a strong role in this context is the fear of being accused of a 'government by judges', a concern that is magnified in international settings with their weak institutional backdrop and hence rather tenuous legitimacy feedback loop. A commonly held view is that,

---

[106] See e.g. *Chevron Corporation (USA) and Texaco Corporation (USA)* v. *Republic of Ecuador*, PCA Case No. 34877, Partial Award on the Merits of 30 Mar. 2010 (Böckstiegel, Brower, van den Berg) (para. 163); *Burlington Resources Inc.* v. *Republic of Ecuador*, ICSID Case No. ARB/08/05, Decision on Jurisdiction of 2 Jun. 2010 (Kaufmann-Kohler, Orrego Vicuña, Stern) (para. 100) (with further references); *Saba Fakes* v. *Republic of Turkey*, ICSID Case No. ARB/07/20, Award of 14 Jul. 2010 (Gaillard, van Houtte, Lévy) (para. 96); *Enron Creditors Recovery Corp. and Ponderosa Assets LP* v. *Argentine Republic*, ICSID Case No. ARB/01/3, Decision on Annulment of 30 Jul. 2010 (Griffith, Robinson, Tresselt) (para. 66); *Chemtura Corporation* v. *Government of Canada*, Ad Hoc NAFTA Arbitration under UNCITRAL Rules, Award of 2 Aug. 2010 (Kaufmann-Kohler, Brower, Crawford) (para. 109).

[107] For such an approach see *International Thunderbird Gaming Corporation* v. *United Mexican States*, Ad Hoc NAFTA Arbitration under UNCITRAL Rules, Separate Opinion of Arbitrator Wälde of 26 Jan. 2006 (para. 129) (in the context of NAFTA Art. 1131(1)).

[108] North American Free Trade Agreement of 17 Dec. 1992 ('NAFTA'), in force since 1 Jan. 1994, 32 ILM 289 (1993), 32 ILM 605 (1993).

[109] Convention on the Settlement of Disputes between States and Nationals of Other States of 18 Mar. 1965 ('ICSID Convention'), in force since 14 Oct. 1966, last amended effective 10 Apr. 2006, http://icsid.worldbank.org/ICSID/ICSID/RulesMain.jsp.

despite the odd 'pathological' cases, this 'soft' approach to precedent has ensured a fairly high degree of consistency, stability and predictability;[110] in short, the best of both worlds. The main consequence is a rather rudimentary classification of tribunals' reference practice as 'de facto' precedent or *jurisprudence constante*, keenly aware of what is going on yet stranded somewhere in conceptual no man's land.

All the same, given what was already said about precedent up until this point, the mere fact that there is no *stare decisis* doctrine in international (investment) law does not of course preclude precedents from exerting important effects; nor are these limited to the realm of the factual. Despite the prominent denial, commentators virtually universally agree that the ICJ's practice for instance differs rather noticeably from this 'theoretical' licence to decide similar issues contrariwise.[111] It, too, frequently bothers to give reasons for distinguishing and departing from prior cases, despite the NBSM mantra. Certainty, coherence, predictability and reputation loom large. Beyond providing fodder for argumentation or psychological reassurance, the decisions of international courts and tribunals add important legal information by providing answers to legal questions that were previously left open. International law is no different in this very basic epistemic respect than other legal systems. The universalisation of specific points allows precedents to be put to use with respect to many different tasks when faced with novel situations.

Everyone is aware of this slightly awkward bypassing of the NBSM credo. Recalling that adopted panel reports were an important part of the General Agreement on Tariffs and Trade (GATT) *acquis* and that they created legitimate expectations among WTO Members, the WTO Appellate Body once opined that previous reports should be taken into account.[112] Failing to do so might even amount to a violation of the proper discharge of its functions and the obligation to conduct an objective assessment under DSU Art. 11.[113] Similarly, in a prime example of blending

---

[110] See A. Reinisch, 'The Issues Raised by Parallel Proceedings and Possible Solutions' in M. Waibel *et al.* (eds.), *The Backlash against Investment Arbitration: Perceptions and Reality* (Wolters Kluwer, Alphen aan den Rijn, 2010), p. 126.

[111] See e.g. M. Bos, 'The Interpretation of International Judicial Decisions', *Revista Española de Derecho Internacional*, 33 (1981), 11, 47; M. Shahabuddeen, *Precedent in the World Court* (Cambridge University Press, 1996), pp. 29–31; Bernhardt (n. 95 above), p. 1244.

[112] WT/DS8/AB/R, WT/DS10/AB/R and WT/DS11/AB/R, *Japan: Taxes on Alcoholic Beverages*, 4 Oct. 1996 (p. 14).

[113] WT/DS344/AB/R, *United States–Final Anti-Dumping Measures on Stainless Steel from Mexico*, 30 Apr. 2008 (para. 162) (expressing deep concern about 'the Panel's decision to depart from well-established Appellate Body jurisprudence'). For more detail on the

substance and method, the ECtHR has stated that although there was no right to an established or well-reasoned jurisprudence, capricious departures might in certain circumstances even amount to a failure to satisfy the requirements of a fair trial.[114] All of this has led one commentator to call the platitude on the absence of the *stare decisis* doctrine in international law a 'myth built on myths'.[115] So where, if at all, does the ECJ fit in?

C The ECJ

Express departures by the ECJ are rare. But they exist. This gives rise to the seemingly paradoxical finding that the Court does not consider itself bound, yet appears to follow its own precedents far more dutifully than many common law courts do theirs.

i The view of the academy

Despite widespread acceptance of their practical importance, it is conventionally said that the ECJ is not bound by its own previous decisions.[116]

WTO see R. Bhala, 'The Power of the Past: Towards De Jure Stare Decisis in WTO Adjudication (Part Three of a Trilogy)', *George Washington International Law Review*, 33 (2001), 873 (arguing for a 'truly grand' *de jure* doctrine of *stare decisis* to end what he considers hypocritical attitudes, although without requiring appellate bodies to be a source of law).

[114] See ECtHR, *Atanasovski v. The Former Yugoslav Republic of Macedonia*, Application No. 36815/03, Judgment of 14 Jan. 2010 (para. 38).

[115] Bhala (n. 113 above), p. 976.

[116] See e.g. F. Dumon and F. Rigaux, 'La Cour de justice des Communautés européennes et les jurisdictions des états membres', *Annales de Droit et de Sciences Politiques*, 19 (1959), 7, 38; P. Hay, 'European Economic Community: *Res Judicata* and Precedent in the Court of Justice of the Common Market', *American Journal of Comparative Law*, 12 (1963), 404, 408; G. Bebr, *Development of Judicial Control of the European Communities* (Nijhoff, The Hague, 1981), p. 9; A. J. Mackenzie Stuart and J.-P. Warner, 'Judicial Decision as a Source of Community Law' in W. G. Grewe, H. Rupp and H. Schneider (eds.), *Europäische Gerichtsbarkeit und nationale Verfassungsgerichtsbarkeit: Festschrift zum 70. Geburtstag von Hans Kutscher* (Nomos, Baden-Baden 1981), p. 276; A. G. Toth, 'The Authority of Judgments of the European Court of Justice: Binding Force and Legal Effects', *Yearbook of European Law*, 4 (1985), 1, 19–20, 69; G. Slynn, 'The Court of Justice of the European Communities', *International and Comparative Law Quarterly*, 33 (1984), 409, 423; A. G. Toth, *The Oxford Encyclopaedia of European Community Law*, 3 vols. (Clarendon Press, Oxford 1990), I, pp. 343, 465, 494–5; R. Cross and J. W. Harris, *Precedent in English Law* (4th edn, Clarendon Press, Oxford, 1991), pp. 16–17; A. Arnull, 'Owning up to Fallibility: Precedent and the European Court of Justice', *Common Market Law Review*, 30 (1993), 247, 248; N. M. Hunnings, *The European Courts* (Cartermill, London, 1996), p. 144; J. J. Barceló, 'Precedent in European Community Law' in N. MacCormick and

Doubts remain how far to take this statement,[117] and what is notable regarding the overwhelming assumption is that denials are rarely if ever expressed without reservation. An abundance of qualifiers are mobilised. The Court is not 'formally', 'legally', 'technically' or 'as such' bound by its jurisprudence. Leaving aside unthinking or defensive language for a moment, this suggests that the ECJ *is* bound in a sense. This most likely springs from the recognition of the argumentative burdens that precedents impose even in the absence of any grand doctrine to that effect. Quite to what extent is however rarely discussed in detail, with intellectual curiosity often sated by reference to practical convenience and the facticity of frequent citation, which in turn serves as an affirmation of the general negative view.

According to the predominant conceptual framework, the matter is not particularly demanding to resolve. Only certain legal materials can claim authority, usually – but not inevitably – those imbued with popular approval, in other words essentially the treaties. Much of the analysis thus revolves around an accepted split between normativity and factual effect. This is supplemented by concerns that granting the ECJ too much power would betray fundamental democratic tenets. The problems are artificiality and absolution of responsibility.

R. Summers (eds.), *Interpreting Precedents: A Comparative Study* (Ashgate, Aldershot, 1997), p. 420; U. Everling, 'On the Judge-Made Law of the European Community's Courts' in D. O'Keeffe and A. Bavasso (eds.), *Judicial Review in European Union Law: Liber Amicorum in Honour of Lord Slynn of Hadley*, 2 vols. (Kluwer Law International, The Hague, London and Boston 2000), I, pp. 31, 39; L. N. Brown and T. Kennedy, *The Court of Justice of the European Communities* (5th edn, Sweet & Maxwell, London, 2000), pp. 369–72; Schermers and Waelbroeck (n. 9 above), pp. 133–6; T. Ojanen, 'Between Precedent and the Present', *Turku Law Journal*, 3 (2001), 105, 107; R. Schulze and U. Seif, 'Einführung' in R. Schulze and U. Seif (eds.), *Richterrecht und Rechtsfortbildung in der Europäischen Rechtsgemeinschaft* (Mohr Siebeck, Tübingen, 2003), p. 11; K. P. E. Lasok and T. Millett, *Judicial Control in the EU: Procedures and Principles* (Richmond Law & Tax, Richmond, 2004), m.n. 684; Müller and Christensen (n. 2 above), pp. 308–10; T. Oppermann, C. D. Classen and M. Nettesheim, *Europarecht* (4th edn, C. H. Beck, Munich, 2009), p. 199; T. C. Hartley, *The Foundations of European Union Law* (7th edn, Oxford University Press, 2010), pp. 70–1; D. Chalmers, G. Davies and G. Monti, *European Union Law: Text and Materials* (2nd edn, Cambridge University Press, 2010), p. 169: S. Pötters and R. Christensen, 'Das Unionsrecht als Hybridform zwischen case law und Gesetzesrecht', *Juristenzeitung*, 67 (2012), 289, 290.

[117] See M. Gutsche, *Die Bindungswirkung der Urteile des Europäischen Gerichtshofes* (Institut für Völkerrecht, Göttingen 1967), pp. 45, 108–9, 115, 216–20; T. Koopmans, 'Stare Decisis in European Law' in D. O'Keeffe and H. G. Schermers (eds.), *Essays in European Law and Integration* (Kluwer, Deventer, 1982), p. 27; A. Bleckmann, *Europarecht* (6th edn, Carl Heymanns, Cologne, 1997), pp. 343–5.

ii The view from within

Judging by its own pronouncements, the ECJ is somewhere between silence and denial as to the normativity of its decisions. At the same time, it is evidently under no illusion as to the law-making dimension of its work. Nor is it true that the Court never refers to past decisions as 'precedents'.[118] But when it comes to explaining the normative quality of its cases, it remains cagey.

The *locus classicus* is often considered to be *Da Costa*, a preliminary ruling in which the ECJ was asked a question identical to one it had only recently answered in *van Gend*, where judgment had been handed down only fifty days earlier.[119] Although the Court considered that there was 'no ground for giving a new interpretation of Art. 12 EEC', it nevertheless entertained the reference. It did not shut the door outright on a new construction, thus declining anything resembling simplistic *stare decisis*.[120] Given the proper ground, things might be decided differently. But therein lies the rub. The Court equally did not assert a naked licence to depart without more from its prior jurisprudence whenever it saw fit. As elaborated earlier, even courts operating in a system of 'formally' binding precedent recognise various grounds when earlier decisions need not be followed, certainly when they are instances of last resort.[121] The question hence becomes precisely what 'ground' would warrant a new interpretation of EEC Art. 12. That however was not addressed in *Da Costa* beyond the hazy observation as to the identity of the questions posed and the lack of 'new factor[s]'.

Unfortunately, neither has the ECJ since felt the need to express itself directly on the matter in more categorical fashion, which accords with its self-depiction as a legal worker that settles practical disputes instead of expounding theories *in abstracto*. This ethos is for example manifest in

---

[118] See e.g. Case C-197/09 RX-II *M* v. *European Medicines Agency (EMEA)* (Third Chamber) [2009] ECR I-12033 (para. 62) (on the GC); Case 370/07 *Commission* v. *Council ('CITES')* (Second Chamber) [2009] ECR I-8917 (para. 54). One of the earlier references to 'precedent' is Case 1252/79 *SpA Acciaierie e Ferriere Lucchini* v. *Commission* [1980] ECR 3753 (para. 15). But see Barceló (n. 116 above), p. 417.

[119] Joined Cases 28 to 30–62 *Da Costa en Schaake NV and ors* v. *Nederlandse Belastingadministratie* [1963] ECR 31; Case 26–62 *NV Algemene Transport- en Expeditie Onderneming van Gend & Loos* v. *Netherlands Inland Revenue Administration* [1963] ECR 1.

[120] See B. Schima, 'Zur Wirkung von Auslegungsentscheidungen des Gerichtshofes der Europäischen Gemeinschaften' in B. Feldner and N. Forgó (eds.), *Norm und Entscheidung* (Springer, Vienna and New York, 2000), p. 295.

[121] See Ch. 6.

its jurisprudence requiring preliminary references to deal with an actual legal dispute, even if engineered, rather than a hypothetical question.[122] Irrespective of its wisdom, such aversion to 'science for the sake of science' and the 'purely academic' is not uncommon amongst adjudicatory bodies, the function of which is often at most extolled as 'dispensing justice', itself a functional task.[123] The judicial toolbox is well stocked to ward off such exercises, mainly through exclusionary concepts such as party submissions, procedural devices, competences and applicable law. Of course this pragmatic self-portrayal does not mean that the ECJ is unaware of how to leverage its position strategically. Professional, not professorial, is the keyword for its *modus operandi*. Abstract pronouncements are prone to have wide-ranging effects. This can cut both ways. While they can serve to entrench a desirable legal proposition – especially when this is neither immediately apparent nor applied, and thus less exposed to potential opposition[124] – they can also come back to subsequently haunt the unsuspecting decision-maker, which is why they need to be employed with care. In this respect the position of a permanent body like the ECJ differs from that of *ad hoc* tribunals.

Nevertheless, various Advocates General have tackled the point, largely weighing in on the side of the denialists. One of the earlier statements is that by AG Lagrange in *Da Costa*.[125] Although couching his observations in terms of *res judicata* and *erga omnes* obligations and thus amalgamating different concepts, the Advocate General asserted that the ECJ should 'retain the legal right' to depart from a leading judgment and could always, as of right, overrule itself. The door was hence never shut on 'spontaneous rethinking'. The strong categorical flavour of these statements is dressed in mollifying accoutrements. For one, 'no one will expect that . . . the Court

---

[122] On the ECJ's professed dislike of entertaining hypotheticals see K.-D. Borchardt, *Die rechtlichen Grundlagen der Europäischen Union* (4th edn, Facultas, Vienna, 2010), p. 327 (listing select exceptions).

[123] Recall however that the US Supreme Court for instance has not shied away from such debates.

[124] This is of course the famed US SC, *Marbury* v. *Madison* 5 US (1 Cranch) 137 (1803) manoeuvre: sacrificing immediate victory to win a long-term war. A more recent example is Case C-409/06 *Winner Wetten GmbH* v. *Bürgermeisterin der Stadt Bergheim* (Grand Chamber) [2010] ECR I-8015 (paras. 63–6), where the Court opened the door for future arguments that the transitional application of national legislation contravening EU law might be warranted in exceptional circumstances, while ruling this out as concerned the present litigation.

[125] Joined Cases 28 to 30–62 *Da Costa en Schaake NV and ors* v. *Nederlandse Belastingad-ministratie* [1963] ECR 31, Opinion of AG Lagrange (pp. 42–3).

will depart' from its jurisprudence, he maintained. Plus, any revisiting of precedents would require 'strong reasons'.

It is immediately apparent that expectations and reasons play an important role in precedent-following at the ECJ, something not captured by caricaturesque archetypes or by pigeonholing the Court as a totally free or completely bound decision-maker. The context matters, more so than any legal entitlement. Two further factors are noticeable in the Advocate General's opinion. First, it is filled with references to the collaborative and mutually respectful nature of the preliminary ruling procedure, displaying a keen awareness that the ECJ constantly has to bargain for acceptance by the Member States and their courts. A more strict doctrine of precedent that would have denied national courts the possibility of referring matters if the ECJ had already ruled on them could have offended these. The Court also picked up on this. It accordingly refused to simply dismiss the reference for lack of purpose, something the Commission had in fact put forward in light of the virtually identical reference in *van Gend*. This set a more co-operative tone than a hierarchical *stare decisis* argument might have struck.[126] Secondly, AG Lagrange praised the more conventional virtues of a lithe doctrine of precedent that essentially seeks to keep a check on the outer perimeters of judicial activity without meddling with decisional freedom as such. He considered this approach conducive to the dynamic evolution of what is now EU law through adjudicators who could take new economic and social developments into account. This again displays a desire for situational responsiveness rather than doctrinal rigour. Hence, he advocated asymmetry: creative powers with few, if any, formalistic constraints. But this can itself of course strain the collaborative effort just outlined.

A few years later in *Manzoni*, AG Warner offered a classic examination of the binding quality of the Court's decisions.[127] The ECJ had been invited to interpret – and in one instance, effectively reconsider – its prior jurisprudence in four EEC Art. 177 references concerning pension discrimination on the grounds of nationality and residence. Siding with academic opinion, AG Warner first took care to distinguish the effect of a ruling in a preliminary reference from that of an annulment decision.[128]

---

[126] See U. Haltern, *Europarecht: Dogmatik im Kontext* (2nd edn, Mohr Siebeck, Tübingen, 2007), p. 233.

[127] Case 112/76 *Renato Manzoni v. Fonds National de Retraite des Ouvriers Mineurs* [1977] ECR 1647, Opinion of AG Warner (pp. 1661–3).

[128] *Ibid.* p. 1661.

This allows for a differentiation between the effects of a potential precedent and more direct forms of *erga omnes* effects of judgments. Provided
that the Court has not stated other effects, annulment means that a measure is retroactively (*ex tunc*) expunged from the Unional legal system.[129]
The Court's very first few cases demonstrate that a measure that has
already been annulled cannot compromise rights and cannot be annulled
again.[130] A ruling in a preliminary reference, however, does not possess
the same invasive quality; indeed, the Court's jurisdiction does not even
extend to affecting Member State measures. Clearly, there is a difference
between the formal legal effect of judgments and any precedential quality
they might enjoy.[131]

AG Warner was quick to follow this up with a remark dispelling the
notion that an interpretative EEC Art. 177 judgment had no effect whatsoever beyond the individual case.[132] The second distinction he thus
drew was between precedential effect and *res judicata*. Referring to the
function of the preliminary reference procedure as a 'dialogue between
[c]ourts', the Advocate General observed that while such a ruling was
binding on the referring court, that was not the same thing as saying that
it only affected the referring court, something the notion of *res judicata*
implicitly expresses in its limited focus on the parties to particular proceedings. It would however be an overextension of *res judicata* to draw
the inverse conclusion from its *inter partes* bindingness, that is to say that
a preliminary ruling does not affect other courts. Indeed, the *inter partes*
construction does not at all fit well with the idea of interpretive guidance
that underlies the preliminary reference procedure. As has often been
stated, its central tenets are the uniform interpretation and application of
EU law. In a similar vein, AG Warner drew attention to the fact that other
Member States and institutions can and often do submit observations in
such proceedings, for exactly that reason.

---

[129] See e.g. Case C-550/09 *Criminal proceedings against E and F* [2010] ECR I-6213, Opinion
of AG Mengozzi (para. 105).

[130] See Case 3–54 *Associazione Industrie Siderurgiche Italiane (ASSIDER)* v. *High Authority
of the European Coal and Steel Community* [1955] ECR 63, 70; Case 5–54 *Industrie
Siderurgiche Associate (ISA)* v. *High Authority of the European Coal and Steel Community*
[1955] ECR 91, 97; Case 2–54 *Italian Republic* v. *High Authority of the European Coal and
Steel Community* [1954] ECR 37, 55.

[131] See A. G. Toth, 'The Authority of Judgments of the European Court of Justice' (n. 116
above), pp. 5, 45.

[132] Case 112/76 *Renato Manzoni* v. *Fonds National de Retraite des Ouvriers Mineurs* [1977]
ECR 1647, Opinion of AG Warner, p. 1662.

Having considered that neither *erga omnes* nor *res judicata* satisfactorily explained the precedential force the Court's decisions are imbued with, AG Warner then turned to the third Latin phrase frequently employed in this context, *stare decisis*. As the first British Advocate General at the ECJ, he was familiar with such approaches, and it is no coincidence that he immediately discarded a widely held misconception by stating that *stare decisis* did not categorically rule out all flexibility and varied conspicuously in its precise emanation depending on the courts in question and their specific legal environment.[133] He argued that while other courts generally had to abide by the ECJ's reasoning regarding matters of interpretation,[134] this still left open various avoidance techniques such as distinguishing and the like. Besides ensuring uniformity, this would also avoid the perplexing situation in the pre-*CILFIT* era whereby inferior courts were privileged over national courts of last resort, given the wording of what is now TFEU Art. 267.

The ECJ itself was however free to reconsider its prior rulings.[135] Wary of rough analogies and noting that the ECJ was in a unique position, the Advocate General was nonetheless prepared to liken the Court in this respect to what was formerly the UK House of Lords, which no longer considered itself inescapably constrained by its own precedents. In its result AG Warner's opinion in *Manzoni* thus conforms to the orthodox view of the Court not being 'strictly' bound by its own decisions. It is of particular interest because it examines three familiar concepts (*erga omnes*, *res judicata*, and *stare decisis*) and rejects a simple imposition thereof in the EU context. Another valuable point that emerges is that departure was held to be consequential upon reconsideration. Reconsidering is a justificatory process, which reinforces the notion of prior jurisprudence imposing an argumentative burden.

Turning to another case, in *Sema Sürül* AG La Pergola was adamant that *stare decisis* had not been incorporated into the supranational judicial

---

[133] *Ibid.*

[134] In the UK this is explicitly reflected in statutory law. See European Communities Act 1972 (c. 68), s. 3(1): 'For the purposes of all legal proceedings any question as to the meaning or effect of any of the Treaties, or as to the validity, meaning or effect of any EU instrument, shall be treated as a question of law (and if not referred to the European Court, be for determination as such *in accordance with the principles laid down by and any relevant decision of the European Court*)' (emphasis added).

[135] Case 112/76 *Renato Manzoni* v. *Fonds National de Retraite des Ouvriers Mineurs* [1977] ECR 1647, Opinion of AG Warner, p. 1663.

system.[136] The case concerned a request from a German court for inter-pretive guidance on a decision of the Association Council set up between the EEC and Turkey in order to assess the entitlement of a Turkish national residing in Germany to certain family allowances. One question that arose was whether the provision in the decision guaranteeing equal treatment had direct effect. Five Member States denied this. They cited *Taflan-Met*, a case where the ECJ had previously expressed the view that the decision was generally intended to be supplemented and implemented in what was then still the Community by a subsequent act of the Council.[137]

The Advocate General was not swayed. His rejection was essentially twofold. First, he called into question the Member States' wide literal reading of *Taflan-Met* (where he had also delivered an opinion), although ostensibly declining to play the *obiter/ratio* game. Of particular interest in the present context however is his second point that, even if the gov-ernments were right in their understanding of that case, one should not attach too much attention to what the Court had previously said on the matter.[138] Despite stressing continuity, logical compatibility and freedom from contradiction, he insisted that the ECJ was 'not technically bound by its earlier judgments'. It followed that the Court could in a preliminary reference give a different answer to a question it had already previously dealt with '*if* such a result [was] justified by new matters brought to its attention in the later proceedings' (emphasis added).

This last twist is curious. It would seem from this condition that the Court is precisely *not* at (complete) liberty to decide previously referred matters differently. Besides, even for proponents of precedent-enforced decisional exclusivity 'new matters' can even in the absence of direct overruling provide grounds for evading a supposed precedent, be it on account of a relevant distinction, changed conditions, obsolescence or because the correctness of the prior decision was assumed without full argument, then said to have been rendered *per incuriam*.[139]

AG La Pergola's reformulation in the next paragraph is also not as con-clusive as might have been expected given his apparent basic take on the subject, although the use of the qualifier 'technically' in fact already sig-nalled a compromising stance from the outset. According to the Advocate

---

[136] Case C-262/96 *Sema Sürül* v. *Bundesanstalt für Arbeit* [1999] ECR I-2685, Opinion of AG La Pergola (para. 36).

[137] Case C-277/94 *Z. Taflan-Met and ors* v. *Bestuur van de Sociale Verzekeringsbank* [1996] ECR I-4085 (paras. 33–7).

[138] *Ibid.* Paras. 36–7.

[139] See Dias (n. 88 above), pp. 77–8; Cross and Harris (n. 116 above), pp. 158–63.

General, a 'position [previously] adopted by the Court could be reviewed, *provided* that the approach taken was based on appropriate and logical grounds and conformed with the relevant precedents' (emphasis added).

Conformity with similar cases might seem an odd demand in a train of thought seeking to establish the opposite, yet it is mirrored in the care the Advocate General subsequently took to reconcile his view with his prior opinion in *Taflan-Met* and his insistence that the rival interpretation would have marked a clandestine departure from established precedent. Even if this last requirement is dismissed as a Freudian slip, the technique is not different in kind from that of courts of last resort of various common law legal orders, including the US, UK and Irish Supreme Courts, all of which have not incontrovertibly felt constrained to strictly follow precedent in all situations.

In a similar manner, AG Ruiz-Jarabo Colomer once cautioned against 'overextending the principle of *stare decisis*', while in the same breath adducing an earlier case as a further argument why the defendant's contention failed that EC Art. 226 (now TFEU Art. 258) was the wrong legal basis for the Commission's action.[140] The Commission had asked the ECJ to declare that several Member States had failed to fulfil various obligations by refusing to make payments in respect of customs duties incurred through the importation of military equipment. One objection was that the Commission should have used the special procedure provided for in EC Art. 298 (now TFEU Art. 348). Apart from referring to the merely permissive wording of said provision as well as its purpose, the Advocate General in response drew attention to the fact that the ECJ had previously not used that procedure in a comparable case. There is a telling ambiguity in his notion of not 'overextending' the doctrine of binding precedent, which suggests that it might actually apply, albeit to a limited yet unclear extent.

At first glance this would not seem to hold up. Adopting a binary or puristic view of normativity, a precedent can either bind a successive court or not. This simplicity is in fact one of the key reasons why bindingness is often presented as mechanistically as flicking a light switch. But if one is prepared to assume that the notion of constrained judicial decision-making is in fact more complex and allows for degrees of bindingness between and beyond these conceptual extremes, the Advocate General's position becomes a lot more plausible.

---

[140] Case C-284/05 *Commission* v. *Republic of Finland* [2009] ECR I-11705, Opinion of AG Ruiz-Jarabo Colomer (para. 42, fn. 30).

In *Merck*, AG Fennelly devoted several paragraphs of his lengthy opinion to the bindingness issue and the latitude for departures from prior
interpretations.[141] Arguing in a reference concerning the free movement
of pharmaceutical products in connection with the accession of Spain
and Portugal that the ECJ should no longer follow an earlier decision,
which in his view had unjustifiably stressed free movement to the detriment patent protection, the Advocate General observed that '[a]s a matter of principle, the Court is of course not bound by its own previous
judgments'.[142]

Once again there is hedging in the form of a qualifier, although this
time getting very close to a duty on the ECJ to follow prior cases or a
presumption to that extent. Correspondingly, judge-made law featured
heavily in the Advocate General's opinion, showing the close connection between positive and negative precedent. In his view, this 'matter
of principle' was offset by a 'matter of practice', whereby it was 'obvious
that the Court should . . . follow its previous case-law *except* where there
are *strong reasons* for not doing so'.[143] The emphasis on context is conspicuous. The absence of such a circumstance would appear to constrain
judicial decision-making. AG Fennelly seemed to consider these statements self-evident. But can it really be said that the 'matter of principle'
follows legally, whereas the 'matter of practice' is somehow outside of
this, in other words pure habit or convenience? The Advocate General
did not venture that far, choosing to compare the role of the Court's own
precedents to pronouncements of courts of last resort in common law
jurisdictions.

In *Internationaler Hilfsfonds*, AG Trstenjak traced this absence of 'formally' binding precedent or strict *stare decisis* to two reasons.[144] Her first
argument was the historical fact that the founding Member States were
all part of the Continental European civil law tradition. Indeed, so are
nearly all of its close to thirty legal orders today. Secondly, she noted that
its would not be fitting for a court from which there is no appeal to not
be able to make necessary changes, given how difficult it is to amend
the treaties and in light of the need to remain flexible when faced with
constitutional objections by the Member States. In spite of everything,

---

[141] Joined Cases C-267/95 and C-268/95 *Merck & Co. Inc. and ors* v. *Primecrown Ltd and ors*
[1996] ECR I-6285 Opinion of AG Fennelly (paras. 138–47).
[142] *Ibid.* para. 139.   [143] *Ibid.* para. 142 (emphasis added).
[144] Case C-331/05 P *Internationaler Hilfsfonds eV* v. *Commission* [2005] ECR I-5475, Opinion
of AG Trstenjak (para. 85) (apparently also dealing with *res judicata*).

the Court would 'endeavour in principle to give a coherent interpretation to the law'. The exhortation is patent.

The second argument seems more compelling. While the EU's dominant pedigree is plain, there is little beyond historical determinism to suggest that the institutions of this supranational entity, which represents the most innovative modern project of governance beyond the nation state, could not develop along different lines. Moreover, as explained before, bindingness is an equally complex issue in civil law systems. Conversely, the flexibility argument holds true for all courts of last resort.

In sum, the ECJ repeatedly professes not to be 'legally' or 'strictly' bound by its own output. It knows of the vital importance of having a pressure valve. At the same time, the Court is also 'naturally hesitant to depart'[145] from precedents, preferring to be 'circumspect'[146] when considering a *revirement*. It, too, values stability and coherence, but it refuses to be 'absolute' about negative precedent or to openly acknowledge any binding effect. It will depart from prior cases where it considers this necessary, which is a broader inquiry than a purely doctrinal one. A modest starting point is that fresh interpretations must be argued for, rather than abiding by previous ones, which is essentially a presumption in favour of coherence.[147] Where it does decide that adaptation is required, the Court might consider it exceptionally warranted to limit the effects of a judgment to the future in order to maintain a degree of legal certainty and protect legitimate expectations.[148] But a more thorough reconstruction of the ECJ's normative output is required. It follows next.

iii Reconstruction

How can the findings above be conceived in positivistic (i.e. evincing fidelity to legal text) and conceptual (i.e. focusing on the abstract

---

[145] See e.g. Case C-163/09 *Repertoire Culinaire Ltd* v. *The Commissioners of Her Majesty's Revenue & Customs* [2010] ECR I-12717, Opinion of AG Kokott (para. 61).

[146] Joined Cases C-94/04 and C-202/04 *Federico Cipolla* v. *Rosaria Fazari (née Portolese)* [2006] ECR I-11421, Opinion of AG Poiares Maduro (paras. 28–9) (suggesting respect for cases in the interest of 'values of cohesion, uniformity and legal certainty').

[147] See Case 28–67 *Firma Molkerei-Zentrale Westfalen/Lippe GmbH* v. *Hauptzollamt Paderborn* [1968] ECR 143, 155 ('no grounds').

[148] See only Case C-163/09 *Repertoire Culinaire Ltd* v. *The Commissioners of Her Majesty's Revenue & Customs* [2010] ECR I-12717, Opinion of AG Kokott (para. 62). That option in itself counters an argument that strict *stare decisis* necessarily ought to follow from a supposed guarantee of perfect previsibility or absolute protection of legitimate expectations.

structure of law rather than purely its contents or consequences) terms?[149] Given the complexities outlined earlier, it is not satisfactory to bluntly brand the Court with inaccurate stereotypes concerning the normativity of precedents. The challenge lies in understanding legal reasoning in a way that takes technical lawyering and interpretation *lege artis* seriously, supplementing instead of supplanting it with theory,[150] yet without surrendering to plain description of what legal workers at the Court do or should do.

(a) Denial of law-making

A preliminary and often implicit line of defence, declaratory cognitivism, has already been assessed in Chapter 2. Recapping briefly, if the ECJ's decisions are not 'law properly so called', there might be little reason to afford them any special significance outside the immediate dispute that is being settled. Accordingly, the Court simply polices, interprets and renders concrete EU law. The shortcomings of such models have been pointed out, and the ECJ evidently does not itself subscribe to such a view. Moreover, ways exist to contest and channel this activity.[151] Quite apart from such a general jurisprudential claim, however, more specific arguments as to why the Court is not 'formally' bound by its own decisions can be drawn from the normative materials of the Union. These are analysed now.

(b) Entrenched negation

A first attempt would look for provisions that can be interpreted to rule out 'strict' *stare decisis*. But just as it lacks a single comprehensive provision on legal sources akin to ICJ Statute Art. 38(1), there is no plain inhibition similar to Art. 5 of the French civil code or ICJ Statute Art. 59 or NAFTA Art. 1136(1). It is however possible to read TEU Art. 19(1), which stipulates that the ECJ shall ensure that 'the law' is observed in the application and interpretation of the treaties, in a way reminiscent of Art. 20(3) of the German Basic Law. Judges' ultimate fidelity is then owed to something that is not exhaustively described by one particular legal artefact, including precedents. In fact, few would earnestly claim

---

[149] Cf. M. I. Niemi, 'Form and Substance in Legal Reasoning: Two Conceptions', *Ratio Juris*, 23 (2010), 479, 480.

[150] Cf. M. Jestaedt, 'Warum in die Ferne schweifen, wenn der Maßstab liegt so nah? Verfassungshandwerkliche Anfragen an das Lissabon-Urteil des BVerfG', *Der Staat*, 48 (2009), 497, 498–499, 510.

[151] Alluded to in Ch. 2, E.ii.(c) above.

adjudicators to be the sole font of law and justice. This applies equally to common law jurisdictions, where 'the law' is sometimes treated in an almost reverential manner as metaphysically floating above the land and legal process. This injects the flexibility necessary for departures.

(c) Legality and limited mandate

Further arguments relate to the EU's celebrated proclamation as a 'community of law' in which the rule of law, sometimes termed the 'principle of legality', obtains.[152] This is put on an explicit primary law footing in TEU Art. 2 and frequently sounds in the jurisprudence of the Court.[153] The constitutional imperative finds practical expression in EU administrative law and a growing concern for due process and proper procedural safeguards.[154] A powerful argument is that inevitably abiding by decisions, even if they are wrong, is untenable since it flies in the face of the principle of legality. Another point parallels an argument refuting the setting of precedents through ECJ judgments: the Court, as an institution of the Union, shall act only within the limits of the competences conferred upon it by the Member States in the treaties.[155] Autonomous authority is beyond its reach. Accepting the positivistic premise that 'legal' or 'formal' bindingness in the context of law is not an inherent quality but must be afforded artificially, one is driven to scour EU law for such a provision imbuing ECJ pronouncements with such authority. Any such bindingness must stem from the treaties, even if this is not expressly recorded in a single provision. Since the deck has been stacked against it through this presupposition, it no longer matters that the EU does not have an explicit negation, as noted above.

Combing through primary law in search for express or implied affirmation, it would appear that by occasionally referring to the notion of 'legally binding' acts of the Union the treaty system envisages that not all

---

[152] See F. C. Mayer, 'Europa als Rechtsgemeinschaft' in G. F. Schuppert and M. Bach (eds.), *Europawissenschaft* (Nomos, Baden-Baden, 2005), p. 429.

[153] For more recent pronouncements to that effect see Case C-232/05 *Commission* v. *French Republic* (First Chamber) [2006] ECR I-10071 (para. 57); Case C-521/06 P *Athinaïki Techniki AE* v. *Commission* (Fourth Chamber) [2008] ECR I-5829 (para. 45); Joined Cases C-402/05 P and C-415/05 P *Yassin Abdullah Kadi and Al Barakaat International Foundation* v. *Council and Commission* (Grand Chamber) [2008] ECR I-6351 (para. 316).

[154] See e.g. A. Simonati, 'The Principles of Administrative Procedure and the EU Courts: An Evolution in Progress?', *Review of European Administrative Law*, 4 (2011), 45, 80 (discerning a shift from *effet utile* to procedural principles protecting individuals).

[155] See TEU Art. 5(2).

acts of the EU qualify as such.[156] In fact, the treaties seem to be relatively clear when it comes to affording certain acts special legal force. This also includes specifying the respective addressees. TFEU Art. 288 states that regulations and (non-judicial) decisions are binding in their entirety. The latter are binding only on addressees, even if others could arguably be treated the same way according to the spirit and purpose of the decisions in question.[157] Directives are binding as to the result to be achieved. On the other hand, recommendations and opinions explicitly 'shall have no binding force'. In light of the positivistic approach one might consider that last provision a redundant restatement, but it underlines the basic take that acts of the EU do not simply compel obedience by virtue of their origin. Unlike the Member States, the Union cannot play the 'inherent sovereignty' trump to ground the binding force of any of its acts.

What about judicial decisions? TFEU Art. 288 does not mention judgments of the Court. Nevertheless, given that presumption this silence is not neutral. Quite the contrary, the positivistic outlook holds that absent deliberate authorisation binding force is denied. Consider only what AG Lagrange had to say almost fifty years ago: 'In the Treaty of Rome I find no special provision derogating from the principle that *res judicata* binds only the case in question.'[158] The treaty provisions stipulating the effects of the ECJ's judgments and dealing with enforcement touch upon the compulsion exerted by its pronouncements, but they do not mention any obligation vis-à-vis the Court itself.[159] Historically, this might not be particularly startling, as has been noted before: none of the original six

---

[156] See e.g. TEFU Arts. 2, 216 and 291.

[157] See Case C-327/09 *Mensch und Natur AG* v. *Freistaat Bayern* [2011] ECR I-2897, Opinion of AG Jääskinen (paras. 42, 49) (arguing that any resulting fragmentation could be avoided if regulations were used instead).

[158] Joined Cases 28 to 30–62 *Da Costa en Schaake NV and ors* v. *Nederlandse Belastingadministratie* [1963] ECR 31, Opinion of AG Lagrange (p. 41). There is of course a difference between *res judicata* and precedential force, with the former being a more limited procedural device precluding actions where there is an identity of parties, cause and subject matter. See e.g. Case C-526/08 *Commission* v. *Grand Duchy of Luxembourg* (Grand Chamber) [2010] ECR I-6151 (paras. 22–9); Art. 1351 of the French *Code civil*: 'L'autorité de la chose jugée n'a lieu qu'à l'égard de ce qui a fait l'objet du jugement. Il faut que la chose demandée soit la même; que la demande soit fondée sur la même cause; que la demande soit entre les mêmes parties, et formée par elles et contre elles en la même qualité.' The point here is the positivistic presumption.

[159] See e.g. TFEU Arts. 260, 266, 280, 299. Cf. F. A. Schockweiler, 'L'Exécution des arrêts de la Cour' in F. Capotorti *et al.* (eds.), *Du droit international au droit de l'intégration: Liber amicorum Pierre Pescatore* (Nomos, Baden-Baden, 1987), pp. 613–35.

Member States generally accept such exclusory binding force of judicial decisions in their respective domestic legal orders.[160]

The same applies to explanatory notes by the Commission such as those relating to the Combined Nomenclature (previously the Common Customs Tariff) used for tariff classification purposes, which are habitually denied binding force and relegated to 'mere' aids to interpretation.[161] The CFREU was treated similarly prior to the Treaty of Lisbon. Again, the main purpose of this restrictive positivism is to make determination without involvement the exception rather than the rule. Less noble motivations might include avoiding any potentially unforeseen loss of power as a consequence of tying one's own hands as well as making token commitments for strategic reasons.

Looking further, the ECJ Rules of Procedure state in Art. 91(1) that '[a] judgment shall be binding from the date of its delivery'. Could this be an endorsement of 'pure' precedential force?[162] A first observation would be that this provision is worded more broadly than ICSID Convention Art. 53(1), since it does not specify that it should be binding 'on the parties'.[163] All the more, it differs from NAFTA Art. 1136(1) and ICJ Statute Art. 59, which conversely speak of 'no binding force except between the (disputing) parties'. Evidently, however, Art. 91 does not state that a judgment should bind *the Court*. What is more, 'judgment(s)' are said to be binding. This could equally well refer to actual rulings (i.e. the operative part), rather than any reasons contained therein and thus evoke more commonplace notions of preclusion. Since bindingness vis-à-vis the involved parties in the more limited sense of *res judicata* is to be expected from an institutionalised court whose judgments are not only advisory, the emphasis rather appears to be on the temporal aspect, namely the date of delivery. This finds support in a purposive interpretation. No appeals

---

[160] See Case C-331/05 P *Internationaler Hilfsfonds eV* v. *Commission* [2005] ECR I-5475, Opinion of AG Trstenjak (para. 85); C. Tomuschat, *Die gerichtliche Vorabentscheidung nach den Verträgen über die europäischen Gemeinschaften* (Carl Heymanns, Cologne, 1964), p. 187. As argued above, such comparison has its limits.

[161] See e.g. Case C-173/08 *Kloosterboer Services BV* v. *Inspecteur van de Belastingdienst/ Douane Rotterdam* (Fifth Chamber) [2009] ECR I-5347 (para. 25); Case C-370/08 *Data I/O GmbH* v. *Hauptzollamt Hannover* (Second Chamber) [2010] ECR I-4401 (para. 30). See also Lasok and Millett (n. 16 above), m.n. 715.

[162] See to that effect Gutsche (n. 117 above), pp. 10–31.

[163] See also the formulation contained in Art. 18 of the Consolidated Version of the Treaty Establishing the European Atomic Energy Community ('Euratom Treaty') [2010] OJ C84: 'The final decisions of the Arbitration Committee shall have the force of res judicata between the parties concerned.'

lie against decisions of the ECJ, hence there is no need for a time limit to have lapsed for the judgment to become binding. Its finality hence falls on the date of delivery.

Moreover, in terms of its location within the legal materials, it seems unlikely that a provision of such eminent importance mandating decisional exclusivity would have to be mined from one line in the midst of the Court's Rules of Procedure – sandwiched between service of an order and publication in the Official Journal – and not mentioned more prominently, that is to say higher up in the normative ladder.[164] Although they have a primary law flavour on account of the Council having to give its approval,[165] in contrast to the CJEU Statute, the ECJ Rules of Procedure are established by the Court itself and hence hybrid in nature. Arguably, reading binding force in the form of 'pure' precedent into this violates a cardinal tenet of attributed positivism. Finally, assuming *arguendo* that Art. 91(1) is indeed a provision affirming the forever compelling quality of the ECJ's judgments, the question arises why it is not utilised as such on a daily basis by, before and against the Court?

That view is also not shaken by Art. 99 of the ECJ Rules of Procedure. This enables the Court to reply by reasoned order in situations where a question posed by a national court in preliminary ruling procedures is 'identical' to a question on which the ECJ has already ruled, where the answer to such a question can be 'clearly deduced' from existing case law or where the answer admits of 'no reasonable doubt'. This provision, originally introduced in 1991 and simplified in 2012, developed and codified the Court's practice of dealing with repetitive references in an economical fashion.[166] While this is a plain recognition of the precedential web spun by the ECJ, it does not compel the Court to abide by its earlier jurisprudence. The wording is not mandatory, neither as concerns the issuing of an order nor in respect of its contents. It certainly does not state that the Court could not change its mind on the matter referred. Quite the contrary, if the ECJ was itself bound by its decisions, it would seem rather bizarre that the Union's system of co-operative legal protection evidently does not prevent Member States from referring the same issue again and again, perhaps in the hope of ultimately getting a different answer.[167]

---

[164] But note that such an argument is generally rejected in respect of ICJ Statute Art. 59.
[165] See TFEU Art. 253.   [166] Cf. ECJ Rules of Procedure Art. 182 in the context of appeals.
[167] On resubmitting see M. P. Broberg and N. Fenger, *Preliminary References to the European Court of Justice* (Oxford University Press, 2010), pp. 190–1.

(d) Substantive support

The case against 'formally' binding precedent at the ECJ can be shored up by more substantive arguments as to why it would be implausible or undesirable for the Court's pronouncements to be self-binding. Through purposive interpretation this can also be threaded into the analysis of the provisions just sketched.

One of the most prominent reasons marshalled in this respect is that self-bindingness would usher in a repugnant degree of stasis and effectively freeze legal relations, to the point that they would have to remain in place even if they were structured wrongly in the past.[168] This insistence on progressive interpretation is occasionally referred to as the 'living tree' doctrine elsewhere, in particular in the human and fundamental rights context. It conflicts starkly with classical Benthamite positivism, which shares its reformist thrust but abhors the idea of judges stepping in for legislators.

In the context of the EU, this flexibility argument carries particular weight. The Union now penetrates a bewildering array of subject matters of modern life, with the ECJ ruling on issues ranging from the core organisation of the European economic and political landscape to the welfare of live bovine animals during sea transport.[169] More so than executive-driven processes of decision-making, fundamental politico-legislative change is difficult to co-ordinate in a legal space that takes pride in its evident diversity, especially where this would involve treaty amendment; a feat that, by design, is beyond even the most influential Member States when acting on their own and that can readily be blocked. Absolute decisional rigidity becomes an increasingly unpalatable and unlikely choice the more difficult the correction or redirection of judicial decisions becomes. Strict doctrines to that effect are hence only applied rigorously to courts of inferior jurisdiction, where appeals are the obvious counteractive mechanism. At the highest tiers, inflexibility is unwarranted without a satisfactory political corrective.

---

[168] See Tomuschat (n. 160 above), p. 188; M. Poiares Maduro and L. Azoulai, 'Introduction' in M. Poiares Maduro and L. Azoulai (eds.), *The Past and Future of EU Law* (Hart, Oxford and Portland, 2010), p. xviii ('law changes even when legal texts remain unchanged').

[169] On the former see e.g. Opinion 1/91 *Draft Agreement Between the Community and the Countries of the European Free Trade Association Relating to the Creation of the European Economic Area* [1991] ECR I-6079. For the latter see Case C-207/06 *Schwaninger Martin Viehhandel – Viehexport* v. *Zollamt Salzburg, Erstattungen* (Third Chamber) [2008] ECR I-5561.

Without seeking to detract from the intricacies of domestic political manoeuvring, such remedial efforts are particularly cumbersome in the EU given its additional structural complexity and lack of a single centralised legislature that could swiftly wipe the slate clean. Of course there is a great deal of informal interaction between the Court and the other organs of the Union, such as when the Commission refocuses its strategies following important judgments. It expressly did so following the *Cassis de Dijon* ruling.[170] But open instances of a direct negative reaction to ECJ jurisprudence through the Member States acting collectively are not that common, particularly outside secondary legislation.

A rare example is Protocol (No. 33) Concerning Article 157 of the Treaty on the Functioning of the European Union, the so called 'Barber Protocol'.[171] Its origin lies in an eponymous reference for a preliminary ruling by the English Court of Appeal concerning retirement pensions and equal pay. The ECJ decided that contracted-out occupational pensions effectively substituting state schemes came within the scope of what is now TFEU Art. 157.[172] Consequently, the principle of equal pay without discrimination based on sex applied. What really worried the Member States, however, was the retroactive effect the judgment might have and the serious financial consequences such a finding might entail, given that what was then still EEC Art. 119 was directly effective and could be relied upon before national courts. Tensions flaring, the ECJ was exceptionally moved to restrict the temporal effect of its judgment in the interest of legal certainty to the extent that, save for proceedings previously initiated, EEC Art. 119 could not be relied upon to claim entitlement to a pension with effect from a date prior to that of the judgment. Nonetheless, a protocol was afterwards annexed to the Treaty of Maastricht to rule out any retroactive effect, stating that all benefits under occupational social security schemes are not to be considered as remuneration if and in so far as they are attributable to periods of employment prior to 17 May

---

[170] Case 120/78 *Rewe-Zentral AG* v. *Bundesmonopolverwaltung für Branntwein* [1979] ECR 649. The ECJ's introduction of 'mutual recognition' into free movement of goods law was readily embraced by the Commission as a viable alternative to the adoption of harmonising measures dealing with minimum requirements: *Completing the Internal Market: White Paper from the Commission to the European Council* COM(85) 310 final (para. 61).

[171] [2010] OJ C83/319. See J. H. H. Weiler and U. Haltern, 'The Autonomy of the Community Legal Order: Through the Looking Glass', *Harvard International Law Journal*, 37 (1996), 411, 416.

[172] Case C-262/88 *Douglas Harvey Barber* v. *Guardian Royal Exchange Assurance Group* [1990] ECR I-1889.

1990 (i.e. the date the *Barber* judgment was handed down). The Court has subsequently not challenged this.[173]

There are other reasons besides the plain need to avoid a sclerotic ultimate arbiter. With the appropriate qualification for preliminary references, the ECJ will only opine on those matters which are necessary for it to settle a dispute. Even in requests under TFEU Art. 267 it will not at present spend a great amount of time exploring and weighing a broad range of 'non-legal' arguments.

Yet another argument is based on the structure of the European system of legal protection. The ECJ is not hierarchically superimposed above the courts of the Member States, which are not courts of inferior jurisdiction. Despite popular clamouring to the contrary and notwithstanding the many rough edges, the relationship is fundamentally one of interactive co-ordination and mutual accommodation on multiple levels – in short, post-national.[174] Of course this does not imply that such collaboration is free from friction or fully complementary. In particular national constitutional courts have fired various warning shots aimed at the Court; the interminable tug-of-war is well-documented.[175] It is also apparent that with growing familiarity between the different layers institutional bashfulness has faded and competitive brio increased, but this can in turn be seen as a sign of progressively more mature and robust relations. As the more recent jurisprudence of the German FCC evinces, the overall trajectory has edged towards co-operation rather than towards collision.[176] Indeed, the FCC was criticised at home for bending over backwards methodologically and stylistically in its obliging efforts.[177] Be that as it may, judicial

---

[173] See e.g. Joined Cases C-4/02 and C-5/02 *Hilde Schönheit* v. *Stadt Frankfurt am Main and Silvia Becker* v. *Land Hessen* (Fifth Chamber) [2003] ECR I-12575 (paras. 101–4); Case C-236/09 *Association Belge des Consommateurs Test-Achats and ors* v. *Conseil des ministres* [2011] ECR I-773, Opinion of AG Kokott (para. 82).

[174] See I. Pernice, 'Europäisches und nationales Verfassungsrecht', *Veröffentlichungen der Vereinigung der deutschen Staatsrechtslehrer*, 60 (2001), 148, 155.

[175] See e.g. M. Kumm, 'The Jurisprudence of Constitutional Conflict: Constitutional Supremacy in Europe Before and After the Constitutional Treaty', *European Law Journal*, 11 (2005), 262, 264–5 (identifying three main areas of conflict: fundamental rights, *Kompetenz-Kompetenz* (i.e. the ultimate power to invalidate *ultra vires* EU law), and other provisions of primary and secondary EU law). For a political science perspective see Stone Sweet and Brunell in A. Stone Sweet (ed.), *The Judicial Construction of Europe* (Oxford University Press, 2004), pp. 81–94.

[176] See e.g. BVerfG, 2 BvE 2/08, *Lissabon*, 2nd Senate, 30 Jun. 2009; BVerfG, 2 BvR 2661/06, *Honeywell*, 2nd Senate, 6 Jul. 2010.

[177] See e.g. Jestaedt (n. 150 above).

rivalries will most likely continue, but this multiplicity is the EU's federalist state of being and not an ailment that has befallen it and needs to be cured.[178] To consider it deficient amounts to adopting a statist mindset, either in an isolated nationalistic form or as megalomaniac super-statism, extreme projects from which a Union 'united in diversity' has continually distanced itself.[179] The Court hence needs to be supple enough to react to pointers it receives from its judicial partners in Europe – think only fundamental rights – and to accommodate different takes on the shared legal space. This pluralistic order would be seriously undermined if the ECJ was self-bound, since this would effectively also impose decisional exclusivity on other actors.

All of this leads to the conclusion that precedents of the ECJ do not have 'strictly' or 'technically' binding force in the sense of precluding departures. That however neither rules out normative or precedential effect of the Court's cases altogether, nor does it even remotely address the prevalence and complexity of precedent-handling.

(e) Normative effect beyond bindingness

Just as there is much to be said for differentiating between bindingness and more direct legal effects of an ECJ judgment,[180] there is little to be gained from eliding bindingness and precedential effect or even normativity as a whole. The latter need not be reduced to the former. What matters is not the total absence of choice but the justification of constraint. The Court's decisions and the legal position of parties can be prejudiced through previous adjudication without there being a clear commitment to a legal doctrine or theoretical concept of bindingness. In other words, that ECJ pronouncements exert no 'strictly' or 'formally' binding force does not rule a precedent's normative effect out altogether. This is hinted at by the Court when it speaks of the need for coherence and consistency in the same breath as disavowing *stare decisis*.

---

[178] See D. Halberstam, 'Pluralism in *Marbury* and *Van Gend*' in M. Poiares Maduro and L. Azoulai (eds.), *The Past and Future of EU Law* (Hart, Oxford and Portland, 2010), p. 32.

[179] This is plain to see in the preliminary reference procedure. It is also manifest in the 'primacy' – as opposed to the 'supremacy' – of EU law.

[180] See A. G. Toth, 'The Authority of Judgments of the European Court of Justice' (n. 116 above), pp. 5, 44–5. The legal effects of the ECJ's decisions are often spelled out in the treaties, e.g. in TFEU Arts. 260, 266, 280, 299. E.g. following successful infringement procedures, Member States are required to take the necessary measures to comply with a judgment. The same applies to Union institutions whose acts have been declared void or whose failures to act have been declared contrary to the treaties. *Ex tunc* nullity also generally applies.

(i) **The authority of interpretation.** Such an effect is particularly noticeable in preliminary reference proceedings concerning the interpretation of the treaties. The French term *question préjudicielle* is a not so subtle tip-off: something is judged beforehand. Sometimes likened to a 'central nervous system' of the multi-tiered Unional legal system,[181] the procedure that is now found in TFEU Art. 267 has proved to be an integral part of ensuring the widespread and effective monitoring and application of EU law by presenting an ingenious and fundamental counterpart to more obviously curative procedures such as infringement actions. Its specificities and functioning are well-documented.[182] The undeniable popularity and success of the reference procedure as a vehicle of European integration is attributable to a stick-and-carrot strategy that liberally mixes inter-judicial dialogue, persuasion, baiting, reprimanding, horse-trading and reciprocal empowerment.[183] For the Court, it has proved to be a tool for ensuring uniformity and economising through decentralisation, but also for the exercise of authority; a major attraction for national courts lies in the shifting of responsibility to Luxembourg and the use of an external agent to leapfrog – and sometimes profoundly upset – national judicial hierarchies and political strictures. It can thus reduce the status of traditional domestic 'custodians' of constitutional review, some of whom have become notorious hold-outs in the process.[184]

In such proceedings, the Court does not technically settle a dispute. But through abstraction (and frequently reformulation) it elevates questions and answers to the point where there are many more cases that could come under that rubric. This is ideally suited to *arrêts de principes*. Interpretations made in this context are binding on the national judge making the reference. But they are effectively 'canons of interpretation', that is to say legal information, for all courts and authorities

---

[181] A. Stone Sweet, 'The Juridical *Coup d'État* and the Problem of Authority: *CILFIT* and *Foto-Frost*' in M. Poiares Maduro and L. Azoulai (eds.), *The Past and Future of EU Law* (Hart, Oxford and Portland, 2010), p. 201.

[182] See only P. J. G. Kapteyn, 'Administration of Justice' in P. J. G. Kapteyn and P. VerLoren van Themaat (eds.), *The Law of the European Union and the European Communities* (4th edn, Kluwer Law International, Alphen aan den Rijn, 2008), pp. 479–99.

[183] See e.g. T. Koopmans, 'La procédure préjudicielle – victime de son succès?' in F. Capotorti and others (eds.), *Du droit international au droit de l'intégration: Liber amicorum Pierre Pescatore* (Nomos, Baden-Baden, 1987), pp. 347–50; K. J. Alter, *Establishing the Supremacy of European Law: The Making of an International Rule of Law in Europe* (Oxford University Press, 2001), pp. 45–63.

[184] See Editorial, 'Judicial Ego', *International Journal of Constitutional Law*, 9 (2011), 1 (for a biting critique of the German FCC in this respect).

in the EU.[185] Where these are not respected, or where courts of last resort fail to request preliminary rulings, this could even trigger state liability.

This bears elaboration. One of the issues left open by the original EEC Art. 177, the current provision's precursor, was whether national courts whose decisions are final might at times be entitled not to make such a reference.[186] In a decision that recognised and solidified the precedential effect of such ECJ decisions and had crucial ramifications for the intricate relationship between national and supranational adjudication, the ECJ in *CILFIT* famously carved out two exceptions besides irrelevance to the obligation to refer.[187] They have become known as the doctrines of *acte clair* and *acte éclairé* and involve situations in which there is no reasonable doubt about the correct application of EU law or where the question raised is materially identical to one that has been answered previously by the Court.[188]

To appreciate this holding one needs to recall the foundational period of the Court and the equally important, if sometimes sidelined, case of *Da Costa*.[189] Here the Dutch *Tariefcommissie* (the Administrative Court for Customs and Excise) had posed questions that were identical to those that the ECJ had in the meantime answered in *van Gend*.[190] The written observations were the same and no new circumstances had since emerged. Aqueous emulsion of ureaformaldehyde there, halogenous derivates of

---

[185] A. Rosas, 'The European Court of Justice in Context: Forms and Patterns of Judicial Dialogue', *European Journal of Legal Studies*, 1 (2007), 1, 7.

[186] The provision enshrines an obligation ('shall') on national courts of last resort to refer to the ECJ questions the resolution of which are necessary to enable them to give judgment. For inferior courts this is worded as an option ('may').

[187] Case 283/81 *Srl CILFIT and Lanificio di Gavardo SpA* v. *Ministry of Health* [1982] ECR 3415.

[188] In fact, the Court in *CILFIT* did not use either expression. AG Capotorti even criticised the theory of *acte clair* in general, noting its inherent circularity (*ibid.* p. 3436). Hence some commentators regret the importation of the term into EU law vocabulary. See D. Edward, '*CILFIT* and *Foto-Frost* in their Historical and Procedural Context' in M. Poiares Maduro and L. Azoulai (eds.), *The Past and Future of EU Law* (Hart, Oxford and Portland, 2010), p. 179 (preferring a test based on 'reasonable doubt' and common sense). The terms have however gained currency with Advocates General, judges and commentators, which is why they will be used here subject to the disclaimer that they have their own Unional flavour.

[189] Joined Cases 28 to 30/62 *Da Costa en Schaake NV and ors* v. *Nederlandse Belastingadministratie* [1963] ECR 31.

[190] Case 26/62 *NV Algemene Transport- en Expeditie Onderneming van Gend & Loos* v. *Netherlands Inland Revenue Administration* [1963] ECR 1.

hydrocarbons here;[191] hardly a suspicious difference. Once more, the question was whether EEC Art. 12 produced direct effect, which again was necessary for the claimants to oppose a hike in import duties. Unable to shake off a sense of déjà vu, the Commission argued that the reference should be dismissed for lack of substance. The French Advocate General had the *acte clair* doctrine in mind, in other words that a 'self-evident' point obviated any need for interpretation.[192]

But the Court in *Da Costa* plotted a different course, shrewdly permitting national courts to refer such questions even if they had already been answered. Not only was this in line with the ostensibly 'unreserved' primary law requirement for courts of last resort to make references, this also handily avoided turning down the co-operative obligingness of domestic courts. Nevertheless, in order not to be caught between a rock (affronting national courts) and a hard place (entertaining a plethora of essentially redundant references time and again), the ECJ added that 'the authority of an interpretation under [TFEU Art. 267] already given by the Court may deprive the obligation of its purpose and thus empty it of its substance. Such is the case especially when the question raised is materially identical with a question which has already been the subject of a preliminary ruling in a similar case.'[193] The message, dripping with precedential reasoning, is clear: unless there is a relevant dissimilarity, there is no need for a further reference. Because the answer to X has already been given as Y, every time X comes up the answer will be Y. In *Da Costa*, the Court concluded that if a reference was made nonetheless, it would simply give judgment on the application in like fashion, which it swiftly proceeded to do, explicitly noting in the *dispositif* that there was 'no new ground for giving a new interpretation'.

Roughly twenty years later, the ECJ elaborated upon this nascent appreciation of precedent in *CILFIT*. It extended the exemption from seeking guidance to proceedings of a different nature where the questions are 'not strictly identical'. The *Corte Suprema di Cassazione* (the Italian Supreme

---

[191] The goods being imported into the Netherlands from Germany in the two other cases joined in *Da Costa* were bakelite material and certain chemical powder products. Here, too, abstraction allowed for relevant similarity.

[192] Joined Cases 28 to 30/62 *Da Costa en Schaake NV and ors v. Nederlandse Belastingadministratie* [1963] ECR 31, Opinion of AG Lagrange (p. 45).

[193] Joined Cases 28 to 30/62 *Da Costa en Schaake NV and ors v. Nederlandse Belastingadministratie* [1963] ECR 31, 38. The French original is even more to the point, speaking of a deprivation of the *cause* of the obligation on the domestic court to refer.

Court of Cassation) had referred a question in the context of a legal dispute between importers of wool and the Italian ministry of health, which had levied fixed health inspection charges. The importing textile firms insisted that wool was subject to the common organisation of agricultural markets by virtue of being 'animal products'. The levy was accordingly impermissible. The respondent ministry not only contended that wool was outside the scope of that regulation, but that this was in fact so obvious that there was no need for a preliminary reference to the ECJ. Unfazed, the Italian court referred a question on the scope of the third paragraph of what is now TFEU Art. 267 and the requisite degree of interpretive doubt.

The ECJ seized the opportunity to explain when a legal issue was woolly enough to demand a reference. Recalling *Da Costa* and reproducing the above extract verbatim, it asserted that a question could be deprived of its substance where previous decisions had already dealt with the point of law in question.[194] Three things are worth noting.

First, the focus shifts from the identity of the questions asked to the answers given by the Court. The link between two situations which should be treated alike is now the ECJ's jurisprudence. While this was already hinted at in *Da Costa*, the Court in *CILFIT* was more outspoken as to who the central actor is in this system of precedent, which might be a sign of the greater confidence displayed by a more mature court. After all, *Da Costa* was hot on the heels of the case that is widely considered to have awoken the slumbering giant. Primacy was only budding in those early days. By contrast, the two decades preceding *CILFIT* had seen the supranational legislator doze off again, so that much of the law-making had been up to a more assertive Court.

Secondly, the requirement of congruence necessary for an analogous imputation that is characteristic of precedential reasoning is refined in *CILFIT*. The Court noted that a reference could be deprived of its purpose (or *cause*) through a previous decision 'even though the questions at issue are not strictly identical'. Again, this was already implicit in *Da Costa*, since 'materially' identical denotes that there has to be equivalence with respect to the relevant parts rather than perfect identity. The negative formulation chosen in *CILFIT* however accentuates the leeway and constant process of reinterpretation that is built into precedential argumentation. This does not necessarily require one particular

---

[194] Case 283/81 *Srl CILFIT and Lanificio di Gavardo SpA* v. *Ministry of Health* [1982] ECR 3415 (para. 14).

precedent that is absolutely identical, assuming such a thing were ever possible. Ultimately, what matters is that the reference is not devoid of substance, in other words that there is still a point that can veritably be argued.

This broader conception of precedent is today brought out clearly by Art. 99 of the ECJ Rules of Procedure, which allows for a reasoned order not only where a question is 'identical' to a matter on which the Court has already ruled, but also where an answer may be 'clearly deduced' from existing case law or where it 'admits of no reasonable doubt'. Similarly, Art. 182 allows for reasoned orders and express reference to 'the relevant case-law' for manifestly well-founded appeals or cross-appeals. This is a clear appreciation of precedent being not only, or even predominantly, about strict authority, bindingness or dictation but rather revolving around legal information and normative justification in the sense of providing fodder for law as an argumentative practice. It further supports the view that the same result can be reached – in this case, a proposition of law be established obviating the need for a preliminary ruling – no matter whether cases are effectively treated as law ('*identical to* a question on which the Court has already ruled'; emphasis added) or whether cases are seen as evidence of the law ('*deduced from* existing case-law'; emphasis added). The generous implementation of the *CILFIT acte éclairé* logic strongly suggests that little heed is paid to theoretical distinctions between 'true' sources of law and 'merely evidentiary' sources of law, a distinction borne out by the German terms *Rechtsquelle* and *Rechtserkenntnisquelle* and still popular in public international law.[195] But the EU legal system, freed from the artificiality of anything akin to ICJ Statute Art. 38(1)(d), has concocted a melange of different conceptions that converge in Art. 99 of the ECJ Rules of Procedure, which further shows that precedent argumentation tends to shake out as practical reasoning and utility rather than religious adherence to conceptual extremes.[196]

---

[195] See e.g. A. Pellet, 'Article 38' in A. Zimmermann, K. Oellers-Frahm and C. Tomuschat (eds.), *The Statute of the International Court of Justice: A Commentary* (Oxford University Press, 2006), p. 784. But see G. G. Fitzmaurice, 'Some Problems Regarding the Formal Sources of Law' in F. M. van Asbeck (ed.), *Symbolae Verzijl: présentées au Prof. J. H. W. Verzijl, á l'occasion de son LXX-ième anniversaire* (Nijhoff, La Haye, 1958), p. 174. For a classic critique of the malleable concept of a legal 'source' see H. Kelsen, *Reine Rechtslehre* (Franz Deuticke, Leipzig and Vienna, 1934), p. 78. Cf. Ch. 2.

[196] Cf. K. Schiemann, *Vom Richter des Common Law zum Richter des Europäischen Rechts* (Vorträge und Berichte Nr 145, Zentrum für Europäisches Wirtschaftsrecht, Rheinische Friedrich-Wilhelms-Universität, Bonn 2005), p. 8. See also Ch. 6 and Ch. 8, B. above.

The Court in *CILFIT* also held that a reference would be unnecessary where there was 'no scope for any reasonable doubt' as to the manner in which a question regarding the correct application of EU law ought to be resolved.[197] This is not infrequently considered a grudging acceptance of the *acte clair* doctrine, which had in various guises long been a staple of certain national courts, chiefly the French *Conseil d'État*. It is now essentially contained in the second variant of Art. 99 of the ECJ Rules of Procedure. Lest this be considered an abrogation of its authority or a peril to the uniform application of supranational law, the ECJ appended certain restrictions seeking to curb the ambit of said doctrine. These have been the subject of heated debate, often sparked by the Court's own Advocates General, largely targeting the supposed lack of clarity and difficulty of meeting the criteria, which are occasionally alleged to practically emaciate national discretion.[198]

What is of interest here is that *acte éclairé* is essentially a species of such *acte clair*. Both implore that there be sufficient legal information regarding the manner in which a point of law ought to be decided. In the former case a prior decision (i.e. the adoption of an externally developed rationality) will be the reason for this absence of reasonable doubt. The latter term has thus come to be associated with others situations in which this might be the case, for instance on the basis of what may be considered unmistakably clear-cut wording.[199] Be that as it may, a question might equally be 'clear' because of a precedent. The methodological eclecticism and argumentative approach inherent in the split *acte éclairé* part is magnified and mirrored by the fact that it sits next to *acte clair* in Art. 99, so that it is hard to escape the impression that it ultimately does not matter which device is used to make a legal point, be it a case or otherwise.[200]

---

[197] Case 283/81 *Srl CILFIT and Lanificio di Gavardo SpA* v. *Ministry of Health* [1982] ECR 3415, para. 16.

[198] See e.g. Case C-338/95 *Wiener S.I. GmbH* v. *Hauptzollamt Emmerich* [1997] ECR I-6495, Opinion of AG Jacobs (paras. 58–65); Case C-461/03 *Gaston Schul Douane-expediteur BV* v. *Minister van Landbouw, Natuur en Voedselkwaliteit* [2005] ECR I-10513, Opinion of AG Ruiz-Jarabo Colomer (paras. 48–59); Case C-495/03 *Intermodal Transports BV* v. *Staatssecretaris van Financiën* [2005] ECR I-8151, Opinion of AG Stix-Hackl (paras. 83– 107). See also H. Rasmussen, 'Remedying the Crumbling EC Judicial System', *Common Market Law Review*, 37 (2000), 1071, 1107–9 (arguing for a reversal of *CILFIT*).

[199] See Haltern (n. 126 above), p. 237. This will, in turn, of course depend on what one's position is on the determinacy of legal language. See also M. Broberg and N. Fenger, 'L'Application de la doctrine de l'acte clair par les juridictions des états membres', *Revue Trimestrielle de Droit Européen* 46 (2010), 861.

[200] Although in an *acte clair* situation the involved parties will also be heard besides the Advocate General.

Cases are just one tool for making normative claims, but perfectly appropriate ones. The fact that they are explicitly singled out highlights their undeniable popularity and importance.

The third point about *CILFIT* is that the ECJ noted that the prior settling of a point of law was not dependent on a particular type of proceeding. *L'autorité de la chose interprétée* is not shackled to what is now TFEU Art. 267. That may not be self-evident, given that preliminary references are special in that the ECJ will *ex officio* consider all possible circumstances leading to a decision. In infringement proceedings, the Court is much more dependent on the submissions of the parties. Nonetheless, precedents can just as well result from those actions. Whether or not a reference is deprived of its *cause* is an issue that transcends the nature of proceedings. It becomes a matter of convincingly distilling and comparing the essence of cases.[201] This is important since it emancipates ECJ precedents from preliminary references, which as a model of path-dependency and interpretive guidance lend themselves well to such a methodology; but by no means do they set the outer limits for its use. Legal information can be found in all forms of adjudicatory reasoning, regardless of procedure. The Court's precedents are hence of similar value when the case in question is a direct action.[202]

(ii) **The authority of the interpreter.** Does this recognition of precedential effect say anything about the import of the ECJ's precedents with respect to its own decision-making? Or is the *Da Costa* and *CILFIT* approach confined to the relationship between national courts and the supranational level?

Two points militate against a restrictive view. The first has to do with the nature of EU law. It is a single, autonomous body of law that is interpreted and applied both centrally and decentrally in the thousands of domestic courts of the EU. Although not in form, national judges are in essence also Unional judges.[203] There is not one type of law for the Member States and one for the supranational level. If a question of EU law is indeed apparent because it has already been dealt with or because it allows for no reasonable doubt as to the manner in which it ought to be resolved, then this is the case regardless of who is considering the matter.

---

[201] See Edward (n. 188 above), p. 178.
[202] Cf. Mackenzie Stuart and Warner (n. 116 above), p. 281.
[203] See U. Everling, 'Die Europäische Union als föderaler Zusammenschluss von Staaten und Bürgern' in A. von Bogdandy and J. Bast (eds.), *Europäisches Verfassungsrecht* (2nd edn, Springer, Heidelberg, 2009), p. 995.

This differs from rigidly hierarchical and institutionalised *stare decisis* approaches.[204]

The second point is similar, but relates more generally to the nature of precedent. It is difficult to see why a question that is materially identical to another should be treated differently – *ceteris paribus* – merely on account of the identity of the interpreter. It is precisely this inherently transcending aspect of analogous reasoning, from which precedent heavily borrows, that supported the Court's remark in *CILFIT* that precedential effect can arise 'irrespective of the nature of proceedings which led to those decisions'.[205]

In this, the ECJ continues the delicate balancing exercise between asserting too much and too little authority. For instance, the Court has often stressed that, in preliminary reference proceedings, it is not actually deciding an individual dispute before national courts through the application of rules of EU law. Indeed, its jurisdiction under TFEU Art. 267 plainly does not extend that far. In light of this, it will reformulate references that appear to be oblivious of this caveat. Of course the line between actually deciding a dispute and providing a pivotal answer for a national court will often be thin in practice, not least since judgments that are not references also often come to be seen as important precedents. Yet it remains an important difference nonetheless, with varying consequences relating to substance, procedure and costs.[206]

But although a preliminary ruling is generally speaking only binding on the referring court and any other national court that is subsequently seized of the matter,[207] this technique has been central to the spinning of a web of precedents that now covers almost all areas of EU law.[208] The official statistics for the year 2011 list 7,428 references for a preliminary

---

[204] See Editorial, 'Les Juges constituants', *European Constitutional Law Review*, 6 (2010), 171, 172.

[205] Case 283/81 *Srl CILFIT and Lanificio di Gavardo SpA* v. *Ministry of Health* [1982] ECR 3415, para. 14.

[206] Cf. the similar take of the ICJ regarding its advisory opinions: ICJ, *Legality of the Threat or Use of Nuclear Weapons*, Advisory Opinion of 8 Jul. 1996, ICJ Rep 1996, 226 (para. 15) ('[t]he purpose of the [ICJ's] advisory opinion is not to settle – at least directly – disputes between States, but to offer legal advice to the organs and institutions requesting the opinion').

[207] See Borchardt (n. 122 above), p. 333. Special considerations apply to rulings on the validity of EU law.

[208] Cf. P. P. Craig and G. de Búrca, *EU Law: Text, Cases, and Materials* (4th edn, Oxford University Press, 2007), p. 477.

ruling since 1953.[209] In recent years, there have been consistently more references than direct actions before the Court, especially now that the GC is primarily responsible for the latter.[210]

National courts are thereby actively encouraged to stand by the ECJ's precedents, but at the same time it is still open to them to try their luck and seek the counsel of the oracle, although there is the very real possibility that they will receive short shrift in the form of a reasoned order.[211] This is in fact not that different from the operation of precedent even if *stare decisis* were to be assumed, where prior reasoning is abbreviated by a quick reference to a precedent. There, too, nothing stops a party from attempting to revisit a point that has already been decided. Such an argument is not inadmissible, but it will require effort to persuade a court that its reasoning can be avoided, be it because it is not materially identical (i.e. distinguishable) or because it is no longer considered to have been decided correctly or to represent 'good law' (i.e. ought to be overruled).

Of course the Court enjoys a privileged position. It is the spider sitting at the middle of this precedential web. That alone means that it cannot ignore it but has to watch and anticipate any reverberations with great care. Its position is further enhanced by the judgment in *Foto-Frost*, according to which the ECJ alone can decide on the validity of acts of the Union's institutions.[212] National courts cannot abstain from seeking a preliminary ruling in such a situation. That the Court takes uniformity and coherence – or, to put it more bluntly, its own central function – seriously is evident from *Gaston Schul*, where the apparent contradiction between the precedential effect recognised in *CILFIT* and the ECJ's monopoly on invalidating Unional acts harking back to *Foto-Frost* came to a head.[213] The Court decided that the latter trumped the former: questions relating to validity have to be referred even where the ECJ has already declared analogous provisions invalid. It retains a monopoly on

---

[209] Court of Justice of the European Union, *Annual Report 2011* (Luxembourg, 2012) 116, http://curia.europa.eu.

[210] Excluding the judicial year 2003, this has been the case ever since 1993. The first time that there were more references for a preliminary ruling than direct actions was 1967. In 2011, there were only eighty-one direct actions compared to 423 preliminary references.

[211] See B. Wägenbaur, *EuGH VerfO: Satzung und Verfahrensordnungen EuGH / EuG – Kommentar* (C. H. Beck, Munich, 2008), p. 236.

[212] Case 314/85 *Foto-Frost* v. *Hauptzollamt Lübeck-Ost* [1987] ECR 4199.

[213] Case C-461/03 *Gaston Schul Douane-expediteur BV* v. *Minister van Landbouw, Natuur en Voedselkwaliteit* (Grand Chamber) [2005] ECR I-10513 (para. 19).

reviewing the legality of acts of the Union institutions, the purpose being maintenance of uniformity.[214] That does not however detract from a general recognition of precedent, the point simply being that in this special situation other countervailing interests are considered to weigh heavily. Precedent and legislative judicial review are distinct but not exclusive concepts.

Although *acte éclairé* might be the most obvious example of an official recognition of the normative effect of precedents in EU law, various hints are littered throughout the system besides the patent popularity of case invocations in legal reasoning. One example where this further becomes plain to see is in the staying of proceedings pending delivery of another judgment. Following delivery, referring courts often no longer consider a separate reply necessary.[215] Moreover, in state liability, an indicator of whether a breach of EU law is 'sufficiently serious' is that it has persisted despite a preliminary ruling or 'settled case-law of the Court on the matter' from which it is clear that the conduct in question amounts to an infringement.[216]

D Sacramental fiction

Concluding on the binding force of ECJ precedents, it is hard to escape the view that this is often a sideshow to much of what precedent at the Court is really about, both from a theoretical perspective and concerning how it plays out in practice. The fascination is rooted in the age-old attraction that normativity and compulsion exert on lawyers.[217] But the latter does not exhaust the former. Five points stand out.

First, no inter- or supranational court or tribunal – including the ECJ – purports to abide by a strict doctrine of binding precedent, namely so-called *stare decisis*. This is corroborated by the earlier examination

---

[214] See Joined Cases C-188/10 and C-189/10 *Aziz Melki and Sélim Abdeli* (Grand Chamber) [2010] ECR I-5667 (para. 54).

[215] See only Case C-137/08 *VB Pénzügyi Lízing Zrt* v. *Ferenc Schneider* (Grand Chamber) [2010] ECR I-10847 (paras. 21–2).

[216] See Joined Cases C-46/93 and C-48/93 *Brasserie du Pêcheur SA* v. *Bundesrepublik Deutschland* [1996] ECR I-1029 (para. 57); Case C-429/09 *Günter Fuß* v. *Stadt Halle* (Second Chamber) [2010] ECR I-12167 (para. 52).

[217] See C. K. Allen, 'Precedent and Logic', *Law Quarterly Review*, 41 (1925), 329, 334 (noting that bindingness had become 'a kind of sacramental phrase which contains a large element of fiction').

of precedent treatment.[218] Even most common law attitudes are not absolutist in this respect, and even if complete decisional exclusivity is indeed accepted as a possibility, it is very much the exception. The archetypes are in the end not that dissimilar. An important reason behind this is that the more rigid an adjudicatory body is in its jurisprudence, the less likely it is to endure, in particular if the stakes are high. The ECJ is aware of this. Denying *stare decisis* often means tilting at windmills.

Secondly, an obsession with *stare decisis* cannot account for many of the routine features of precedent employment by the ECJ, including the wide variety of uses sketched previously. A reductionist approach makes little sense from the standpoint of prototype-based reasoning and is comparable to describing birds by reference to a penguin (flightless) or fruit by reference to an avocado (not sweet) – not wrong but missing important information.

Thirdly, like all phenomena, the workings of a legal system can be reconstructed either from the normal case or from the exception. Precedent is no different in this respect. It lends itself to a Hegelian or Schmittian perspective, depending on whether one focuses on regular application or on the unusual instances of forced compulsion. Both are not without peril if pursued exclusively. The former exaggerates the 'cunning of history'; it recognises yet readily sanctions everyday practice as a rational order and uncritical achievement, bereft of an emancipatory sting.[219] It is the ECJ's preferred approach when it comes to precedent (dis)application. As to the shortcomings of obsessing about a lack of strict bindingness, it ignores the 'cross-pollination' or *acculturation juridique* taking place in many areas of law in the form of professionalised cross-border dialogue and consensus-building.[220] This is the orthodox standpoint of much international law, which tends to fail to account for normative evolution in the first place.

Fourthly, whether or not a precedent is 'strictly' binding in the sense of mandating decisional exclusivity is not the same thing as whether or not it exerts normative (or precedential) effect altogether. The latter is not dependent on the former. This can be traced in many of the remarks made by the ECJ's Advocates General. It becomes difficult otherwise to explain

---

[218] Of course that does not mean that some bodies may follow their precedents more rigidly than others. Cf. Kaufmann-Kohler (n. 105 above), pp. 365–6 (on international sports arbitration).

[219] Cf. R. M. Unger, *What Should Legal Analysis Become?* (Verso, London, 1996), p. 72.

[220] Cf. W. W. Park, *Arbitration of International Business Disputes* (Oxford University Press, 2006), p. viii.

why such actors bother to distinguish precedents or provide reasons for departures. To use a homely metaphor, precedents are like a wedding vow between the Court and its jurisprudence. They impose an 'ought'. This can be broken, but it will likely give rise to costs, condemnation and a guilty conscience. Such a conception of precedents need not confine itself to the 'merely' factual, cultural or psychological. It can be conceptualised as a legal argument that derives its gravitational force from considerations relating to the system of EU law, be it on account of an elementary absence of logical contradiction or because of ambitious forms of substantive justification that flow from broader substantive considerations.[221] Either way, systemic fit becomes the real battleground instead of 'strict' bindingness.[222]

Fifthly, the purist's version of bindingness need not follow *per definitionem* from the law-making role of the ECJ outlined elsewhere. That would be an oversimplification. For one, saying the Court makes law is not equivalent to saying its judgments are 'the law'; the eternal question of what precisely constitutes the latter is left open and not monopolised by the concept of legal information. Furthermore, that would presuppose parity of judicial law-making with treaties and legislation. Reasons militating against such an understanding have already been canvassed.[223] In any event, legislatures constantly undo their own prior output. It would also underhandedly dismiss without more an entire mode of regulation that has, unhappily or not, become known as 'soft law', which is considered capable of producing normative effects without being binding.[224] This nowadays makes up much of inter- and supranational normativity,

---

[221] For a model of the latter approach see e.g. R. Dworkin, *Taking Rights Seriously* (Duckworth, London, 1977), pp. 113–17.

[222] That does not require giving up on bindingness altogether. Cf. J. Klabbers, 'Goldmann Variations' in A. von Bogdandy, P. Dann and M. Goldmann (eds.), *The Exercise of Public Authority by International Institutions* (Springer, Heidelberg, 2010), pp. 722–3 ('shorthand inextricably tied up with legal thought').

[223] See Ch. 2, F.i.

[224] On the idea of legal relevance in international law without bindingness per se see D. Thürer, '"Soft Law" – eine neue Form von Völkerrecht?', *Zeitschrift für Schweizerisches Recht*, 104 (1985), 429; S. H. Nasser, *Sources and Norms of International Law: A Study on Soft Law* (Galda & Wilch, Berlin, 2008). A prominent example within EU law would be the CFREU prior to TEU Art. 6(1). See Case C-34/09 *Gerardo Ruiz Zambrano* v. *Office national de l'emploi (ONEm)* [2011] ECR I-1177, Opinion of AG Sharpston (para. 154). See also M. Bothe, 'Soft Law in den Europäischen Gemeinschaften?' in I. von Münch (ed.), *Staatsrecht, Völkerrecht, Europarecht: Festschrift für Hans-Jürgen Schlochauer zum 75. Geburtstag* (de Gruyter, Berlin, 1981), p. 761; F. Beveridge and S. Nott, 'A Hard Look at Soft Law' in P. P. Craig and C. Harlow (eds.), *Lawmaking in the European Union*

including recommendations and opinions as mentioned in TFEU Art. 288 as well as the so-called Open Method of Co-ordination.[225] It can produce normative effects, even if it 'in principle' is deemed to have 'no legally binding force'.[226]

(Kluwer Law International, London, 1998), pp. 288–96; B. van Vooren, 'A Case Study of "Soft Law" in EU External Relations', *European Law Review*, 34 (2009), 696.

[225] See J. Schwarze, 'Soft Law im Recht der Europäischen Union', *Europarecht*, (2011), 3, 4–6 (noting that, if anything, 'no law' would be a better antonym than 'hard law').

[226] See F. Snyder, 'Soft Law and Institutional Practice in the European Community' in S. Martin (ed.), *The Construction of Europe: Essays in Honour of Emile Noël* (Kluwer, Dordrecht, 1994) 198.

9

Conclusions and suggestions

Precedent at the ECJ is unfinished business, both conceptually and in practice. This book has sought to address several recurrent problems, hoping to lay the groundwork for a more informed debate. First, the Court's precedents are neither irrelevant, be it normatively or otherwise, nor immovable decrees. Precedent is a prime vehicle for conveying information about law, but it is an argumentative device that requires work. Secondly, what the ECJ does when employing case-based reasoning cannot adequately be described by focusing only on the disapplication of precedents or by reference to supposed civil law or common law archetypes. Thirdly, its precedent technique and the normativity of its prior cases are rooted in the broader context in which it operates rather than in refined theoretical or methodological concepts.

Several implications apply to, but also transcend, the ECJ's specific situation. These include the inevitability of judicial law-making and the blurring of cognition and creation in adjudication; the multiplicity of law-making actors; the limited significance of 'activism' charges; the move from top-down hierarchical modes of reasoning to multiple heterarchies of legal information; the relative impotence of theories of sources and validity concerning precedents; the move from text to system and back again; the move from depersonalisation to personalisation and back again; the devaluation and convergence of rigid inductive and deductive archetypes; the mutual influencing of precedent and context by bleeding form into substance and vice versa; the link between substantive precedent use and open disagreement; the importance of appreciating and accommodating the asymmetrical impact of certain adjudicatory bodies; the move from the ontology of a norm to justifications of coercion; and the attendant shift from exegesis to persuasion.

Back at the ECJ, it is no secret that its success over the past decades is for the most part not owed to the strength of its legal reasoning, but due to its pragmatic co-operation with other entities.[1] In many respects this is also reflected in its precedent use. Consistency frequently serves as a palliative in the absence of deeper engagement and discursiveness. Yet surface coherence and the oubliette technique are demanding their toll, and the ECJ's reasoning can become inscrutable.[2] This jeopardises the perception that it is legitimately exercising its function as allocated by the treaties. While it may still be an effective dispute resolution body, it is harming the norm-compliance aspect of its efforts in the long run.

This criticism is fundamentally different from worn 'teleology bashing' that assumes that text or (fabricated) intention exhausts meaning. On the contrary, the Court should make its argument richer and deeper, rather than more technical and shallow. The point is to make the justification open enough to be assessable and persuasive enough to withstand fair and informed criticism. One certainly need not imply improper motives or inability: perfectly well-intended and rational judges can come to perfectly reasonable yet conflicting decisions.[3]

With this in mind, the following proposals focus specifically on the ECJ's precedent practice, which provides an excellent starting point, and would help to remedy much of the general disaffection.[4] They would radically transform the Court's current precedent technique.

First, the ECJ should cut back on general precedent mentions. In particular broad case references intoning 'integration' and its aims are

---

[1] Examples where national judicial actors plainly pursued internal agendas include Case C-118/08 *Transportes Urbanos y Servicios Generales SAL* v. *Administración del Estado* (Grand Chamber) [2010] ECR I-635 and Joined Cases C-188/10 and C-189/10 *Aziz Melki and Sélim Abdeli* (Grand Chamber) [2010] ECR I-5667.

[2] See J. Fejø, 'How Does the ECJ Cite its Previous Judgments in Competition Law Cases?' in M. Johansson, N. Wahl and U. Bernitz (eds.), *Liber Amicorum in Honour of Sven Norberg: A European for All Seasons* (Bruylant, Brussels, 2007), pp. 203–4, 216–7 (taking a dim view as to a rational answer to his own question).

[3] Cf. Mill's reference to Cicero on forensic success and the difference between a case being watertight and a case being comprehensive: 'Their reasons may be good, and no one may have been able to refute them. But if they are equally unable to refute the reasons on the opposite side, and if they do not so much as know what they are, they have no ground for preferring either opinion.' J. S. Mill, *On Liberty* (Agora, Millis, 2003 (1859)), p. 43.

[4] For general critiques of the Court's reasoning see J. H. H. Weiler, 'Epilogue: The Judicial Après Nice' in G. de Búrca and J. Weiler (eds.), *The European Court of Justice* (Oxford University Press, 2001), pp. 222–6; V. Perju, 'Reason and Authority in the European Court of Justice', *Virginia Journal of International Law*, 49 (2009), 307, 338–41; G. M. Berrisch, 'Die neue Verfahrensordnung des EuGH – Verfahrensbeschleunigung auf Kosten des Anhörungsrechts', *Europäische Zeitschrift für Wirtschaftsrecht*, (2012), 881, 883 (urging quality rather than speed).

unsatisfactory. Although a popular means of justification,[5] this device is inherently one-sided and finds little resonance in European philosophy or democratic pluralism.[6]

Secondly, the Court should resile from its excessive use of parenthetical string citations and instead opt for more substantial citations. That does not mean that it needs to describe precedents in detail when dealing with a point as established as primacy or direct effect, nor does it imply that judicial minimalism cannot have a point. But the mere invocation of a case does not convincingly explain or justify a statement. Of course, well-written, lucid and discursive reasoning is no guarantee for 'correct' precedent use and legal decisions.[7] The point relates to the relationship between the ECJ and its wider audience rather than between the Court and the available legal materials. Reasoning that is accessible and comprehensible places the cards on the table so that they can be scrutinised, thereby improving the reception and, ultimately, legitimacy of the ECJ. A court that decides important matters internally or incomprehensibly loses the respect and trust of its addressees. Issues to bear in mind when referring to a putative precedent would be to state in appropriate detail what the essence of that case is considered to be, why it is relevantly similar or not to the present context and what the precise use for that precedent is in the current litigation. The emphasis should be on quality rather than quantity.

Thirdly and turning to the precise use of precedents, the ECJ should attempt to avoid invoking precedents to make bald statements of law or to blandly affirm a conclusion after it has already been stated. It is preferable to draw upon cases in the process of interpreting provisions and in order to tease out specificities that justify tipping a close call in a certain direction. There is also little point in spending time on refutations of precedents' normative quality. Most importantly, coherence between cases alone adds little to nothing. Consistency is better thought of as a

---

[5] See U. Everling, 'Richterliche Rechtsfortbildung in der Europäischen Gemeinschaft', *Juristenzeitung*, 55 (2000), 217, 223.

[6] Even from an internal perspective integration is a highly variable concept. In some spheres, negative integration (i.e. the abolition of barriers) is insufficient. While market integration can conceivably rest to a large extent on negative integration, European integration in criminal matters, for instance, is unlikely to be achieved that way. Preventing and punishing crime demands more active measures. See A. Hinarejos, 'Integration in Criminal Matters and the Role of the Court of Justice', *European Law Review*, 36 (2011), 420, 425.

[7] See F. Schauer, 'Opinions as Rules', *University of Chicago Law Review*, 62 (1995), 1455, 1466.

limited negative test that can show inconsistencies, that is to say areas where further argumentative effort needs to be particularly thorough; it alone does not make a good or 'right' decision. A multipolar concept of systemic adequacy is a better frame of reference.

Fourthly, the Court needs to be disabused of the misunderstanding that a departure from prior decisions is a systemic failure. That is an inevitable occurrence in all moderately complex and active legal systems. A technique of reasoned, explicit overruling causes less damage and contributes more to legal certainty than silently ignoring difficult points. It also lessens the urge to slather judgments with (largely meaningless) string references, as if their absence would otherwise indicate a departure. Nor does reliable planning necessarily depend on complete previsibility – assuming for a moment such a thing was possible – given that not all statements induce reliance and since contingencies can be and frequently are accommodated in advance.[8] The oubliette however is the antithesis of transparency and justice. This is where the ECJ could further reap the benefits from more substantive precedent citation. When it starts to explain in more detail what the pertinent few cases are really about and what troubled the Court at the time, there will be less speculation, thus mandating less need for departures in the long run. The low rates of departures at the German FCC and the US and UK Supreme Courts show that even in complex legal systems with vast regulatory outputs a ready acceptance of overruling is manageable.

In abandoning a precedent the ECJ should express itself plainly as to the grounds for doing so, elaborate both upon the factors that militate against a departure as well as those that favour overruling and state why it considers the latter to carry the day. Circular statements to the effect that 'the treaties imply' a departure are hardly satisfactory. Nothing turns on the ontology of a norm when intelligible justification is absent. It is not required of the ECJ to be disloyal to the European project. In fact, the Court is welcome to pour as much time, skill and work as possible into 'giving effect' to the treaties. But, and herein lies the rub, it must actually make the argumentative effort.[9] This requires neither a commitment to legal indeterminacy nor to a singularly correct interpretation. Nor is this irredeemably ideological or an abnegation of the judicial role. There are

---

[8] See M. A. Eisenberg, *The Nature of the Common Law* (Harvard University Press, London, 1988), pp. 157–8.

[9] There is no difference, logically or otherwise, between justifying and arguing a decision in this respect.

ample tools, normative and concrete, to make such arguments in legal discourse.

This leads to a fifth suggestion. Separate and dissenting opinions should be allowed to show greater argumentative effort, amplify legal information[10] and demonstrate that alternative case rationalities were considered. Leaving aside the technical point of amending the CJEU Statute, fragmentation is not a convincing objection. First of all, fragility alone can hardly excuse poor performance.[11] Moreover, if the Union or the ECJ did indeed falter because out-voted judges were to publicly speak their mind, then more fundamental problems are afoot. Various national constitutional and supreme courts have managed to avoid serious fraction, as have international courts such as the ICJ and ECtHR. International investment arbitration is certainly not collapsing because of this practice. At the ECJ, nobody seriously suggests the Advocates General have had a deleterious effect. On the contrary, plurality or minority opinions can contain useful legal information. There is no reason to believe that opinions will become impossibly truculent or extreme. That argument forgets that what matters is quality of reasoning, not the veneer of authority. It also has little faith in the abilities of current and future judges and the capacity of outside commentators to tell an overblown or bad dissent from a good, measured one. Richer legal discourse and a multiplicity of views are not defects that need to be expunged. At the very least, the losing side can often take comfort from a well-reasoned dissent.

The point that is the least worry concerning dissents is that of endangering judicial independence in light of the dangling carrot of re-election. This could in any event be abandoned and replaced with longer tenure coupled with a Europe-wide merits appointment that is either based on a quota system or entirely nationality-blind, a move that would set the supranational EU apart from traditional international legal orders.[12] Likewise, given their import, the current idiosyncratic employment of *référendaires* ought to be reconsidered.

---

[10] Cf. G. Slynn, 'Critics of the Court: A Reconsideration' in M. T. Andenæs and F. G. Jacobs (eds.), *European Community Law in the English Courts* (Clarendon Press, Oxford and New York, 1998), p. 9.

[11] Cf. J. Habermas *et al.*, 'Europa und die neue Deutsche Frage', *Blätter für deutsche und internationale Politik*, 56 (2011), 45.

[12] On the 'soft-balancing' strategy that explains the disproportionate influence of weaker states see E. Benvenisti and G. W. Downs, 'The Empire's New Clothes: Political Economy and the Fragmentation of International Law', *Stanford Law Review*, 60 (2007), 595, 621–3.

This proposed reform of precedent practice would ideally be flanked by institutional reform, one aspect of which has just been mentioned. Various general proposals have been canvassed elsewhere as to how workload and budget could be tweaked.[13] Probably the most promising attempt to focus more on quality of adjudication rather than quantity would be to supplement the numbers of the GC and give it first instance jurisdiction to hear preliminary references. The number of judges at the ECJ could further be decided on a functional rather than a representational basis, for example by reducing it to a more workable number in light of the possibility of issuing dissents. Special chambers could be introduced. If the above recommendations were adopted, the office of the Advocate General could be abolished since her job would essentially be merged with the judges' function. Finally, even the French-language sacred cow could be eyed keenly. Given that it is more likely after successive waves of enlargement that future European generations will speak English rather than French, the internal working language might be changed in the interest of attracting the best candidates and ensuring a wider and more satisfactory space for legal discourse.

Viewed in light of the global 'rise of regulators',[14] dealing with complexity via undiscerning precedent use is an unfortunate managerial trend that confuses means with ends and has learnt little from the emancipatory potential unleashed by the fundamental Kantian insight. Translated into legal technique and looking to the future, neither 'relentless category-grinding'[15] nor a supposedly predetermined logic of cases are a substitute for broader legal and political imagination. Precedents are always tools, never masters. Using them, even affirmatively, means taking a stance, and demands an explanation why this is appropriate in the present situation. The key lies in shifting the essence of legal analysis from a discipline preoccupied with hermeneutics and truth towards an open-ended but rigorous discipline centred on human activity that is concerned with solving acute problems through law. Ritualised exchanges need to be questioned and the issues as such confronted. A first but indispensable step in this is consciously tackling the unfinished business of precedents.

---

[13] See e.g. H. Rasmussen, 'Remedying the Crumbling EC Judicial System', *Common Market Law Review*, 37 (2000), 1071, 1110–1; T. C. Hartley, *The Foundations of European Union Law* (7th edn, Oxford University Press, 2010), pp. 76–7.

[14] On this development see J. Katz Cogan, 'The Regulatory Turn in International Law', *Harvard International Law Journal*, 52 (2011), 322.

[15] R. M. Unger, 'Legal Analysis as Institutional Imagination', *Modern Law Review*, 59 (1996), 1 (referring to the German pandectists).

Appendix A

ECJ Grand Chamber data

i Precedents

Number	Case	Name	Date	Number of paras.	Proceedings[1]
1	C-225/08	*Wolf*	12.01.2010	48	PR
2	C-341/08	*Petersen*	12.01.2010	82	PR
3	C-555/07	*Kücükdeveci*	19.01.2010	57	PR
4	C-118/08	*Transportes Urbanos*	26.01.2010	49	PR
5	C-362/08 P	*Internationaler Hilfsfonds*	26.01.2010	69	P
6	C-310/08	*Ibrahim*	23.02.2010	61	PR
7	C-480/08	*Teixeira*	23.02.2010	90	PR
8	C-135/08	*Rottman*	02.03.2010	65	PR
9	Jc C-175/08, C-176/08, C-178/08, C-179/08	*Abdulla*	02.03.2010	101	PR
10	C-518/07	*Commission v. Germany*	09.03.2010	58	I
11	C-378/08	*Raffinerie Mediterranee*	09.03.2010	79	PR
12	Jc C-379/08, C-380/08	*Raffinerie Mediterranee*	09.03.2010	93	PR
13	C-325/08	*Olympique Lyonnais*	16.03.2010	51	PR
14	Jc C-236/08 to C-238/08	*Google France*	23.03.2010	121	PR
15	C-73/08	*Bressol*	13.04.2010	97	PR
16	C-91/08	*Wall*	13.04.2010	72	PR

(continued)

(continued)

Number	Case	Name	Date	Number of paras.	Proceedings[1]
17	C-246/07	Commission v. Sweden	20.04.2010	112	I
18	C-265/08	Federutility	20.04.2010	48	PR
19	C-533/08	TNT Express	04.05.2010	65	PR
20	Jc C-570/07, C-571/07	Pérez	01.06.2010	126	PR
21	C-58/08	Vodafone	08.06.2010	81	PR
22	C-211/08	Commission v. Spain	15.06.2010	82	I
23	C-31/09	Bolbol	17.06.2010	57	PR
24	Jc C-188/10, C-189/10	Melki, Abdeli	22.06.2010	76	PR
25	C-139/07 P	Commission v. TGI	29.06.2010	74	P
26	C-441/07 P	Commission v. Alrosa	29.06.2010	123	P
27	C-28/08 P	Commission v. Bavarian Lager	29.06.2010	89	P
28	C-526/08	Commission v. Luxembourg	29.06.2010	74	I
29	C-550/09	Criminal proceedings E and F	29.06.2010	81	PR
30	C-428/08	Monsanto	06.07.2010	78	PR
31	C-271/08	Commission v. Germany	15.07.2010	108	I
32	C-409/06	Winner Wetten	08.09.2010	71	PR
33	Jc C-316/07, C-358/07 to C-360/07, C-409/07, C-410/07	Stoß	08.09.2010	117	PR
34	C-46/08	Carmen Media	08.09.2010	112	PR
35	C-550/07 P	Akzo Nobel	14.09.2010	125	P
36	C-48/09 P	Lego Juris	14.09.2010	88	P

Number	Case	Name	Date	Number of paras.	Proceedings[1]
37	Jc C-514/07 P, C-528/07 P, C-532/07 P	*Sweden* v. *API*	21.09.2010	166	P
38	C-512/08	*Commission* v. *France*	05.10.2010	72	I
39	C-173/09	*Elchinov*	05.10.2010	82	PR
40	C-499/08	*Ingeniørforeningen*	12.10.2010	50	PR
41	C-45/09	*Rosenbladt*	12.10.2010	81	PR
42	C-482/08	*UK* v. *Council*	26.10.2010	72	A
43	C-97/09	*Schmelz*	26.10.2010	78	PR
44	C-137/08	*VB Pénzügyi*	09.11.2010	57	PR
45	C-540/08	*Mediaprint*	09.11.2010	48	PR
46	Jc C-57/09, C-101/09	*Germany* v. *B and D*	09.11.2010	122	PR
47	Jc C-92/09, C-93/09	*Schecke, Eifert*	09.11.2010	110	PR
48	C-261/09	*Mantello*	16.11.2010	52	PR
49	C-145/09	*BW* v. *Tsakouridis*	23.11.2010	57	PR
50	C-439/08	*VEBIC*	07.12.2010	65	PR
51	C-585/08	*Pammer*	07.12.2010	95	PR
52	C-285/09	*Criminal proceedings R*	07.12.2010	56	PR
				4243	

[1] Key: PR = preliminary reference; P = appeal; I = infringement proceedings.

ii Citation and avoidance

Number	Individual	Substantive	General	Distinguished	Overruled
1	7	0	3		
2	16	0	8		
3	27	1	14	1	
4	22	0	16		
5	4	0	6		
6	18	2	12		
7	22	4	13		
8	16	1	3	1	
9	1	0	1		
10	6	0	3		
11	11	0	10		
12	21	0	9		
13	18	0	11		
14	34	0	16		
15	32	0	24		
16	23	0	17		
17	16	0	5	1	
18	2	0	4		
19	28	0	11		
20	34	0	23		
21	21	0	9		
22	34	2	26	2	
23	2	0	0		
24	25	0	15		
25	4	1	3	1	
26	0	0	1	1	
27	1	0	1		
28	6	0	5		
29	19	1	10	1	
30	3	0	3		
31	16	0	13	2	
32	37	1	34		
33	56	3	45		
34	40	3	32	2	
35	27	4	7		(considered)
36	19	3	8		
37	32	1	14		

Number	Individual	Substantive	General	Distinguished	Overruled
38	43	2	19		
39	61	0	34		
40	4	0	1		
41	18	0	11	1	
42	5	0	3		
43	20	0	14		
44	23	2	7		
45	4	0	3	1	
46	5	0	1		
47	18	0	11		
48	11	0	6		
49	19	0	12		
50	5	0	3		
51	9	1	8		
52	32	0	14		
	977	32	582		

iii Use[1]

Number	C	ID	L	I(L)	I(P)	I(C)	J(I)	F	A
1	1		4		2				
2			5		4	1		2	4
3	2		19		3		1	1	1
4			9	6	6				1
5			2		1				1
6			3		6	3	3		3
7					10	9			3
8			11		4	1			
9							1		
10			3		3				
11			5		5			1	
12			18		3				
13			6		4		1	3	4
14	4		6	3	16			2	3
15			21		5	1		4	1
16		7	9		2			4	1
17			7		8	1			
18			1		1				
19		5	20		3				
20			13	2	6		2	7	4
21		2	13		6				
22		1	4		9	2		7	11
23					2				
24			17		4		1		3
25			1		2	1			
26									
27					1				
28			4		1				1
29			4		6	1	3		5
30			2		1				
31	2			4	2			3	5
32			11	3	11	1	1		10
33			17	1	9	5		8	16
34	2		18	3	9	2		1	5
35			19		1	6			1
36			6	2	6	2	2		1
37			11	2	10		3	3	3

Number	C	ID	L	I(L)	I(P)	I(C)	J(I)	F	A
38	1	4	10		7	5	2	5	9
39		2	20		21		1	4	13
40			3					1	
41			3	2	6	1		4	2
42	2		2						1
43		7	5		6				2
44			5	3	8	2	2	1	2
45					2				2
46					4		1		
47			11	2	2			2	1
48			1	1	7		1		1
49		2	7		5			5	
50			1		4				
51					7				2
52			13	2	12		3	2	0
	14	**30**	**370**	**36**	**263**	**44**	**28**	**70**	**122**
%	1.4	3.1	37.9	3.7	26.9	4.5	2.9	7.2	12.5

[1] Key: C = classifying a legal issue or fact; ID = identifying relevant legal provisions; L = stating the law; I(L) = interpreting the law; I(P) = interpreting specific provisions; I(C) = interpreting prior cases; J(I) = justifying interpretation; F = asserting facts; A = affirming conclusions.

Appendix B

Investment Tribunal data

i Precedents

Number	Case	Name	Date	Number of paras.	Stage[1]	Rules
1	ARB/06/3	*Rompetrol v. Romania*	14.01.2010	27	D (Participation of a Counsel)	ICSID C+AR
2	ARB/06/18	*Lemire v. Ukraine*	14.01.2010	514	D (Jurisdiction and Liability)	ICSID C+AR
3	ARB/07/5	*Beccara v. Argentina*	27.01.2010	153	PO3 (Confidentiality)	ICSID C+AR
4	ARB/06/2	*Quiborax v. Bolivia*	26.02.2010	165	D (Provisional Measures)	ICSID C+AR
5	ARB/05/18, ARB/07/15	*Kardassopoulos, Fuchs v. Georgia*	03.03.2010	693	A	ICSID C+AR
6	ARB/08/15	*Cemex v. Venezuela*	03.03.2010	73	D (Provisional Measures)	ICSID C+AR
7	ARB08/8	*Inmaris v. Ukraine*	08.03.2010	149	D (Jurisdiction)	ICSID C+AR
8	ARB/07/16	*Alpha v. Ukraine*	19.03.2010	85	D (Disqualification)	ICSID C+AR
9	ARB/05/16	*Kazakhstan v. Rumeli*	25.03.2010	184	D (Annulment)	ICSID C+AR
10	PCA Case No 34877	*Chevron, Texaco v. Ecuador*	30.03.2010	557	PA (Merits)	UNCITRAL AR
11	ICSID Admin	*Merrill v. Canada*	31.03.2010	271	A	UNCITRAL AR
12	PCA Case No 34877	*Chevron, Texaco v. Ecuador*	31.03.2010	9	PO8 (Expert Procedure)	UNCITRAL AR
13	ARB/08/12	*Caratube v. Kazakhstan*	26.04.2010	16	PO2 (Document Production)	ICSID C+AR
14	ARB/98/2	*Casado v. Chile*	05.05.2010	35	D (Stay of Enforcement)	ICSID C+AR
15	PCA Case No 2009–23	*Chevron, Texaco v. Ecuador*	14.05.2010	3	O (Interim Measures)	UNCITRAL AR
16	ARB/07/23	*RDC v. Guatemala*	18.05.2010	157	D2 (Objections to Jurisdiction)	ICSID C+AR
17	ARB/08/2	*ATA v. Jordan*	18.05.2010	133	A	ICSID C+AR

Number	Case	Name	Date	Number of paras.	Stage[1]	Rules
18	ARB(AF)/07/3	Anderson v. Costa Rica	19.05.2010	66	A	ICSID C+AFR
19	ARB/08/12	Caratube v. Kazakhstan	26.05.2010	11	PO3	ICSID C+AR
20	ARB/08/5	Burlington v. Ecuador	02.06.2010	342	D (Jurisdiction)	ICSID C+AR
21	SCC Case No V (064/2008)	Al-Bahloul v. Tajikistan	08.06.2010	123	FA	SCC AR
22	ARB/07/27	Mobil v. Venezuela	10.06.2010	209	D (Jurisdiction)	ICSID C+AR
23	ARB/05/19	Helnan v. Egypt	14.06.2010	73	D (Annulment)	ICSID C+AR
24	ARB/07/24	Hamester v. Ghana	18.06.2010	362	A	ICSID C+AR
25	ARB/02/16	Sempra v. Argentina	29.06.2010	229	D (Annulment)	ICSID C+AR
26	ARB/07/20	Fakes v. Turkey	14.07.2010	156	A	ICSID C+AR
27	ARB/07/13	S&T v. Romania	16.07.2010	32	O (Discontinuance)	ICSID C+AR
28	ARB/08/20	Millicom v. Senegal	16.07.2010	122	D (Jurisdiction)	ICSID C+AR
29	ARB/03/17	Suez, AGBAR, InterAgua v. Argentina	30.07.2010	248	D (Liability)	ICSID C+AR
30	ARB/03/19; ICSID Admin	Suez, AGBAR, Vivendi v. Argentina; AWG v. Argentina	30.07.2010	276	D (Liability)	ICSID C+AR; UNCITRAL AR
31	ARB/01/3	Enron v. Argentina	30.07.2010	427	D (Annulment)	ICSID C+AR
32	ARB/09/12	Pac Rim v. El Salvador	02.08.2010	266	D (Preliminary Objections)	ICSID C+AR
33	PCA Case No 2009–21	Howard v. Canada	02.08.2010	83	O (Termination of Proceedings and Award of Costs)	UNCITRAL AR
34	PCA Case No 2009–21	Howard v. Canada	09.08.2010	6	C	UNCITRAL AR
35	Ad Hoc	Chemtura v. Canada	02.08.2010	273	A	UNCITRAL AR
36	ARB(AF)/07/1	Foresti v. South Africa	04.08.2010	133	A	ICSID C+AFR
37	ARB/97/3	Aguas del Aconquija, Vivendi v. Argentina	20.08.2010	269	D (Annulment)	ICSID C+AR
38	ARB/07/26	Urbaser v. Argentina	12.08.2010	59	D (Disqualification)	ICSID C+AR
39	SCC Case No V (079/2005)	RosInvest v. Russian Federation	12.09.2010	702	FA	SCC AR
40	ARB/07/22	AES v. Hungary	23.09.2010	310	A	ICSID C+AR

(*continued*)

(continued)

Number	Case	Name	Date	Number of paras.	Stage[1]	Rules
41	ARB/10/6	*RSM* v. *Grenada*	14.10.2010	46	D (Security for Costs)	ICSID C+AR
42	PCA Case No 2008–13	*Eureko* v. *Slovakia*	26.10.2010	293	A (Jurisdiction, Arbitrability, Suspension)	UNCITRAL AR
43	ARB/07/16	*Alpha* v. *Ukraine*	08.11.2010	519	A	ICSID C+AR
44	ARB/05/18, ARB/07/15	*Kardassopoulos, Fuchs* v. *Georgia*	12.11.2010	45	D (Stay of Enforcement)	ICSID C+AR
45	ARB/09/11	*Global Trading* v. *Ukraine*	01.12.2010	59	A	ICSID C+AR
46	ARB/10/6	*RSM* v. *Grenada*	10.12.2010	181	A	ICSID C+AR
47	ARB/08/4	*Murphy* v. *Ecuador*	15.12.2010	161	A (Jurisdiction)	ICSID C+AR
48	ICSID Admin	*Apotex* v. *US*	16.12.2010	67	PO1 (Appointment)	UNCITRAL AR
49	ARB/10/5	*Tidewater* v. *Venezuela*	23.12.2010	73	D (Disqualification)	ICSID C+AR
50	ARB/03/25	*Fraport* v. *Philippines*	23.12.2010	286	D (Annulment)	ICSID C+AR
51	ARB/04/1	*Total* v. *Argentina*	27.12.2010	484	D (Liability)	ICSID C+AR
52	ABR/08/15	*Cemex* v. *Venezuela*	30.12.2010	160	D (Jurisdiction)	ICSID C+AR
				10375		

[1] Key: D = decision; PO = procedural order; A = award; FA = final award; PA = partial award; C = correction of order; O = order.

ii Citation and avoidance

Number	Individual	Substantive	General	Distinguished	Departed
1	12	9	0	1	2
2	25	4	4	1	
3	16	5	3	1	1
4	24	0	3		
5	46	12	6	5	
6	38	10	13		
7	36	4	8	2	1
8	28	3	4		
9	32	3	5	1	
10	14	1	1	1	
11	64	13	15	5	
12	0	0	0		
13	0	0	0		
14	10	0	1		
15	0	0	0		
16	22	5	9	1	
17	13	4	0		
18	6	0	3		
19	0	0	0		
20	49	20	2	5	
21	5	2	0		
22	74	13	19		
23	23	6	5		1
24	42	19	13	1	
25	11	0	6	1	
26	32	8	10	2	2
27	0	0	0		
28	6	0	4		
29	88	40	23	5	2
30	83	40	23	5	2
31	95	37	8	4	
32	4	0	1	4	
33	2	0	0		
34	0	0	0		
35	14	4	2	1	
36	0	0	0		

(*continued*)

(continued)

Number	Individual	Substantive	General	Distinguished	Departed
37	12	2	1		
38	4	1	1		
39	11	3	3	2	
40	10	3	2		
41	12	7	2		1
42	7	0	2	2	
43	45	9	11		1
44	4	0	1		
45	14	4	3		
46	13	1	2		
47	9	4	1		2
48	0	0	0		
49	23	2	5	3	
50	56	6	22	2	
51	107	12	20	4	1
52	54	8	20	2	
	1295	**324**	**287**		

iii Use[1]

Number	C	ID	L	I(L)	I(P)	I(C)	J(I)	F	A
1			1	1	1	8		1	
2			4	2	14	4	1		
3		3	3		6	3		1	
4			4	11	8				1
5		5	12	2	9	10	3	5	
6				6	20	5	2		5
7	4	3		4	11	3	6	3	2
8		6			14			3	5
9				13	6	3	6		4
10			2	3	6	1	1	1	
11			1	19	35	5		4	
12									
13									
14					5		1	4	
15									
16			2	7	8	3		2	
17	1	1	3	1		4			3
18				1	5				
19									
20	1		5		14	20	2	2	5
21	1			3				1	
22	1	2	30	15	6	15		2	3
23					15	6		1	1
24	7	5	10	2	8	3	1	6	
25					11				
26			3		22	6	1		
27									
28			4		1		1		
29	2	1	7		37	23	3	2	13
30	2	1	5		35	23	2	2	13
31	2	1	13	2	42	27	3	2	3
32					4				
33					1			1	
34									
35				3	8	2			1
36									

(continued)

(continued)

Number	C	ID	L	I(L)	I(P)	I(C)	J(I)	F	A
37					4	4	1	2	1
38				1				2	1
39				2		1	6	2	
40			5	1	3		1		
41					10		1	1	
42		1	2	2			2		
43		2	3	2	20	9	2	4	3
44					4				
45					13	1			
46			3	1	7	1	1		
47					3	3	2	1	
48									
49	1			3	3	3	4	7	2
50	1	5	11	4	26	4		2	3
51	4		20	5	38	8	6	13	13
52		8	25	3	7	9	2		
	27	44	178	119	490	217	61	77	82
%	2.1	3.4	13.7	9.2	37.8	16.8	4.7	5.9	6.3

[1] Key: C = classifying a legal issue or fact; ID = identifying relevant legal provisions; L = stating the law; I(L) = interpreting the law; I(P) = interpreting specific provisions; I(C) = interpreting prior cases; J(I) = justifying interpretation; F = asserting facts; A = affirming conclusions.

BIBLIOGRAPHY

Aarnio, A., 'Precedent in Finland' in N. MacCormick and R. Summers (eds.), *Interpreting Precedents: A Comparative Study* (Ashgate, Aldershot, 1997)

Albors-Llorens, A., 'The European Court of Justice: More than a Teleological Court', *The Cambridge Yearbook of European Legal Studies*, 2 (1999), 373

Alexander, L., 'Precedential Constraint, Its Scope and Strength: A Brief Survey of the Possibilities and Their Merits' in T. Bustamente and C. Bernal Pulido (eds.), *On the Philosophy of Precedent* (Franz Steiner, Stuttgart, 2012)

Alexy, R., *A Theory of Legal Argumentation* (Clarendon Press, Oxford, 1989)

Alexy R., and R. Dreier, 'Precedent in the Federal Republic of Germany' in N. MacCormick and R. Summers (eds.), *Interpreting Precedents* (Ashgate, Aldershot, 1997)

Allan, T. R. S., 'Judicial Deference and Judicial Review: Legal Doctrine and Legal Theory', *Law Quarterly Review*, 127 (2011), 96

Allen, C. K., 'Precedent and Logic', *Law Quarterly Review*, 41 (1925), 329
Law in the Making (6th edn, Clarendon Press, Oxford, 1958)

Alter, K., *Establishing the Supremacy of European Law: The Making of an International Rule of Law in Europe* (Oxford University Press, 2001)
'Agents or Trustees? International Courts in their Political Context', *European Journal of International Relations*, 14 (2008), 33

Alter, K. and L. R. Helfer, 'Legal Integration in the Andes: Law-Making by the Andean Tribunal of Justice', *European Law Journal*, 17 (2011), 701

Alter K., and S. Meunier-Aitsahalia, 'Judicial Politics in the European Community: European Integration and the Pathbreaking Cassis de Dijon Decision', *Comparative Political Studies*, 26 (1994), 535

Amaya, A., 'Legal Justification by Optimal Coherence', *Ratio Juris*, 24 (2011), 304

Arnull, A., 'Owning up to Fallibility: Precedent and the European Court of Justice', *Common Market Law Review*, 30 (1993), 247
The European Union and its Court of Justice (2nd edn, Oxford University Press, 2006)
'Me and My Shadow: The European Court of Justice and the Disintegration of European Union Law', *Fordham International Law Journal*, 31 (2008), 1174

Atiyah, P. S., *Pragmatism and Theory in English Law* (The Hamlyn Lectures, Stevens, London, 1987)

Atiyah, P. S., and R. Summers, *Form and Substance in Anglo-American Law* (Clarendon Press, Oxford, 1987)

Augsberg, I., *Die Lesbarkeit des Rechts* (Velbrück, Weilerswist, 2009)

'Methoden des europäischen Verwaltungsrechts' in J. P. Terhechte (ed.), *Verwaltungsrecht der Europäischen Union* (Nomos, Baden-Baden, 2011)

Azizi, J., 'Unveiling the EU Courts' Internal Decision-Making Process: A Case for Dissenting Opinions?', *ERA Forum*, 12 (2011), 49

Bader Ginsburg, R., 'The Role of Dissenting Opinions', *Minnesota Law Review*, 95 (2010), 1

Baker, J. H., *An Introduction to English Legal History* (4th edn, Butterworths, London, 2002)

Bankowski, Z. *et al.*, 'Rationales for Precedent' in N. MacCormick and R. Summers (eds.), *Interpreting Precedents: A Comparative Study* (Ashgate, Aldershot, 1997)

Banks, C. P., 'The Supreme Court and Precedent: An Analysis of Natural Courts and Reversal Trends', *Judicature*, 75 (1992), 262

Barak, A., *The Judge in a Democracy* (Princeton University Press, 2006)

Baratta, R., 'National Courts as "Guardians" and "Ordinary Courts" of EU Law: Opinion 1/09 of the ECJ', *Legal Issues of Economic Integration*, 38 (2011), 297

Barceló, J. J., 'Precedent in European Community Law' in N. MacCormick and R. Summers (eds.), *Interpreting Precedents: A Comparative Study* (Ashgate, Aldershot, 1997)

Barnard, C., *The Substantive Law of the EU: The Four Freedoms* (3rd edn, Oxford University Press, 2010)

Bast, J., *Aufenthaltsrecht und Migrationssteuerung* (Mohr Siebeck, Tübingen, 2011)

Bebr, G., *Development of Judicial Control of the European Communities* (Nijhoff, The Hague, 1981)

Beckett, W. E., 'Les Questions d'intérêt général au point de vue juridique dans la jurisprudence de la Cour Permanente de Justice Internationale', *Recueil des Cours/Académie de Droit International de La Haye*, 39 (1932), 135

Behrendt, C., *Le Juge constitutionnel, un législateur-cadre positif* (Bruylant, Brussels, 2006)

Bell, J., *French Legal Cultures* (Butterworths, London, 2001)

Judiciaries within Europe (Cambridge University Press, 2006)

Benda, E., and E. Klein, *Verfassungsprozessrecht* (2nd edn, C.F. Müller, Heidelberg, 2001)

Bengoetxea, J., N. MacCormick and L. Moral Soriano, 'Integration and Integrity in the Legal Reasoning of the European Court of Justice' in G. de Búrca and J. Weiler (eds.), *The European Court of Justice* (Oxford University Press, 2001)

Bentham, J., 'Truth versus Ashhurst' in J. Bowring (ed.), *The Works of Jeremy Bentham* (William Tait, Edinburgh, 1843)

Benvenisti, E., and G. W. Downs, 'The Empire's New Clothes: Political Economy and the Fragmentation of International Law', *Stanford Law Review*, 60 (2007), 595

'National Courts, Domestic Democracy, and the Evolution of International Law', *European Journal of International Law*, 20 (2009), 59

'Prospects for the Increased Independence of International Tribunals', *German Law Journal*, 12 (2011), 1057

Bergel, J.-L., *Théorie générale du droit* (4th edn, Dalloz, Paris, 2003)

Berman, H. J., *Law and Revolution*, II: *The Impact of the Protestant Reformations on the Western Legal Tradition* (Harvard University Press, Cambridge, MA, 2006)

Bermann, G. A., 'Reconciling European Union Law Demands with the Demands of International Arbitration', *Fordham International Law Journal*, 34 (2011), 1193

Bernhardt, R., 'Article 59' in A. Zimmermann, K. Oellers-Frahm and C. Tomuschat (eds.), *The Statute of the International Court of Justice: A Commentary* (Oxford University Press, 2006)

Bernstorff, J. von, *The Public International Law Theory of Hans Kelsen: Believing in Universal Law* (Cambridge University Press, 2010)

Berrisch, G. M., 'Die neue Verfahrensordnung des EuGH – Verfahrensbeschleunigung auf Kosten des Anhörungsrechts', *Europäische Zeitschrift für Wirtschaftsrecht* (2012), 881

Besson, S., 'European Legal Pluralism after "Kadi"', *European Constitutional Law Review*, 5 (2009), 237

'Theorizing the Sources of International Law' in S. Besson and J. Tasioulas (eds.), *The Philosophy of International Law* (Oxford University Press, 2010)

Beveridge, F. and S. Nott, 'A Hard Look at Soft Law' in P. P. Craig and C. Harlow (eds.), *Lawmaking in the European Union* (Kluwer Law International, London, 1998)

Bhala, R., 'The Power of the Past: Towards De Jure Stare Decisis in WTO Adjudication (Part Three of a Trilogy)', *George Washington International Law Review*, 33 (2001), 873

Bleckmann, A., *Europarecht* (6th edn, Carl Heymanns, Cologne, 1997)

Völkerrecht (Nomos, Baden-Baden, 2001)

Bocheński, I. M., *Ancient Formal Logic* (North-Holland, Amsterdam, 1951)

Bogdandy, A. von, *Gubernative Rechtsetzung* (Mohr Siebeck, Tübingen, 2000)

'Founding Principles' in A. von Bogdandy and J. Bast (eds.), *Principles of European Constitutional Law* (2nd edn, Hart and C. H. Beck, Oxford and Munich, 2010)

Bogdandy, A. von, S. Cassese and P. M. Huber (eds.), *Handbuch Ius Publicum Europaeum*, 8 vols. planned (C. F. Müller, Heidelberg, 2010), III

Bogdandy, A. von and M. Jacob, 'The Judge as Law-Maker: Thoughts on Bruno Simma's Declaration in the Kosovo Opinion' in U. Fastenrath *et al.* (eds.), *From Bilateralism to Community Interest: Essays in Honour of Judge Bruno Simma* (Oxford University Press, 2011)

Bogdandy, A. von and I. Venzke, 'Beyond Dispute: International Judicial Institutions as Lawmakers', *German Law Journal*, 12 (2011), 979

Borchardt, K.-D., 'Richterrecht durch den Gerichtshof der Europäischen Gemeinschaften' in A. Randelzhofer, R. Scholz and D. Wilke (eds.), *Gedächtnisschrift für Eberhard Grabitz* (C. H. Beck, Munich 1995)

'Auslegung, Rechtsfortbildung und Rechtsschöpfung' in R. Schulze, M. Zuleeg and S. Kadelbach (eds.), *Europarecht: Handbuch für die deutsche Rechtspraxis* (2nd edn, Nomos, Baden-Baden, 2010)

Die rechtlichen Grundlagen der Europäischen Union (4th edn, Facultas, Vienna, 2010)

Borgsmidt, K., 'The Advocate General at the European Court of Justice: A Comparative Study', *European Law Review*, 13 (1988), 106

Borrás, A., 'Legislation through Individual Case Law: The ECJ's Handwriting in the Brussels I Regulation', *The European Legal Forum*, 5(6) (2010), 241

Bos, M., 'The Interpretation of International Judicial Decisions', *Revista Española de Derecho Internacional*, 33 (1981), 11

Bothe, M., 'Soft Law in den Europäischen Gemeinschaften?' in I. von Münch (ed.), *Staatsrecht, Völkerrecht, Europarecht: Festschrift für Hans-Jürgen Schlochauer zum 75. Geburtstag* (de Gruyter, Berlin, 1981)

Boyle, A. E. and C. M. Chinkin, *The Making of International Law* (Oxford University Press, 2007)

Brenner, S. and H. J. Spaeth, *Stare Indecisis: The Alteration of Precedent on the Supreme Court, 1946–1992* (Cambridge University Press, 1995)

Broberg, M. and N. Fenger, 'L'Application de la doctrine de l'acte clair par les juridictions des Etats membres', *Revue Trimestrielle de Droit Européen* 46 (2010), 861

Preliminary References to the European Court of Justice (Oxford University Press, 2010)

Brown, L. N. and T. Kennedy, *The Court of Justice of the European Communities* (5th edn, Sweet & Maxwell, London, 2000)

Bryde, B.-O., *Verfassungsentwicklung: Stabilität und Dynamik im Verfassungsrecht der Bundesrepublik Deutschland* (Nomos, Baden-Baden, 1982)

Bung, J., *Subsumtion und Interpretation* (Nomos, Baden-Baden, 2004)

Burrows, A., 'The Relationship Between Common Law and Statute Law in the Law of Obligations', *Law Quarterly Review*, 128 (2012), 232

Burrows, N. and R. Greaves, *The Advocate General and EC Law* (Oxford University Press, 2007)

Bydlinski, F., *Juristische Methodenlehre und Rechtsbegriff* (2nd edn, Springer, Vienna, 1991)

Grundzüge der Juristischen Methodenlehre (WUV, Vienna, 2005)

Calabresi, G., *A Common Law for the Age of Statutes* (Harvard University Press, Cambridge, MA, 1982)

Caldeira, G. A., 'Legal Precedent: Structures of Communication between State Courts', *Social Networks*, 10 (1988), 29

Cappelletti, M., 'Is the European Court of Justice "Running Wild"?', *European Law Review*, 12 (1987), 3

Cardozo, B. N., *The Nature of the Judicial Process* (Yale University Press, New Haven, 1925)

Chalmers, D., 'The Secret Delivery of Justice', *European Law Review*, 33 (2008), 773

Chalmers, D., G. Davies and G. Monti, *European Union Law: Text and Materials* (2nd edn, Cambridge University Press, 2010)

Chiassoni, P., 'The Philosophy of Precedent: Conceptual Analysis and Rational Reconstruction' in T. Bustamente and C. Bernal Pulido (eds.), *On the Philosophy of Precedent* (Franz Steiner, Stuttgart, 2012)

Chieu, T., 'Class Actions in the European Union?', *Cardozo Journal of International and Comparative Law*, 18 (2010), 123

Christensen, R., *Was heißt Gesetzesbindung?* (Duncker & Humblot, Berlin, 1989)

'Postmoderne Methodik oder: Überlebt der König seine Enthauptung in der Regel?', *Kritische Justiz*, 43 (2010), 223

Cichowski, R. A., *The European Court and Civil Society: Litigation, Mobilization and Governance* (Cambridge University Press, New York, 2007)

Cohen, F. S., 'The Problems of a Functional Jurisprudence', *Modern Law Review*, 1 (1937), 5

Coing, H., 'Philologie und Jurisprudenz: Eine Analyse der "Dialogi" des Gentilis' in D. Simon (ed.), *Gesammelte Aufsätze zu Rechtsgeschichte, Rechtsphilosophie und Zivilrecht: 1947–1975*, 2 vols. (Klostermann, Frankfurt 1982), II

Europäisches Privatrecht, 2 vols. (C. H. Beck, Munich, 1985), I

Europäisches Privatrecht, 2 vols. (C. H. Beck, Munich, 1989), II

Coke, E., *The First Part of the Institutes of the Laws of England: or, a Commentary upon Littleton* (15th edn, E. and R. Brooke, London, 1794)

Constantinesco, V., 'The ECJ as a Law-Maker: Praeter aut Contra Legem?' in D. O'Keeffe and A. Bavasso (eds.), *Judicial Review in European Union Law: Liber Amicorum in Honour of Lord Slynn of Hadley*, 2 vols. (Kluwer Law International, The Hague, London and Boston, 2000), I

Conway, G., 'Levels of Generality in the Legal Reasoning of the European Court of Justice', *European Law Journal*, 14 (2008), 787

Coppel, J. and A. O'Neill, 'The European Court of Justice: Taking Rights Seriously?', *Legal Studies*, 12 (2006), 227

Costello, C., 'Metock: Free Movement and "Normal Family Life" in the Union', *Common Market Law Review*, 46 (2009), 587

Coutron, L., *La Contestation incidente des actes de l'Union européenne* (Bruylant, Brussels, 2008)

'Style des arrêts de la Cour de justice et normativité de la jurisprudence communautaire', *Revue Trimestrielle de Droit Européen*, 45 (2009), 643

Craig, P. P., 'Competence and Member State Autonomy: Causality, Consequence and Legitimacy' in H. W. Micklitz and B. de Witte (eds.), *The European Court of Justice and the Autonomy of Member States* (Oxford Legal Studies Research Paper No 57/2009, 2010)

'The ECJ and *Ultra Vires* Action: A Conceptual Analysis', *Common Market Law Review*, 48 (2011), 395

Craig, P. P. and G. de Búrca, *EU Law: Text, Cases, and Materials* (4th edn, Oxford University Press, 2007)

Cross, R., and J. W. Harris, *Precedent in English Law* (4th edn, Clarendon Press, Oxford, 1991)

Danwitz, T. von, 'Zur Entwicklung der gemeinschaftlichen Staatshaftung', *Juristenzeitung*, 49 (1994), 335

Verwaltungsrechtliches System und europäische Integration (Mohr, Tübingen, 1996)

Dänzer-Vanotti, W., 'Unzulässige Rechtsforbildung des Europäischen Gerichtshofs', *Recht der Internationalen Wirtschaft* (1992), 733

D'Aspremont, J., *Formalism and the Sources of International Law* (Oxford University Press, 2011)

Davies, D. J., *The Book of English Law* (John Murray, London, 1953)

Dawson, J. P., *The Oracles of the Law* (University of Michigan Press, Ann Arbor, 1968)

Dederichs, M., *Die Methodik des EuGH: Häufigkeit und Bedeutung Methodischer Argumente in den Begründungen des Gerichthofes der Europäischen Gemeinschaften* (Nomos, Baden-Baden, 2004)

Deleuze, G. and F. Guattari, *A Thousand Plateaus* (reprint edn, Continuum, London, 2003 (1987))

Demaret, P., 'Le Juge et le jugement dans l'Europe d'aujourd'hui: la Cour de justice des Communautés européennes' in R. Jacob (ed.), *Le Juge et le jugement dans les traditions juridiques européennes* (Libr. Générale de Droit et le Jurisprudence, Paris, 1996)

Denning, A. T. D., *The Family Story* (Hamlyn, Feltham, 1982)

Dias, R. W. M., *Jurisprudence* (3rd edn, Butterworths, London, 1970)

Di Fabio, U., *Das Recht offener Staaten. Grundlinien einer Staats- und Rechtstheorie* (Mohr Siebeck, Tübingen 1998)

Dolzer R., and C. Schreuer, *Principles of International Investment Law* (Oxford University Press, 2008)

Dumon, F. and F. Rigaux, 'La Cour de justice des Communautés européennes et les jurisdictions des etats membres', *Annales de Droit et de Sciences Politiques*, 19 (1959), 7

Duxbury, N., *The Nature and Authority of Precedent* (Cambridge University Press, 2008)

Dworkin, R., *Taking Rights Seriously* (Duckworth, London, 1977)
A Matter of Principle (Oxford University Press, 1985)
Law's Empire (reprint edn, Hart, Oxford 1998 (1986))

Dyzenhaus, D. and M. Taggart, 'Reasoned Decisions and Legal Theory' in D. E. Edlin (ed.), *Common Law Theory* (Cambridge University Press, 2007)

Eckertz-Höfer, M., '"Vom guten Richter" – Ethos, Unabhängigkeit, Professionalität', *Die Öffentliche Verwaltung*, 62 (2009), 729

Editorial, 'Les Juges constituants', *European Constitutional Law Review*, 6 (2010), 171
'The Court of Justice as the Guardian of National Courts – or Not?', *European Law Review*, 36 (2011), 319
'Judicial Ego', *International Journal of Constitutional Law*, 9 (2011), 1

Edward, D., 'How the Court of Justice Works', *European Law Review*, 20 (1995), 539
'Richterrecht in Community Law' in R. Schulze and U. Seif (eds.), *Richterrecht und Rechtsfortbildung in der Europäischen Rechtsgemeinschaft* (Mohr Siebeck, Tübingen 2003)
'CILFIT and Foto-Frost in their Historical and Procedural Context' in M. Poiares Maduro and L. Azoulai (eds.), *The Past and Future of EU Law* (Hart, Oxford and Portland, 2010)

Eisenberg, M. A., *The Nature of the Common Law* (Harvard University Press, London, 1988)

Elsuwege, P. van, 'Shifting the Boundaries? European Union Citizenship and the Scope of Application of EU Law', *Legal Issues of Economic Integration*, 38 (2011), 263

Eskridge, W. N. Jr, 'Overruling Statutory Precedents', *Georgetown Law Journal*, 76 (1987–1988), 1361

Esser, J., *Grundsatz und Norm in der richterlichen Fortbildung des Privatrechts* (Mohr, Tübingen, 1956)
Vorverständnis und Methodenwahl in der Rechtsfindung (Athenäum, Frankfurt, 1970)

Evans, J., 'Change in the Doctrine of Precedent during the Nineteenth Century' in L. Goldstein (ed.), *Precedent in Law* (Clarendon Press, Oxford, 1987)

Everling, U., 'On the Judge-Made Law of the European Community's Courts' in D. O'Keeffe and A. Bavasso (eds.), *Judicial Review in European Union Law: Liber Amicorum in Honour of Lord Slynn of Hadley*, 2 vols. (Kluwer Law International, The Hague, London and Boston, 2000), I

'Richterliche Rechtsfortbildung in der Europäischen Gemeinschaft', *Juristenzeitung*, 55 (2000), 217

'Die Europäische Union als föderaler Zusammenschluss von Staaten und Bürgern' in A. von Bogdandy and J. Bast (eds.), *Europäisches Verfassungsrecht* (2nd edn, Springer, Heidelberg, 2009)

Fallon, R. H., 'Stare Decisis and the Constitution', *New York University Law Review*, 76 (2001), 570

Fauchald, O. K., 'The Legal Reasoning of ICSID Tribunals: An Empirical Analysis', *European Journal of International law*, 19 (2008), 301

Fejø, J., 'How Does the ECJ Cite its Previous Judgments in Competition Law Cases?' in M. Johansson, N. Wahl and U. Bernitz (eds.), *Liber Amicorum in Honour of Sven Norberg: A European for All Seasons* (Bruylant, Brussels, 2007)

Fikentscher, W., *Methoden des Rechts in vergleichender Darstellung*, 5 vols. (Mohr, Tübingen 1977), IV

Fitzmaurice, G. G., 'Some Problems Regarding the Formal Sources of Law' in F. M. van Asbeck (ed.), *Symbolae Verzijl: présentées au Prof. J. H. W. Verzijl, á l'occasion de son LXX-ième anniversaire* (Nijhoff, La Haye, 1958)

Flume, W., *Gewohnheitsrecht und Römisches Recht* (Westdeutscher Verlag, Opladen, 1975)

Flyvbjerg, B., *Making Social Science Matter* (Cambridge University Press, 2001)

Fon, V., F. Parisi and B. Depoorter, 'Litigation, Judicial Path-Dependence, and Legal Change', *European Journal of Law and Economics*, 20 (2005), 43

Forsthoff, U., *Niederlassungsfreiheit für Gesellschaften* (Nomos, Baden-Baden, 2006)

Fowler, J. H. *et al.*, 'Network Analysis and the Law: Measuring the Legal Importance of Precedents at the U.S. Supreme Court', *Political Analysis*, 15 (2007), 324

Frank, J., *Law and the Modern Mind* (Brentano, New York, 1930)

Frankenberg, G., 'Stranger Than Paradise: Identity & Politics in Comparative Law', *Utah Law Review* (1997), 259

Freedman, D., R. Pisani and R. Purves, *Statistics* (4th edn, W.W. Norton, New York, 2007)

Friedman, L. M. *et al.*, 'State Supreme Courts: A Century of Style and Citation', *Stanford Law Review*, 33 (1980–1981), 773

Friedmann, W. G., 'General Course in Public International Law', *Recueil des Cours/Académie de Droit International de La Haye*, 127 (1969), 41

Frowein, J. A., 'Die Verfassung der Europäischen Union aus der Sicht der Mitgliedstaaten', *Europarecht*, 30 (1995), 315

'Kritische Bemerkungen zur Lage des deutschen Staatsrechts aus rechtsvergleichender Sicht', *Die Öffentliche Verwaltung*, 51 (1998), 806

Garner, B. A. (ed.), *Black's Law Dictionary* (8th edn, Thomson West, St Paul, MN, 2004)

Geldart, W., W. S. Holdsworth and H. G. Hanbury, *Elements of English Law* (6th edn, Oxford University Press, London, 1959)

Gény, F., *Méthode d'interprétation et sources en droit privé positif,* 2 vols. (Libr. Générale de Droit et de Jurisprudence, Paris, 1919), I

Gerhardt, M. J., *The Power of Precedent* (Oxford University Press, 2008)

Germelmann, C. F., *Die Rechtskraft von Gerichtsentscheidungen in der Europäischen Union* (Mohr Siebeck, Tübingen, 2009)

Glenn, H. P., *Legal Traditions of the World* (4th edn, Oxford University Press, 2010)

Goldmann, M., 'Inside Relative Normativity: From Sources to Standard Instruments for the Exercise of International Public Authority' in A. von Bogdandy, P. Dann and M. Goldmann (eds.), *The Exercise of Public Authority by International Institutions* (Springer, Heidelberg, 2010)

Goodheart, A., 'Determining the Ratio Decidendi of a Case' in A. Goodheart (ed.), *Essays in Jurisprudence and the Common Law* (Cambridge University Press, 1931)

Gordon, R., *EC Law in Judicial Review* (Oxford University Press, 2007)

Graf Vitzthum, W., 'Begriff, Geschichte und Rechtsquellen des Völkerrechts' in W. Graf Vitzthum (ed.), *Völkerrecht* (5th edn, De Gruyter, Berlin, 2010)

Grawert, R., 'Das Grundgesetz im Lichte seiner Grundrechte. Eine judikative Entwicklungsgeschichte', *Der Staat,* 49 (2010), 507

Grewe, W., *Epochen der Völkerrechtsgeschichte* (Nomos, Baden-Baden, 1984)

Grimmel, A. and C. Jakobeit (eds.), *Politische Theorien der Europäischen Integration* (VS Verlag, Wiesbaden, 2009)

Grzeszick, B., 'Art 20 VI' in R. Herzog *et al.* (eds.), *(Maunz/Dürig) Grundgesetz Kommentar* (C. H. Beck, Munich, 2007)

Guillaume, G., 'Le Précédent dans la justice et l'arbitrage international', *Journal du Droit International,* 137 (2010), 685

Gundel, J., 'Keine Durchbrechung nationaler Verfahrensfristen zugunsten von Rechten aus nicht umgesetzten EG-Richtlinien', *Neue Zeitschrift für Verwaltungsrecht,* 17 (1998), 910

Gutsche, M., *Die Bindungswirkung der Urteile des Europäischen Gerichtshofes* (Institut für Völkerrecht, Göttingen, 1967)

Haasbeek, L., 'Soft Drugs under Scrutiny: How "Easy Going" is the Court?', *Legal Issues of Economic Integration,* 38 (2011), 389

Habermas, J., 'A Short Reply', *Ratio Juris,* 12 (1999), 445

Habermas, J. *et al.,* 'Europa und die neue Deutsche Frage', *Blätter für deutsche und internationale Politik,* 56 (2011), 45

Haferkamp, H.-P., *Georg Friedrich Puchta und die "Begriffsjurisprudenz"* (Klostermann, Frankfurt am Main, 2004)

Hager, G., *Rechtsmethoden in Europa* (Mohr Siebeck, Tübingen 2009)

Halberstam, D., 'Constitutional Heterarchy: The Centrality of Conflict in the European Union and the United States' in J. L. Dunoff and J. P. Trachtman (eds.), *Ruling the World? Constitutionalism, International Law, and Global Governance* (Cambridge University Press, 2009)

'Pluralism in Marbury and Van Gend' in M. Poiares Maduro and L. Azoulai (eds.), *The Past and Future of EU Law* (Hart, Oxford and Portland, 2010)

Halberstam, D. and E. Stein, 'The United Nations, the European Union, and the King of Sweden: Economic Sanctions and Individual Rights in a Plural World Order', *Common Market Law Review*, 46 (2009), 13

Hale, M., *The History of the Common Law of England* (reprint edn, Rothman, Littleton, 1987 (1713))

Hallstein, W., *Die Europäische Gemeinschaft* (5th edn, Econ, Düsseldorf and Vienna, 1979)

Haltern, U., *Europarecht und das Politische* (Mohr Siebeck, Tübingen, 2005)

Europarecht: Dogmatik im Kontext (2nd edn, Mohr Siebeck, Tübingen, 2007)

'On Finality' in A. von Bogdandy and J. Bast (eds.), *Principles of European Constitutional Law* (2nd edn, Hart and C. H. Beck, Oxford and Munich, 2010)

Hanschmann, F., *Der Begriff der Homogenität in der Verfassungslehre und Europarechtswissenschaft* (Springer, Berlin and Heidelberg, 2008)

Harris, P., 'Difficult Cases and the Display of Authority', *Journal of Law, Economics & Organization*, 1 (1985), 209

Hart, H. L. A., *The Concept of Law* (2nd edn, Oxford University Press, 1997)

Hartley, T. C., *The Foundations of European Union Law* (7th edn, Oxford University Press, 2010)

Hathaway, O. A., 'Path Dependence in the Law: The Course and Pattern of Legal Change in a Common Law System', *Iowa Law Review*, 86 (2001), 101

Hatje, A., 'The Economic Constitution within the Internal Market' in A. von Bogdandy and J. Bast (eds.), *Principles of European Constitutional Law* (2nd edn, Hart and C. H. Beck, Oxford and Munich, 2010)

Hay, P., 'European Economic Community – Res Judicata and Precedent in the Court of Justice of the Common Market', *American Journal of Comparative Law*, 12 (1963), 404

Healy, T., 'Stare Decisis and the Consitution: Four Questions and Answers', *Notre Dame Law Review*, 83 (2008), 1173

Hegel, G. W. F., *Outlines of the Philosophy of Right* (Oxford University Press, 2008 (1821))

Heiskanen, V., *International Legal Topics* (Lakimiesliiton Kustannus, Helsinki, 1992)

Heller, T., *Logik und Axiologie der analogen Rechtsanwendung* (De Gruyter, Berlin and Cologne, 1961)

Herzog, R. and L. Gerken, 'Stoppt den Europäischen Gerichtshof' *Frankfurter Allgemeine Zeitung* (Frankfurt, 8 September 2008)

Hesselink, M. W., 'A Toolbox for European Judges', *European Law Journal*, 17 (2011), 441

Higgins, R., *Problems and Process: International Law and How We Use It* (Clarendon Press, Oxford, 1994)

Hillmann, J., 'An Emerging International Rule of Law? – The WTO Dispute Set-tlement System's Role in its Evolution', *Ottawa Law Review*, 42 (2010–2011), 269

Hilpold, P., 'Unionsbürgerschaft und Bildungsrechte oder: Der EuGH-Richter als "Künstler"' in G. H. Roth and P. Hilpold (eds.), *Der EuGH und die Sou-veränität der Mitgliedstaaten* (Stämpfli, Bern, 2008)

Hinarejos, A., 'Integration in Criminal Matters and the Role of the Court of Justice', *European Law Review*, 36 (2011), 420

Hirschl, R., 'The New Constitutionalism and the Judicialization of Pure Politics Worldwide', *Fordham Law Review*, 75 (2006–2007), 721

Hoffmann, B., *Das Verhältnis von Gesetz und Recht* (Duncker & Humblot, Berlin, 2003)

Hoffmann, R., 'Der Oberste Gerichtshof Dänemarks und die europäische Integra-tion', *Europäische Grundrechte-Zeitschrift*, 26 (1999), 1

Hofmann, R. and P. B. Donath, 'Die Asylverfahrensrichtlinie unter beson-derer Berücksichtigung völkerrechtlicher Standards' in R. Hofmann (ed.), *Europäisches Flüchtlings- und Einwanderungsrecht* (Nomos, Baden-Baden, 2008)

Holland, T. E., *The Elements of Jurisprudence* (13th edn, Oxford University Press, 1924)

Holzleithner, E. and V. Mayer-Schönberger, 'Das Zitat als grundloser Grund rechtlicher Legitimität' in B. Feldner and N. Forgó (eds.), *Norm und Entschei-dung* (Springer, Vienna and New York, 2000)

Hong, Q. L., 'Constitutional Review in the Mega-Leviathan: A Democratic Foun-dation for the European Court of Justice', *European Law Journal*, 16 (2010), 695

Horspool, M. and M. Humphreys, *European Union Law* (6th edn, Oxford University Press, 2010)

Hudson, M. O., *The Permanent Court of International Justice 1920–1942* (Macmillan, New York, 1943)

Hughes, C. E., *The Supreme Court of the United States* (4th print edn, Columbia University Press, New York, 1947)

Hunnings, N. M., *The European Courts* (Cartermill, London, 1996)

Hunter, D., 'No Wilderness of Single Instances: Inductive Inference in Law', *Journal of Legal Education*, 48 (1998), 365

IMF, *World Economic Outlook (September 2011): Slowing Growth, Rising Risks* (IMF, Washington, 2011)

Isensee, J., *Das Volk als Grund der Verfassung: Mythos und Relevanz der Lehre von der verfassunggebenden Gewalt* (Westdeutscher Verlag, Opladen, 1995)

Jacob, H., *Courts, Law, and Politics in Comparative Perspective* (Yale University Press, New Haven, 1996)

Jacqué, J.-P., 'Les Verts v The European Parliament' in M. Poiares Maduro and L. Azoulai (eds.), *The Past and Future of EU Law* (Hart, Oxford and Portland, 2010)

Jellinek, G., *Allgemeine Staatslehre* (3rd edn, Springer, Berlin, 1922)

Jennings, R. Y. and A. Watts, *Oppenheim's International Law*, I: *Peace* (9th edn, Longman, Harlow, 1992)

Jestaedt, M., 'Warum in die Ferne schweifen, wenn der Maßstab liegt so nah? Verfassungshandwerkliche Anfragen an das Lissabon-Urteil des BVerfG', *Der Staat*, 48 (2009), 497

Johnson, C. A., 'Citations to Authority in Supreme Court Opinions', *Law & Policy*, 7 (1985), 509

'Follow-up Citations in the US Supreme Court', *Western Political Quarterly*, 39 (1986), 538

Joliet, R. and D. T. Keeling, 'Trade Mark Law and the Free Movement of Goods: The Overruling of the Judgment in Hag I', *International Review of Industrial Property and Copyright Law* (1991), 303

Kadelbach, S., 'Union Citizenship' in A. von Bogdandy and J. Bast (eds.), *Principles of European Constitutional Law* (2nd edn, Hart and C. H. Beck, Oxford and Munich, 2010)

Kähler, L., *Strukturen und Methoden der Rechtsprechungsänderung* (2nd edn, Nomos, Baden-Baden, 2011)

Kakouris, C. N., 'La Cour de Justice des Communautés européennes comme Cour Constitutionnelle: trois observations' in O. Due, M. Lutter and J. Schwarze (eds.), *Festschrift für Ulrich Everling*, 2 vols. (Nomos, Baden-Baden 1995), I

Kalman, L., *The Strange Career of Legal Liberalism* (Yale University Press, New Haven and London, 1996)

Kant, I., *Critique of Pure Reason* (Hackett, Indianapolis, 1996 (1781))

Kapteyn, P. J. G., 'Administration of Justice' in P. J. G. Kapteyn and P. VerLoren van Themaat (eds.), *The Law of the European Union and the European Communities* (4th edn, Kluwer Law International, Alphen aan den Rijn, 2008)

Katz Cogan, J., 'The Regulatory Turn in International Law', *Harvard International Law Journal*, 52 (2011), 322

Kau, M., *United States Supreme Court und Bundesverfassungsgericht* (Springer, Berlin and Heidelberg, 2007)

Kaufmann, A., *Analogie und "Natur der Sache"* (2nd edn, R. v. Decker & C. F. Müller, Heidelberg, 1982)

Kaufmann-Kohler, G., 'Arbitral Precedent: Dream, Necessity or Excuse?', *Arbitration International*, 23 (2007), 357

Kelsen, H., *Reine Rechtslehre* (Franz Deuticke, Leipzig and Vienna, 1934)

Kennedy, David, 'Theses about International Legal Discourse', *German Yearbook of International Law*, 23 (1980), 353

'The Move to Institutions', *Cardozo Law Review*, 8 (1987), 841

Kennedy, Duncan, *A Critique of Adjudication: Fin de Siècle* (Harvard University Press, Cambridge, MA, 1997)

'Two Globalizations of Law & Legal Thought: 1850–1968', *Suffolk University Law Review*, 36 (2003), 631

The Dark Sides of Virtue (Princeton University Press, 2004)

'A Left Phenomenological Alternative to the Hart/Kelsen Theory of Legal Interpretation' in D. Kennedy (ed.), *Legal Reasoning: Collected Essays* (Davies, Aurora 2008)

Kenney, S. J., 'Beyond Principals and Agents: Seeing Courts as Organizations by Comparing Référendaires at the European Court of Justice and Law Clerks at the US Supreme Court', *Comparative Political Studies*, 33 (2000), 593

Kingsbury, B., 'International Courts: Uneven Judicialisation in Global Order' in J. Crawford and M. Koskenniemi (eds.), *The Cambridge Companion to International Law* (Cambridge University Press, 2012)

Kirchhof, P., 'Recht Sprechen ist Sprechen über das Gesetz' in G. Müller, E. Osterloh and T. Stein (eds.), *Festschrift für Günter Hirsch zum 65. Geburtstag* (C. H. Beck, Munich, 2008)

Klabbers, J., 'Goldmann Variations' in A. von Bogdandy, P. Dann and M. Goldmann (eds.), *The Exercise of Public Authority by International Institutions* (Springer, Heidelberg, 2010)

Klatt, M., *Making the Law Explicit: The Normativity of Legal Argumentation* (Hart, Oxford, 2008)

Koch, H.-J. and H. Rüßmann, *Juristische Begründungslehre* (C. H. Beck, Munich, 1982)

Komarek, J., 'Precedent and Judicial Lawmaking in Supreme Courts: The Court of Justice Compared to the US Supreme Court and the French Cour de Cassation', *The Cambridge Yearbook of European Legal Studies*, 11 (2009), 399

'Questioning Judicial Deliberations', *Oxford Journal of Legal Studies*, 29 (2009), 805

'Judicial Lawmaking and Precedent in Supreme Courts', *LSE Law, Society and Economy Working Papers 4/2011* (2011)

Koopmans, T., 'Stare Decisis in European Law' in D. O'Keeffe and H. G. Schermers (eds.), *Essays in European Law and Integration* (Kluwer, Deventer, 1982)

'La Procédure préjudicielle – victime de son succès?' in F. Capotorti *et al.* (eds.), *Du droit international au droit de l'intégration: Liber amicorum Pierre Pescatore* (Nomos, Baden-Baden, 1987)

'The Birth of European Law at the Crossroads of Legal Traditions', *American Journal of Comparative Law*, 39 (1991), 493

Koskenniemi, M., *From Apology to Utopia* (reissue edn, Cambridge University Press, 2005)

'Constitutionalism as Mindset: Reflections on Kantian Themes about International Law and Globalization', *Theoretical Inquiries in Law*, 8 (2007), 9

Kötz, H., 'Contract Law in Europe and the United States: Legal Unification in the Civil Law and Common Law', *The Tulane European and Civil Law Forum*, 27 (2012), 1

Kreindler, R. H., *Transnational Litigation: A Basic Primer* (Oceana, New York, 1998)

Kriele, M., 'Das demokratische Prinzip im Grundgesetz', *Veröffentlichungen der Vereinigung der deutschen Staatsrechtslehrer*, 29 (1971), 46

    Theorie der Rechtsgewinnung (2nd edn, Duncker & Humblot, Berlin, 1976)

Kumm, M., 'The Jurisprudence of Constitutional Conflict: Constitutional Supremacy in Europe Before and After the Constitutional Treaty', *European Law Journal*, 11 (2005), 262

Ladeur, K.-H., 'Der "Eigenwert" des Rechts – Die Selbstorganisationsfähigkeit der Gesellschaft und die relationale Rationalität des Rechts' in C. J. Meier-Schatz (ed.), *Die Zukunft des Rechts* (Helbing & Lichtenhahn, Basel, Geneva and Munich, 1999)

Lagrange, M., 'La Cour de justice des Communautés européennes', *Études et Documents du Conseil d'État*, 17 (1963), 55

Lakshminath, A., *Precedent in Indian Law* (3rd edn, Eastern Book, Lucknow, 2009)

Lamond, G., 'Do Precedents Create Rules?', *Legal Theory*, 11 (2005), 1

    'Precedent and Analogy in Legal Reasoning' Stanford Encyclopedia of Philosophy, http://plato.stanford.edu/

Landa, D. and J. R. Lax, 'Legal Doctrine on Collegial Courts', *Journal of Politics*, 71 (2009), 946

Langbein, J. H., 'Blackstone on Judging' in W. Prest (ed.), *Blackstone and his Commentaries: Biography, Law, History* (Hart, Oxford, 2009)

Langenbucher, K., *Die Entwicklung und Auslegung von Richterrecht* (C. H. Beck, Munich, 1996)

Langton, R., *Kantian Humility: Our Ignorance of Things in Themselves* (Oxford University Press, 1998)

Larenz, K. and C.-W. Canaris, *Methodenlehre der Rechtswissenschaft* (3rd edn, Springer, Berlin and Heidelberg, 1995)

Lasok, K. P. E. and T. Millett, *Judicial Control in the EU: Procedures and Principles* (Richmond Law & Tax, Richmond, 2004)

Lasser, M., *Judicial Deliberations: A Comparative Analysis of Judicial Transparency and Legitimacy* (Oxford University Press, 2004)

    'The European Pasteurization of French Law', *Cornell Law Review*, 90 (2005), 995

Lauterpacht, E., 'Principles of Procedure in International Law', *Recueil des Cours/Académie de Droit International de La Haye*, 345 (2009), 391

Lauterpacht, H., *The Function of Law in the International Community* (Clarendon Press, Oxford, 1933)

    The Development of International Law by the International Court (Stevens, London, 1958)

Lauwaars, R. H., 'Institutional Structure' in P. J. G. Kapteyn and P. VerLoren van Themaat (eds.), *The Law of the European Union and the European Communities* (4th edn, Kluwer Law International, Alphen aan den Rijn, 2008)

Lax, J. R. and C. M. Cameron, 'Bargaining and Opinion Assignment on the US Supreme Court', *Journal of Law, Economics & Organization*, 23 (2007), 276

Lecourt, R., *L' Europe des juges* (reprint edn, Bruylant, Brussels, 2008 (1976))

Lemmens, K., 'But Pasteur was French: Comments on Mitchel Lasser's The European Pasteurization of French Law' in N. Huls, M. Adams and J. Bomhoff (eds.), *The Legitimacy of Highest Courts' Rulings: Judicial Deliberations and Beyond* (TMC Asser Press, The Hague, 2009)

Lenaerts, K., 'Interlocking Legal Orders in the European Union and Comparative Law', *International and Comparative Law Quarterly*, 52 (2003), 873

'The Basic Constitutional Charter of a Community Based on the Rule of Law' in M. Poiares Maduro and L. Azoulai (eds.), *The Past and Future of EU Law* (Hart, Oxford and Portland, 2010)

'Federalism and the Rule of Law: Perspective from the European Court of Justice', *Fordham International Law Journal*, 33 (2010), 1338

Lenaerts, K. and J. A. Gutiérrez-Fons, 'The Constitutional Allocation of Powers and General Principles of EU Law', *Common Market Law Review*, 47 (2010), 1629

Lenaerts, K. and K. Gutman, '"Federal Common Law" in the European Union: A Comparative Perspective from the United States', *American Journal of Comparative Law*, 54 (2006), 1

Lenz, C. O., 'Das Amt des Generalanwalts am Europäischen Gerichtshof' in O. Due, M. Lutter and J. Schwarze (eds.), *Festschrift für Ulrich Everling*, 2 vols. (Nomos, Baden-Baden, 1995), I

Lepsius, O., 'Die maßstabsetzende Gewalt' in M. Jestaedt *et al.* (eds.), *Das entgrenzte Gericht: Eine kritische Bilanz nach sechzig Jahren Bundesverfassungsgericht* (Suhrkamp, Berlin, 2011)

Levinson, S., 'Looking Abroad when Interpreting the US Constitution: Some Reflections', *Texas International Law Journal*, 39 (2004), 353

Lieberman, D., *The Province of Legislation Determined* (Cambridge University Press, 1989)

Lindblom, C. E., 'The Science of "Muddling Through"', *Public Administration Review*, 19 (1959), 79

Llewellyn, K. N., *The Bramble Bush* (Oceana, New York, 1930)

'On What is Wrong with So-Called Legal Education', *Columbia Law Review*, 35 (1935), 651

The Common Law Tradition: Deciding Appeals (4th edn, Little, Brown, Boston, 1960)

Lorenzen, E. G., 'The Qualification, Classification, or Characterization Problem in Conflict of Laws', *Yale Law Journal*, 50 (1941), 743

Lowe, V., 'The Function of Litigation in International Society', *International and Comparative Law Quarterly*, 61 (2012), 209

Luhmann, N., 'Spontane Ordnungsbildung' in F. Morstein Marx (ed.), *Verwaltung: Eine einführende Darstellung* (Duncker & Humblot, Berlin, 1965)

  Soziale Systeme: Grundriß einer allgemeinen Theorie (Suhrkamp, Frankfurt am Main, 1984)

  'Die Paradoxie des Entscheidens', *Verwaltungsarchiv*, 84 (1993), 287

  Das Recht der Gesellschaft (5th edn, Suhrkamp, Frankfurt am Main, 1995)

Lundmark, T., '*Stare decisis* vor dem Bundesverfassungsgericht', *Rechtstheorie*, 28 (1997), 315

Lupu, Y. and E. Voeten, 'Precedent in International Courts: A Network Analysis of Case Citations by the European Court of Human Rights', *British Journal of Political Science*, 42 (2012), 413

Luts, L. A., 'Typologies of Modern Legal Systems of the World', *Journal of Comparative Law*, 5 (2010), 28

MacCormick, N., 'Why Cases Have Rationes and What These Are' in L. Goldstein (ed.), *Precedent in Law* (Clarendon Press, Oxford 1987)

Mackenzie, R., C. Romano and Y. Shany, *Manual on International Courts and Tribunals* (2nd edn, Oxford University Press, 2010)

Mackenzie Stuart, A. J. and J.-P. Warner, 'Judicial Decision as a Source of Community Law' in W. G. Grewe, H. Rupp and H. Schneider (eds.), *Europäische Gerichtsbarkeit und nationale Verfassungsgerichtsbarkeit: Festschrift zum 70. Geburtstag von Hans Kutscher* (Nomos, Baden-Baden, 1981)

McLachlan, C., L. Shore and M. Weiniger, *International Investment Arbitration: Substantive Principles* (Oxford University Press, 2007)

McNamara, K. R., 'Constructing Authority in the European Union' in D. D. Avant, M. Finnemore and S. K. Sell (eds.), *Who Governs the Globe?* (Cambridge University Press, 2010)

Maine, H. S., *Ancient Law* (Routledge, London, 1905)

Malaurie, P. and P. Morvan, *Droit civil: introduction générale* (3rd edn, Defrénois, Paris, 2009)

Malenovský, J., 'L'Indépendance des juges internationaux', *Recueil des Cours/ Académie de Droit International de La Haye*, 349 (2010), 9

Mancini, F., 'The Making of a Constitution for Europe', *Common Market Law Review*, 26 (1989), 595

Mancini, G. F. and D. T. Keeling, 'Language, Culture and Politics in the Life of the European Court of Justice', *Columbia Journal of European Law*, 1 (1995), 397

Mann, M. E., 'Schutz unternehmensinterner Anwaltskorrespondenz', *Zeitschrift für vergleichende Rechtswissenschaft/Archiv für Internationales Wirtschaftsrecht*, 110 (2011), 302

Marshall, G., 'What is Binding in a Precedent' in N. MacCormick and R. Summers (eds.), *Interpreting Precedents: A Comparative Study* (Ashgate, Aldershot, 1997)

Mattei, U., 'The Issue of European Civil Codification and Legal Scholarship', *Hastings International & Comparative Law Review*, 21 (1998), 883

Maveety, N., 'The Study of Judicial Behaviour and the Discipline of Political Science' in N. Maveety (ed.), *The Pioneers of Judicial Behaviour* (University of Michigan Press, Ann Arbor, 2003)

Mayer, F. C., 'Europa als Rechtsgemeinschaft' in G. F. Schuppert and M. Bach (eds.), *Europawissenschaft* (Nomos, Baden-Baden, 2005)

'Art. 19 EUV' in E. Grabitz, M. Hilf and M. Nettesheim (eds.), *Das Recht der Europäischen Union* (C. H. Beck, Munich, 2010)

Mehdi, R., 'Le Revirement jurisprudentiel en droit communautaire' in J. Bourrinet (ed.), *L' Intégration européenne au XXIe siècle: en hommage à Jacques Bourrinet* (La Documentation Française, Paris, 2004)

Mei, A. P. van der, 'Cross-Border Access to Healthcare and Entitlement to Complementary "*Vanbraekel* Reimbursement"', *European Law Review*, 36 (2011), 431

Merrills, J. G., *International Dispute Settlement* (3rd edn, Cambridge University Press, 1998)

Metzger, E., 'Roman Judges, Case Law, and Principles of Procedure', *Law and History Review*, 22 (2004), 243

Mill, J. S., *On Liberty* (Agora, Millis, 2003 (1859))

Möllers, C., *Die drei Gewalten: Legitimation der Gewaltengliederung in Verfassungsstaat, europäischer Integration und Internationalisierung* (Velbrück, Weilerswist, 2008)

Monaghan, H. P., 'Stare Decisis and Constitutional Adjudication', *Columbia Law Review*, 88 (1988), 723

Montesquieu, *De l'ésprit des lois*, 31 vols. (Éditions Gallimard, Paris 1995 (1758)), XI

Morrison, T. W., 'Stare Decisis in the Office of Legal Counsel', *Columbia Law Review*, 100 (2010), 101

Moser, M. K., 'Allgemeine Rechtsgrundsätze in der Rechtsprechung des EuGH als Katalysatoren einer europäischen Wertegemeinschaft', *Zeitschrift für Europarecht, Internationales Privatrecht & Rechtsvergleichung*, 53 (2012), 4

Müller, F. and R. Christensen, *Juristische Methodik: Grundlagen* (9th edn, Duncker & Humblot, Berlin, 2004)

Juristische Methodik: Europarecht (2nd edn, Duncker & Humblot, Berlin, 2007)

Müller, F., R. Christensen and M. Sokolowski, *Rechtstext und Textarbeit* (Duncker & Humblot, Berlin, 1997)

Murkens, J. E. K., 'Identity Trumps Integration: The Lisbon Treaty in the German Federal Constitutional Court', *Der Staat*, 48 (2009), 517

Naômé, C., *Le Renvoi préjudiciel en droit européen: guide pratique* (Larcier, Brussels, 2007)

Nasser, S. H., *Sources and Norms of International Law: A Study on Soft Law* (Galda & Wilch, Berlin, 2008)

Neill, P., 'The European Court of Justice: A Case Study in Judicial Activism' (European Policy Forum, 1995)

Neumann, U., *Juristische Argumentationslehre* (Wiss. Buchges., Darmstadt, 1986)
  Recht als Struktur und Argumentation (Nomos, Baden-Baden, 2008)

Neyer, J. and D. Wolf, 'The Analysis of Compliance with International Rules: Definitions, Variables, and Methodology' in M. Zürn and C. Joerges (eds.), *Law and Governance in Postnational Europe: Compliance Beyond the Nation-State* (Cambridge University Press, 2005)

Niemi, M. I., 'Form and Substance in Legal Reasoning: Two Conceptions', *Ratio Juris*, 23 (2010), 479

Notaro, N., 'Case C-188/95, Fantask A/S and Others v. Industriministeriet (Erhvervsministeriet): Annotation', *Common Market Law Review*, 35 (1998), 1385

Obermaier, A. J., *The End of Territoriality? The Impact of ECJ Rulings on British, German and French Social Policy* (Ashgate, Farnham, 2009)

Ojanen, T., 'Between Precedent and the Present', *Turku Law Journal*, 3 (2001), 105

Oppermann, T., C. D. Classen and M. Nettesheim, *Europarecht* (4th edn, C. H. Beck, Munich, 2009)

Ossenbühl, F., 'Der gemeinschaftsrechtliche Staatshaftungsanspruch', *Deutsches Verwaltungsblatt*, 107 (1992), 993

Palmer, B. W., 'Judicial Review: Usurpation or Abdication?', *ABA Journal*, 46 (1960), 881

Parfit, D., *Reasons and Persons* (Clarendon Press, Oxford, 1987)

Park, W. W., *Arbitration of International Business Disputes* (Oxford University Press, 2006)

Patterson, D., 'The Poverty of Interpretive Universalism: Towards the Reconstruction of Legal Theory', *Texas Law Review*, 72 (1993), 1

Paulsen, M. S., 'The Worst Constitutional Decision of All Time', *Notre Dame Law Review*, 78 (2003), 995

Peczenik, A., 'Jumps and Logic in the Law', *Artificial Intelligence and Law*, 4 (1996), 297

Pellet, A., 'Article 38' in A. Zimmermann, K. Oellers-Frahm and C. Tomuschat (eds.), *The Statute of the International Court of Justice: A Commentary* (Oxford University Press, 2006)

Perelman, C., *Logique juridique: Nouvelle rhétorique* (2nd edn, Dalloz, Paris, 1999)

Perju, V., 'Reason and Authority in the European Court of Justice', *Virginia Journal of International Law*, 49 (2009), 307

Pernice, I., 'Europäisches und nationales Verfassungsrecht', *Veröffentlichungen der Vereinigung der deutschen Staatsrechtslehrer*, 60 (2001), 148

Perry, S. R., 'Judicial Obligation, Precedent and the Common Law', *Oxford Journal of Legal Studies*, 7 (1987), 215

Pescatore, P., 'Les Droits de l'homme et l'intégration européenne', *Cahiers de Droit Européen*, 4 (1968), 629

The Law of Integration (Sijthoff, Leiden, 1974)

'Le Recours, dans la jurisprudence de la Cour de justice des Communautés européennes, à des normes déduites de la comparaison des droits des Etats membres', *Revue Internationale de Droit Comparé*, 32 (1980), 337

'Van Gend en Loos, 3 February 1963 – A View from Within' in M. Poiares Maduro and L. Azoulai (eds.), *The Past and Future of EU Law* (Hart, Oxford and Portland, 2010)

Peterson, J., 'Unpacking Show Trials: Situating the Trial of Saddam Hussein', *Harvard International Law Journal*, 48 (2007), 257

Picod, F., 'La Nouvelle Approche de la Cour de justice en matière d'entraves aux échanges', *Revue Trimestrielle de Droit Européen*, 34 (1998), 169

Plucknett, T. F. T., *A Concise History of the Common Law* (5th edn, Little, Brown, Boston, 1956)

Poiares Maduro, M., *We the Court: The European Court of Justice and the European Economic Constitution* (Hart, Oxford, 1998)

Poiares Maduro, M. and L. Azoulai, 'Introduction' in M. Poiares Maduro and L. Azoulai (eds.), *The Past and Future of EU Law* (Hart, Oxford and Portland, 2010)

Poiares Maduro, M. and L. Azoulai (eds.), *The Past and Future of EU Law: The Classics of EU Law Revisited on the 50th Anniversary of the Rome Treaty* (Hart, Oxford, 2010)

Pollock, F., *The Genius of the Common Law* (Lawbook Exchange, Union, 2000 (1912))

Posner E. A. and J. Yoo, 'Judicial Independence in International Tribunals', *California Law Review*, 93 (2005), 1

Posner, R. A., 'The Deprofessionalization of Legal Teaching and Scholarship', *Michigan Law Review*, 91 (1993), 1921

'Pragmatic Adjudication' in M. Dickstein (ed.), *The Revival of Pragmatism: New Essays on Social Thought, Law, and Culture* (Duke University Press, Durham, 1998)

Economic Analysis of Law (7th edn, Wolters Kluwer, Austin, 2007)

How Judges Think (Harvard University Press, Cambridge, MA, 2008)

Postema, G. J., *Bentham and the Common Law Tradition* (Clarendon Press, Oxford, 1986)

'"Protestant" Interpretation and Social Practices', *Law and Philosophy*, 6 (1987), 283

Pötters, S. and R. Christensen, 'Das Unionsrecht als Hybridform zwischen case law und Gesetzesrecht', *Juristenzeitung*, 67 (2012), 289

Radbruch, G., 'Die Natur der Sache als juristische Denkform' in G. C. Hernmarck (ed.), *Festschrift zu Ehren von Rudolf Laun* (Toth, Hamburg, 1948)

Rasmussen, H., *On Law and Policy in the European Court of Justice* (Nijhoff, Dordrecht, 1986)

'Between Self-Restraint and Activism: A Judicial Policy for the European Court', *European Law Review*, 13 (1988), 28

'Remedying the Crumbling EC Judicial System', *Common Market Law Review*, 37 (2000), 1071

Raz, J., 'Interpretation without Retrieval' in A. Marmor (ed.), *Law and Interpretation* (Oxford University Press, 1995)

The Authority of Law (2nd edn, Oxford University Press, 2009)

Reed, L., J. Paulsson and N. Blackaby, *Guide to ICSID Arbitration* (2nd edn, Kluwer Law International, Alphen aan den Rijn, 2011)

Reinisch, A., 'The Issues Raised by Parallel Proceedings and Possible Solutions' in M. Waibel *et al.* (eds.), *The Backlash Against Investment Arbitration: Perceptions and Reality* (Wolters Kluwer, Alphen aan den Rijn, 2010)

Reisman, W. M., 'Judge Shigeru Oda: A Tribute to an International Treasure', *Leiden Journal of International Law*, 16 (2003), 57

Richardson, I., 'What Makes a "Leading" Case', *Victoria University of Wellington Law Review*, 41 (2010), 317

Roellecke, G., 'Zur Unterscheidung von Rechtsdogmatik und Theorie', *Juristenzeitung*, 66 (2011), 645

Romashov, R. A., 'The Concepts of "Jus" and "Lex": Historical and Legal Linguistic Aspects', *Journal of Comparative Law*, 5 (2010), 145

Rosas, A., 'With a Little Help from My Friends: International Case-Law as a Source of Reference for the EU Courts', *The Global Community Yearbook of International Law and Jurisprudence*, 5 (2005), 203a

'The European Court of Justice in Context: Forms and Patterns of Judicial Dialogue', *European Journal of Legal Studies*, 1 (2007), 1

'Separation of Powers in the European Union', *The International Lawyer*, 41 (2007), 1033

'The European Union and Fundamental Rights/Human Rights' in C. Krause and M. Scheinin (eds.), *International Protection of Human Rights: A Textbook* (Åbo Akademi University Institute for Human Rights, Turku, 2009)

'Justice in Haste, Justice Denied? The European Court of Justice and the Area of Freedom, Security and Justice', *The Cambridge Yearbook of European Legal Studies*, 11 (2009), 1

'Finis Europae Socialis?' in J.-C. Piris *et al.* (eds.), *Chemins d'Europe: mélanges en l'honneur de Jean-Paul Jacqué* (Dalloz, Paris, 2010)

'Life after Dassonville and Cassis: Evolution but No Revolution' in M. Poiares Maduro and L. Azoulai (eds.), *The Past and Future of EU Law* (Hart, Oxford and Portland, 2010)

Rosenfeld, M., 'Comparing Constitutional Review by the European Court of Justice and the US Supreme Court' in I. Pernice, J. Kokott and C. Saunders (eds.), *The Future of the European Judicial System in a Comparative Perspective* (Nomos, Baden-Baden, 2006)

Rosenne, S., *The Law and Practice of the International Court 1920–2005* 4 vols. (4th edn, Martinus Nijhoff, Leiden, 2006), III

Ross, R. J., 'The Commoning of the Common Law: The Renaissance Debate over Printing English Law, 1520–1640', *University of Pennsylvania Law Review*, 146 (1998), 323

Rubin, P. H. (ed.), *The Evolution of Efficient Common Law* (Elgar, Cheltenham, 2007)

Ruffert, M. (ed.), *The Transformation of Administrative Law in Europe* (Sellier, Munich, 2007)

Sachs, M., *Die Bindung des Bundesverfassungsgerichts an seine Entscheidungen* (Vahlen, Munich, 1977)

Salacuse, J. W., *The Law of Investment Treaties* (Oxford University Press, 2010)

Sampaio Ferraz, T. Jr, 'On Sense and Sensibility in Legal Interpretation', *Rechtstheorie*, 42 (2011), 139

Sands, P., 'Turtles and Torturers: The Transformation of International Law', *New York University Journal of International Law & Politics*, 33 (2001), 527

'Introduction and Acknowledgments' in R. Mackenzie, C. Romano and Y. Shany (eds.), *Manual on International Courts and Tribunals* (2nd edn, Oxford University Press, 2010)

Sarmiento, D., 'The Silent Lamb and the Deaf Wolves' in M. Avbelj and J. Komarek (eds.), *Constitutional Pluralism in the European Union and Beyond* (Hart, Oxford, 2012)

Sartor, G., 'Syllogism and Defeasibilty', *Northern Ireland Legal Quarterly*, 59 (2008), 21

Sauer, W., *Juristische Methodenlehre: Zugleich eine Einleitung in die Methodik der Geisteswissenschaften* (Enke, Stuttgart, 1940)

Saul, B., 'Legislating from a Radical Hague: The United Nations Special Tribunal for Lebanon Invents an International Crime of Transnational Terrorism', *Leiden Journal of International Law*, 24 (2011), 677

Savigny, F. C. von, *Vom Beruf unsrer Zeit für Gesetzgebung und Rechtswissenschaft* (2nd edn, J. C. B. Mohr, Heidelberg, 1828)

System des heutigen Römischen Rechts, 9 vols. (Veit, Berlin, 1840), I

Schauer, F., 'Precedent', *Stanford Law Review*, 39 (1986–1987), 571

'Opinions as Rules', *University of Chicago Law Review*, 62 (1995), 1455

Schauer, F. and V. J. Wise, 'Legal Positivism as Legal Information', *Cornell Law Review*, 82 (1996–1997), 1080

Schepel, H. and E. Blankenburg, 'Mobilizing the European Court of Justice' in G. de Búrca and J. Weiler (eds.), *The European Court of Justice* (Oxford University Press, 2001)

Schermers, H. G. and D. F. Waelbroeck, *Judicial Protection in the European Union* (6th edn, Kluwer Law International, The Hague, 2001)

Schiemann, K., *Vom Richter des Common Law zum Richter des Europäischen Rechts* (Vorträge und Berichte Nr 145, Zentrum für Europäisches Wirtschaftsrecht, Rheinische Friedrich-Wilhelms-Universität, Bonn, 2005)

'The Functioning of the Court of Justice in an Enlarged Union and the Future of the Court' in A. Arnull, P. Eeckhout and T. Tridimas (eds.), *Continuity and Change in EU Law* (Oxford University Press, 2008)

Schima, B., 'Zur Wirkung von Auslegungsentscheidungen des Gerichtshofes der Europäischen Gemeinschaften' in B. Feldner and N. Forgó (eds.), *Norm und Entscheidung* (Springer, Vienna and New York, 2000)

Schlink, B., 'Die Entthronung der Staatsrechtswissenschaft durch die Verfassungsgerichtsbarkeit', *Der Staat*, 28 (1989), 161

Schlüchter, E., *Mittlerfunktion der Präjudizien* (de Gruyter, Berlin, 1986)

Schmidt, S. K., 'Gefangen im "lock in"? Zur Pfadabhängigkeit der Rechtsprechung des Europäischen Gerichtshofs', *Der Moderne Staat*, 2 (2010), 455

Schmitt, C., *Gesetz und Urteil: Eine Untersuchung zum Problem der Rechtspraxis* (Liebmann, Berlin, 1912)

Schneiderman, D., 'Judicial Politics and International Investment Arbitration: Seeking an Explanation for Conflicting Outcomes', *Northwestern Journal of International Law & Business*, 30 (2010), 383

Schockweiler, F. A., 'L'Exécution des arrêts de la Cour' in F. Capotorti *et al.* (eds.), *Du droit international au droit de l'intégration: Liber amicorum Pierre Pescatore* (Nomos, Baden-Baden, 1987)

Schönfeld, K. M., 'Rex, Lex et Judex: Montesquieu and *la bouche de la loi* Revisited', *European Constitutional Law Review*, 4 (2008), 274

Schreuer, C., *The ICSID Convention: A Commentary* (2nd edn, Cambridge University Press, 2009)

Schreuer, C. and M. Weiniger, 'Conversations across Cases: Is There a Doctrine of Precedent in Investment Arbitration?', *Transnational Dispute Management*, 5 (2008), 1

Schulze, R. and U. Seif, 'Einführung' in R. Schulze and U. Seif (eds.), *Richterrecht und Rechtsfortbildung in der Europäischen Rechtsgemeinschaft* (Mohr Siebeck, Tübingen, 2003)

From Dual to Cooperative Federalism: The Changing Structure of European Law (Oxford University Press, 2009)

Schulze-Fielitz, H., 'Art 20' in H. Dreier (ed.), *Grundgesetz Kommentar*, 3 vols. (Mohr Siebeck, Tübingen, 2006), II

Schwarze, J., 'Grenzen des Richterrechts in der Europäischen Rechtsordnung' in G. Müller, E. Osterloh and T. Stein (eds.), *Festschrift für Günter Hirsch zum 65. Geburtstag* (C. H. Beck, Munich, 2008)

'Soft Law im Recht der Europäischen Union', *Europarecht*, (2011), 3

Schwebel, S. M., 'The Contribution of the International Court of Justice to the Development of International Law' in W. P. Heere (ed.), *International Law and The Hague's 750th Anniversary* (TMC Asser Press, The Hague, 1999)

Sendler, H., 'Über sog. humoristische Urteile', *Neue Juristische Wochenschrift*, (1995), 847

Shaffer, G. and T. Ginsburg, 'The Empirical Turn in International Legal Scholarship', *American Journal of International Law*, 106 (2012), 1

Shahabuddeen, M., *Precedent in the World Court* (Cambridge University Press, 1996)

Shany, Y., 'No Longer a Weak Department of Power? Reflections on the Emergence of a New International Judiciary', *European Journal of International Law*, 20 (2009), 73

Shapiro, M., 'Judges as Liars', *Harvard Journal of Law & Public Policy*, 17 (1994), 155

'Law, Courts and Politics' in T. Ginsburg and R. A. Kagan (eds.), *Institutions and Public Law: Comparative Approaches* (Lang, New York, 2005)

Shapiro, M. and A. Stone Sweet, *On Law, Politics, and Judicialization* (Oxford University Press, 2002)

Sharpston, E., 'The Changing Role of the Advocate General' in A. Arnull, P. Eeckhout and T. Tridimas (eds.), *Continuity and Change in EU Law* (Oxford University Press, 2008)

Shaw, J., 'A View of the Citizenship Classics: Martinez Sala and Subsequent Cases on Citizenship of the Union' in M. Poiares Maduro and L. Azoulai (eds.), *The Past and Future of EU Law* (Hart, Oxford and Portland, 2010)

Siltala, R., *A Theory of Precedent: From Analytical Positivism to a Post-Analytical Philosophy of Law* (Hart, Oxford, 2000)

Simon, D., 'Alle Quixe sind Quaxe – Aristoteles und die juristische Argumentation', *Juristenzeitung*, 66 (2011), 697

Simonati, A., 'The Principles of Administrative Procedure and the EU Courts: An Evolution in Progress?', *Review of European Administrative Law*, 4 (2011), 45

Simonds, G., 'Law' in E. Barker (ed.), *The Character of England* (Clarendon Press, Oxford, 1947)

Skouris, V., 'Self-Conception, Challenges and Perspectives of the EU Courts' in I. Pernice, J. Kokott and C. Saunders (eds.), *The Future of the European Judicial System in a Comparative Perspective* (Nomos, Baden-Baden, 2006)

Slaughter, A.-M., 'A Global Community of Courts', *Harvard International Law Journal*, 44 (2003), 191

Slynn, G., 'The Court of Justice of the European Communities', *International and Comparative Law Quarterly*, 33 (1984), 409

'Critics of the Court: A Reconsideration' in M. T. Andenæs and F. G. Jacobs (eds.), *European Community Law in the English Courts* (Clarendon Press, Oxford and New York, 1998)

Snyder, F., 'Soft Law and Institutional Practice in the European Community' in S. Martin (ed.), *The Construction of Europe: Essays in Honour of Emile Noël* (Kluwer, Dordrecht, 1994)

Solanke, I., '"Stop the ECJ"?: An Empirical Analysis of Activism at the Court', *European Law Journal*, 17 (2011), 764

Somek, A., *Rechtliches Wissen* (Suhrkamp, Frankfurt am Main, 2006)

'The Spirit of Legal Positivism', *German Law Journal*, 12 (2011), 729

Sommermann, K.-P., 'Art 20 Abs 3' in C. Starck (ed.), *(Mangoldt/Klein) Kommentar zum Grundgesetz*, 3 vols. (5th edn, C. H. Beck, Munich, 2005), II

Sørensen, M., *Les Sources du droit international: étude sur la jurisprudence de la Cour Permanente de Justice Internationale* (Einar Munksgaard, Copenhagen, 1946)

Sornarajah, M., *The International Law on Foreign Investment* (3rd edn, Cambridge University Press, 2010)

Stein, E., 'Lawyers, Judges, and the Making of a Transnational Constitution', *American Journal of International Law*, 75 (1981), 1

Steiner, U., 'Richterliche Rechtsfortbildung und Grundgesetz' in G. Müller, E. Osterloh and T. Stein (eds.), *Festschrift für Günter Hirsch zum 65. Geburtstag* (C. H. Beck, Munich, 2008)

Steingruber, A. M., *Consent in International Arbitration* (Oxford University Press, 2012)

Stern, K., *Das Staatsrecht der Bundesrepublik Deutschland*, 5 vols. (C. H. Beck, Munich, 1980), II

Stolleis, M., *The Law under the Swastika* (University of Chicago Press, Chicago and London, 1998)

Stone, J., *Precedent and Law* (Butterworths, Sydney, 1985)

Stone Sweet, A., 'Conclusion' in A. Stone Sweet (ed.), *The Judicial Construction of Europe* (Oxford University Press, 2004)

'The European Court and Integration' in A. Stone Sweet (ed.), *The Judicial Construction of Europe* (Oxford University Press, 2004)

'The Juridical Coup d'État and the Problem of Authority: CILFIT and Foto-Frost' in M. Poiares Maduro and L. Azoulai (eds.), *The Past and Future of EU Law* (Hart, Oxford and Portland, 2010)

Stone Sweet, A. and T. Brunell, 'Constructing a Supranational Constitution' in A. Stone Sweet (ed.), *The Judicial Construction of Europe* (Oxford University Press, 2004)

Streinz, R., 'Does the European Court of Justice Keep the Balance Between Individual and Community Interest in Kadi?' in U. Fastenrath *et al.* (eds.), *From Bilateralism to Community Interest: Essays in Honour of Judge Bruno Simma* (Oxford University Press, 2011)

Summers, R. and M. Taruffo, 'Interpretation and Comparative Analysis' in N. Mac-Cormick and R. Summers (eds.), *Interpreting Statutes* (Dartmouth, Aldershot, 1991)

Sunstein, C. R., 'On Analogical Reasoning', *Harvard Law Review*, 106 (1993), 741

Tamanaha, B., *Beyond the Formalist-Realist Divide: The Role of Politics in Judging* (Princeton University Press, 2010)

Taruffo, M., 'Institutional Factors Influencing Precedents' in N. MacCormick and R. Summers (eds.), *Interpreting Precedents: A Comparative Study* (Ashgate, Aldershot, 1997)

Tennyson, A, *Aylmer's Field* (Macmillan, London and New York, 1891)

Thayer, E. R., 'Judicial Legislation: Its Legitimiate Function in the Development of the Common Law', *Harvard Law Review*, 5 (1891), 172

Thomas, E. W., *The Judicial Process* (Cambridge University Press, 2005)

Thürer, D., '"Soft Law" – eine neue Form von Völkerrecht?', *Zeitschrift für Schweizerisches Recht*, 104 (1985), 429

Timmermans, C. W. A., 'General Aspects of the European Union and the European Communities' in P. J. G. Kapteyn and P. VerLoren van Themaat (eds.), *The Law of the European Union and the European Communities* (4th edn, Kluwer Law International, Alphen aan den Rijn, 2008)

Tomuschat, C., *Die gerichtliche Vorabentscheidung nach den Verträgen über die europäischen Gemeinschaften* (Carl Heymanns, Cologne, 1964)

'Das Europa der Richter' in J. Bröhmer *et al.* (eds.), *Internationale Gemeinschaft und Menschenrechte: Festschrift für Georg Ress zum 70. Geburtstag* (Carl Heymanns, Cologne, 2005)

Toth, A. G., 'The Authority of Judgments of the European Court of Justice: Binding Force and Legal Effects', *Yearbook of European Law*, 4 (1985), 1

The Oxford Encyclopaedia of European Community Law, 3 vols. (Clarendon Press, Oxford, 1990), I

Tribe, L. H., *American Constitutional Law* (2nd edn, Foundation Press, Mineola, 1988)

Tridimas, T., 'The Role of the Advocate General in the Development of Community Law: Some Reflections', *Common Market Law Review*, 34 (1997), 1349

The General Principles of EU Law (2nd edn, Oxford University Press, 2006)

Troper, M. and C. Grzegorczyk, 'Precedent in France' in N. MacCormick and R. Summers (eds.), *Interpreting Precedents: A Comparative Study* (Ashgate, Aldershot, 1997)

Twining, W., *General Jurisprudence* (Cambridge University Press, 2009)

Twiss, T. (ed.), *Henrici de Bracton: De Legibus et Consuetudinibus Angliae*, 6 vols. (William S. Hein, Buffalo 1990 (1878)), I

Unger, R. M., 'Legal Analysis as Institutional Imagination', *Modern Law Review*, 59 (1996), 1

What Should Legal Analysis Become? (Verso, London, 1996)

The Self Awakened: Pragmatism Unbound (Harvard University Press, Cambridge, MA, 2007)

Vanderlinden, J., *Le Concept de code en Europe occidentale du XIII. au XIX. siècle* (Editions de l'Institut de Sociologie, Université Libre de Bruxelles, Brussels, 1967)

Vauchez, A., 'The Transnational Politics of Judicialization. *Van Gend en Loos* and the Making of EU Polity', *European Law Journal*, 16 (2010), 1

Verdross, A. and B. Simma, *Universelles Völkerrecht: Theorie und Praxis* (3rd edn, Duncker & Humblot, Berlin, 1984)

Vermeule, A., *Judging under Uncertainty* (Harvard University Press, Cambridge, MA, 2006)

Vesting, T., *Rechtstheorie* (C. H. Beck, Munich, 2007)

Vogenauer, S., *Die Auslegung von Gesetzen in England und auf dem Kontinent*, 2 vols. (Mohr Siebeck, Tübingen, 2001), I

Vooren, B. van, 'A Case Study of "Soft Law" in EU External Relations', *European Law Review*, 34 (2009), 696

Wachsmann, P., 'La Volonté de l'interprète', *Droits*, 28 (1998), 29

Wägenbaur, B., *EuGH VerfO: Satzung und Verfahrensordnungen EuGH/EuG – Kommentar* (C. H. Beck, Munich, 2008)

Waldock, H. M., 'General Course on Public International Law', *Recueil des Cours/Académie de Droit International de La Haye*, 106 (1962), 1

Waldron, J., *The Law* (Routledge, London, 1990)

Law and Disagreement (Clarendon Press, Oxford, 1999)

Walsh, D. J., 'On the Meaning and Pattern of Legal Citations: Evidence from State Wrongful Discharge Precedents', *Law & Society Review*, 31 (1997), 337

Walter, K. F., *Rechtsfortbildung durch den EuGH* (Duncker & Humblot, Berlin, 2009)

Wambaugh, E., *The Study of Cases* (2nd edn, Little, Brown, Boston, 1894)

Ward, A. and D. L. Weiden, *Sorcerers' Apprentices: 100 Years of Law Clerks at the United States Supreme Court* (New York University Press, 2006)

Wattel, P., '*Köbler*, *CILFIT* and *Welthgrove*: We Can't Go On Meeting Like This', *Common Market Law Review*, 41 (2004), 177

Weiler, J. H. H., 'The Transformation of Europe', *Yale Law Journal*, 100 (1990–1991), 2403

'European Models: Polity, People and System' in P. Craig and C. Harlow (eds.), *Lawmaking in the European Union* (Kluwer Law International, London, The Hague and Boston, 1998)

'Epilogue: The Judicial Après Nice' in G. de Búrca and J. Weiler (eds.), *The European Court of Justice* (Oxford University Press, 2001)

'The Geology of International Law: Governance, Democracy and Legitimacy', *Zeitschrift für ausländisches öffentliches Recht und Völkerrecht*, 64 (2004), 547

Weiler, J. H. H. and U. Haltern, 'The Autonomy of the Community Legal Order: Through the Looking Glass', *Harvard International Law Journal*, 37 (1996), 411

Weinreb, L. L., *Legal Reason: The Use of Analogy in Legal Argument* (Cambridge University Press, 2005)

Weischedel, W., *Die philosophische Hintertreppe* (38th edn, DTV, Munich, 2009)

Wenzel, J., '§ 563' in T. Rauscher, P. Wax and J. Wenzel (eds.), *Münchener Kommentar zur Zivilprozessordnung* (3rd edn, C. H. Beck, Munich, 2007)

Wichern, N. J., 'A Court of Clerks, Not of Men: Serving Justice in the Media Age', *DePaul Law Review*, 49 (1999), 621

Wieacker, F., *Privatrechtsgeschichte der Neuzeit* (2nd edn, Vandenhoeck & Ruprecht, Göttingen, 1967)

Williams, A., *The Ethos of Europe: Values, Law and Justice in the EU* (Cambridge University Press, 2010)

Williams, G., *Salmond on Jurisprudence* (11th edn, Sweet & Maxwell, London, 1957)

Zander, M., *The Law-Making Process* (6th edn, Cambridge University Press, 2004)

Zimmermann, R., 'Codification: History and Present Significance of an Idea', *European Review of Private Law*, 3 (1995), 95

Zuleeg, M., 'The Advantages of the European Constitution' in A. von Bogdandy and J. Bast (eds.), *Principles of European Constitutional Law* (Hart and C. H. Beck, Oxford and Munich, 2010)

INDEX